CLASSICAL MYTHOLOGY

H. A. GUERBER

HOMER. François Gérard.

CLASSICAL MYTHOLOGY

H. A. GUERBER

FALL RIVER PRESS

New York

FALL RIVER PRESS

New York

An Imprint of Sterling Publishing Co., Inc.
1166 Avenue of the Americas
New York, NY 10036

Originally published as
The Myths of Greece and Rome (1907)

ISBN 978-1-4351-6288-4

Manufactured in the United States of America

4   6   8   10   9   7   5   3

www.sterlingpublishing.com

CONTENTS

LIST OF ILLUSTRATIONS   xx

PREFACE   xxiii

I. The Beginning of All Things

MYTHS OF CREATION   1

CHAOS AND NYX   2

EREBUS, ÆTHER, AND HEMERA   2

CREATION OF GÆA AND URANUS   3

THE EGG MYTH   5

MOUNT OLYMPUS AND THE RIVER OCEANUS   5

THE HYPERBOREANS   5

THE ETHIOPIANS AND THE ISLES OF THE BLEST   6

URANUS AND GÆA   7

TITANS, CYCLOPES, AND CENTIMANI   7

THE TITANS REVOLT   8

CRONUS AND RHEA   8

BIRTH OF JUPITER   10

JUPITER'S INFANCY   11

JUPITER'S SUPREMACY   12

THE GIANTS' WAR   12

THE DEATH OF TYPHŒUS   13

DEFEAT OF ENCELADUS   14

JUPITER DIVIDES HIS REALM   15

STORY OF PROMETHEUS   15

STORY OF EPIMETHEUS AND PANDORA   18

THE FOUR AGES   23

THE DELUGE   25

STORY OF DEUCALION AND PYRRHA   26

II. Jupiter

JUPITER'S TITLES   29

JUPITER'S ATTENDANTS   31

STORY OF PHILEMON AND BAUCIS   32

JUPITER KIDNAPS EUROPA   34

SEARCH FOR EUROPA   35

FOUNDING OF THEBES   37

WORSHIP OF JUPITER   38

III. Juno

JUNO'S MARRIAGE   41
STORY OF CALLISTO AND ARCAS   41
JUNO'S ATTENDANT   42
WORSHIP OF JUNO   42
STORY OF CLEOBIS AND BITON   44

IV. Minerva

BIRTH OF MINERVA   45
NAMING OF ATHENS   47
STORY OF ARACHNE   48
WORSHIP OF MINERVA   50

V. Apollo

STORY OF CORONIS   52
ÆSCULAPIUS   53
ADMETUS AND ALCESTIS   54
THE WALLS OF TROY   55
APOLLO SLAYS PYTHON   55
APOLLO AND HYACINTHUS   57
APOLLO AND CYPARISSUS   57
APOLLO AND DAPHNE   58
CEPHALUS AND PROCRIS   60
CLYTIE   62
APOLLO AND MARSYAS   63
APOLLO AND PAN   64
ORPHEUS AND EURYDICE   66
STORY OF AMPHION   71
ARION   71
STORY OF PHAETON   73
THE HELIADES   77
THE NINE MUSES   78
STORY OF AURORA AND TITHONUS   80
WORSHIP OF APOLLO   81

VI. Diana

STORY OF NIOBE   85
DIANA'S AVOCATIONS   88
STORY OF ENDYMION   88

STORY OF ORION   90
STORY OF ACTEON   92

VII. Venus

VENUS' BIRTH   95
VENUS AND VULCAN   98
STORY OF ALECTRYON   98
VENUS' CHILDREN   99
VENUS AND ADONIS   101
VENUS AND ANCHISES   103
STORY OF HERO AND LEANDER   103
PYRAMUS AND THISBE   109
ECHO AND NARCISSUS   110
PYGMALION AND GALATEA   112
CUPID AND PSYCHE   113
PSYCHE FORSAKEN   118
PSYCHE'S JOURNEY TO HADES   119
BERENICE'S HAIR   121
WORSHIP OF VENUS   122

VIII. Mercury

BIRTH OF MERCURY   123
MERCURY'S THEFT   124
MERCURY'S WAND, CAP, AND SHOES   124
STORY OF IO   126
ARGUS' WATCH   128
MERCURY'S OFFICES AND WORSHIP   129

IX. Mars

MARS' CHARACTER   131
MARS' ATTENDANTS   131
STORY OF OTUS AND EPHIALTES   132
THE AREOPAGUS   132
MARS' CHILDREN   133
ROMULUS AND REMUS   133
QUIRINUS   135
THE ANCILE   135
WORSHIP OF MARS   136

X. Vulcan

VULCAN'S FALL   137

VULCAN'S FORGE   138

THE GOLDEN THRONE   138

VULCAN'S LOVES   140

XI. Neptune

NEPTUNE'S EXILE   144

STORY OF HESIONE   146

NEPTUNE'S CONTESTS   146

NEPTUNE'S POWER   147

NEPTUNE'S WIVES   147

AMPHITRITE   148

STORY OF IDAS AND MARPESSA   149

NEPTUNE'S ATTENDANTS   151

PROTEUS   151

WORSHIP OF NEPTUNE   152

XII. Pluto

WORSHIP OF PLUTO   154

HADES   154

RIVERS OF HADES   155

THE JUDGES   156

THE FURIES   156

THE FATES   159

TARTARUS   160

THE DANAIDES   160

TANTALUS   161

SISYPHUS   162

SALMONEUS   163

TITYUS   163

IXION   164

ELYSIAN FIELDS   165

XIII. Bacchus

STORY OF SEMELE   167

BIRTH OF BACCHUS   170

BACCHUS' ATTENDANTS   170

BACCHUS AND THE PIRATES   172
THE CURSE OF GOLD   173
NAXOS   175
BACCHUS AND ARIADNE   176
STORY OF PENTHEUS   176
WORSHIP OF BACCHUS   178

XIV. Ceres and Proserpina

CERES AND PROSERPINA   179
PLUTO KIDNAPS PROSERPINA   179
CERES' SEARCH   183
CERES AND TRIPTOLEMUS   184
ARETHUSA AND ALPHEUS   186
CERES' MOURNING   189
THE POMEGRANATE SEEDS   190
PROSERPINA'S RETURN   191
WORSHIP OF CERES   191
STORY OF ERISICHTHON   192
CERES AND STELLIO   193

XV. Vesta

WORSHIP OF VESTA   195
VESTAL VIRGINS   195
FESTIVALS   199
LARES, MANES, AND PENATES   199

XVI. Janus

JANUS' TWO FACES   201
WORSHIP OF JANUS   202
ANCIENT DIVISIONS OF TIME   203

XVII. Somnus and Mors

CAVE OF SLEEP   205
SOMNUS AND MORPHEUS   205
DREAMS AND NIGHTMARES   208
STORY OF CEYX AND HALCYONE   208
MORS   209
MORPHEUS   210

XVIII. Æolus

ÆOLUS' CHILDREN   211
TEMPLE OF ÆOLUS   213

XIX. Hercules

JUNO PERSECUTES HERCULES   215
HERCULES' CHOICE   217
HERCULES' MADNESS   218
HERCULES IN SERVITUDE   218
NEMEAN LION   219
HYDRA OF LERNA   219
STAG OF CERYNEA   220
ERYMANTHIAN BOAR   220
AUGEAN STABLES   220
CRETAN BULL   222
DIOMEDES' STEEDS   222
HIPPOLYTE'S GIRDLE   223
STYMPHALIAN BIRDS   225
CATTLE OF GERYONES   225
HESPERIAN APPLES   225
PYGMIES   226
ATLAS   227
OLYMPIAN GAMES   228
HERCULES AND OMPHALE   229
HERCULES AND DEIANEIRA   231
STORY OF NESSUS   233
NESSUS' ROBE   235
DEIANEIRA'S JEALOUSY   236
HERCULES' DEATH   236
WORSHIP OF HERCULES   238

XX. Perseus

ACRISIUS AND DANAE   239
THE SHOWER OF GOLD   239
BIRTH OF PERSEUS   240
DANAE AT SERIPHUS   241
THE GORGONS   241
PERSEUS' QUEST   242

The Grææ   243
Death of Medusa   243
Birth of Snakes   243
Atlas Petrified   245
Story of Andromeda   246
Phineus Petrified   247
Return to Argos   247

XXI. Theseus

Periphetes   251
Sinis   252
Sciron   252
Cercyon and Procrustes   253
Medea's Draught   253
Tribute to the Minotaur   254
Dædalus and Icarus   254
Talus   257
Ariadne's Clew   257
Theseus and the Minotaur   258
Theseus' Escape   258
Ariadne Forsaken   258
Theseus' Punishment   260
Theseus' Reign and Marriage   260
Centaurs and Lapithæ   261
Theseus in Hades   261
Phædra and Hippolytus   263
Death of Theseus   263

XXII. Jason

Jason's Vow   265
The One Sandal   266
Phryxus and Helle   267
The Golden Fleece   267
The Speaking Oak   268
The Argo and Crew   268
Story of Hylas   269
Phineus and the Harpies   269
The Symplegades   269

ARRIVAL AT COLCHIS   270
MEDEA'S AID   270
THE FLEECE CAPTURED   272
DEATH OF ABSYRTUS   274
PELIAS DETHRONED   275
THE MAGIC RECIPE   275
DEATH OF JASON   276

XXIII. The Calydonian Hunt

BIRTH OF MELEAGER   277
THE HUNTERS   277
MELEAGER SLAYS HIS UNCLES   278
ATALANTA'S RACE   278
THE GOLDEN APPLES   278
CASTOR AND POLLUX   280

XXIV. Œdipus

ŒDIPUS CONSULTS THE ORACLE   284
ŒDIPUS LEAVES CORINTH   285
DEATH OF LAIUS   285
THE SPHINX   286
THE RIDDLE   286
ŒDIPUS MARRIES HIS MOTHER   288
THE PLAGUE   288
DEATH OF JOCASTA   289
DEATH OF ŒDIPUS   289
ETEOCLES AND POLYNICES   290
THE SEVEN CHIEFS BEFORE THEBES   290
ANTIGONE'S DEVOTION   291
ANTIGONE AND HÆMON   293

XXV. Bellerophon

ANTEIA'S TREACHERY   295
THE CHIMÆRA   296
MINERVA'S ADVICE   296
PEGASUS BRIDLED   298
CHIMÆRA SLAIN   298
BELLEROPHON'S FALL   299

XXVI. Minor Divinities

NAIADES AND OREADES	301
NAPÆÆ AND DRYADES	301
STORY OF DRYOPE	302
SATYRS AND PAN	304
STORY OF SYRINX	304
SILVAN DEITIES	305
FLORA AND ZEPHYRUS	305
VERTUMNUS AND POMONA	306
SEA DEITIES	306
STORY OF GLAUCUS	308

XXVII. The Trojan War

JUPITER AND THETIS	309
THE APPLE OF DISCORD	310
PARIS AND ŒNONE	311
JUDGMENT OF PARIS	311
PARIS' RETURN TO TROY	314
PARIS SAILS FOR GREECE	314
HELEN'S SUITORS	315
ABDUCTION OF HELEN	316
PREPARATIONS FOR WAR	318
ULYSSES FEIGNS MADNESS	318
AGAMEMNON MADE CHIEF	318
ACHILLES' EARLY LIFE	319
ULYSSES DISCOVERS ACHILLES	320
SACRIFICE OF IPHIGENIA	320
ARRIVAL AT TROY	321
PROTESILAUS AND LAODAMIA	321
CHRYSEIS AND BRISEIS	323
ACHILLES' WRATH	324
AGAMEMNON MISLED	324
MENELAUS AND PARIS FIGHT	325
HECTOR AND ANDROMACHE	327
GREEKS REPELLED	328
PATROCLUS DONS ACHILLES' ARMOR	329
DEATH OF PATROCLUS	330
ACHILLES' GRIEF	331

ACHILLES' ARMOR   332

DEATH OF HECTOR   332

THE GODS' DECREE   334

RETURN OF HECTOR'S BODY   334

DEATH OF PENTHESILEA   335

DEATH OF ACHILLES   335

PHILOCTETES' ARROWS   336

DEATH OF PARIS AND ŒNONE   336

THE PALLADIUM   337

THE WOODEN HORSE   338

DEATH OF LAOCOON   338

FALL OF TROY   340

RETURN OF THE GREEKS   341

XXVIII. Adventures of Ulysses

SIEGE OF ISMARUS   343

THE LOTUS-EATERS   344

POLYPHEMUS AND GALATEA   346

POLYPHEMUS' CAVE   349

ULYSSES BLINDS POLYPHEMUS   350

ULYSSES' ESCAPE   350

GIFT OF ÆOLUS   352

THE LÆSTRYGONIANS   353

CIRCE, THE ENCHANTRESS   353

ULYSSES AND CIRCE   354

ULYSSES VISITS CIMMERIA   356

THE SIRENS   357

CHARYBDIS AND SCYLLA   357

CATTLE OF THE SUN   359

ULYSSES AND CALYPSO   360

NAUSICAA AND ULYSSES   361

THE PETRIFIED SHIP   361

ULYSSES' RETURN TO ITHACA   362

PENELOPE'S WEB   362

ULYSSES' BOW   364

DEATH OF THE SUITORS   364

ULYSSES' LAST JOURNEY   365

XXIX. Adventures of Æneas

ÆNEAS GOES TO SAVE PRIAM   368

VENUS APPEARS TO ÆNEAS   369

ANCHISES' ESCAPE   369

CREUSA'S GHOST   370

ARRIVAL IN THRACE   370

DELOS AND CRETE   371

ÆNEAS' VISION   371

CELÆNO, THE HARPY   372

RESCUE OF ACHEMENIDES   372

THE TEMPEST   373

ARRIVAL IN LIBYA   374

ÆNEAS AND DIDO   374

DEATH OF DIDO   375

FUNERAL GAMES   377

APPARITION OF ANCHISES   378

THE CUMÆAN SIBYL   378

ARRIVAL IN LATIUM   380

WAR WITH THE LATINS   381

STORY OF CAMILLA   381

NISUS AND EURYALUS   382

THE ARMOR   382

ÆNEAS' ARRIVAL   383

JUNO'S TREACHERY   383

ÆNEAS' PROWESS   383

ÆNEAS' WOUND   384

DEATH OF TURNUS   384

ÆNEAS' PROGENY   385

XXX. Analysis of Myths

EARLY THEORIES   387

MODERN THEORIES   388

ANTHROPOLOGICAL THEORY   388

PHILOLOGICAL THEORY   390

SKY MYTHS   393

     Uranus   393

     Jupiter   393

     Juno   393

     Argus   394

SUN AND DAWN MYTHS   394
    Europa   394
    Apollo   394
    Coronis   395
    Daphne   395
    Cephalus and Procris   395
    Orpheus and Eurydice   396
    Phaeton   396
    Endymion   397
    Adonis   397
    Tantalus   397
    Sisyphus   398
    Ixion   398
    Hercules   398
    Iole   398
    Deianeira   399
    Perseus   399
    Theseus   400
    Argonauts   400
    Medea   400
    Glauce   401
    Meleager   401
    Œdipus   401
    Eumenides   402
    Bellerophon   402
    Trojan War   403
    Ulysses   404
    Minerva   404
MOON MYTHS   404
    Diana, Io, and Circe   404
EARTH MYTHS   405
    Gæa and Rhea   405
    Ceres and Proserpina   405
    Danae and Semele   405
SEA MYTHS   406
    Oceanus and Neptune   406
    Nereus   406
CLOUD MYTHS   406
    Charon   406

Niobe 406

FIRE MYTHS 407

Cyclopes 407

Titans 407

Prometheus 407

Vulcan 408

Vesta 408

WIND MYTHS 408

Mercury 408

Mars 409

Otus and Ephialtes 409

Pan, Æolus, and the Harpies 409

UNDERWORLD MYTHS 410

Cerberus and Pluto 410

GENEALOGICAL TABLE 411

INDEX TO POETICAL QUOTATIONS 413

GLOSSARY AND INDEX 415

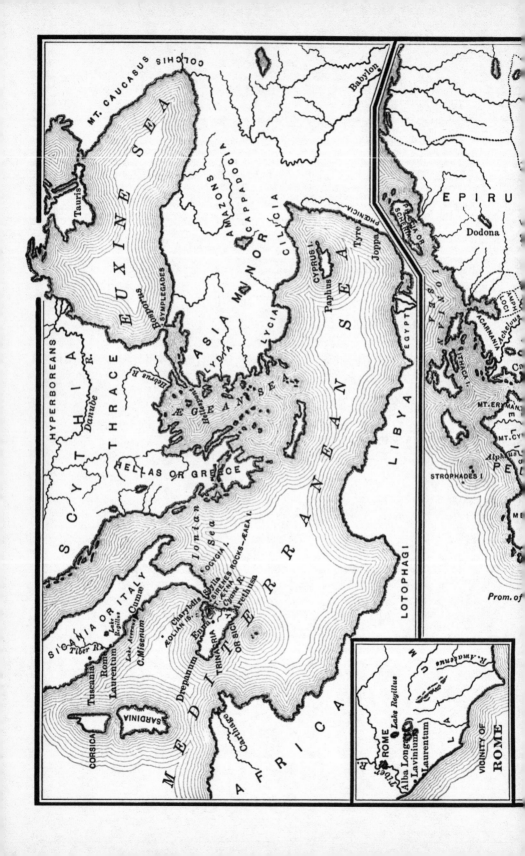

LIST OF ILLUSTRATIONS

HOMER	ii
AMOR	4
FOUNTAIN OF CYBELE (RHEA)	9
MINERVA AND PROMETHEUS	16
PANDORA	20
HOPE	24
OLYMPIAN ZEUS	30
GANYMEDE AND THE EAGLE	33
THE ABDUCTION OF EUROPA	36
JUNO	40
IRIS	43
MINERVA	46
APOLLO BELVEDERE	56
APOLLO AND DAPHNE	59
ORPHEUS AND EURYDICE	68
FARNESE BULL	72
AURORA	76
APOLLO AND THE MUSES	79
DIANA OF VERSAILLES	84
NIOBE	87
VENUS DE MILO	94
FOURTH HOUR OF THE NIGHT	97
SLEEPING LOVE	100
HERO AND LEANDER	106
CUPID AWAKENING PSYCHE	117
CHARON AND PSYCHE	120
FLYING MERCURY	125
VENUS DE MILO AND MARS	134
FORGE OF VULCAN	139
FOUNTAIN OF NEPTUNE	145
FATHER NILE	151
THE FURIES	157
THE THREE FATES	158
BACCHUS	171
MARRIAGE OF BACCHUS AND ARIADNE	177

ABDUCTION OF PROSERPINA	181
CERES	185
A NYMPH	187
SCHOOL OF THE VESTAL VIRGINS	196
THE VESTAL TUCCIA	198
GENIUS OF DEATH	207
HERCULES AN INFANT	216
FARNESE HERCULES	221
MOUNTED AMAZON GOING TO THE CHASE	224
HERCULES AT THE FEET OF OMPHALE	230
FORTUNA	232
HERCULES AND CENTAUR	234
PERSEUS	244
PERSEUS AND ANDROMEDA	248
DÆDALUS AND ICARUS	255
ARIADNE	259
THESEUS	262
JASON AND THE DRAGON	271
MEDEA	273
ATALANTA'S RACE	279
ŒDIPUS AND THE SPHINX	287
ANTIGONE AND ISMENE	292
CHIMÆRA	297
VERTUMNUS AND POMONA	307
PARIS	313
ABDUCTION OF HELEN	317
PARTING OF HECTOR AND ANDROMACHE	326
THETIS BEARING THE ARMOR OF ACHILLES	333
LAOCOON	339
TRIUMPH OF GALATEA	347
ACIS AND GALATEA (EVENING)	348
CIRCE AND THE FRIENDS OF ULYSSES	355
SIREN	358
PENELOPE	363
ÆNEAS AT THE COURT OF DIDO	376
CUMÆAN SIBYL	379

PREFACE

The myths of Greece and Rome have inspired so much of the best thought in English literature that a knowledge of them is often essential to the understanding of what we read.

"When Byron calls Rome," says Thomas Bulfinch, "'the Niobe of nations,' or says of Venice, 'She looks a Sea-Cybele fresh from Ocean,' he calls up to the mind of one familiar with our subject illustrations more vivid and striking than the pencil could furnish, but which are lost to the reader ignorant of mythology." Literature abounds in such poetic borrowings from the classics, and it is impossible to enjoy fully the works of some of our best writers if we cannot immediately appreciate their imagery.

Again, expressions such as "the heel of Achilles" are part of the common language, but their meaning is lost upon those to whom the myths from which they are derived are unfamiliar.

But apart from the practical utility of the myths, as necessary to the comprehension of much that we read and hear, they have a great aesthetic value, presenting, as they do, a mine of imaginative material whose richness and beauty cannot fail to appeal even to the colder sensibilities of this more prosaic age. It would be difficult, indeed, to exaggerate the importance of these old-world stories, with their wonderful admixture of pagan faith and riotous imagination, in correcting the tendency to mere utilitarianism in the education of the young, and there is need to lay stress upon this because of the increased attention now being given to science and modern languages at the expense of the classics.

Translations of the exquisite writings of the Greek and Latin poets cannot, of course, convey the same rich impressions. They are, at the best, weak and imperfect vehicles for reproducing the literary and imaginative wealth of a golden age; but they are, nevertheless, capable of imparting something of the atmosphere of the great originals, and, in whatever tongue they may be told, the stories themselves cannot easily be spoilt; they will assuredly appeal to thousands to whom the ancient languages of Greece and Rome are as a sealed book.

The writings of many of the great English classical translators, it may be added, are instinct with the spirit of the ancients. We might fancy that they, too, had caught sight of Proteus rising from the sea, and had heard

Old Triton blow his wreathéd horn.

But properly to understand even these translations we first require a knowledge of mythology which it would take a lifetime to acquire piece by piece from general reading, and the aims, therefore, of this book are: first, to present outlines of the stories in a simple form pleasurable to the reader who has no desire further than to obtain a general knowledge of the myths, or to be entertained; and, second, to furnish a practical guide for the student who wishes to prosecute his mythological studies, and who desires to acquire the means whereby he will be enabled to follow intelligently the allusions to other myths which meet him at every turn, and to know something of the origin and significance of the stories.

The numerous quotations throughout will show the way to the noble pasturage from which these "flowers of Parnassus" have been culled, and they will enable the reader to appreciate the great influence of the myths upon our literature. The large selection of reproductions from famous pictures and statuary, also, will show something of the debt which art, both ancient and modern, owes to the same inspiration.

The myths are told as graphically and accurately as possible, great care being taken, however, to avoid the more repulsive features of heathen mythology; and when two or more versions of the same myth occur, the preference has invariably been given to the most popular, that is to say, to the one which has inspired the greatest works.

Both the Latin and the Greek forms of proper names are given, but the Latin names are usually retained throughout the narrative, because more frequently used in poetry and art.

The closing chapter includes an analysis of myths by the light of philology and comparative mythology, and the philological explanation of the stories related in the preceding chapters.

A map, genealogical table, and complete glossary and index adapt this volume for constant use in the library, the school, and the arm-chair.

Chapter I

THE BEGINNING OF ALL THINGS

Mythology is the science which treats of the early traditions, or myths, relating to the religion of the ancients, and includes, besides a full account of the origin of their gods, their theory concerning the beginning of all things.

MYTHS OF CREATION

Among all the nations scattered over the face of the earth, the Hebrews alone were instructed by God, who gave them not only a full account of the creation of the world and of all living creatures, but also a code of laws to regulate their conduct. All the questions they fain would ask were fully answered, and no room remained for conjecture.

It was not so, however, with the other nations. The Greeks and Romans, for instance, lacking the definite knowledge which we obtain from the Scriptures, and still anxious to know everything, were forced to construct, in part, their own theory. As they looked about them for some clue to serve as guide, they could not help but observe and admire the wonders of nature. The succession of day and night, summer and winter, rain and sunshine; the fact that the tallest trees sprang from tiny seeds, the greatest rivers from diminutive streams, and the most beautiful flowers and delicious fruits from small green buds,—all seemed to tell them of a superior Being, who had fashioned them to serve a definite purpose.

They soon came to the conclusion that a hand mighty enough to call all these wonders into life, could also have created the beautiful Earth whereon they dwelt. These thoughts gave rise to others; suppositions became certainties; and soon the following myth or fable was evolved, to be handed down from generation to generation.

At first, when all things lay in a great confused mass,—

Ere earth, and sea, and covering heavens, were known,
The face of nature, o'er the world, was one;
And men have call'd it Chaos; formless, rude,
The mass; dead matter's weight, inert, and crude;
Where, in mix'd heap of ill-compounded mold,
The jarring seeds of things confusedly roll'd.

OVID (Elton's tr.)

The Earth did not exist. Land, sea, and air were mixed up together; so that the earth was not solid, the sea was not fluid, nor the air transparent.

No sun yet beam'd from yon cerulean height;
No orbing moon repair'd her horns of light;
No earth, self-poised, on liquid ether hung;
No sea its world-enclasping waters flung;
Earth was half air, half sea, an embryo heap;
Nor earth was fix'd, nor fluid was the deep;
Dark was the void of air; no form was traced;
Obstructing atoms struggled through the waste;
Where cold, and hot, and moist, and dry rebell'd;
Heavy the light, and hard the soft repell'd.

OVID (Elton's tr.)

CHAOS AND NYX

Over this shapeless mass reigned a careless deity called Chaos, whose personal appearance could not be described, as there was no light by which he could be seen. He shared his throne with his wife, the dark goddess of Night, named Nyx or Nox, whose black robes, and still blacker countenance, did not tend to enliven the surrounding gloom.

EREBUS, ÆTHER, AND HEMERA

These two divinities wearied of their power in the course of time, and called their son Erebus (Darkness) to their assistance. His first act was to dethrone and supplant Chaos; and then, thinking he would be happier with a helpmeet, he married his own mother, Nyx. Of course, with our present views, this marriage was a heinous sin; but the ancients, who at first had no fixed laws, did not consider this union unsuitable, and recounted how Erebus and Nyx ruled over the chaotic world together, until their two beautiful children, Æther (Light) and Hemera (Day), acting in concert, dethroned them, and seized the supreme power.

CREATION OF GÆA AND URANUS

Space, illumined for the first time by their radiance, revealed itself in all its uncouthness. Æther and Hemera carefully examined the confusion, saw its innumerable possibilities, and decided to evolve from it a "thing of beauty"; but quite conscious of the magnitude of such an undertaking, and feeling that some assistance would be desirable, they summoned Eros (Amor or Love), their own child, to their aid. By their combined efforts, Pontus (the Sea) and Gæa (Ge, Tellus, Terra), as the Earth was first called, were created.

In the beginning the Earth did not present the beautiful appearance that it does now. No trees waved their leafy branches on the hillsides; no flowers bloomed in the valleys; no grass grew on the plains; no birds flew through the air. All was silent, bare, and motionless. Eros, the first to perceive these deficiencies, seized his life-giving arrows and pierced the cold bosom of the Earth. Immediately the brown surface was covered with luxuriant verdure; birds of many colors flitted through the foliage of the new-born forest trees; animals of all kinds gamboled over the grassy plains; and swift-darting fishes swam in the limpid streams. All was now life, joy, and motion.

Gæa, roused from her apathy, admired all that had already been done for her embellishment, and, resolving to crown and complete the work so well begun, created Uranus (Heaven).

> Her first-born Earth produc'd,
> Of like immensity, the starry Heaven:
> That he might sheltering compass her around
> On every side.
>
>   HESIOD (Elton's tr.)

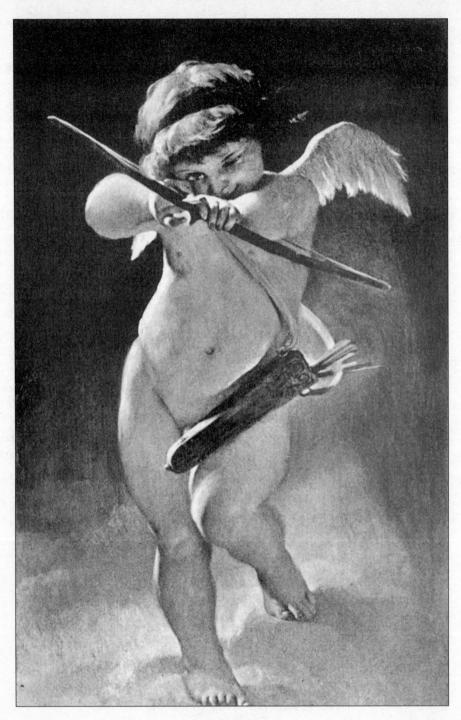

AMOR. Martin.

THE EGG MYTH

This version of the creation of the world, although but one of the many current with the Greeks and Romans, was the one most generally adopted; but another, also very popular, stated that the first divinities, Erebus and Nyx, produced a gigantic egg, from which Eros, the god of love, emerged to create the Earth.

> In the dreary chaotical closet
> Of Erebus old, was a privy deposit,
> By Night the primæval in secrecy laid;
> A Mystical Egg, that in silence and shade
> Was brooded and hatched; till time came about:
> And Love, the delightful, in glory flew out.
>
> ARISTOPHANES (Frere's tr.)

MOUNT OLYMPUS AND THE RIVER OCEANUS

The Earth thus created was supposed by the ancients to be a disk, instead of a sphere as science has proved. The Greeks fancied that their country occupied a central position, and that Mount Olympus, a very high mountain, the mythological abode of their gods, was placed in the exact center. Their Earth was divided into two equal parts by Pontus (the Sea,—equivalent to our Mediterranean and Black Seas); and all around it flowed the great river Oceanus in a "steady, equable current," undisturbed by storm, from which the Sea and all the rivers were supposed to derive their waters.

THE HYPERBOREANS

The Greeks also imagined that the portion of the Earth directly north of their country was inhabited by a fortunate race of men, the Hyperboreans, who dwelt in continual bliss, and enjoyed a never-ending springtide. Their homes were said to be "inaccessible by land or by sea." They were "exempt from disease, old age, and death," and were so virtuous that the gods frequently visited them, and even condescended to share their feasts and games. A people thus favored could not fail to be happy, and many were the songs in praise of their sunny land.

I come from a land in the sun-bright deep,
    Where golden gardens grow;
Where the winds of the north, becalm'd in sleep,
    Their conch shells never blow.

So near the track of the stars are we,
    That oft, on night's pale beams,
The distant sounds of their harmony
    Come to our ears, like dreams.

The Moon, too, brings her world so nigh,
    That when the night-seer looks
To that shadowless orb, in a vernal sky,
    He can number its hills and brooks.

To the Sun god all our hearts and lyres
    By day, by night, belong;
And the breath we draw from his living fires
    We give him back in song.

                                        MOORE

THE ETHIOPIANS AND THE ISLES OF THE BLEST

South of Greece, also near the great river Oceanus, dwelt another nation, just as happy and virtuous as the Hyperboreans,—the Ethiopians. They, too, often enjoyed the company of the gods, who shared their innocent pleasures with great delight.

And far away, on the shore of this same marvelous river, according to some mythologists, were the beautiful Isles of the Blest, where mortals who had led virtuous lives, and had thus found favor in the sight of the gods, were transported without tasting of death, and where they enjoyed an eternity of bliss. These islands had sun, moon, and stars of their own, and were never visited by the cold wintry winds that swept down from the north.

> The Isles of the Blest, they say,
>   The Isles of the Blest,
> Are peaceful and happy, by night and by day,
>   Far away in the glorious west.
>
> They need not the moon in that land of delight,
>   They need not the pale, pale star;
> The sun is bright, by day and night,
>   Where the souls of the blessed are.
>
> They till not the ground, they plow not the wave,
>   They labor not, never! oh, never!
> Not a tear do they shed, not a sigh do they heave,
>   They are happy, for ever and ever!
>
> PINDAR

URANUS AND GÆA

Chaos, Erebus, and Nyx were deprived of their power by Æther and Hemera, who did not long enjoy the possession of the scepter; for Uranus and Gæa, more powerful than their progenitors, soon forced them to depart, and began to reign in their stead. They had not dwelt long on the summit of Mount Olympus, before they found themselves the parents of twelve gigantic children, the Titans, whose strength was such that their father, Uranus, greatly feared them. To prevent their ever making use of it against him, he seized them immediately after their birth, hurled them down into a dark abyss called Tartarus, and there chained them fast.

TITANS, CYCLOPES, AND CENTIMANI

This chasm was situated far under the earth; and Uranus knew that his six sons (Oceanus, Cœus, Crius, Hyperion, Iapetus, and Cronus), as well as his six daughters, the Titanides (Ilia, Rhea, Themis, Thetis, Mnemosyne, and Phœbe), could not easily escape from its cavernous depths. The Titans did not long remain sole occupants of Tartarus, for one day the brazen doors were again thrown wide open to admit the Cyclopes,—Brontes (Thunder), Steropes (Lightning), and Arges (Sheet-lightning),—three later-born children of Uranus and Gæa, who helped the Titans to make the darkness hideous with their incessant clamor for freedom. In due time their number was increased by the three terrible Centimani (Hundred-handed), Cottus, Briareus, and Gyes, who were sent thither by Uranus to share their fate.

Greatly dissatisfied with the treatment her children had received at their father's hands, Gæa remonstrated, but all in vain. Uranus would not grant her request to set the giants free, and, whenever their muffled cries reached his ear, he trembled for his own safety. Angry beyond all expression, Gæa swore revenge, and descended into Tartarus, where she urged the Titans to conspire against their father, and attempt to wrest the scepter from his grasp.

THE TITANS REVOLT

All listened attentively to the words of sedition; but none were courageous enough to carry out her plans, except Cronus, the youngest of the Titans, more familiarly known as Saturn or Time, who found confinement and chains peculiarly galling, and who hated his father for his cruelty. Gæa finally induced him to lay violent hands upon his sire, and, after releasing him from his bonds, gave him a scythe, and bade him be of good cheer and return victorious.

Thus armed and admonished, Cronus set forth, came upon his father unawares, defeated him, thanks to his extraordinary weapon, and, after binding him fast, took possession of the vacant throne, intending to rule the universe forever. Enraged at this insult, Uranus cursed his son, and prophesied that a day would come when he, too, would be supplanted by his children, and would suffer just punishment for his rebellion.

CRONUS AND RHEA

Cronus paid no heed to his father's imprecations, but calmly proceeded to release the Titans, his brothers and sisters, who, in their joy and gratitude to escape the dismal realm of Tartarus, expressed their willingness to be ruled by him. Their

FOUNTAIN OF CYBELE (RHEA). (Madrid.)

satisfaction was complete, however, when he chose his own sister Rhea (Cybele, Ops) for his consort, and assigned to each of the others some portion of the world to govern at will. To Oceanus and Thetis, for example, he gave charge over the ocean and all the rivers upon earth; while to Hyperion and Phœbe he entrusted the direction of the sun and moon, which the ancients supposed were daily driven across the sky in brilliant golden chariots.

Peace and security now reigned on and around Mount Olympus; and Cronus, with great satisfaction, congratulated himself on the result of his enterprise. One fine morning, however, his equanimity was disturbed by the announcement that a son was born to him. The memory of his father's curse then suddenly returned to his mind. Anxious to avert so great a calamity as the loss of his power, he hastened to his wife, determined to devour the child, and thus prevent him from causing further annoyance. Wholly unsuspicious, Rhea heard him inquire for his son. Gladly she placed him in his extended arms; but imagine her surprise and horror when she beheld her husband swallow the babe!

Birth of Jupiter

Time passed, and another child was born, but only to meet with the same cruel fate. One infant after another disappeared down the capacious throat of the voracious Cronus,—a personification of Time, who creates only to destroy. In vain the bereaved mother besought the life of one little one: the selfish, hard-hearted father would not relent. As her prayers seemed unavailing, Rhea finally resolved to obtain by stratagem the boon her husband denied; and as soon as her youngest son, Jupiter (Jove, Zeus), was born, she concealed him.

Cronus, aware of his birth, soon made his appearance, determined to dispose of him in the usual summary manner. For some time Rhea pleaded with him, but at last pretended to yield to his commands. Hastily wrapping a large stone in swaddling clothes, she handed it to Cronus, simulating intense grief. Cronus was evidently not of a very inquiring turn of mind, for he swallowed the whole without investigating the real contents of the shapeless bundle.

> To th' imperial son of Heaven,
> Whilom the king of gods, a stone she gave
> Inwrapt in infant swathes; and this with grasp
> Eager he snatch'd, and in his ravening breast
> Convey'd away: unhappy! nor once thought
> That for the stone his child behind remain'd
> Invincible, secure; who soon, with hands
> Of strength o'ercoming him, should cast him forth
> From glory, and himself th' immortals rule.
>
> HESIOD (Elton's tr.)

Ignorant of the deception practiced upon him, Cronus then took leave, and the overjoyed mother clasped her rescued treasure to her breast. It was not sufficient, however, to have saved young Jupiter from imminent death: it was also necessary that his father should remain unconscious of his existence.

JUPITER'S INFANCY

To insure this, Rhea intrusted her babe to the tender care of the Melian nymphs, who bore him off to a cave on Mount Ida. There a goat, Amalthea, was procured to act as nurse, and fulfilled her office so acceptably that she was eventually placed in the heavens as a constellation, a brilliant reward for her kind ministrations. To prevent Jupiter's cries being heard in Olympus, the Curetes (Corybantes), Rhea's priests, uttered piercing screams, clashed their weapons, executed fierce dances, and chanted rude war songs.

The real significance of all this unwonted noise and commotion was not at all understood by Cronus, who, in the intervals of his numerous affairs, congratulated himself upon the cunning he had shown to prevent the accomplishment of his father's curse. But all his anxiety and fears were aroused when he suddenly became aware of the fraud practiced upon him, and of young Jupiter's continued existence. He immediately tried to devise some plan to get rid of him; but, before he could put it into execution, he found himself attacked, and, after a short but terrible encounter, signally defeated.

JUPITER'S SUPREMACY

Jupiter, delighted to have triumphed so quickly, took possession of the supreme power, and aided by Rhea's counsels, and by a nauseous potion prepared by Metis, a daughter of Oceanus, compelled Cronus to produce the unfortunate children he had swallowed; i.e., Neptune, Pluto, Vesta, Ceres, and Juno.

Following the example of his predecessor, Jupiter gave his brothers and sisters a fair share of his new kingdom. The wisest among the Titans—Mnemosyne, Themis, Oceanus, and Hyperion—submitted to the new sovereign without murmur, but the others refused their allegiance; which refusal, of course, occasioned a deadly conflict.

> When gods began with wrath,
> And war rose up between their starry brows,
> Some choosing to cast Cronus from his throne
> That Zeus might king it there, and some in haste
> With opposite oaths that they would have no Zeus
> To rule the gods forever.
>
> E. B. BROWNING

THE GIANTS' WAR

Jupiter, from the top of Mount Olympus, discerned the superior number of his foes, and, quite aware of their might, concluded that reënforcements to his party would not be superfluous. In haste, therefore, he released the Cyclopes from Tartarus, where they had languished so long, stipulating that in exchange for their freedom they should supply him with thunderbolts,—weapons which only they knew how to forge. This new engine caused great terror and dismay in the ranks of the enemy, who, nevertheless, soon rallied, and struggled valiantly to overthrow the usurper and win back the sovereignty of the world.

During ten long years the war raged incessantly, neither party wishing to submit to the dominion of the other, but at the end of that time the rebellious Titans were obliged to yield. Some of them were hurled into Tartarus once more, where they were carefully secured by Neptune, Jupiter's brother, while the young conqueror joyfully proclaimed his victory.

League all your forces then, ye powers above,
Join all, and try th' omnipotence of Jove:
Let down our golden everlasting chain,
Whose strong embrace holds heaven and earth and main:
Strive all, of mortal and immortal birth,
To drag, by this, the Thunderer down to earth,
Ye strive in vain! if I but stretch this hand,
I heave the gods, the ocean, and the land;
I fix the chain to great Olympus' height,
And the vast world hangs trembling in my sight!
For such I reign, unbounded and above;
And such are men and gods, compar'd to Jove.

HOMER (Pope's tr.)

The scene of this mighty conflict was supposed to have been in Thessaly, where the country bears the imprint of some great natural convulsion; for the ancients imagined that the gods, making the most of their gigantic strength and stature, hurled huge rocks at each other, and piled mountain upon mountain to reach the abode of Jupiter, the Thunderer.

Mountain on mountain, as the Titans erst,
My brethren, scaling the high seat of Jove,
Heaved Pelion upon Ossa's shoulders broad
In vain emprise.

LOWELL

Saturn, or Cronus, the leader and instigator of the revolt, weary at last of bloodshed and strife, withdrew to Italy, or Hesperia, where he founded a prosperous kingdom, and reigned in peace for many long years.

THE DEATH OF TYPHŒUS

Jupiter, having disposed of all the Titans, now fancied he would enjoy the power so unlawfully obtained; but Gæa, to punish him for depriving her children of their birthright, created a terrible monster, called TyphŒus, or Typhon, which she sent to attack him. This TyphŒus was a giant, from whose trunk one hundred dragon heads arose; flames shot from his eyes, nostrils, and mouths; while he incessantly uttered such blood-curdling screams, that the gods, in terror, fled from Mount Olympus and sought refuge in Egypt. In mortal fear lest this terror-inspiring monster would pursue them, the gods there assumed the forms of different animals; and Jupiter became a ram, while Juno, his sister and queen, changed herself into a cow.

The king of the gods, however, soon became ashamed of his cowardly flight, and resolved to return to Mount Olympus to slay TyphŒus with his terrible thunderbolts. A long and fierce struggle ensued, at the end of which, Jupiter, again victorious, viewed his fallen foe with boundless pride; but his triumph was very short-lived.

Defeat of Enceladus

Enceladus, another redoubtable giant, also created by Gæa, now appeared to avenge TyphŒus. He too was signally defeated, and bound with adamantine chains in a burning cave under Mount Ætna. In early times, before he had become accustomed to his prison, he gave vent to his rage by outcries, imprecations, and groans: sometimes he even breathed forth fire and flames, in hopes of injuring his conqueror. But time, it is said, somewhat cooled his resentment; and now he is content with an occasional change of position, which, owing to his huge size, causes the earth to tremble over a space of many miles, producing what is called an earthquake.

> 'Tis said, that thunder-struck Enceladus,
> Groveling beneath the incumbent mountain's weight,
> Lies stretched supine, eternal prey of flames;
> And, when he heaves against the burning load,
> Reluctant, to invert his broiling limbs,
> A sudden earthquake shoots through all the isle,
> And Ætna thunders dreadful under ground,
> Then pours out smoke in wreathing curls convolved,
> And shades the sun's bright orb, and blots out day.
>
> Addison

JUPITER DIVIDES HIS REALM

Jupiter had now conquered all his foes, asserted his right to the throne, and could at last reign over the world undisturbed; but he knew that it would be no small undertaking to rule well heaven, earth, and sea, and resolved to divide the power with his brothers. To avoid quarrels and recriminations, he portioned the world out into lots, allowing each of his brothers the privilege of drawing his own share.

Neptune thus obtained control over the sea and all the rivers, and immediately expressed his resolve to wear a symbolic crown, composed exclusively of marine shells and aquatic plants, and to abide within the bounds of his watery realm.

Pluto, the most taciturn of the brothers, received for his portion the scepter of Tartarus and all the Lower World, where no beam of sunlight was ever allowed to find its way; while Jupiter reserved for himself the general supervision of his brothers' estates, and the direct management of Heaven and Earth.

Peace now reigned throughout all the world. Not a murmur was heard, except from the Titans, who at length, seeing that further opposition would be useless, grew reconciled to their fate.

In the days of their prosperity, the Titans had intermarried. Cronus had taken Rhea "for better or for worse"; and Iapetus had seen, loved, and wedded the fair Clymene, one of the ocean nymphs, or Oceanides, daughters of Oceanus. The latter pair became the proud parents of four gigantic sons,—Atlas, Menetius, Prometheus (Forethought), and Epimetheus (Afterthought),—who were destined to play prominent parts in Grecian mythology.

STORY OF PROMETHEUS

At the time of the creation, after covering the new-born Earth with luxuriant vegetation, and peopling it with living creatures of all kinds, Eros perceived that it would be necessary to endow them with instincts which would enable them to preserve and enjoy the life they had received. He therefore called the youngest two sons of Iapetus to his aid, and bade them make a judicious distribution of gifts to all living creatures, and create and endow a superior being, called Man, to rule over all the others.

Prometheus' and Epimetheus' first care was, very naturally, to provide for the beings already created. These they endowed with such reckless generosity, that

MINERVA AND PROMETHEUS. Thorwaldsen.
(Copenhagen.)

all their favors were soon dispensed, and none remained for the endowment of man. Although they had not the remotest idea how to overcome this difficulty, they proceeded to fashion man from clay.

> Prometheus first transmuted
> Atoms culled for human clay.
> HORACE

They first molded an image similar in form to the gods; bade Eros breathe into its nostrils the spirit of life, and Minerva (Pallas) endow it with a soul; whereupon man lived, and moved, and viewed his new domain.

Justly proud of his handiwork, Prometheus observed man, and longed to bestow upon him some great power, unshared by any other creature of mortal birth, which would raise him far above all other living beings, and bring him nearer to the perfection of the immortal gods. Fire alone, in his estimation, could effect this; but fire was the special possession and prerogative of the gods, and Prometheus knew they would never willingly share it with man, and that, should any one obtain it by stealth, they would never forgive the thief. Long he pondered the matter, and finally determined to obtain fire, or die in the attempt.

One dark night, therefore, he set out for Olympus, entered unperceived into the gods' abode, seized a lighted brand, hid it in his bosom, and departed unseen, exulting in the success of his enterprise. Arrived upon earth once more, he consigned the stolen treasure to the care of man, who immediately adapted it to various purposes, and eloquently expressed his gratitude to the benevolent deity who had risked his own life to obtain it for him.

> Of Prometheus, how undaunted
>   On Olympus' shining bastions
> His audacious foot he planted,
> Myths are told and songs are chanted,
>   Full of promptings and suggestions.

> Beautiful is the tradition
>   Of that flight through heavenly portals,
> The old classic superstition
>   Of the theft and the transmission
>   Of the fire of the Immortals.
>
> LONGFELLOW

From his lofty throne on the topmost peak of Mount Olympus Jupiter beheld an unusual light down upon earth. Anxious to ascertain its exact nature, he watched it closely, and before long discovered the larceny. His anger then burst forth, terrible to behold; and the gods all quailed when they heard him solemnly vow he would punish the unhappy Prometheus without mercy. To seize the offender in his mighty grasp, bear him off to the Caucasian Mountains, and bind him fast to a great rock, was but a moment's work. There a voracious vulture was summoned to feast upon his liver, the tearing of which from his side by the bird's cruel beak and talons caused the sufferer intense anguish. All day long the vulture gorged himself; but during the cool night, while the bird slept, Prometheus' suffering abated, and the liver grew again, thus prolonging the torture, which bade fair to have no end.

Disheartened by the prospect of long years of unremitting pain, Prometheus at times could not refrain from pitiful complaints; but generation after generation of men lived on earth, and died, blessing him for the gift he had obtained for them at such a terrible cost. After many centuries of woe, Hercules, son of Jupiter and Alcmene, found Prometheus, killed the vulture, broke the adamantine chains, and liberated the long-suffering god.

STORY OF EPIMETHEUS AND PANDORA

The first mortals lived on earth in a state of perfect innocence and bliss. The air was pure and balmy; the sun shone brightly all the year; the earth brought forth delicious fruit in abundance; and beautiful, fragrant flowers bloomed everywhere. Man was content. Extreme cold, hunger, sickness, and death were unknown. Jupiter, who justly ascribed a good part of this beatific condition to the gift conferred by Prometheus, was greatly displeased, and tried to devise some means to punish mankind for the acceptance of the heavenly fire.

With this purpose in view, he assembled the gods on Mount Olympus, where, in solemn council, they decided to create woman; and, as soon as she had been artfully fashioned, each one endowed her with some special charm, to make her more attractive.

> The crippled artist-god,
> Illustrious, molded from the yielding clay
> A bashful virgin's image, as advis'd
> Saturnian Jove.

*   *   *   *   *

> But now when the fair mischief, seeming-good,
> His hand had perfected, he led her forth
> Exulting in her grac'd attire, the gift
> Of Pallas, in the midst of gods and men.
> On men and gods in that same moment seiz'd
> The ravishment of wonder, when they saw
> The deep deceit, th' inextricable snare.
>
> HESIOD (Elton's tr.)

Their united efforts were crowned with the utmost success. Nothing was lacking, except a name for the peerless creature; and the gods, after due consideration, decreed she should be called Pandora. They then bade Mercury take her to Prometheus as a gift from heaven; but he, knowing only too well that nothing good would come to him from the gods, refused to accept her, and cautioned his brother Epimetheus to follow his example. Unfortunately Epimetheus was of a confiding disposition, and when he beheld the maiden he exclaimed, "Surely so beautiful and gentle a being can bring no evil!" and accepted her most joyfully.

The first days of their union were spent in blissful wanderings, hand in hand, under the cool forest shade; in weaving garlands of fragrant flowers; and in refreshing themselves with the luscious fruit, which hung so temptingly within reach.

One lovely evening, while dancing on the green, they saw Mercury, Jupiter's messenger, coming towards them. His step was slow and weary, his garments

PANDORA. Sichel.

dusty and travel-stained, and he seemed almost to stagger beneath the weight of a huge box which rested upon his shoulders. Pandora immediately ceased dancing, to speculate with feminine curiosity upon the contents of the chest. She nudged Epimetheus, and in a whisper begged him to ask Mercury what brought him thither. Epimetheus complied with her request; but Mercury evaded the question, asked permission to deposit his burden in their dwelling for safekeeping, professing himself too weary to convey it to its destination that day, and promised to call for it shortly. The permission was promptly granted. Mercury, with a sigh of relief, placed the box in one corner, and then departed, refusing all hospitable offers of rest and refreshment.

He had scarcely crossed the threshold, when Pandora expressed a strong desire to have a peep at the contents of the mysterious box; but Epimetheus, surprised and shocked, told her that her curiosity was unseemly, and then, to dispel the frown and pout seen for the first time on the fair face of his beloved, he entreated her to come out into the fresh air and join in the merry games of their companions. For the first time, also, Pandora refused to comply with his request. Dismayed, and very much discouraged, Epimetheus sauntered out alone, thinking she would soon join him, and perhaps by some caress atone for her present willfulness.

Left alone with the mysterious casket, Pandora became more and more inquisitive. Stealthily she drew near, and examined it with great interest, for it was curiously wrought of dark wood, and surmounted by a delicately carved head, of such fine workmanship that it seemed to smile and encourage her. Around the box a glittering golden cord was wound, and fastened on top in an intricate knot. Pandora, who prided herself specially on her deft fingers, felt sure she could unfasten it, and, reasoning that it would not be indiscreet to untie it if she did not raise the lid, she set to work. Long she strove, but all in vain. Ever and anon the laughing voices of Epimetheus and his companions, playing in the luxuriant shade, were wafted in on the summer breeze. Repeatedly she heard them call, and beseech her to join them; yet she persisted in her attempt. She was just on the point of giving it up in despair, when suddenly the refractory knot yielded to her fumbling fingers, and the cord, unrolling, dropped on the floor.

Pandora had repeatedly fancied that sounds like whispers issued from the box. The noise now seemed to increase, and she breathlessly applied her ear to the lid to ascertain whether it really proceeded from within. Imagine, therefore, her surprise when she distinctly heard these words, uttered in the most pitiful accents: "Pandora, dear Pandora, have pity upon us! Free us from this gloomy prison! Open, open, we beseech you!"

Pandora's heart beat so fast and loud, that it seemed for a moment to drown all other sounds. Should she open the box? Just then a familiar step outside made her start guiltily. Epimetheus was coming, and she knew he would urge her again to come out, and would prevent the gratification of her curiosity. Precipitately, therefore, she raised the lid to have one little peep before he came in.

Now, Jupiter had malignantly crammed into this box all the diseases, sorrows, vices, and crimes that afflict poor humanity; and the box was no sooner opened, than all these ills flew out, in the guise of horrid little brown-winged creatures, closely resembling moths. These little insects fluttered about, alighting, some upon Epimetheus, who had just entered, and some upon Pandora, pricking and stinging them most unmercifully. Then they flew out through the open door and windows, and fastened upon the merrymakers without, whose shouts of joy were soon changed into wails of pain and anguish.

Epimetheus and Pandora had never before experienced the faintest sensation of pain or anger; but, as soon as these winged evil spirits had stung them, they began to weep, and, alas! quarreled for the first time in their lives. Epimetheus reproached his wife in bitterest terms for her thoughtless action; but in the very midst of his vituperation he suddenly heard a sweet little voice entreat for freedom. The sound proceeded from the unfortunate box, whose cover Pandora had dropped again, in the first moment of her surprise and pain. "Open, open, and I will heal your wounds! Please let me out!" it pleaded.

The tearful couple viewed each other inquiringly, and listened again. Once more they heard the same pitiful accents; and Epimetheus bade his wife open the box and set the speaker free, adding very amiably, that she had already done so much harm by her ill-fated curiosity, that it would be difficult to add materially to its evil consequences, and that, perchance, the box contained some good spirit, whose ministrations might prove beneficial.

It was well for Pandora that she opened the box a second time, for the gods, with a sudden impulse of compassion, had concealed among the evil spirits one kindly creature, Hope, whose mission was to heal the wounds inflicted by her fellow-prisoners.

> Hope sole remain'd within, nor took her flight,
> Beneath the vessel's verge conceal'd from light.
>
> HESIOD (Elton's tr.)

Lightly fluttering hither and thither on her snowy pinions, Hope touched the punctured places on Pandora's and Epimetheus' creamy skin, and relieved their suffering, then quickly flew out of the open window, to perform the same gentle office for the other victims, and cheer their downcast spirits.

Thus, according to the ancients, evil entered into the world, bringing untold misery; but Hope followed closely in its footsteps, to aid struggling humanity, and point to a happier future.

> Hope rules a land forever green:
> All powers that serve the bright-eyed Queen
> Are confident and gay;
> Clouds at her bidding disappear;
> Points she to aught?—the bliss draws near,
> And Fancy smooths the way.
>
> WORDSWORTH

During many centuries, therefore, Hope continued to be revered, although the other divinities had ceased to be worshiped.

According to another version, Pandora was sent down to man, bearing a vase in which the evil spirits were imprisoned, and on the way, seized by a fit of curiosity, raised the cover, and allowed them all to escape.

THE FOUR AGES

Little by little the world was peopled; and the first years of man's existence upon earth were, as we have seen, years of unalloyed happiness. There was no occasion for labor, for the earth brought forth spontaneously all that was necessary for man's subsistence. "Innocence, virtue, and truth prevailed; neither were there any laws to restrict men, nor judges to punish." This time of bliss has justly borne the title of Golden Age, and the people in Italy then throve under the wise rule of good old Saturn, or Cronus.

HOPE. Thorwaldsen.

Unfortunately, nothing in this world is lasting; and the Golden Age was ollowed by another, not quite so prosperous, hence called the Silver Age, when the year was first divided into seasons, and men were obliged to toil for their daily bread.

> Succeeding times a silver age behold,
> Excelling brass, but more excell'd by gold.
> Then summer, autumn, winter, did appear,
> And spring was but a season of the year;
> The sun his annual course obliquely made,
> Good days contracted, and enlarg'd the bad.
> The air with sultry heats began to glow,
> The wings of winds were clogg'd with ice and snow;
> And shivering mortals into houses driven,
> Sought shelter from the inclemency of heaven.
> Those houses, then, were caves or homely sheds,
> With twining osiers fenc'd, and moss their beds.
> Then plows, for seed, the fruitful furrows broke,
> And oxen labor'd first beneath the yoke.
>
> OVID (Dryden's tr.)

Yet, in spite of these few hardships, the people were happy, far happier than their descendants during the Age of Brass, which speedily followed, when strife became customary, and differences were settled by blows.

But by far the worst of all was the Iron Age, when men's passions knew no bounds, and they even dared refuse all homage to the immortal gods. War was waged incessantly; the earth was saturated with blood; the rights of hospitality were openly violated; and murder, rape, and theft were committed on all sides.

THE DELUGE

Jupiter had kept a close watch over men's actions during all these years; and this evil conduct aroused his wrath to such a point, that he vowed he would annihilate the human race. But the modes of destruction were manifold, and, as he could not decide which would eventually prove most efficacious, he summoned the gods to deliberate and aid him by their counsels. The first suggestion offered, was to destroy the world by fire, kindled by Jupiter's much-dreaded thunderbolts; and the king of gods was about to put it into instant execution, when his arm was stayed by the objection that the rising flames might set fire to his own abode, and reduce its magnificence to unsightly ashes. He therefore rejected the plan as impracticable, and bade the gods devise other means of destruction.

After much delay and discussion, the immortals agreed to wash mankind off the face of the earth by a mighty deluge. The winds were instructed to gather together the rain clouds over the earth. Neptune let loose the waves of the sea, bidding them rise, overflow, and deluge the land. No sooner had the gods spoken, than the elements obeyed: the winds blew; the rain fell in torrents; lakes, seas, rivers, and oceans broke their bonds; and terrified mortals, forgetting their petty quarrels in a common impulse to flee from the death which threatened them, climbed the highest mountains, clung to uprooted trees, and even took refuge in the light skiffs they had constructed in happier days. Their efforts were all in vain, however; for the waters rose higher and higher, overtook them one after another in their ineffectual efforts to escape, closed over the homes where they might have been so happy, and drowned their last despairing cries in their seething depths.

> Now hills and vales no more distinction know,
> And level'd nature lies oppress'd below;
> The most of mortals perish in the flood.
>
> OVID (Dryden's tr.)

STORY OF DEUCALION AND PYRRHA

The rain continued to fall, until, after many days, the waves covered all the surface of the earth except the summit of Mount Parnassus, the highest peak in Greece. On this mountain, surrounded by the ever-rising flood, stood the son of Prometheus, Deucalion, with his faithful wife Pyrrha, a daughter of Epimetheus and Pandora. From thence they, the sole survivors, viewed the universal desolation with tear-dimmed eyes.

In spite of the general depravity, the lives of this couple had always been pure and virtuous; and when Jupiter saw them there alone, and remembered their piety, he decided not to include them in the general destruction, but to save their lives. He therefore bade the winds return to their cave, and the rain to cease. Neptune, in accordance with his decree, blew a resounding blast upon his conch shell to recall the wandering waves, which immediately returned within their usual bounds.

> At length the world was all restor'd to view,
> But desolate, and of a sickly hue;
> Nature beheld herself, and stood aghast,
> A dismal desert and a silent waste.
>
> Ovid (Dryden's tr.)

Deucalion and Pyrrha followed the receding waves step by step down the steep mountain side, wondering how they should repeople the desolate earth. As they talked, they came to the shrine of Delphi, which alone had been able to resist the force of the waves. There they entered to consult the wishes of the gods. Their surprise and horror were unbounded, however, when a voice exclaimed, "Depart from hence with veiled heads, and cast your mother's bones behind you!" To obey such a command seemed sacrilegious in the extreme; for the dead had always been held in deep veneration by the Greeks, and the desecration of a grave was considered a heinous crime, and punished accordingly. But, they reasoned, the gods' oracles can seldom be accepted in a literal sense; and Deucalion, after due thought, explained to Pyrrha what he conceived to be the meaning of this mysterious command.

"The Earth," said he, "is the mother of all, and the stones may be considered her bones." Husband and wife speedily decided to act upon this premise, and continued their descent, casting stones behind them. All those thrown by Deucalion were immediately changed into men, while those cast by Pyrrha became women.

Thus the earth was peopled for the second time with a blameless race of men, sent to replace the wicked beings slain by Jupiter. Deucalion and Pyrrha shortly after became the happy parents of a son named Hellen, who gave his name to all the Hellenic or Greek race; while his sons Æolus and Dorus, and grandsons Ion and Achæus, became the ancestors of the Æolian, Dorian, Ionian, and Achaian nations.

Other mythologists, in treating of the deluvian myths, state that Deucalion and Pyrrha took refuge in an ark, which, after sailing about for many days, was stranded on the top of Mount Parnassus. This version was far less popular with the Greeks, although it betrays still more plainly the common source whence all these myths are derived.

> Who does not see in drown Deucalion's name,
> When Earth her men and Sea had lost her shore,
> Old Noah!
>
> FLETCHER

Chapter II

JUPITER

JUPITER'S TITLES

Jupiter, Jove, or Zeus, king of the gods, supreme ruler of the universe, the special deity of mankind, the personification of the sky and of all the phenomena of the air, and the guardian of political order and peace, was the most prominent of all the Olympian divinities: the others were obliged to submit to his will, and trembled at his all-powerful nod.

> He, whose all-conscious eyes the world behold,
> The eternal Thunderer sat, enthroned in gold.
> High heaven the footstool of his feet he makes,
> And wide beneath him all Olympus shakes.
>
> He spoke, and awful bends his sable brows,
> Shakes his ambrosial curls, and gives the nod,
> The stamp of fate and sanction of the god:
> High heaven with trembling the dread signal took,
> And all Olympus to the center shook.
>
> —HOMER (Pope's tr.)

The Fates and Destiny alone dared oppose Jupiter's sovereign will, and they continued to issue their irrevocable decrees, even after he supplanted his father and began to rule over all.

In common with all other Greek and Roman divinities, Jupiter, though immortal, was subject to pleasure, pain, grief, and anger, and a prey to all the passions which rule the hearts of men.

It was he who presided at the councils held on the top of "many-peaked Olympus," and summoned the gods whenever he wished to discuss with them any matter of importance, or to indulge in a sumptuous repast, when they ate the celestial ambrosia and quaffed the fragrant nectar.

OLYMPIAN ZEUS. Flaxman.

He is generally represented as a fine majestic figure, with long curling hair and beard, clad in flowing drapery, his redoubtable thunderbolts or scepter in one hand, and a statue of Victory in the other. The world is his footstool; and the eagle, emblem of strength and power, is generally seen close beside him.

JUPITER'S ATTENDANTS

Jupiter had his own special attendants, such as Victoria, or Nice, the goddess of victory, who was ever ready to obey his slightest behest, and it is said her master loved her so dearly, that he generally held an image of her in his hand.

The hundred-tongued goddess of fame, Fama, trumpet in hand, proclaimed, at his bidding, anything he wished, never questioning whether it were true or false.

> Fame than who never plague that runs
> 　Its way more swiftly wins:
> Her very motion lends her power:
> She flies and waxes every hour.
> At first she shrinks, and cowers for dread:
> 　Ere long she soars on high:
> Upon the ground she plants her tread,
> 　Her forehead in the sky.
> 　　　　　VIRGIL (Conington's tr.)

Close by Jupiter's side was sometimes seen Fortuna, goddess of fortune, poised on a constantly revolving wheel, whereon she journeyed throughout the world, scattering with careless hands her numerous gifts, and lavishing with indifference her choicest smiles; while Hebe, or Juventas, the goddess of youth, was ever ready at his wish to pour out the nectar, in which the gods were wont to pledge each other.

> Hebe, honored of them all,
> Ministered nectar, and from cups of gold
> They pledged each other.
> 　　　　　HOMER (Bryant's tr.)

But this fair goddess awkwardly tripped and fell on a solemn occasion, and was forced to resign her office. To replace her, the father of the gods was obliged to go in quest of another cup-bearer.

To facilitate his search, he assumed the form of an eagle, and winged his flight over the earth. He had not flown far, before he beheld a youth of marvelous beauty, alone on a neighboring hill. To swoop down, catch him up in his mighty talons, and bear him safely off to Olympus, was but a moment's work; and there the kidnapped youth Ganymede, the son of a king of Troy, was carefully instructed in the duties he was called upon to perform in the future.

> And godlike Ganymede, most beautiful
> Of men; the gods beheld and caught him up
> To heaven, so beautiful was he, to pour
> The wine to Jove, and ever dwell with them.
>   HOMER (Bryant's tr.)

STORY OF PHILEMON AND BAUCIS

Solicitous for the welfare of mankind, Jupiter often visited the earth, taking great care to assume some disguise which would enable him to ascertain all he wished without any risk of detection. One day he and Mercury, his special messenger and favorite among the gods, took the forms of needy, belated travelers, and entered the lowly hut of a worthy old couple, Philemon and Baucis.

Eager to offer their best to the strangers, these poor people decided to kill their sole remaining goose; but their efforts to secure it were vain, and finally the persecuted fowl took refuge between Jupiter's knees. Touched with their zeal, yet anxious to prevent the death of the confiding goose, Jupiter revealed himself to his faithful worshipers, and in gratitude for their intended sacrifice bade them ask any boon, promising by the great river Styx—the most binding and solemn oath a god could utter—to grant their request.

Contrary to the custom current in similar cases, Philemon and Baucis made a modest and judicious choice, and proffered a timid request that they might serve the gods as long as life and strength endured, and finally die together. This most reasonable wish was immediately granted; and Jupiter, moreover, changed their humble abode into a superb temple, where they could offer daily sacrifices on his altars.

GANYMEDE AND THE EAGLE. (National Museum, Naples.)

Their little shed, scarce large enough for two,
Seems, from the ground increased, in height and bulk to grow.
A stately temple shoots within the skies,
The crotches of their cot in columns rise;
The pavement polish'd marble they behold,
The gates with sculpture grac'd, the spires and tiles of gold.

Ovid (Dryden's tr.)

After many years of faithful service, when age had made them long for death, Philemon and Baucis were transformed into majestic oaks, which stood for many a century in front of the temple, monuments of the love and faith which had bound the pair through life.

Although married to Juno, Jupiter often indulged in love affairs with other goddesses, and even with mortal maidens. The ancients themselves did not practice polygamy, but their gods were supposed to be able to indulge all their passions with impunity. As the personification of the sky, Jupiter, therefore, consorted at times with Juno (the Atmosphere), with Dione (Moisture), with Themis (Justice), etc., without incurring any reproach; for these marriages, in their estimation, were all symbolical.

But Juno being of a jealous disposition, Jupiter was forced to conduct his courtships with great secrecy and circumspection, and therefore generally adopted the precaution of a disguise. To win Europa, the fair daughter of Agenor, for instance, he became a bull.

The gods themselves,
Humbling their deities to love, have taken
The shapes of beasts upon them. Jupiter
Became a bull, and bellow'd.

SHAKESPEARE

JUPITER KIDNAPS EUROPA

One day Europa was playing in her father's meadows with her three brothers, Cadmus, PhŒnix, and Cilix, when she suddenly saw a white bull coming towards her; not with fiery eyes and lowered horns, but gently, as if to express a mute request to be petted. The maiden, delighted, stroked the beast, and decked him with bright garlands of meadow-blossoms. Then, seeing him kneel, as if to invite her to mount, she lightly sprang upon his broad back, calling to her companions to follow her example; but, before they could do as she wished, the bull had risen to his feet, and galloped off towards the sea with his fair burden on his back.

Instead of turning when he saw the foam-crested waves, he plunged into the midst of them, and in a few minutes disappeared from view, so rapidly did he swim away. To reassure the frightened girl, the bull now spoke in gentle accents, bidding her dismiss all fear, for he was the great Jupiter in disguise.

> Take courage, gentle maid! nor fear the tide:
> I, though near-seen a bull, am heavenly Jove:
> I change my shape at will.
>
> MOSCHUS (Elton's tr.)

Pleased with the novelty of her situation, and flattered by the god's evident admiration, Europa ceased to struggle, wound her arms more closely around the bull's neck to prevent the waves from washing her off her perilous seat, and allowed herself to be carried away.

Jupiter finally deposited his fair burden upon the shores of a new land, to which he gallantly gave her name, Europe. He then resumed his wonted form, explained at length his reasons for so unceremoniously kidnapping her, and finally won her consent to their union. Their three sons were Minos, Rhadamanthus, and Sarpedon. The two former were subsequently appointed judges in the Infernal Regions, while the third found an early but glorious death during the Trojan war.

SEARCH FOR EUROPA

All unconscious of their sister's fate, the young princes had returned in haste to their father's palace to announce her sudden involuntary departure. Agenor, whose favorite she had always been, rent his garments for grief, and bade his sons go forth and seek her, and not to return till they had found her. Accompanied by their mother, Telephassa, they immediately set out on their journey, inquiring of all they met if they had seen their sister. Search and inquiry proved equally fruitless.

THE ABDUCTION OF EUROPA. Albani.
(Uffizi Palace, Florence.)

At last, weary of this hopeless quest, PhŒnix refused his further aid, and allowed his sorrowing relatives to continue without him, remaining in a land which from him was called PhŒnicia. Cilix, too, soon followed his example, and settled in a fertile country which they had reached, hence called Cilicia; and finally Telephassa, worn out with grief and fatigue, lay down to die, charging her oldest son to go on alone.

Cadmus wandered on till he came to Delphi, where he consulted the oracle; but, to his great dismay, the only reply he received was, "Follow the cow, and settle where she rests."

In deep perplexity he left the temple, and, from force of habit, journeyed on, patiently questioning all he met. Soon he perceived a cow leisurely walking in front of him, and, mindful of the oracle, he ceased his search and followed her. Urged by curiosity, many adventurers joined him on the way, and, when the cow at last lay down in the land since called BŒotia, they all promised to aid Cadmus, their chosen leader, to found their future capital, which was to be called Thebes.

Founding of Thebes

Parched with thirst after their long walk, the men then hastened to a neighboring spring, but, to Cadmus' surprise, time passed and still they did not return. Armed with his trusty sword, he finally went down to the spring to discover the cause of their delay, and found that they had all been devoured by a huge dragon, which lived in the hollow. The prince raised his sword to avenge their death, and dealt the dragon such a deadly blow upon the head, that he put an immediate end to its existence.

While Cadmus stood there contemplating his lifeless foe, a voice bade him extract the dragon's teeth, and sow them in the ground already broken for his future city. No human being was within sight: so Cadmus knew the order proceeded from the immortal gods, and immediately prepared to obey it. The dragon's teeth were no sooner planted, than a crop of giants sprang from the soil, full grown, and armed to the teeth. They were about to fall upon Cadmus, when the same voice bade him cast a stone in the midst of their close-drawn phalanx. Cadmus, seeing the giants were almost upon him, and that no time was to be lost, quickly threw a stone. The effect produced was almost instantaneous; for the giants, each fancying it had been thrown by his neighbor, began fighting among themselves. In a few minutes the number of giants was reduced to five, who sheathed their bloodstained weapons, and humbly tendered their services to Cadmus. With their aid, the foundations of the city were laid; but their labor was not very arduous, as the gods caused some of the public buildings to rise up out of the ground, all complete, and ready for use.

To reward Cadmus for his loving and painstaking search for Europa, Jupiter gave him the hand of the fair princess Harmonia, a daughter of Mars and Venus, in marriage. Cadmus, the founder of Thebes, is supposed to have invented the alphabet, and introduced its use into Greece. Although his career was very prosperous at first, he finally incurred the wrath of the gods by forgetting, on a solemn occasion, to offer them a suitable sacrifice; and, in anger at his dereliction, they changed him and Harmonia into huge serpents.

Worship of Jupiter

Jupiter was, of course, very widely and generally worshiped by the ancients; and his principal temples—the Capitol at Rome, and the shrine of Jupiter Ammon in Libya—have been world-renowned. He also had a noted temple at Dodona, where an oak tree gave forth mysterious prophecies, which were supposed to have been inspired by the king of gods; this long lost shrine has recently been discovered.

> Oh, where, Dodona! is thine aged grove,
> Prophetic fount, and oracle divine?
> What valley echoed the response of Jove?
> What trace remaineth of the Thunderer's shrine?
> All, all forgotten!
>
> BYRON

A magnificent temple at Olympia, on the Peloponnesus, was also dedicated to Jupiter; and here every fifth year the people of Greece were wont to assemble to celebrate games, in honor of Jupiter's great victory over the Titans. These festivals were known as the Olympian Games; and the Greeks generally reckoned time by olympiads, that is to say, by the space of time between the celebrations. Within the temple at Olympia stood a wonderful statue of gold and ivory, the work of Phidias. Its proportions and beauty were such, that it was counted one of the Seven

Wonders of the ancient world. It is said, too, that the artist, having completed this masterpiece, longed for some sign of approval from heaven, and fervently prayed for a token that the god accepted his labor. Jupiter, in answer to this prayer, sent a vivid flash of lightning, which played about the colossal image, illuminating it, but leaving it quite unharmed.

The Greeks were indebted to Phidias for many of their most exquisite statues of the gods; but none of the others equaled this figure of Jupiter in size, dignity of attitude, or elaborate finish.

> Wise Phidias, thus his skill to prove,
> Through many a god advanc'd to Jove,
> And taught the polish'd rocks to shine
> With airs and lineaments divine;
> Till Greece, amaz'd, and half afraid,
> Th' assembled deities survey'd.
>
> ADDISON

JUNO.
(Vatican, Rome.)

Chapter III

JUNO

Juno's Marriage

Juno (Hera, Here), queen of heaven, and goddess of the atmosphere and of marriage, was the daughter of Cronus and Rhea, and consequently the sister of Jupiter; but, as soon as the latter had dethroned his parents and seized the scepter, he began to look about him for a suitable helpmate. Juno won his affections by her great beauty; and he immediately began his courtship, which he carried on in the guise of a cuckoo, to infuse a little romance into it. He evidently found favor in her sight, and won her consent to share his throne; for shortly afterward their wedding was celebrated with great pomp on Mount Olympus. It was on this solemn occasion that the immortal conclave of the gods declared that Juno should be henceforth honored as goddess of marriage.

> Juno, who presides
> Supreme o'er bridegrooms and o'er brides.
> Virgil (Conington's tr.)

But although in the beginning this union seemed very happy, there soon arose subjects for contention; for unfortunately Jupiter was inclined to be faithless, and Juno jealous, and, like the element she personified, exceedingly variable in her moods. On such occasions she gave way to her violent temper, and bitterly reproached her husband, who, impatient of her censure, punished her severely, and, instead of reforming, merely continued his numerous intrigues with renewed zest.

Story of Callisto and Arcas

On one occasion he fell deeply in love with a maiden named Callisto, gentle, fair, and slender; but, in spite of all the precautions which he took when visiting her, Juno discovered the object of his affections. Night and day she thought and planned, until she devised a species of revenge which seemed adequate. The graceful girl was suddenly bereft of speech, changed into a rough, ungainly bear, and driven out into the solitudes of the great forests, which were from that time forth to be her home. Jupiter vainly sought his missing ladylove, and it was only long afterward that he discovered her and her little bear son Arcas. In pity for all they had suffered, he transferred them both to the sky, where they are still known as the constellations of the Great and Little Bear.

Juno's Attendant

Juno, like her husband, had also her special attendant, Iris (the Rainbow), whom she frequently employed as messenger,—a task which this deity accomplished with as much celerity as Mercury. Her flight through the air was so rapid, that she was seldom seen; and no one would have known she had passed, had it not been for the brilliant trail her many-colored robe left behind her in the sky.

> Like fiery clouds, that flush with ruddy glare,
> Or Iris, gliding through the purple air;
> When loosely girt her dazzling mantle flows,
> And 'gainst the sun in arching colors glows.
>
> FLACCUS (Elton's tr.)

Juno is the mother of Mars, Hebe, and Vulcan, and is always described and represented as a beautiful, majestic woman, clad in flowing robes, with a diadem and scepter. The peacock and cuckoo were both sacred to her, and are therefore often seen at her side.

Worship of Juno

Her principal places of worship were at Mycenæ, Sparta, Argos, Rome, and Heræum. She had also numerous other sanctuaries scattered throughout the ancient world, and was worshiped in the same temples as Jupiter. Many fine statues of this goddess were found in Greece and Italy, some of which are still extant, and serve to show the ancients' exalted conception of the Queen of Heaven.

IRIS. Tito Conti.

Story of Cleobis and Biton

Juno's festivals, the Matronalia, in Rome, were always celebrated with great pomp. Less important feasts were held in each city where a temple was dedicated to her. On one of these occasions an old priestess was very anxious to go to the temple at Argos, where she had ministered to the goddess for many years, and which she had left only to be married. The way was long and dusty: so the aged woman, who could no longer walk such a distance, bade her sons, Cleobis and Biton, harness her white heifers to her car. The youths hastened to do her bidding; but, although they searched diligently, the heifers could not be found. Rather than disappoint their aged mother, who had set her heart upon attending the services, these kind-hearted sons harnessed themselves to the cart, and drew her through the city to the temple gates, amid the acclamations of all the people, who admired this trait of filial devotion.

The mother was so touched by her sons' affection, that, as she knelt before the altar, she fervently prayed Juno to bestow upon them the greatest boon in her power. At the conclusion of the services the ex-priestess went into the portico, where her sons had thrown themselves to rest after their unwonted exertions; but instead of finding them merely asleep, as she expected, she found them dead. The Queen of Heaven had transported them while asleep to the Elysian Fields, the place of endless bliss, where such as they enjoyed eternal life.

Chapter IV

MINERVA

Birth of Minerva

Although immortal, the gods were not exempt from physical pain. One day Jupiter suffered intensely from a sudden headache, and, in hopes that some mode of alleviation would be devised, he summoned all the gods to Olympus. Their united efforts were vain, however; and even the remedies suggested by Apollo, god of medicine, proved inefficacious. Unwilling, or perchance unable, to endure the racking pain any longer, Jupiter bade one of his sons, Vulcan, cleave his head open with an ax. With cheerful alacrity the dutiful god obeyed; and no sooner was the operation performed, than Minerva (Pallas, Athene) sprang out of her father's head, full-grown, clad in glittering armor, with poised spear, and chanting a triumphant song of victory.

> From his awful head
> Whom Jove brought forth, in warlike armor drest,
> Golden, all radiant.
>
> Shelley

The assembled gods recoiled in fear before this unexpected apparition, while at the same time a mighty commotion over land and sea proclaimed the advent of a great divinity.

The goddess, who had thus joined the inhabitants of Olympus, was destined to preside over peace, defensive war, and needlework, to be the incarnation of wisdom, and to put to flight the obscure deity called Dullness, who until then had ruled the world.

MINERVA.
(National Museum, Naples.)

Ere Pallas issu'd from the Thund'rer's head,
Dullness o'er all possess'd her ancient right,
Daughter of Chaos and eternal Night.

POPE

Minerva, having forced her unattractive predecessor to beat an ignominious retreat, quickly seized the scepter, and immediately began to rule in her stead.

NAMING OF ATHENS

Not long after her birth, Cecrops, a PhŒnician, came to Greece, where he founded a beautiful city in the province since called Attica. All the gods watched his undertaking with great interest; and finally, seeing the town promised to become a thriving place, each wished the privilege of naming it. A general council was held, and after some deliberation most of the gods withdrew their claims. Soon none but Minerva and Neptune were left to contend for the coveted honor.

To settle the quarrel without evincing any partiality, Jupiter announced that the city would be intrusted to the protection of the deity who would create the most useful object for the use of man. Raising his trident, Neptune struck the ground, from which a noble horse sprang forth, amid the exclamations of wonder and admiration of all the spectators. His qualities were duly explained by his proud creator, and all thought it quite impossible for Minerva to surpass him. Loudly they laughed, and scornfully too, when she, in her turn, produced an olive tree; but when she had told them the manifold uses to which wood, fruit, foliage, twigs, etc., could be applied, and explained that the olive was a sign of peace and prosperity, and therefore far more desirable than the horse, the emblem of war and wretchedness, they could but acknowledge her gift the most serviceable, and award her the prize.

To commemorate this victory over her rival, Minerva gave her own name of Athene to the city, whose inhabitants, from that time forth, were taught to honor her as their tutelary goddess.

Ever at Jupiter's side, Minerva often aided him by her wise counsels, and in times of war borrowed his terrible shield, the Ægis, which she flung over her shoulder when she sallied forth to give her support to those whose cause was just.

> Her shoulder bore
> The dreadful Ægis with its shaggy brim
> Bordered with Terror. There was Strife, and there
> Was Fortitude, and there was fierce Pursuit,
> And there the Gorgon's head, a ghastly sight,
> Deformed and dreadful, and a sign of woe.
>
> HOMER (Bryant's tr.)

The din of battle had no terrors for this doughty goddess, and on every occasion she was wont to plunge into the thickest of the fray with the utmost valor.

STORY OF ARACHNE

These virile tastes were, however, fully counterbalanced by some exclusively feminine, for Minerva was as deft with her needle as with her sword. In Greece there lived in those olden times a maiden by the name of Arachne. Pretty, young, and winsome, she would have been loved by all had it not been for her inordinate pride, not in her personal advantages, but in her skill as a needlewoman.

Arachne, in her conceit, fancied that no one could equal the work done by her deft fingers, so she boasted far and wide that she would have no fear to match her skill with Minerva's. She made this remark so loudly and so frequently, that the goddess was finally annoyed, and left her seat in high Olympus to come down upon earth and punish the maiden. In the guise of an old crone, she entered Arachne's house, seated herself, and began a conversation. In a few minutes the maiden had resumed her usual strain, and renewed her rash boast. Minerva gently advised her to be more modest, lest she should incur the wrath of the gods by her presumptuous words; but Arachne was so blinded by her conceit, that she scorned the well-meant warning, saucily tossed her head, and declared she wished the goddess would hear her, and propose a contest, in which she would surely be able to prove the truth of her assertions. This insolent speech so incensed Minerva, that she cast aside her disguise and accepted the challenge.

Both set up their looms, and began to weave exquisite designs in tapestry: Minerva choosing as her subject her contest with Neptune; and Arachne, the kidnapping of Europa. In silence the fair weavers worked, and their webs grew apace under their practiced fingers. The assembled gods, the horse, the olive tree, seemed to live and move under Minerva's flashing shuttle.

> Emongst these leaves she made a Butterflie,
> With excellent device and wondrous slight,
> Fluttring among the Olives wantonly,
> That seem'd to live, so like it was in sight:
> The velvet nap which on his wings doth lie,
> The silken downe with which his backe is dight,
> His broad outstretched hornes, his hayrie thies,
> His glorious colours, and his glistering eies.
>
> SPENSER

Arachne, in the mean while, was intent upon her swimming bull, against whose broad breast the waves splashed, and upon a half-laughing, half-frightened girl, who clung to the bull's horns, while the wind played with her flowing tresses and garments.

> Sweet Europa's mantle blew unclasp'd,
> From off her shoulder backward borne:
> From one hand droop'd a crocus: one hand grasp'd
> The mild bull's golden horn.
>
> TENNYSON

The finishing touches all given, each turned to view her rival's work, and at the very first glance Arachne was forced to acknowledge her failure. To be thus outstripped, after all her proud boasts, was humiliating indeed. Bitterly did Arachne now repent of her folly; and in her despair she bound a rope about her neck, and hung herself. Minerva saw her discomfited rival was about to escape: so she quickly changed her dangling body into a spider, and condemned her to weave and spin without ceasing,—a warning to all conceited mortals.

Worship of Minerva

Minerva, the goddess of wisdom, was widely worshiped. Temples and altars without number were dedicated to her service, the most celebrated of all being the Parthenon at Athens. Naught but the ruins of this mighty pile now exist; but they suffice to testify to the beauty of the edifice, which served, in turn, as temple, church, mosque, and finally as powder magazine.

> Fair Parthenon! yet still must Fancy weep
> For thee, thou work of nobler spirits flown.
> Bright, as of old, the sunbeams o'er thee sleep
> In all their beauty still—and thine is gone!
> Empires have sunk since thou wert first revered.
> And varying rites have sanctified thy shrine.
> The dust is round thee of the race that rear'd
> Thy walls; and thou—their fate must soon be thine!
>
> HEMANS

Statues of Minerva—a beautiful, majestic woman, fully clothed and armed—were very numerous. The most celebrated of all, by the renowned Greek sculptor Phidias, measured full forty feet in height. Festivals were celebrated in honor of Minerva wherever her worship was held,—some, the Greek Panathenæa, for instance, only every four years; others, such as the Minervalia and Quinquatria, every year. At these festivals the Palladium, a statue of the goddess, said to have fallen from heaven, was carried in procession through the city, where the people hailed its appearance with joyful cries and songs of praise.

Chapter V

APOLLO

The most glorious and beautiful among all the gods was Apollo (PhŒbus, Sol, Helios, Cynthius, Pytheus), god of the sun, of medicine, music, poetry, and all fine arts.

> Bright-hair'd Apollo!—thou who ever art
> A blessing to the world—whose mighty heart
> Forever pours out love, and light, and life;
> Thou, at whose glance, all things of earth are rife
> With happiness; to whom, in early spring,
> Bright flowers raise up their heads, where'er they cling
> On the steep mountain side, or in the vale
> Are nestled calmly. Thou at whom the pale
> And weary earth looks up, when winter flees,
> With patient gaze: thou for whom wind-stripped trees
> Put on fresh leaves, and drink deep of the light
> That glitters in thine eye: thou in whose bright
> And hottest rays the eagle fills his eye
> With quenchless fire, and far, far up on high
> Screams out his joy to thee, by all the names
> That thou dost bear—whether thy godhead claims
> PhŒbus or Sol, or golden-hair'd Apollo,
> Cynthian or Pythian, if thou dost follow
> The fleeing night, oh, hear
> Our hymn to thee, and willingly draw near!
>
> PIKE

Apollo was the son of Jupiter and Latona, or Leto, the goddess of dark nights. Juno's jealousy had been aroused by Jupiter's preference for her rival. To avenge herself, she banished Latona to earth, and declared that if any one, mortal or immortal, showed her any pity or gave her any assistance, he would incur her lasting resentment.

After long, painful wanderings on earth, poor Latona, weary and parched with thirst, drew near a small pool by the wayside to refresh herself; but, urged by Juno, some reapers bade her pass on, and then, seeing she paid no heed to their commands, they sprang into the shallow waters, and stirred up the mud at the bottom until it was quite unpalatable. With tear-dimmed eyes, Latona prayed these cruel men might never leave the spot whereon they now stood; and Jupiter, in answer to her prayer, immediately transformed them into huge green frogs, which creatures have since then showed great preference for muddy pools.

Driven on once more by Juno's unrelenting hatred, Latona finally came to the seashore, where she stretched out imploring hands to Neptune, who sent a dolphin to bear her in safety to the floating island of Delos, raised in her behalf from the depths of the sea. The rocking motion, however, proving disagreeable to the goddess, Neptune chained the island fast in the Ægean Sea; and there in that delightful climate, justly praised by poets, were born to Jupiter and Latona twin children, Apollo and Diana, the divinities of the sun and moon.

STORY OF CORONIS

Apollo, having attained manhood, could not avoid the usual lot of the gods, as well as of mortal men,—the pangs of love. They were first inspired by Coronis, a fair maiden, who kindled within his breast an ardent flame. The sun god wooed the girl warmly and persistently, and at length had the deep satisfaction of seeing his affections returned. His bliss, however, proved but fleeting; for Coronis, reasoning, that, if one lover were so delightful, two would be doubly so, secretly encouraged another suitor.

> Flirted with another lover
>   (So at least the story goes)
> And was wont to meet him slyly,
>   Underneath the blushing rose.
>   SAXE

Although so cleverly managed, these trysts could not escape the bright eyes of Apollo's favorite bird, the snowy raven,—for such was his hue in those early times,—so *he* flew off in haste to his master to report the discovery he had made. Desperate with love and jealousy, Apollo did not hesitate, but, seizing his bow and deadly arrows, shot Coronis through the heart.

The deed was no sooner accomplished, than all his love returned with tenfold power; and, hastening to Coronis' side, he vainly tried all his remedies (he was god of medicine) to recall her to life.

> The god of Physic
> Had no antidote; alack!
> He who took her off so deftly
> Couldn't bring the maiden back!
>   SAXE

Bending over the lifeless body of his beloved one, he bewailed his fatal haste, and cursed the bird which had brought him the unwelcome tidings of her faithlessness.

> Then he turned upon the Raven,
>   "Wanton babbler! see thy fate!
> Messenger of mine no longer,
>   Go to Hades with thy prate!
>
> "Weary Pluto with thy tattle!
>   Hither, monster, come not back;
> And—to match thy disposition—
>   Henceforth be thy plumage black!"
>   SAXE

ÆSCULAPIUS

The only reminder of this unfortunate episode was a young son of Apollo and Coronis, Æsculapius (Asklepios), who was carefully instructed by Apollo in the healing art. The disciple's talent was so great, that he soon rivaled his master, and even, it is said, recalled the dead to life. Of course, these miracles did not long remain concealed from Jupiter's all-seeing eye; and he, fearing lest the people would forget him and worship their physician, seized one of his thunderbolts, hurled it at the clever youth, and thus brought to an untimely end his brilliant medical career.

> Then Jove, incensed that man should rise
> From darkness to the upper skies,
> The leech that wrought such healing hurled
> With lightning down to Pluto's world.
>   VIRGIL (Conington's tr.)

Æsculapius' race was not entirely extinct, however, for he left two sons—Machaon and Podalirius, who inherited his medical skill—and a daughter, Hygeia, who watched over the health of man.

ADMETUS AND ALCESTIS

Maddened with grief at the unexpected loss of his son, Apollo would fain have wreaked his vengeance upon the Cyclopes, the authors of the fatal thunderbolt; but ere he could execute his purpose, Jupiter interfered, and, to punish him, banished him to earth, where he entered the service of Admetus, King of Thessaly. One consolation alone now remained to the exiled god,—his music. His dulcet tones soon won the admiration of his companions, and even that of the king, who listened to his songs with pleasure, and to reward him gave him the position of head shepherd.

> Then King Admetus, one who had
>   Pure taste by right divine,
> Decreed his singing not too bad
> To hear between the cups of wine:
>
> And so, well pleased with being soothed
>   Into a sweet half sleep
> Three times his kingly beard he smoothed
> And made him viceroy o'er his sheep.
>   LOWELL

Time passed. Apollo, touched by his master's kindness, wished to bestow some favor in his turn, and asked the gods to grant Admetus eternal life. His request was complied with, but only on condition, that, when the time came which had previously been appointed for the good king's death, some one should be found willing to die in his stead. This divine decree was reported to Alcestis, Admetus' beautiful young wife, who in a passion of self-sacrifice offered herself as substitute, and cheerfully gave her life for her husband. But immortality was too dearly bought at such a price; and Admetus mourned until Hercules, pitying his grief, descended into Hades, and brought her back from the tomb.

> Did not Hercules by force
> Wrest from the guardian Monster of the tomb
> Alcestis, a reanimated Corse,
> Given back to dwell on earth in vernal bloom?
> WORDSWORTH

THE WALLS OF TROY

Apollo, after endowing Admetus with immortality, left his service, and went to assist Neptune, who had also been banished to earth, to build the walls of Troy. Scorning to perform any menial tasks, the God of Music seated himself near by, and played such inspiring tunes that the stones waltzed into place of their own accord.

APOLLO SLAYS PYTHON

Then, his term of exile being ended, he returned to heaven, and there resumed his wonted duties. From his exalted position he often cast loving glances down upon men, whose life he had shared for a short time, whose every privation he had endured; and, in answer to their prayers, he graciously extended his protection over them, and delivered them from misfortunes too numerous to mention. Among other deeds done for men was the slaying of the monster serpent Python, born from the slime and stagnant waters which remained upon the surface of the earth after the Deluge. None had dared approach the monster; but Apollo fearlessly drew near, and slew him with his golden shafts. The victory over the terrible

APOLLO BELVEDERE.
(Vatican, Rome.)

Python won for Apollo the surname of Pytheus (the Slayer), by which appellation he was frequently invoked.

This annihilation of Python is, of course, nothing but an allegory, illustrating the sun's power to dry up marshes and stagnant pools, thus preventing the lurking fiend malaria from making further inroads.

Apollo has always been a favorite subject for painters and sculptors. The most beautiful statue of him is the Apollo Belvedere, which represents him at the moment of his conquest of the Python.

APOLLO AND HYACINTHUS

Although successful in war, Apollo was very unfortunate indeed in friendship. One day he came down to earth to enjoy the society of a youth of mortal birth, named Hyacinthus. To pass the time agreeably, the friends began a game of quoits, but had not played long, before Zephyrus, god of the south wind, passing by, saw them thus occupied. Jealous of Apollo, for he too loved Hyacinthus, Zephyrus blew Apollo's quoit aside so violently that it struck his playmate, and felled him to the ground. Vainly Apollo strove to check the stream of blood which flowed from the ghastly wound. Hyacinthus was already beyond aid, and in a few seconds breathed his last in his friend's arms. To keep some reminder of the departed, Apollo changed the fallen blood drops into clusters of flowers, ever since called, from the youth's name, hyacinths; while Zephyrus, perceiving too late the fatal effect of his jealousy, hovered inconsolable over the sad spot, and tenderly caressed the dainty flowers which had sprung from his friend's lifeblood.

> Zephyr penitent,
> Who now, ere PhŒbus mounts the firmament,
> Fondles the flower.
>
> KEATS

APOLLO AND CYPARISSUS

To divert his mind from the mournful fate of Hyacinthus, Apollo sought the company of Cyparissus, a clever young hunter; but this friendship was also doomed to a sad end, for Cyparissus, having accidentally killed Apollo's pet stag, grieved so sorely over this mischance, that he pined away, and finally died. Apollo then changed his lifeless clay into a cypress tree, which he declared should henceforth be used to shade the graves of those who had been greatly beloved through life.

APOLLO AND DAPHNE

Some time after this episode, Apollo encountered in the forest a beautiful nymph by the name of Daphne, the daughter of the river god Peneus. Love at first sight was the immediate consequence on Apollo's part, and he longed to speak to the maid and win her affections. He first tried to approach her gently, so as not to frighten her; but, before he could reach her side, she fled, and he, forgetful of all else, pursued her flying footsteps. As he ran, he called aloud to Daphne, entreating her to pause were it only for a moment, and promising to do her no harm.

> Abate, fair fugitive, abate thy speed,
> Dismiss thy fears, and turn thy beauteous head;
> With kind regard a panting lover view;
> Less swiftly fly, less swiftly I'll pursue:
> Pathless, alas! and rugged is the ground,
> Some stone may hurt thee, or some thorn may wound.
>
> You fly, alas! not knowing whom you fly;
> No ill-bred swain, nor rustic clown, am I.
>
> PRIOR

The terrified girl paid no heed to promises or entreaties, but sped on until her strength began to fail, and she perceived, that, notwithstanding her utmost efforts, her pursuer was gaining upon her. Panting and trembling, she swerved aside, and rushed down to the edge of her father's stream, calling out loudly for his protection. No sooner had she reached the water's edge, than her feet seemed rooted to the ground. A rough bark rapidly inclosed her quivering limbs, while her trembling hands were filled with leaves. Her father had granted her prayer by changing her into a laurel tree.

Apollo, coming up just then with outstretched arms, clasped nothing but a rugged tree trunk. At first he could not realize that the fair maiden had

APOLLO AND DAPHNE. Remini.
(Villa Borghese, Rome.)

vanished from his sight forever; but, when the truth dawned upon him, he declared that from henceforth the laurel would be considered his favorite tree, and that prizes awarded to poets, musicians, etc., should consist of a wreath of its glossy foliage.

> I espouse thee for my tree:
> Be thou the prize of honor and renown;
> The deathless poet, and the poem, crown;
> Thou shalt the Roman festivals adorn,
> And, after poets, be by victors worn.
>
> OVID (Dryden's tr.)

This story of Apollo and Daphne was an illustration of the effect produced by the sun (Apollo) upon the dew (Daphne). The sun is captivated by its beauty, and longs to view it more closely; the dew, afraid of its ardent lover, flies, and, when its fiery breath touches it, vanishes, leaving nothing but verdure in the selfsame spot where but a moment before it sparkled in all its purity.

CEPHALUS AND PROCRIS

The ancients had many analogous stories, allegories of the sun and dew, amongst others the oft-quoted tale of Cephalus and Procris. Cephalus was a hunter, who fell in love with and married one of Diana's nymphs, Procris. She brought him as dowry a hunting dog, Lelaps, and a javelin warranted never to miss its mark. The newly married pair were perfectly happy; but their content was viewed with great displeasure by Eos (Aurora), goddess of dawn, who had previously tried, but without success, to win Cephalus' affections, and who now resolved to put an end to the bliss she envied.

All day long Cephalus hunted in the forest, and, when the evening shadows began to fall, joined his loving wife in their cozy dwelling. Her marriage gifts proved invaluable, as Lelaps was swift of foot, and tireless in the chase. One day, to test his powers, the gods from Olympus watched him course a fox, a special creation of theirs; and so well were both animals matched in speed and endurance, that the chase bade fair to end only with the death of one or both of the participants. The gods, in their admiration for the fine run, declared the animals deserved to be remembered forever, and changed them into statues, which retained all the spirited action of the living creatures.

In the warm season, when the sun became oppressive, Cephalus was wont to rest during the noon hour in some shady spot, and as he flung himself down upon the short grass he often called for a breeze, bidding it cool his heated brow.

> A hunter once in that grove reclin'd,
>   To shun the noon's bright eye,
> And oft he woo'd the wandering wind,
>   To cool his brow with its sigh.
> While mute lay ev'n the wild bee's hum,
>   Nor breath could stir the aspen's hair,
> His song was still, "Sweet air, oh come!"
>   While Echo answer'd, "Come, sweet air!"
>
> MOORE

Eos heard of this habit, and was fully aware that he merely addressed the passing wind; nevertheless she sought Procris, and informed her that her husband was faithless, and paid court to a fair maid, who daily met him at noonday in the forest solitudes. Procris, blinded by sudden jealousy, gave credit to the false story, and immediately resolved to follow her husband.

The morning had well-nigh passed, and the sun was darting its perpendicular rays upon the earth, when Cephalus came to his usual resort, near which Procris was concealed.

"Sweet air, oh come!" the hunter cried; and Procris, cut to the heart by what she considered an infallible proof of his infidelity, sank fainting to the ground. The rustle caused by her swoon attracted Cephalus' attention. Under the mistaken impression that some wild beast was lurking there, ready to pounce upon him, he cast his unerring javelin into the very midst of the thicket, and pierced the faithful bosom of his wife. Her dying moan brought him with one bound to her side; ere she breathed her last, an explanation was given and received; and Procris died with the blissful conviction that her husband had not deserved her unjust suspicions, and that his heart was all her own.

There are, of course, many other versions of these selfsame myths; but one and all are intended to illustrate the same natural phenomena, and are subject to the same interpretation.

Apollo's principal duty was to drive the sun chariot. Day after day he rode across the azure sky, nor paused on his way till he reached the golden boat awaiting him at the end of his long day's journey, to bear him in safety back to his eastern palace.

> Helios all day long his allotted labor pursues;
>> No rest to his passionate heart and his panting horses given,
> From the moment when roseate-fingered Eos kindles the dews
>> And spurns the salt sea-floors, ascending silvery the heaven,
> Until from the hand of Eos Hesperos, trembling, receives
>> His fragrant lamp, and faint in the twilight hangs it up.
>
> OWEN MEREDITH

CLYTIE

A fair young maiden, named Clytie, watched Apollo's daily journey with strange persistency; and from the moment when he left his palace in the morning until he came to the far western sea in the evening, she followed his course with loving eyes, thought of the golden-haired god, and longed for his love. But, in spite of all this fervor, she never won favor in Apollo's eyes, and languished until the gods, in pity, changed her into a sunflower.

Even in this altered guise, Clytie could not forget the object of her love; and now, a fit emblem of constancy, she still follows with upturned face the glowing orb in its daily journey across the sky.

> No, the heart that has truly lov'd never forgets,
>> But as truly loves on to the close;
> As the sunflower turns on her god when he sets
>> The same look which she turn'd when he rose.
>
> MOORE

APOLLO AND MARSYAS

A young shepherd, lying in the cool grass one summer afternoon, became aware of a distant sound of music, so sweet, so thrilling, that he fairly held his breath to listen. These weird, delightful tones were produced by Minerva, who, seated by the banks of a small stream, was trying her skill on the flute. As she bent over the limpid waters, she suddenly beheld her puffed cheeks and distorted features, and impetuously threw the instrument into the water, vowing never to touch it again.

> Hence, ye banes of beauty, hence!
> What? shall I my charms disgrace
> By making such an odious face?
>   MELANIPPIDES

The sudden break in the entrancing music caused the youth, Marsyas, to start from his abstraction and look about him. He then perceived the rejected flute sailing gently down the stream past his feet. To seize the instrument and convey it to his lips was the work of an instant; and no sooner had he breathed into it, than the magic strain was renewed. No recollection of his pastoral duties could avail to tear Marsyas away from his new-found treasure; and so rapidly did his skill increase, that he became insufferably conceited, and boasted he could rival Apollo, whom he actually challenged to a musical contest.

Intending to punish him for his presumption, Apollo accepted the challenge, and selected the nine Muses—patronesses of poetry and music—as umpires. Marsyas was first called upon to exhibit his proficiency, and charmed all by his melodious strains.

> So sweet that alone the south wind knew,
> By summer hid in green reeds' jointed cells
> To wait imprisoned for the south wind's spells,
> From out his reedy flute the player drew,
> And as the music clearer, louder grew,

Wild creatures from their winter nooks and dells,
Sweet furry things with eyes like starry wells,
Crept wanderingly out; they thought the south wind blew.
With instant joyous trust, they flocked around
His feet who such a sudden summer made,
His eyes, more kind than men's, enthralled and bound
Them there.

H. H.

The Muses bestowed much deserved praise, and then bade Apollo surpass his rival if he could. No second command was necessary. The god seized his golden lyre, and poured forth impassioned strains. Before pronouncing their decision, the Muses resolved to give both musicians a second hearing, and again both strove; but on this occasion Apollo joined the harmonious accents of his godlike voice to the tones of his instrument, causing all present, and the very Muses too, to hail him as conqueror.

And, when now the westering sun
Touch'd the hills, the strife was done,
And the attentive Muses said:
"Marsyas, thou art vanquished!"

MATTHEW ARNOLD

According to a previous arrangement,—that the victor should have the privilege of flaying his opponent alive,—Apollo bound Marsyas to a tree, and slew him cruelly. As soon as the mountain nymphs heard of their favorite's sad death, they began to weep, and shed such torrents of tears, that they formed a new river, called Marsyas, in memory of the sweet musician.

APOLLO AND PAN

The mournful termination of this affair should have served as a warning to all rash mortals. Such was not the case, however; and shortly after, Apollo found himself engaged in another musical contest with Pan, King Midas' favorite flute player.

Upon this occasion Midas himself retained the privilege of awarding the prize, and, blinded by partiality, gave it to Pan, in spite of the marked inferiority of his playing. Apollo was so incensed by this injustice, that he determined to show his opinion of the dishonest judge by causing generous-sized ass's ears to grow on either side of his head.

> The god of wit, to show his grudge,
> Clapt asses' ears upon the judge;
> A goodly pair, erect and wide,
> Which he could neither gild nor hide.
>
> SWIFT

Greatly dismayed by these new ornaments, Midas retreated into the privacy of his own apartment, and sent in hot haste for a barber, who, after having been sworn to secrecy, was admitted, and bidden to fashion a huge wig, which would hide the deformity from the eyes of the king's subjects. The barber acquitted himself deftly, and, before he was allowed to leave the palace, was again charged not to reveal the secret, under penalty of immediate death.

But a secret is difficult to keep; and this one, of the king's long ears, preyed upon the poor barber's spirits, so that, incapable of enduring silence longer, he sallied out into a field, dug a deep hole, and shouted down into the bosom of the earth,—

> "King Midas wears
> (These eyes beheld them, these) such ass's ears!"
>
> HORACE

Unspeakably relieved by this performance, the barber returned home. Time passed. Reeds grew over the hole, and, as they bent before the wind which rustled through their leaves, they were heard to murmur, "Midas, King Midas, has ass's ears!" and all who passed by caught the whisper, and noised it abroad, so that the secret became the general topic of all conversations.

Orpheus and Eurydice

As Apollo had frequent opportunities of meeting the Muses, it is not to be wondered at that he fell a victim to the charms of the fair Calliope, who, in her turn,
loved him passionately, and even wrote verses in his honor. This being the state of
her feelings, she readily consented to their union, and became the proud mother of
Orpheus, who inherited his parents' musical and poetical gifts.

> Orpheus with his lute made trees,
> And the mountain-tops, that freeze,
>   Bow themselves when he did sing:
> To his music plants and flowers
> Ever sprung; as sun and showers
>   There had made a lasting spring.
>
> Everything that heard him play,
> Even the billows of the sea,
>   Hung their heads, and then lay by.
>   Shakespeare

This talent waxed greater as the years passed by, and became so remark-
able, that the youth's fame was very widespread; and when he fell in love with
Eurydice, he brought all his skill into play to serenade her, and wooed her with
voice and glance and with tender, passionate music. Eurydice was touched by
his courtship, and ere long requited the love lavished upon her by conferring her
hand upon Orpheus.

Shortly after their union, while walking alone in the fields, the bride encountered a youth named Aristæus, whose bold admiration proved so distasteful, that
she fled from him as quickly as possible. In her haste she accidentally trod upon
a venomous serpent lurking in the long grass, which immediately turned upon
her, and bit her heel. A short period of agonized suffering ensued; then Eurydice
died, and her spirit was conducted down into the gloomy realms of Pluto, leaving
Orpheus broken-hearted.

Plaintive, heartrending laments now replaced the joyous wedding strains;
but even the charms of music failed to make life endurable, and Orpheus wan-

dered off to Olympus, where he so piteously implored Jupiter to restore his wife
to his longing arms, that the great god's heart was moved to compassion. He
gave him permission, therefore, to go down into the Infernal Regions to seek
his wife, but warned him at the same time that the undertaking was perilous in
the extreme.

Nothing daunted, Orpheus hastened to the entrance of Hades, and there
saw the fierce three-headed dog, named Cerberus, who guarded the gate, and
would allow no living being to enter, nor any spirit to pass out of Hades. As soon
as this monster saw Orpheus, he began to growl and bark savagely, to frighten
him away; but Orpheus merely paused, and began to play such melting chords,
that Cerberus' rage was appeased, and he finally allowed him to pass into Pluto's
dark kingdom.

The magic sounds penetrated even into the remote depths of Tartarus, where
the condemned suspended their toil for a moment, and hushed their sighs and
groans to listen.

> E'en Tantalus ceased from trying to sip
> The cup that flies from his arid lip;
> Ixion, too, the magic could feel,
> And, for a moment, blocked his wheel;
> Poor Sisyphus, doomed to tumble and toss
> The notable stone that gathers no moss,
> Let go his burden, and turned to hear
> The charming sounds that ravished his ear.
>
> SAXE

No living being had ever before penetrated thus into the Infernal Regions,
and Orpheus wandered on until he came to the throne of Pluto, king of these
realms, whereon the stern ruler sat in silence, his wife Proserpina beside him, and
the relentless Fates at his feet.

Orpheus made known his errand in operatic guise, and succeeded in moving
the royal pair to tears, whereupon they graciously consented to restore Eurydice
to life and to her fond husband's care.

ORPHEUS AND EURYDICE. Beyschlag.

Hell consented
To hear the Poet's prayer:
Stern Proserpine relented,
And gave him back the fair.
Thus song could prevail
O'er death, and o'er hell,
A conquest how hard and how glorious!
Tho' fate had fast bound her
With Styx nine times round her,
Yet music and love were victorious.

POPE

But one condition was imposed before he was allowed to depart; i.e., that he should leave the Infernal Regions without turning once to look into his beloved wife's face.

Orpheus accepted the condition joyfully, and wended his way out of Hades, looking neither to the right nor to the left, but straight before him; and as he walked he wondered whether Eurydice were changed by her sojourn in these ray-less depths. His longing to feast his eyes once more upon her loved features made him forget the condition imposed by Pluto, and turn just before he reached the earth; but he only beheld the vanishing form of the wife he had so nearly snatched from the grave.

All was now over. He had tried and failed. No hope remained. In despair, the lonely musician retreated to the forest solitudes, and there played his mournful laments,—

Such strains as would have won the ear
Of Pluto, to have quite set free
His half-regained Eurydice.

MILTON

But there were none to hear except the trees, winds, and wild beasts in the forest, who strove in their dumb way to comfort him as he moved restlessly about, seeking a solace for his bursting heart. At times it seemed to his half-delirious fancy that he could discern Eurydice wandering about in the dim distance, with the selfsame mournful expression of which he had caught a mere glimpse as she drifted reluctantly back into the dark shadows of Hades.

> At that elm-vista's end I trace
> Dimly thy sad leave-taking face,
> Eurydice! Eurydice!
> The tremulous leaves repeat to me
> Eurydice! Eurydice!
>
> LOWELL

At last there dawned a day when some Bacchantes overtook him in the forest, and bade him play some gay music, so they might indulge in a dance. But poor Orpheus, dazed with grief, could not comply with their demands; and the sad notes which alone he now could draw from his instrument so enraged the merrymakers, that they tore him limb from limb, and cast his mangled remains into the Hebrus River.

As the poet-musician's head floated down the stream, the pallid lips still murmured, "Eurydice!" for even in death he could not forget his wife; and, as his spirit drifted on to join her, he incessantly called upon her name, until the brooks, trees, and fountains he had loved so well caught up the longing cry, and repeated it again and again.

Nothing was now left to remind mortals of the sweet singer who had thus perished, except his lute, which the gods placed in the heavens as a bright constellation, Lyra, also called by Orpheus' name.

Another musician celebrated in mythological annals is Amphion, whose skill was reported to be but little inferior to Orpheus'.

> 'Tis said he had a tuneful tongue,
>   Such happy intonation,
> Wherever he sat down and sung
>   He left a small plantation;
> Wherever in a lonely grove
>   He set up his forlorn pipes,
> The gouty oak began to move,
>   And flounder into hornpipes.
>
> TENNYSON

Story of Amphion

This musician, a son of Jupiter and Antiope, had a twin brother Zethus, who, however, shared none of his artistic tastes. Hearing that their mother Antiope had been repudiated by her second husband, Lycus, so that he might marry another wife by the name of Dirce, these youths hastened off to Thebes, where they found the state of affairs even worse than represented; for poor Antiope was now imprisoned, and subject to her rival's daily cruel treatment.

Zethus and Amphion, after besieging and taking the city, put Lycus to death, and, binding Dirce to the tail of a wild bull, let him loose to drag her over briers and stones until she perished. This punishment inflicted upon Dirce is the subject of the famous group once belonging to the Farnese family, and now called by their name.

Amphion's musical talent was of great use to him when he subsequently became King of Thebes, and wished to fortify his capital by building a huge rampart all around it; for the stones moved in rhythmic time, and, of their own volition, marched into their places.

Arion

Second to him only, in musical fame, was Arion, the musician who won untold wealth by his talent. On one occasion, having gone to Sicily to take part in a musical contest which had attracted thither the most famous musicians from all points of the compass, he resolved to return home by sea.

Unfortunately for him, the vessel upon which he had embarked was manned by an avaricious, piratical crew, who, having heard of his treasures, resolved to murder him to obtain possession of them. He was allowed but scant time to prepare for death; but, just as they were about to toss him overboard, he craved permission to play for the last time. The pirates consented. His clear notes floated over the sea, and allured a school of dolphins, which came and played about the ship. The pirates, terrified by the power of his music, and in dread lest their hearts should be moved, quickly laid hands upon him, and hurled him into the water, where he fell upon the broad back of a dolphin, who bore him in safety to the nearest shore.

FARNESE BULL.
(National Museum, Naples.)

Then was there heard a most celestiall sound
Of dainty musicke, which did next ensew
Before the spouse: that was Arion crownd;
Who, playing on his harpe, unto him drew
The eares and hearts of all that goodly crew,
That even yet the Dolphin, which him bore
Through the Agean seas from Pirates vew,
Stood still by him astonisht at his lore,
And all the raging seas for joy forgot to rore.

SPENSER

To commemorate this miracle, the gods placed Arion's harp, together with the dolphin, in the heavens, where they form a constellation.

In the sunny plains of Greece there once dwelt Clymene, a fair nymph. She was not alone, however, for her golden-haired little son Phaeton was there to gladden her heart with all his childish graces.

STORY OF PHAETON

Early in the morning, when the sun's bright orb first appeared above the horizon, Clymene would point it out to her boy, and tell him that his father, Apollo, was setting out for his daily drive. Clymene so often entertained her child with stories of his father's beauty and power, that at last Phaeton became conceited, and acquired a habit of boasting rather loudly of his divine parentage. His playmates, after a time, wearied of his arrogance, and, to avoid the constant repetition of his vain speeches, bade him show some proof of his divine origin, or keep his peace.

Stung to the quick by some insolent taunts which they added, Phaeton hastened to his mother, and begged her to direct him to his father, that he might obtain the desired proof. Clymene immediately gave him all necessary information, and bade him make haste if he would reach his father's palace in the far east before the sun chariot passed out of its portals to accomplish its daily round. Directly eastward Phaeton journeyed, nor paused to rest until he came in view of the golden and jeweled pinnacles and turrets of his father's abode.

The sun's bright palace, on high columns rais'd
With burnish'd gold and flaming jewels blaz'd,
The folding gates diffus'd a silver light,
And with a milder gleam refresh'd the sight.

ADDISON

Quite undazzled by this splendor, the youth still pressed on, straining his eyes to catch the first glimpse of the godly father, whose stately bearing and radiant air his mother had so enthusiastically described.

Apollo, from his golden throne, had watched the boy's approach, and, as he drew nearer, recognized him as his own offspring. Timidly now Phaeton advanced to the steps of his father's throne, and humbly waited for permission to make his errand known. Apollo addressed him graciously, called him his son, and bade him speak without fear. In a few minutes the youth impetuously poured out the whole story, and watched with pleasure the frown which gathered on Apollo's brow when he repeated his companions' taunts. As soon as he had finished his tale, Apollo exclaimed that he would grant him any proof he wished, and confirmed these words by a solemn oath.

"By the terrible Styx" said the angry sire,
While his eyes flashed volumes of fury and fire,
"To prove your reviler an infamous liar,
I swear I will grant you whate'er you desire!"

SAXE

This oath was the most solemn any god could utter, and in case of perjury he was obliged to drink the waters of this river, which would lull him into senseless stupidity for one whole year. During nine years following he was deprived of his office, banished from Olympus, and not allowed to taste of the life-giving nectar and ambrosia.

With a flash of triumph in his dark eyes, Phaeton, hearing this oath, begged permission to drive the sun chariot that very day, stating that all the world would be sure to notice his exalted position, and that none would ever dare doubt his veracity after such a signal mark of Apollo's favor.

When the god heard this presumptuous request, he started back in dismay, for he alone could control the four fiery steeds which drew the golden-wheeled sun car. Patiently he then explained to Phaeton the great danger of such an undertaking, earnestly begging him to select some other, less fatal boon.

> Choose out a gift from seas, or earth, or skies,
> For open to your wish all nature lies;
> Only decline this one unequal task,
> For 'tis a mischief, not a gift, you ask.
>
> ADDISON

But Phaeton, who, like many another conceited youth, fancied he knew better than his sire, would not give heed to the kindly warning, and persisted in his request, until Apollo, who had sworn the irrevocable oath, was obliged to fulfill his promise.

The hour had already come when the Sun usually began his daily journey. The pawing, champing steeds were ready; rosy-fingered Aurora only awaited her master's signal to fling wide the gates of morn; and the Hours were ready to escort him as usual.

Apollo, yielding to pressure, quickly anointed his son with a cooling essence to preserve him from the burning sunbeams, gave him the necessary directions for his journey, and repeatedly and anxiously cautioned him to watch his steeds with the utmost care, and to use the whip but sparingly, as they were inclined to be very restive.

The youth, who had listened impatiently to cautions and directions, then sprang into the seat, gathered up the reins, signaled to Aurora to fling the gates wide, and dashed out of the eastern palace with a flourish.

For an hour or two Phaeton bore in mind his father's principal injunctions, and all went well; but later, elated by his exalted position, he became very reckless, drove faster and faster, and soon lost his way. In finding it again he drove so close to the earth, that all the plants shriveled up, the fountains and rivers were dried in their mossy beds, the smoke began to rise from the parched and blackened earth, and even the people of the land over which he was passing were burned black,— a hue retained by their descendants to this day.

AURORA. Guido Reni. (Rospigliosi Palace, Rome.)

Terrified at what he had done, Phaeton whipped up his steeds, and drove so far away, that all the vegetation which had survived the intense heat came to an untimely end on account of the sudden cold.

The cries of mortals rose in chorus, and their clamors became so loud and importunate, that they roused Jupiter from a profound sleep, and caused him to look around to discover their origin. One glance of his all-seeing eye sufficed to reveal the damaged earth and the youthful charioteer. How had a beardless youth dared to mount the sun chariot? Jupiter could scarcely credit what he saw. In his anger he vowed he would make the rash mortal expiate his presumption by immediate death. He therefore selected the deadliest thunderbolt in his arsenal, aimed it with special care, and hurled it at Phaeton, whose burned and blackened corpse fell from his lofty seat down into the limpid waves of the Eridanus River.

> And Phaethon, caught in mid career,
> And hurled from the Sun to utter sunlessness,
> Like a flame-bearded comet, with ghastliest hiss,
> Fell headlong in the amazed Eridanus,
> Monarch of streams, who on the Italian fields
> Let loose, and far beyond his flowery lips
> Foam-white, ran ruinous to the Adrian deep.
>
> WORSLEY

THE HELIADES

The tidings of his death soon reached poor Clymene, who mourned her only son, and refused to be comforted; while the Heliades, Phaeton's sisters, three in number,—Phaetusa, Lampetia, and Ægle,—spent their days by the riverside, shedding tears, wringing their white hands, and bewailing their loss, until the gods, in pity, transformed them into poplar trees, and their tears into amber, which substance was supposed by the ancients to flow from the poplar trees like teardrops. Phaeton's intimate friend, Cycnus, piously collected his charred remains, and gave them an honorable burial. In his grief he continually haunted the scene of his friend's death, and repeatedly plunged into the river, in the hope of finding some more scattered fragments, until the gods changed him into a swan; which bird is ever sailing mournfully about, and frequently plunging his head into the water to continue his sad search.

Apollo, as the dearly loved leader of the nine Muses,—daughters of Jupiter and Mnemosyne, goddess of memory,—was surnamed Musagetes.

> Whom all the Muses loved, not one alone;—
> Into his hands they put the lyre of gold,
>   And, crowned with sacred laurel at their fount,
>   Placed him as Musagetes on their throne.
>   LONGFELLOW

Although the Muses united at times in one grand song, they had each separate duties assigned them.

THE NINE MUSES

Clio, the Muse of history, recorded all great deeds and heroic actions, with the names of their authors, and was therefore generally represented with a laurel wreath and a book and stylus, to indicate her readiness to note all that happened to mortal men or immortal gods.

Euterpe, the graceful "Mistress of Song," was represented with a flute, and garlands of fragrant flowers.

Thalia, Muse of pastoral poetry, held a shepherd's crook and mask, and wore a crown of wild flowers.

> Mild pastoral Muse!
> That, to the sparkling crown Urania wears,
> And to her sister Clio's laurel wreath,
> Preferr'st a garland culled from purple heath!
>   WORDSWORTH

Her graver sister, Melpomene, who presided over tragedy, wore a crown of gold, and wielded a dagger and a scepter; while Terpsichore, the light-footed Muse of dancing, was represented treading an airy measure.

APOLLO AND THE MUSES. Mengs.

Erato, who preferred lyric poetry to all other styles of composition, was pictured with a lyre; and Polyhymnia, Muse of rhetoric, held a scepter to show that eloquence rules with resistless sway.

Calliope, Muse of heroic poetry, also wore a laurel crown; and Urania, Muse of astronomy, held mathematical instruments, indicative of her love of the exact sciences.

This glorious sisterhood was wont to assemble on Mount Parnassus or on Mount Helicon, to hold their learned debates on poetry, science, and music.

Apollo's favorite attendant was Eos (Aurora), the fair goddess of dawn, whose rose-tipped fingers opened wide the eastern gates of pearl, and who then flashed across the sky to announce her master's coming.

> Hail, gentle Dawn! mild blushing goddess, hail!
> Rejoiced I see thy purple mantle spread
> O'er half the skies; gems pave thy radiant way,
> And orient pearls from every shrub depend.
>
> SOMERVILLE

STORY OF AURORA AND TITHONUS

This dainty goddess loved and married Tithonus, Prince of Troy, and won from the gods the boon of everlasting life to confer upon him. Alas! however, she forgot to ask at the same time for continued youth; and her husband grew older and older, and finally became so decrepit, that he was a burden to her. Knowing he would never die, and wishing to rid herself of his burdensome presence, she changed him into a grasshopper.

At this time the goddess fell in love with Cephalus, the young hunter, and frequently visited him on Mount Hymettus.

"Come," PhŒbus cries, "Aurora, come—too late
Thou linger'st slumbering with thy wither'd mate!
Leave him, and to Hymettus' top repair!
Thy darling Cephalus expects thee there!"
The goddess, with a blush, her love betrays,
But mounts, and, driving rapidly, obeys.

                                        KEATS

WORSHIP OF APOLLO

The principal temples dedicated to the worship of Apollo were at Delos, his birthplace, and at Delphi, where a priestess called Pythia gave out mysterious oracles
purporting to have come from the god. The ancients everywhere could not fail
to recognize the sun's kindly influence and beneficent power, and were therefore
ever ready to worship Apollo.

I marvel not, O sun! that unto thee
In adoration man should bow the knee,
    And pour his prayers of mingled awe and love;
For like a God thou art, and on thy way
Of glory sheddest with benignant ray,
    Beauty, and life, and joyance from above.

                                        SOUTHEY

The most renowned among the numerous festivals held in honor of Apollo
were, without exception, the Pythian Games, celebrated at Delphi every three
years.

A manly, beardless youth of great beauty, Apollo is generally crowned with
laurels, and bears either a bow or a lyre.

Lord of the unerring bow,
The God of life, and poesy, and light—
The Sun in human limbs array'd, and brow
All radiant from his triumph in the fight;
The shaft hath just been shot—the arrow bright
With an immortal's vengeance; in his eye
And nostril beautiful disdain, and might
And majesty, flash their full lightnings by,
Developing in that one glance the Deity.

BYRON

One of the Seven Wonders of the ancient world, the famous Colossus of Rhodes, was a statue of Apollo, his head encircled with a halo of bright sunbeams, and his legs spread wide apart to allow vessels, with all their sails spread, to pass in and out of the harbor, whose entrance he guarded for many a year.

DIANA OF VERSAILLES. (Louvre, Paris.)

Chapter VI

DIANA

Diana (Cynthia, PhŒbe, Selene, Artemis), the fair twin sister of Apollo, was not only goddess of the moon, but also of the chase.

> "Goddess serene, transcending every star!
> Queen of the sky, whose beams are seen afar!
> By night heaven owns thy sway, by day the grove,
> When, as chaste Dian, here thou deign'st to rove."
>
> BYRON

In works of art this goddess is generally represented as a beautiful maiden, clad in a short hunting dress, armed with a bow, a quiver full of arrows at her side, and a crescent on her well-poised head.

Proud of her two children, Apollo and Diana, Latona boasted far and wide that such as hers had never been, for they excelled all others in beauty, intelligence, and power.

STORY OF NIOBE

The daughter of Tantalus, Niobe, heard this boast, and laughed in scorn; for she was the mother of fourteen children,—seven manly sons and seven beautiful daughters. In her pride she called aloud to Latona, and taunted her because her offspring numbered but two.

Shortly after, Niobe even went so far as to forbid her people to worship Apollo and Diana, and gave orders that all the statues representing them in her kingdom should be torn down from their pedestals, and destroyed. Enraged at this insult, Latona called her children to her side, and bade them go forth and slay all her luckless rival's offspring.

Provided with well-stocked quivers, the twins set out to do her bidding; and Apollo, meeting the seven lads out hunting, cut their existence short with his unfailing arrows.

> Phœbus slew the sons
> With arrows from his silver bow, incensed
> At Niobe.
>
> HOMER (Bryant's tr.)

With all proverbial speed the tidings reached Niobe, whose heart failed when she heard that her seven sons, her pride and delight, had fallen under Apollo's shafts, and that they now lay cold and stiff in the forest, where they had eagerly hastened a few hours before, to follow the deer to its cover.

As she mourned their untimely death, she thought her cup of sorrow was full; but long ere her first passion of grief was over, Diana began to slay her daughters.

> But what is this? What means this oozing flood?
> Her daughters, too, are weltering in their blood:
> One clasps her mother's knees, one clings around
> Her neck, and one lies prostrate on the ground;
> One seeks her breast; one eyes the coming woe
> And shudders; one in terror crouches low.
>
> MELEAGER

In vain the poor girls sought to escape the flying arrows. In vain Niobe sought to protect them, and called upon all the gods of Olympus. Her daughters fell one by one, never to rise again. The last clung convulsively to her mother's breast; but, even in that fond mother's passionate embrace, death found and claimed her. Then the gods, touched by the sight of woe so intense, changed Niobe into stone, just as she stood, with upturned face, streaming eyes, and quivering lips.

This statue was placed on Mount Sipylus, close to a stream of running water; and it was said that tears continually flowed down the marble cheeks, for, though changed, Niobe still felt, and wept for her great loss.

NIOBE. (Uffizi Palace, Florence.)

This story is an allegory, in which Niobe, the mother, represents winter, hard, cold, and proud; until Apollo's deadly arrows, the sunbeams, slay her children, the winter months. Her tears are emblems of the natural thaw which comes in spring, when winter's pride has melted.

DIANA'S AVOCATIONS

As soon as the young Goddess of the Moon had been introduced in Olympus, all the gods expressed a wish to marry her; but she refused to listen to their entreaties, begged her father's permission to remain single all her life, and pleaded her cause so ably, that Jupiter was forced to grant her request.

Every evening, as soon as the Sun had finished his course, Diana mounted her moon car, and drove her milk-white steeds across the heavens, watched over and loved by the countless stars, which shone their brightest to cheer her on her way; and as she drove she often bent down to view the sleeping earth, so shadowy and dreamlike, and to breathe the intoxicating perfume of the distant flowers. It always seemed to her then as if Nature, so beautiful during the day, borrowed additional charms from the witching hours of the night.

> 'Twas now the time when Phœbus yields to night,
> And rising Cynthia sheds her silver light,
> Wide o'er the world in solemn pomp she drew
> Her airy chariot hung with pearly dew.

STORY OF ENDYMION

One evening, as she was driving noiselessly along, she suddenly checked her steeds; for there on the hillside she saw a handsome young shepherd, fast asleep, his upturned face illumined by the moon's soft light. Diana wonderingly gazed upon his beauty, and before long felt her heart beat with more than admiration. Gliding gently from her chariot, she floated to his side, bent slowly, and dropped an airy kiss upon his slightly parted lips.

The youth Endymion, only partially awakened by this demonstration, half raised his fringed lids, and for a moment his sleep-dimmed eyes rested wonderingly upon the beautiful vision. That one glance, although it drove Diana away in great haste, kindled in his heart an inextinguishable passion. He rose with a start, and rubbed his sleepy eyes; but when he saw the moon, which he fancied close beside him, sailing away across the deep-blue sky, he felt sure the whole occurrence had been but a dream, but so sweet a dream that he cast himself down upon the sward, hoping to woo it to visit him once more.

It did not come again that night, however; but the next night, as he lay on the selfsame spot, it recurred in all its sweetness; and night after night it was repeated when the pale moonbeams fell athwart his sleeping face.

> Then, as the full orb poised upon the peak,
> There came a lovely vision of a maid,
> Who seemed to step as from a golden car
> Out of the low-hung moon.
>
> LEWIS MORRIS

Diana, fully as enamored as he, could not bear to pass him by without a caress, and invariably left her car for a moment, as it touched the mountain peak, to run to him and snatch a hasty kiss.

> Chaste Artemis, who guides the lunar car,
> The pale nocturnal vigils ever keeping,
> Sped through the silent space from star to star,
> And, blushing, stooped to kiss Endymion sleeping.
>
> BOYESEN

But, even when asleep, Endymion watched for her coming, and enjoyed the bliss of her presence; yet a spell seemed to prevent his giving any sign of consciousness.

Time passed thus. Diana, who could not bear to think of the youth's beauty being marred by want, toil, and exposure, finally caused an eternal sleep to fall upon him, and bore him off to Mount Latmus, where she concealed him in a cave held sacred to her, and never profaned by human gaze. There each night the goddess paused to gaze enraptured upon his beloved countenance, and to press a soft kiss upon his unconscious lips. Such is the tale of Diana and her lowly sweetheart, which has inspired poets of all ages.

Queen of the wide air; thou most lovely queen
Of all the brightness that mine eyes have seen!
As thou exceedest all things in thy shrine,
So every tale, does this sweet tale of thine.

KEATS

STORY OF ORION

Endymion was not, however, the only mortal loved by Diana, for mythologists report that her affections were also bestowed upon a young hunter by the name of Orion. All day long this youth scoured the forest, his faithful dog Sirius at his heels.

One day, in the dense shade of the forest, he met a group of Diana's nymphs, the seven Pleiades, daughters of Atlas. These fair maidens needed but to be seen to be passionately loved, and Orion's heart burned as he sought to approach them; but they were very coy, and, as he drew near and addressed them, turned and fled.

Afraid lest he should never see them again were he now to lose sight of them, he pursued them hotly; but the nymphs sped on, until, their strength failing, they called upon their patroness's aid. Their prayer was no sooner heard than answered, and Orion, panting and weary, came up just in time to see seven snow-white pigeons wing their way up into the azure sky.

There a second transformation overtook the Pleiades, who were changed into a constellation, composed of seven bright stars, and there they shone undimmed for ages; but when Troy fell into the enemy's hands, all grew pale with grief, and one, more timid and impressionable than the rest, withdrew from sight to hide her anguish from the curious eyes of men.

And is there glory from the heavens departed?—
O void unmark'd!—thy sisters of the sky
Still hold their place on high,
Though from its rank thine orb so long hath started
Thou, that no more art seen of mortal eye!

HEMANS

Orion, like a fickle youth, was soon consoled for their disappearance, and loved Merope, daughter of Œnopion, King of Chios, who consented to their union on condition that his future son-in-law should win his bride by some heroic deed. Now, as Orion was anything but a patient man, the delay was very unwelcome indeed, and he made up his mind to abduct his bride instead of marrying her openly; but the plan was frustrated by Œnopion's watchfulness, and Orion was punished by the loss not only of his bride, but also of his eyesight.

Blind, helpless, and alone, he now wandered from place to place, hoping to find some one capable of restoring his sight. At last he reached the Cyclopes' cave, and one of them took pity on him, and led him to the Sun, from whose radiance he borrowed a store of light,—

> When, blinded by Œnopion,
> He sought the blacksmith at his forge,
> And, climbing up the mountain gorge,
> Fixed his blank eyes upon the sun.
>
> LONGFELLOW

Happy once more, he resumed his favorite sport, and hunted from morn till eve. Diana met him in the forest, and, sharing his tastes, soon learned to love him; but this affection was viewed with great displeasure by Apollo, from whose piercing glance nothing that occurred by day could be hidden, and he resolved to put an end to his sister's infatuation. He therefore summoned her to his side. To divert her suspicions, he began to talk of archery, and, under the pretext of testing her skill as a markswoman, bade her shoot at a dark speck rising and falling far out at sea.

Diana seized her bow, feathered her arrow, and sent it with such force and accurate aim, that she touched the point, and saw it vanish beneath the waves, little suspecting that the dark head of Orion, who was refreshing himself by a sea bath, was given her as a target. When she discovered her error, she mourned his loss with many tears, vowed never to forget him, and placed him and his faithful dog Sirius as constellations in the sky.

STORY OF ACTÆON

When Diana had finished her nightly journey in her moon car, she seized her bow and arrows, and, attended by her nymphs, was wont to sally forth to hunt the wild beasts in the forest.

One summer afternoon, after an unusually long and exciting pursuit, Diana and her followers came to one of the still mountain pools where they had often resorted to enjoy a plunge. The cool waters rippled so invitingly, that the goddess and her attendants hastened to divest themselves of their short hunting garments, and lave their heated limbs.

But unfortunately the goddess and her attendant nymphs had not been the only ones out hunting that day. Actæon, the huntsman, had risen at dawn to stalk the deer; and now, weary and parched with thirst, he too sought the well-known mountain spring,

> Deep in the cool recesses of the wood,
> Where the cold crystal of a mossy pool
> Rose to the flowery marge, and gave again
> The soft green lawn where ofttimes, overspent,
> I lay upon the grass and eager bathed
> My limbs in the clear lymph.
>
> LEWIS MORRIS

As he drew near the accustomed spot, Actæon fancied he heard bursts of silvery laughter: so he crept on very cautiously, and soon, gently parting the thick branches of the underbrush, beheld the sporting group.

At the selfsame moment Diana turned to ascertain the cause of the rustle which had caught her practiced ear, and met the admiring gaze of the astonished young hunter. Speechless with indignation that a mortal had beheld her thus, she caught some water in her hollow palm, flung it in his face, and bade him go and declare, if he could, that he had seen Diana disrobed.

The glittering drops had no sooner touched the young man's face, than he turned to obey her command, and found himself transformed into a stag, with slender, sinewy limbs, furry skin, and wide-branching antlers. Nothing remained of his former self except the woeful consciousness of his transformation; and as he stood there, motionless and dismayed, the distant baying of his hounds coming to join him fell upon his ear.

An electric thrill of fear shot through every vein, as, mindful of his new form, he bounded away through the forest. Alas! too late; for the pack had caught one glimpse of his sleek sides, and were after him in full cry.

In vain poor Actæon strained every muscle. His limbs refused their support, and, as he sank exhausted to the ground, the hounds sprang at his quivering throat.

> Nearer they came and nearer, baying loud,
> With bloodshot eyes and red jaws dripping foam;
> And when I strove to check their savagery,
> Speaking with words, no voice articulate came,
> Only a dumb, low bleat. Then all the throng
> Leapt swift on me, and tore me as I lay!
>
> LEWIS MORRIS

Diana was widely worshiped, and temples without number were dedicated to her service; among others, the world-renowned sanctuary of Ephesus. The ancients also celebrated many festivals in honor of this fair goddess of the moon, who was ever ready to extend her protection over all deserving mortals.

VENUS DE MILO.
(Louvre, Paris.)

Chapter VII

VENUS

Venus' Birth

Venus (Dione, Aphrodite, Cytherea), the goddess of beauty, love, laughter, and marriage, is said by some mythologists to be the daughter of Jupiter and Dione, goddess of moisture: others report that she sprang from the foam of the sea.

> Look, look, why shine
> Those floating bubbles with such light divine?
> They break, and from their mist a lily form
> Rises from out the wave, in beauty warm.
> The wave is by the blue-veined feet scarce press'd,
> Her silky ringlets float about her breast,
> Veiling its fairy loveliness; while her eye
> Is soft and deep as the blue heaven is high.
> The Beautiful is born; and sea and earth
> May well revere the hour of that mysterious birth.
>
> Shelley

The ocean nymphs were the first to discover her, cradled on a great blue wave; and they carried her down into their coral caves, where they tenderly nursed her, and taught her with the utmost care. Then, her education being completed, the sea nymphs judged it time to introduce her to the other gods, and, with that purpose in view, carried her up to the surface of the sea,—where Tritons, Oceanides, and Nereides all crowded around her, loudly expressing their ardent admiration,—and offered her pearls and choice bits of coral from the deep, as a tribute to her charms.

Then they pillowed her softly on a great wave, and intrusted her to the care of Zephyrus, the soft south wind, who blew a gentle breath, and wafted her to the Island of Cyprus.

The four beautiful Horæ (the Seasons), daughters of Jupiter and Themis, goddess of justice, stood there on the shore to welcome her.

> An ethereal band
> Are visible above: the Seasons four,—
> Green-kirtled Spring, flush Summer, golden store
> In Autumn's sickle, Winter frosty hoar.
>
> KEATS

And they were not alone to watch for her coming, for the three Charites (Graces, or Gratiæ) were also present.

> "These three on men all gracious gifts bestow,
> Which decke the body or adorne the mynde,
> To make them lovely or well-favoured show;
> As comely carriage, entertainement kynde,
> Sweete semblaunt, friendly offices that bynde,
> And all the complements of curtesie:
> They teach us how to each degree and kynde
> We should our selves demeane, to low, to hie,
> To friends, to foes; which skill men call Civility."
>
> SPENSER

Daughters of Jupiter and Eurynome, these maidens, who bore the respective names of Aglaia, Euphrosyne, and Thalia, longed to show their love for their new mistress. When the wave upon which she reclined came nearer still, the "rosy-bosomed Hours, fair Venus' train," appeared. The wind finally brought the fair goddess in safety to the shore; and, as soon as her foot touched the white sand, all bent in homage to her surpassing beauty, and reverentially watched her dry her hair.

FOURTH HOUR OF THE NIGHT. Raphael.

Idalian Aphrodite beautiful,
Fresh as the foam, new-bathed in Paphian wells,
With rosy slender fingers backward drew
From her warm brows and bosom her deep hair
Ambrosial, golden round her lucid throat
And shoulder: from the violets her light foot
Shone rosy-white, and o'er her rounded form
Between the shadows of the vine bunches
Floated the glowing sunlights, as she moved.

TENNYSON

This hasty and somewhat primitive toilet completed, Venus and her followers set out for Mount Olympus, and on their way thither were joined by Himerus, god of the desire of love; Pothos, god of the amities of love; Suadela, god of the soft speech of love; and Hymen, god of marriage.

VENUS AND VULCAN

A throne had been prepared for the expected goddess, and, when she suddenly appeared to take possession of it, the assembled gods could not restrain a rapturous murmur of admiration. Her beauty took them by storm, and her grace won their hearts; but, although they one and all expressed a desire to marry her, Venus scornfully rejected their proposals. Even the king of gods was slighted, and, to punish her for her pride, he decreed she should marry Vulcan, god of the forge, the most ill-favored of all the heavenly council.

This compulsory union was anything but a happy one; for Venus never showed any affection for her deformed consort, and, instead of being a faithful wife, soon deserted him, and openly declared she would please herself.

STORY OF ALECTRYON

Her first fancy was for Mars, the handsome god of war, who was not slow in reciprocating the fair goddess's affections, and many and sweet were the secret interviews they enjoyed. Yet, fearful lest some of the gods passing by should discover them together, Mars always placed his attendant Alectryon on guard, bidding him give due warning of any one's approach, and especially to call him before the sun rose, as the lovers were particularly anxious that Apollo should not witness their parting caresses.

All prospered according to their desires, until one night the unfortunate Alectryon fell asleep; and so profound were his slumbers, that he did not even stir when Aurora flung open the gates of the east, and Apollo flashed forth to receive the melodious greetings of the feathered denizens of the forest.

The sun god drove rapidly on, glancing right and left, and taking note of all he saw. Nothing escaped his bright and piercing eye, as it flashed its beams hither and thither, and he was soon aware of the sleeping watchman and of the guilty lovers. As fast as his fleet-footed steeds could carry him, Apollo hastened to Vulcan, to whom he vividly described the sight which had greeted his eyes.

The irate husband lost no time, but, seizing a net of linked steel, went in search of his runaway wife. Stealthily he approached the lovers' bower, and deftly flung the net over both sleepers, who were caught in its fine meshes, and could not escape; and there he kept them imprisoned, in spite of their entreaties, until all the gods had seen their humiliating plight, and turned them into ridicule. But when he at last set them free, Mars darted away, vowing vengeance upon the negligent sentinel, who was still blissfully sleeping. Pouncing upon him, Mars awakened him roughly, administered a sharp reproof, changed him into a cock, banished him into the barnyard, and condemned him to give daily warning of the sun's approach.

> And, from out a neighboring farmyard,
> Loud the cock Alectryon crowed.
>
> LONGFELLOW

VENUS' CHILDREN

Several beautiful children were born to Mars and Venus. Hermione, or Harmonia, their daughter, married Cadmus, King of Thebes; and Cupid (Cupido, Eros, Amor), their little son, was appointed god of love. Although nursed with tender solicitude, this second-born child did not grow as other children do, but remained

SLEEPING LOVE. Perrault.

a small, rosy, chubby child, with gauzy wings and roguish, dimpled face. Alarmed for his health, Venus consulted Themis, who oracularly replied, "Love cannot grow without Passion."

In vain the goddess strove to catch the concealed meaning of this answer. It was only revealed to her when Anteros, god of passion, was born. When with his brother, Cupid grew and flourished, until he became a handsome, slender youth; but when separated from him, he invariably resumed his childish form and mischievous habits.

VENUS AND ADONIS

Venus, however, did not lavish all her love upon Mars, for she is said to have felt a tender passion for a young man named Adonis, a bold young hunter, whose rash pursuit of dangerous game caused Venus many anxious alarms. In vain she besought him to forego the pleasures of the chase and remain with her. He laughingly escaped, and continued to join the other hunters in his favorite sport. But, alas! one day, after an exciting pursuit, he boldly attacked a wild boar, which, goaded to madness, turned upon him, buried his strong tusk in the youth's unprotected side, and trampled him to death.

> The white tusk of a boar has transpierced his white thigh.

> *   *   *   *   *

> The youth lieth dead while his dogs howl around,
> And the nymphs weep aloud from the mists of the hill.
> > BION (Mrs. Browning's tr.)

Venus ran straight to the scene of his tragic death, rushing through underbrush and briers, tearing her delicate skin, and her blood tingeing all the white roses along her way to a faint pink. When she arrived, she found her beloved Adonis cold in death, and her passionate caresses met with no response. Then she burst into such a passion of tears, that the wood and water nymphs, the gods, men, and all nature in fact, joined with her to mourn the beloved youth.

> Her loss the Loves deplore:
> Woe, Venus, woe! Adonis is no more.
>
> Bɪᴏɴ (Elton's tr.)

Very reluctantly Mercury at last appeared to lead the soul of the departed down into the Infernal Regions, where it was welcomed by Proserpina, queen of the realm, and led to the place where pure and virtuous mortals enjoyed an eternity of bliss. Venus, still inconsolable, shed countless tears, which, as they dropped upon the ground, were changed to anemones, while the red drops which had fallen from Adonis' side were transformed into red roses.

> As many drops as from Adonis bled,
> So many tears the sorrowing Venus shed:
> For every drop on earth a flower there grows:
> Anemones for tears; for blood the rose.
>
> Bɪᴏɴ (Elton's tr.)

As time did not soften Venus' grief, but, on the contrary, made it more and more unendurable, she went to Olympus, where she fell at Jupiter's feet, imploring him to release Adonis from death's embrace, or allow her to share his lot in Hades.

To allow Beauty to desert the earth was not possible, nor could he resist her pleading: so he finally decreed that Adonis should be restored to her longing arms. But Pluto, whose subject he had now become, refused to yield up Adonis; and after much dispute a compromise was agreed upon, by virtue of which Adonis was allowed to spend one half of the year on earth, providing he spent the remaining six months in the Elysian Fields.

In early spring, therefore, Adonis left the Lower World, and came with bounding tread to join his beloved. On his path the flowers bloomed and the birds sang, to show their joy at his coming. An emblem of vegetation, which rises from the ground in early spring to deck the earth with beautiful foliage and flowers, and cause the birds to sing for gladness, Adonis reluctantly returned to Hades, when Winter, the cruel boar, slew him again with his white tusk, and made nature again droop, and mourn his departure.

But even in death, so strong is Love,
I could not wholly die; and year by year,
When the bright springtime comes, and the earth lives,
Love opens these dread gates, and calls me forth
Across the gulf.

LEWIS MORRIS

VENUS AND ANCHISES

The Goddess of Beauty also loved Anchises, Prince of Troy, but, ashamed of lavishing favors upon a mere mortal, extorted from him a promise that he would never reveal their secret marriage. Unfortunately, however, Anchises was of a boastful disposition, and ere long yielded to temptation and revealed the secret, incurring her wrath to such an extent, that some mythologists accuse her of borrowing one of Jupiter's thunderbolts and slaying him. Others, however, report that Anchises lived to a ripe old age, and escaped from burning Troy on his son Æneas' back. Venus' love was, however, all transferred to her son Æneas, whom she signally protected throughout his checkered career.

STORY OF HERO AND LEANDER

Venus' most ardent admirers and faithful worshipers were the young people, for she delighted in their youthful sentiments, and was ever ready to lend a helping hand to all true lovers when apparently insurmountable obstacles appeared on their path.

This was the case with a lovely maiden by the name of Hero, who was dedicated by her parents to Venus' service, and, as soon as old enough, spent all her time in the temple, ministering to the goddess, or in a lonely tower by the sea, where she dwelt alone with her aged nurse.

Honey-sweet Hero, of a princely race,
Was priestess to Queen Venus in that place;
And at her father's tower, by the sea set—
Herself a Queen of Love, though maiden yet—
Dwelt.

EDWIN ARNOLD

The maiden's beauty increased with her years, until the fame of her loveliness spread throughout her native city Sestus, and even passed over the Hellespont and reached Abydus, where Leander, the bravest and handsomest youth of the town, was fired with a desire to view the charming young priestess.

Just at that time a solemn festival in honor of Venus was to be celebrated at Sestus, to which all the youths and maidens were cordially invited. Under pretext of paying homage to the goddess, Leander entered her temple, and saw the young priestess, whose charms far surpassed all descriptions.

Venus, as has already been stated, was always deeply interested in young lovers; and when she saw these two, so well matched in beauty and grace, she bade Cupid pierce them with his love darts, which behest the mischief-loving god immediately obeyed.

> God Eros, setting notch to string,
> Wounded two bosoms with one shaft-shooting,
> A maiden's and a youth's—Leander he,
> And lovely Hero, Sestos' sweetest, she;
> She of her town, and he of his, the boast;
> A noble pair!
>
> EDWIN ARNOLD

An undying passion was thus simultaneously kindled in both young hearts; and, thanks to Venus' assistance, Leander managed to exchange a few words with Hero, declared his love, implored her to view his suit kindly, and, above all, to grant him a private interview, or he would surely die.

The maiden listened to his pleading with mingled joy and terror, for she knew her parents would never consent to their union. Then, afraid lest some one should notice that she was talking to a stranger, she bade him depart; but he refused to go until he had learned where she lived, and proposed to swim across the Hellespont when the shades of night had fallen, and none could see his goal, and pay her a visit in her lonely tower.

"Sweet! for thy love," he cried, "the sea I'd cleave,
Though foam were fire, and waves with flame did heave,
I fear not billows if they bear to thee;
Nor tremble at the hissing of the sea!
And I will come—oh! let me come—each night,
Swimming the swift flood to my dear delight:
For white Abydos, where I live, doth front
Thy city here, across our Hellespont."

EDWIN ARNOLD

At last his prayers overcame the maiden's scruples, and she arranged to receive him in her sea-girt tower, promising at a given hour to light a torch and hold it aloft to guide him safely across the sea. Then only he departed.

Night came on; darkness stole over the earth; and Leander impatiently paced the sandy shore, and watched for the promised signal, which no sooner appeared, than he exultantly plunged into the dark waves, and parted them with lusty strokes, as he hastened across the deep to join his beloved. At times the huge billows towered above his head; but when he had escaped their threatening depths, and rose up on their foamy crests, he could catch a glimpse of the torch burning brightly, and pictured to himself the shy, sweet blushes which would dye Hero's cheek as he clasped her to his passionate heart.

Leander had no fear—he cleft the wave—
What is the peril fond hearts will not brave!

LANDON

Venus, from the top of "many-peaked Olympus," smilingly viewed the success of her scheme, and nerved Leander's arm to cleave the rapid current. At last he reached the tower steps, and was lovingly greeted by Hero, whose heart had throbbed with anxiety at the thought of the perils her lover was braving for the sake of seeing her once more.

It was only when the dawn began to whiten the east, that the lovers finished their interview and parted, he to return to Abydus, and she to prepare for the daily duties which would soon claim her attention. But separation by day was

HERO AND LEANDER. Bodenhausen.

all these fond lovers could endure, and night after night, as soon as the first stars appeared, Hero lighted her torch, and Leander hastened to her, to linger by her side till dawn.

> Thus pass'd the summer shadows in delight:
> Leander came as surely as the night,
> And when the morning woke upon the sea,
> It saw him not, for back at home was he.
>
> HUNT

No one suspected their meetings; and all went well until the first fierce storms of winter swept down over the Hellespont. Hero, in the gray dawn of a winter's morning, besought her lover not to leave her to battle against the waves, which beat so violently against the stone tower; but he gently laughed at her fears, and departed, promising to return at night as usual.

The storm, which had raged so fiercely already in the early morning, increased in violence as the day wore on, until the waves were lashed into foam, while the wind howled more and more ominously as the darkness came on again; but none of these signs could deter Leander from visiting Hero.

> There came one night, the wildest of the year,
> When the wind smote like edge of hissing spear,
> And the pale breakers thundered on the beach.
>
> EDWIN ARNOLD

All day long Hero had hoped that her lover would renounce his nightly journey; but still, when evening came, she lighted her torch to serve as beacon, should he risk all to keep his word. The wind blew so fiercely, that the torch wavered and flickered, and nearly went out, although Hero protected its feeble flame by standing over it with outstretched robes.

At sight of the wonted signal, Leander, who had already once been beaten back by the waves, made a second attempt to cross the strait, calling upon the gods to lend him their aid. But this time his prayers were unheard, drowned in the fury of the storm; yet he struggled on a while longer, with Hero's name on his lips.

At last, exhausted and ready to sink, he lifted his eyes once more to view the cheering light. It was gone, extinguished by a passing gust of wind. Like a stone Leander sank, once, twice, thrice, and the billows closed forever over his head.

Hero in the mean while had relighted her torch, and, quite unconscious of the tragedy which had taken place, stood on the tower, straining her eyes to pierce the darkness. All night long she waited and watched for the lover who did not come; and, when the first sunbeams shone over the tossing sea, she cast an anxious glance over the waters to Abydus. No one was in sight as far as she could see. She was about to descend to pursue her daily tasks, when, glancing at the foot of the tower, she saw her lover's corpse heaving up and down on the waves.

> As shaken on his restless pillow,
> His head heaves with the heaving billow;
> That hand, whose motion is not life,
> Yet feebly seems to menace strife,
> Flung by the tossing tide on high,
> Then level'd with the wave.
>
> BYRON

Hero's heart broke at this sad sight, and she longed to die, too, that she might not be parted from Leander. To hasten their meeting, she threw herself into the sea, and perished in the waves, close by his side. Thus lived and died the faithful lovers, whose attachment has passed into a proverb.

Byron, the celebrated English bard, attempted Leander's feat of swimming across the Hellespont, and, on his return from that dangerous venture, wrote the following lines, which are so familiar to all English-speaking people:—

> The winds are high on Helle's wave,
> As on that night of stormy water
> When Love, who sent, forgot to save
> The young, the beautiful, the brave,
> The lonely hope of Sestos' daughter.
> Oh! when alone along the sky
> Her turret torch was blazing high,

Though rising gale, and breaking foam,
And shrieking sea-birds warn'd him home;
And clouds aloft and tides below,
With signs and sounds, forbade to go,
He could not see, he would not hear,
Or sound or sign foreboding fear;
His eye but saw that light of love,
The only star it hail'd above;
His ear but rang with Hero's song,
"Ye waves, divide not lovers long!"
That tale is old, but love anew
May nerve young hearts to prove as true.

PYRAMUS AND THISBE

An equally loving and unfortunate pair were Pyramus and Thisbe. Although no waves divided them, and they had the good fortune to occupy adjoining houses in Babylon, their parents having quarreled, they were forbidden to see or speak to each other. This decree wrung their tender hearts; and their continuous sighs finally touched Venus, who prepared to give them her aid. Thanks to this goddess's kind offices, a crack was discovered in the party wall, through which the lovers could peep at each other, converse, and even, it is said, exchange a kiss or two.

Sundry stolen interviews through this crack made them long for uninterrupted and unrestrained meetings: so they made an appointment to meet on a certain day and hour, under a white mulberry tree, just without the city gates.

Thisbe, anxious to see her lover, was the first to reach the trysting place, and, as she slowly paced back and forth to while away the time of waiting, she wondered what had happened to delay Pyramus. Her meditation was suddenly broken by a rustling sound in some neighboring bushes; and, thinking Pyramus was concealed there, she was about to call to him that he was discovered, when, instead of her lover, she saw a lion emerge from the thicket and come towards her, slowly lashing his sides with his tail, and licking his bloody jaws. With one terrified shriek the girl ran away, dropping her veil, which the lion caught in his bloody mouth and tore to shreds, before beating a retreat into the forest.

Shortly after, Pyramus came rushing up, out of breath, and full of loving excuses for Thisbe, who was not there, however, to receive them. Wondering at her absence, Pyramus looked around, and after a short investigation discerned the lion's footprints and the mangled veil. These signs sufficed to convince him that Thisbe had perished, and in a fit of despair he drew his dagger from its sheath and thrust it into his heart.

A few minutes later, Thisbe cautiously drew near, peering anxiously about to discover whether the lion were still lurking near. Her first glance showed her Pyramus stretched dead beneath the mulberry tree, with her bloody veil pressed convulsively to his lips. With a cry of terror she flew to his side, and tried to revive him; but, when assured that all her efforts were in vain, she drew the dagger from his breast, and, plunging it into her own bosom, fell beside him quite lifeless.

> In her bosom plunged the sword,
> All warm and reeking from its slaughtered lord.
> OVID (Eusden's tr.)

Since that ominous day the fruit of the mulberry tree, which had been white, assumed a blood-like hue, dyed by the blood which flowed from the death wounds of Pyramus and Thisbe.

ECHO AND NARCISSUS

The lovely and talkative nymph Echo lived free from care and whole of heart until she met Narcissus, hunting in the forest. This frivolous young lady no sooner beheld the youth, than she fell deeply in love with him, and was proportionately grieved when she saw that he did not return her affections.

All her blandishments were unavailing, and, in her despair at his hard-heartedness, she implored Venus to punish him by making him suffer the pangs of unrequited love; then, melancholy and longing to die, she wandered off into the mountains, far from the haunts of her former companions, and there, brooding continually over her sorrow, pined away until there remained naught of her but her melodious voice.

The gods, displeased at her lack of proper pride, condemned her to haunt rocks and solitary places, and, as a warning to other impulsive maidens, to repeat the last sounds which fell upon her ear.

> But her voice is still living immortal,—
>   The same you have frequently heard
> In your rambles in valleys and forests,
>   Repeating your ultimate word.
>
>   SAXE

Venus alone had not forgotten poor Echo's last passionate prayer, and was biding her time to punish the disdainful Narcissus. One day, after a prolonged chase, he hurried to a lonely pool to slake his thirst.

> In some delicious ramble, he had found
> A little space, with boughs all woven round;
> And in the midst of all, a clearer pool
> Than e'er reflected in its pleasant cool
> The blue sky here, and there, serenely peeping
> Through tendril wreaths fantastically creeping.
>
>   KEATS

Quickly he knelt upon the grass, and bent over the pellucid waters to take a draught; but he suddenly paused, surprised. Down near the pebbly bottom he saw a face so passing fair, that he immediately lost his heart, for he thought it belonged to some water nymph gazing up at him through the transparent flood.

With sudden passion he caught at the beautiful apparition; but, the moment his arms touched the water, the nymph vanished. Astonished and dismayed, he slowly withdrew to a short distance, and breathlessly awaited the nymph's return.

The agitated waters soon resumed their mirror-like smoothness; and Narcissus, approaching noiselessly on tiptoe, and cautiously peeping into the pool, became aware first of curly, tumbled locks, and then of a pair of beautiful, watchful, anxious eyes. Evidently the nymph had just concluded to emerge from her hiding place to reconnoiter.

More prudent this time, the youth gradually bent further over the pool; and, reassured by his kindly glances, the nymph's whole head appeared. In gentle tones the youth now addressed her; and her ruby lips parted and moved as if she were answering, though not a sound came to his ear. In his excitement he began to gesticulate, whereupon two snowy arms repeated his every gesture; but when, encouraged by her loving glances and actions, he tried once more to clasp her in his arms, she vanished as rapidly as the first time.

Time and again the same pantomime was enacted, and time and again the nymph eluded his touch; but the enamored youth could not tear himself away from the spot haunted by this sweet image, whose sensitive face reflected his every emotion, and who grew as pale and wan as he,—evidently, like him, a victim to love and despair.

Even the shades of night could not drive Narcissus away from his post, and, when the pale moonbeams illumined his retreat, he bent over the pool to ascertain whether she too were anxious and sleepless, and saw her gazing longingly up at him.

There Narcissus lingered day and night, without eating or drinking, until he died, little suspecting that the fancied nymph was but his own image reflected in the clear waters. Echo was avenged; but the gods of Olympus gazed compassionately down upon the beautiful corpse, and changed it into a flower bearing the youth's name, which has ever since flourished beside quiet pools, wherein its pale image is clearly reflected.

> A lonely flower he spied,
> A meek and forlorn flower, with naught of pride,
> Drooping its beauty o'er the watery clearness,
> To woo its own sad image into nearness:
> Deaf to light Zephyrus it would not move;
> But still would seem to droop, to pine, to love.
>
> KEATS

PYGMALION AND GALATEA

Pygmalion, King of Cyprus, was a very celebrated sculptor. All his leisure moments were spent in the faithful portrayal of the gods and goddesses. One day his practiced hand fashioned an image of Galatea. It was so beautiful that even before it was entirely finished its author loved it. When completed, Pygmalion admired it still more, deemed it too beautiful to remain inanimate, and besought Venus to give it life, stating that he wished a wife just like it.

As Pygmalion had always been an obdurate bachelor, and had frequently declared he would never marry, Venus was delighted to see him at last a victim of the tender passion, and resolved to grant his request. Pygmalion clasped the exquisite image to his breast to infuse some of his own warmth into the icy bosom, and pressed kiss after kiss upon the chiseled lips, until at last they grew soft and warm at his touch, and a faint color flushed the pale cheeks, as a breath dilated her lungs, and sent her blood coursing along her veins,—

> As once with prayers in passion flowing,
> Pygmalion embraced the stone,
> Till, from the frozen marble glowing,
> The light of feeling o'er him shone.
>
> SCHILLER

Pygmalion's delight at seeing his fair image a living and breathing maiden was unbounded, and after a short but passionate wooing the object of his affections became his happy wife.

CUPID AND PSYCHE

In those same remote ages of "sweet mythology" there lived a king whose three daughters were world-renowned on account of their matchless beauty. Psyche, the youngest of the sisters, was so lovely, that her father's subjects declared her worthy to be called the Goddess of Beauty, and offered to pay homage to her instead of to Venus. Offended by this proposal, which Psyche had good sense enough to refuse, Venus resolved to demonstrate forcibly to that benighted race that the maiden was mortal. She therefore bade her son Cupid slay her.

Armed with his bow and arrows, and provided with a deadly poison, Cupid set out to do her bidding, and at nightfall reached the palace, crept noiselessly past the sleeping guards, along the deserted halls, and came to Psyche's apartment, into which he glided unseen. Stealthily he approached the couch upon which the fair maiden was sleeping, and bent over her to administer the poisoned dose.

A moonbeam falling athwart her face revealed her unequaled loveliness, and made Cupid start back in surprise; but, as he did so, one of his own love arrows came into contact with his rosy flesh, and inflicted a wound, from which he was to suffer for many a weary day.

All unconscious of the gravity of his hurt, he hung enraptured over the sleeping maiden, and let her fair image sink into his heart; then, noiselessly as he had entered, he stole out again, vowing he would never harm such innocence and beauty.

Morning dawned. Venus, who had expected to see the sun illumine her rival's corpse, saw her sporting as usual in the palace gardens, and bitterly realized that her first plan had completely failed. She therefore began to devise various torments of a petty kind, and persecuted the poor girl so remorselessly, that she fled from home with the firm intention of putting an end to the life she could no longer enjoy in peace.

To achieve this purpose, Psyche painfully toiled up a rugged mountain, and, creeping to the very edge of a great precipice, cast herself down, expecting to be dashed to pieces on the jagged rocks below; but Cupid, who had indignantly though helplessly seen all his mother's persecutions, had followed Psyche unseen, and, when he perceived her intention to commit suicide, he called to Zephyrus (the South Wind), and entreated him to catch the maiden in his strong yet gentle arms, and bear her off to a distant isle.

Consequently, instead of a swift, sharp fall and painful death, Psyche felt herself gently wafted over hill and dale, across sparkling waters; and, long before she wearied of this new mode of travel, she was gently laid on a flowery bank, in the midst of an exquisite garden.

Bewildered, she slowly rose to her feet, rubbed her pretty eyes to make sure she was not dreaming, and wonderingly strolled about the beautiful grounds. Ere long she came to an enchanted palace, whose portals opened wide to receive her, while gentle voices bade her enter, and invisible hands drew her over the threshold and waited upon her.

When night came, and darkness again covered the earth, Cupid appeared in search of his beloved Psyche. In the perfumed dusk he confessed his love, and tenderly begged for some return.

Now, although the fading light would not permit her to discern the form or features of her unknown lover, Psyche listened to his soft tones with unconcealed pleasure, and soon consented to their union. Cupid then entreated her to make no attempt to discover his name, or to catch a glimpse of his face, warning her that if she did so he would be forced to leave her, never to return.

> "Dear, I am with thee only while I keep
> My visage hidden; and if thou once shouldst see
> My face, I must forsake thee: the high gods
> Link Love with Faith, and he withdraws himself
> From the full gaze of Knowledge."
>
> LEWIS MORRIS

Psyche solemnly promised to respect her mysterious lover's wishes, and gave herself up entirely to the enjoyment of his company. All night long they talked; and when the first faint streak of light appeared above the horizon, Cupid bade Psyche farewell, promising to return with the welcome shades of night. All day long Psyche thought of him, longed for him, and, as soon as the sun had set, sped to the bower where the birds were sleepily trilling forth their evening song, and breathlessly waited until he came to join her.

> Now on broad pinions from the realms above
> Descending Cupid seeks the Cyprian grove;
> To his wide arms enamor'd Psyche springs,
> And clasps her lover with aurelian wings.
> A purple sash across His shoulder bends,
> And fringed with gold the quiver'd shafts suspends.
>
> DARWIN

Although the hours of day seemed interminable, spent as they were in complete solitude, Psyche found the hours of night all too short in the sweet society of Love. Her every wish was gratified almost as soon as expressed; and at last, encouraged by her lover's evident anxiety to please her, she gave utterance to her longing to see and converse with her sisters once more. The ardent lover could not refuse to grant this request, yet Psyche noticed that his consent seemed somewhat hesitating and reluctant.

The next morning, while enjoying a solitary stroll, Psyche suddenly encountered her two sisters. After rapturous embraces and an incoherent volley of questions and answers, they settled down to enjoy a long talk. Psyche related her desperate attempt at suicide, her miraculous preservation from certain death, her aërial journey, her entrance into the enchanted palace, her love for her mysterious nightly visitor,—all, in short, that had happened since she had left her father's home.

Now, the elder sisters had always been jealous of Psyche's superior beauty; and when they saw her luxurious surroundings, and heard her raptures about her lover, they were envious, and resolved to mar the happiness which they could not enjoy. They therefore did all in their power to convince poor Psyche that her lover must be some monster, so hideous that he dare not brave the broad light of day, lest he should make her loathe him, and further added, that, if she were not very careful, he would probably end by devouring her.

They thereupon advised poor troubled Psyche to conceal a lamp and dagger in her lover's apartment, and to gaze upon him in secret, when his eyes were closed in sleep. If the light of the lamp revealed, as they felt sure it would, the hideous countenance and distorted form of a monster, they bade her use the dagger to kill him. Then, satisfied with their work, the sisters departed, leaving Psyche alone to carry out their evil suggestions.

When safe at home once more, the sisters constantly brooded over the tale Psyche had poured into their ears, and, hoping to secure as luxurious a home and as fascinating a lover, they each hurried off in secret to the mountain gorge, cast themselves over the precipice, and—perished.

Night having come, bringing the usually so welcome Cupid, Psyche, tortured with doubt, could with difficulty conceal her agitation. After repeated efforts to charm her from her silent mood, Cupid fell asleep; and, as soon as his regular breathing proclaimed him lost in slumber, Psyche noiselessly lighted her lamp, seized her dagger, and, approaching the couch with great caution, bent over her sleeping lover. The lamp, which she held high above her head, cast its light full upon the face and form of a handsome youth.

CUPID AWAKENING PSYCHE. Thumann.

Now trembling, now distracted; bold,
And now irresolute she seems;
The blue lamp glimmers in her hold,
And in her hand the dagger gleams.
Prepared to strike, she verges near,
Then, the blue light glimmering from above,
The hideous sight expects with fear—
And gazes on the god of Love.

                                    APOLLONIUS

Psyche's heart beat loudly with joy and pride as she beheld, instead of the monster, this graceful youth; and as she hung over him, enraptured, she forgot all caution. An inadvertent motion tipped her lamp, and one drop of burning oil, running over the narrow brim, fell upon Cupid's naked shoulder.

The sudden pain made him open his eyes with a start. The lighted lamp, the glittering dagger, the trembling Psyche, told the whole story. Cupid sprang from the couch, seized his bow and arrows, and, with a last sorrowful, reproachful glance at Psyche, flew away through the open window, exclaiming,—

"Farewell! There is no Love except with Faith,
And thine is dead! Farewell! I come no more!"

                                    LEWIS MORRIS

PSYCHE FORSAKEN

When he had vanished into the dusky air without, the balmy night winds ceased to blow; and suddenly a tempest began to rage with such fury, that poor frightened Psyche dared not remain alone in the palace, but hastened out into the gardens, where she soon lost consciousness of her misery in a deep swoon. When she opened her eyes once more, the storm had ceased, the sun was high in the heavens, and palace and gardens had vanished.

Poor Psyche lingered there the following and many succeeding nights, vainly hoping for Cupid's return, and shedding many bitter tears of repentance. Finally she resolved to commit suicide, and, with that purpose in view, plunged into a neighboring river; but the god of the stream caught and carried her ashore, where his daughters, the water nymphs, restored her to life. Thus forced to live, Psyche wandered about disconsolate, seeking Cupid, and questioning all she met, the nymphs, Pan, and Ceres, who compassionately listened to her confession of love for her husband.

> Not as the earthly loves which throb and flush
> Round earthly shrines was mine, but a pure spirit,
> Lovelier than all embodied love, more pure
> And wonderful; but never on his eyes
> I looked, which still were hidden, and I knew not
> The fashion of his nature; for by night,
> When visual eyes are blind, but the soul sees,
> Came he, and bade me seek not to inquire
> Or whence he came or wherefore. Nor knew I
> His name. And always ere the coming day,
> As if he were the Sun god, lingering
> With some too well loved maiden, he would rise
> And vanish until eve.
>
> LEWIS MORRIS

Ceres had often seen Cupid, and had heard that very morning that he was having a wound in his shoulder dressed by Venus: so she advised Psyche to go to the Goddess of Beauty, to enter her service, and to perform every task with cheerful alacrity, knowing that such a course would ultimately bring about a meeting and reconciliation between the lovers.

Psyche gratefully accepted and followed Ceres' advice, and labored early and late to satisfy her exacting mistress, who appointed such difficult tasks, that the poor girl would never have been able to accomplish them had she not been aided by all the beasts and insects, who loved her dearly.

PSYCHE'S JOURNEY TO HADES

Venus repeatedly tested her fidelity and endurance, and finally resolved, as a crucial experiment, to send her to Hades to fetch a box of beauty ointment, for which Proserpina alone had the recipe. Directed by Zephyrus, her old friend, Psyche

CHARON AND PSYCHE. Neide.

encountered the terrors of Hades in safety, delivered her message, and in return received a small box. The gates of Hades were closed behind her, and she had nearly finished her last task, when she suddenly fancied that it would be wise to appropriate a little of the magic preparation to efface the traces of sleepless nights and many tears.

The box, however, contained naught but the spirit of Sleep, who, pouncing upon Psyche, laid her low by the roadside. Cupid, passing by, saw her there, marked the ravages of grief, remembered his love and her suffering, and, wrestling with the spirit, forced him to reënter the narrow bounds of his prison, and woke Psyche with a loving kiss.

> "Dear, unclose thine eyes.
> Thou mayst look on me now. I go no more,
> But am thine own forever."
>
> LEWIS MORRIS

Then, hand in hand, they winged their flight to Olympus, entered the council hall; and there Cupid presented Psyche, his chosen bride, to the assembled deities, who all promised to be present at the nuptial ceremony. Venus even, forgetting all her former envy, welcomed the blushing bride, who was happy ever after.

The ancients, for whom Cupid was an emblem of the heart, considered Psyche the personification of the soul, and represented her with butterfly wings; that little insect being another symbol of the soul, which cannot die.

BERENICE'S HAIR

One of the latest myths concerning Venus is that of Berenice, who, fearing for her beloved husband's life, implored the goddess to protect him in battle, vowing to sacrifice her luxuriant hair if he returned home in safety. The prayer was granted, and Berenice's beautiful locks laid upon Venus' shrine, whence they, however, very mysteriously disappeared. An astrologer, consulted concerning the supposed theft, solemnly pointed to a comet rapidly coming into view, and declared that the gods had placed Berenice's hair among the stars, there to shine forever in memory of her wifely sacrifice.

WORSHIP OF VENUS

Venus, goddess of beauty, is represented either entirely naked, or with some scanty drapery called a "cestus." Seated in her chariot, formed of a single pearl shell, and drawn by snow-white doves, her favorite birds, she journeyed from shrine to shrine, complacently admiring the lavish decorations of jewels and flowers her worshipers provided. The offerings of young lovers were ever those which found most favor in her sight.

> Venus loves the whispers
>   Of plighted youth and maid,
> In April's ivory moonlight
>   Beneath the chestnut shade.
>   MACAULAY

Numerous ancient and some modern statues of this goddess grace the various art galleries, but among them all the most perfect is the world-renowned Venus de Milo.

Venus' festivals were always scenes of graceful amusements; and her votaries wore wreaths of fresh, fragrant flowers, the emblem of all natural beauty.

Chapter VIII

MERCURY

Birth of Mercury

As already repeatedly stated in the course of this work, Jupiter was never a strictly faithful spouse, and, in spite of his wife's remonstrances, could not refrain from indulging his caprice for every pretty face he met along his way. It is thus, therefore, that he yielded to the charms of Maia, goddess of the plains, and spent some blissful hours in her society. This divine couple's happiness culminated when they first beheld their little son, Mercury (Hermes, Psychopompus, Oneicopompus), who was born in a grotto on Mount Cyllene, in Arcadia,—

> Mercury, whom Maia bore,
> Sweet Maia, on Cyllene's hoary top.
> Virgil (Cowper's tr.)

This infant god was quite unlike mortal children, as will readily be perceived by the numerous pranks he played immediately after his birth. First he sprang from his mother's knee, grasped a tortoise shell lying on the ground, bored holes in its sides, stretched strings across its concavity, and, sweeping his hands over them, produced strains of sweetest music, thus inventing the first lyre.

> So there it lay, through wet and dry,
> As empty as the last new sonnet,
> Till by and by came Mercury,
> And, having mused upon it,
> "Why here," cried he, "the thing of things
> In shape, material, and dimension!
> Give it but strings, and, lo, it sings,
> A wonderful invention."
> Lowell

Mercury's Theft

Being very hungry toward evening, young Mercury escaped from his sleeping mother, and sallied out in search of food. He had not gone very far, before he came to a wide meadow, where Apollo's herds were at pasture. The oxen were fat and sleek; and the mischievous little god, after satisfying himself that they were young, and therefore promised to be tender and juicy, drove fifty of them off to a secluded spot, taking good care to envelop their feet in leafy branches, so they would leave no traces. Then, his hiding place being reached in safety, Mercury coolly killed two of the oxen, which he proceeded to eat.

Apollo soon missed his cattle, and began to search for some clew to their hiding place or to the thief. He could, however, discover nothing but some broken twigs and scattered leaves. Suddenly he remembered that the babe whose birth had been announced early that morning in high Olympus had been appointed god of thieves. He therefore lost no more time in useless search and conjecture, but strode off to Mount Cyllene, where he found Mercury peacefully sleeping in his cradle. With a rude shake, the sun god roused him from his slumbers, and bade him restore the stolen cattle. Mercury pretended innocence, until Apollo, exasperated, dragged him off to Olympus, where he was convicted of the theft, and condemned to restore the stolen property. Mercury yielded to the decree, produced the remaining oxen, and, in exchange for the two missing, gave Apollo the lyre he had just fashioned.

This, like most other myths, admits of a natural explanation. Apollo (the Sun) was supposed by the ancients to possess great herds of cattle and sheep, the clouds; and Mercury, the personification of the wind, born in the night, after a few hours' existence waxes sufficiently strong to drive away the clouds and conceal them, leaving no trace of his passage except a few broken branches and scattered leaves.

Mercury's Wand, Cap, and Shoes

The gift of the lyre pleased Apollo so well, that he in return wished to make a present to Mercury, and gave him a magic wand, called Caduceus, which had the power of reconciling all conflicting elements. Mercury, anxious to test it, thrust it between two quarreling snakes, who immediately wound themselves in amity

FLYING MERCURY. Bologna.
(National Museum, Florence.)

around it. This so pleased him, that he bade them remain there forever, and used the wand on all occasions.

> A snake-encircl'd wand;
> By classic authors term'd Caduceus
> And highly fam'd for several uses.
>
> GOLDSMITH

Mercury was in due time appointed messenger of the gods, who, to make him fleet of foot, presented him with winged sandals, the Talaria, which endowed him with marvelous rapidity of motion. As these sandals did not seem quite sufficient, however, the gods added the winged cap, Petasus, to the winged shoes.

> Foot-feather'd Mercury appear'd sublime
> Beyond the tall tree tops; and in less time
> Than shoots the slanted hail-storm, down he dropt
> Towards the ground; but rested not, nor stopt
> One moment from his home; only the sward
> He with his wand light touch'd, and heavenward
> Swifter than sight was gone.
>
> KEATS

Mercury was not only the messenger of the gods, but was also appointed god of eloquence, commerce, rain, wind, and the special patron of travelers, shepherds, cheats, and thieves.

STORY OF IO

Jupiter often intrusted to Mercury messages of a delicate nature, and always found him an invaluable ally; but the faithful messenger was never so much needed or so deeply appreciated as during Jupiter's courtship of Io, the peerless daughter of the river god Inachus.

To avoid Juno's recriminations, Jupiter had carried on this affair with even more than his usual secrecy, visiting his beloved only when quite certain that his wife was asleep, and taking the further precaution of spreading a cloud over the spot where he generally met her, to shield her from all chance of being seen from Olympus.

One fine afternoon, all conditions being favorable, Jupiter hastened down to earth to see Io, and began to stroll with her up and down the river edge. They heeded not the noonday heat, for the cloud over their heads screened them from the sun's too ardent rays.

From some cause Juno's slumbers were less protracted than usual, and she soon arose from her couch to look about her realm, the atmosphere, and convince herself that all was well. Her attention was soon attracted by an opaque, immovable cloud near the earth,—a cloud which had no business there, for had she not bidden them all lie still on the blue until she awoke? Her suspicions being aroused by the presence of this cloud, she sought her husband in Olympus, and, not finding him, flew down to earth, brushing the cloud aside in her haste.

Jupiter, thus warned of her coming, had but time to change the maiden beside him into a heifer, ere his wife alighted and inquired what he was doing there. Carelessly the god pointed to the heifer, and declared he had been whiling away the time by creating it; but the explanation failed to satisfy Juno, who, seeing no other living creature near, suspected that her spouse had been engaged in a clandestine flirtation, and had screened its fair object from her wrath only by a sudden transformation.

Dissimulating these suspicions with care, Juno begged her husband to give her his new creation, which request he could not refuse, but granted most reluctantly, thus adding further confirmation to her jealous fears. The Queen of Heaven then departed, taking Io with her, and placed her under the surveillance of Argus, one of her servants, who possessed myriad eyes, but one half of which he closed at a time.

> The eyes of Argus, sentinel of Heaven:
> Those thousand eyes that watch alternate kept,
> Nor all o'er all his body waked or slept.
>
> STATIUS (Elton's tr.)

Argus' Watch

She bade him watch the heifer closely, and report anything unusual in its actions. One day, therefore, as he was watching his charge pasture by the river, Argus heard her relate to her father, Inachus, the story of her transformation, and immediately imparted his discovery to Juno, who, advising still closer watchfulness, sent him back to his post.

Jupiter, in the mean while, was in despair; for days had passed without his being able to exchange a word with Io, or deliver her from her imprisonment. Finally he called Mercury to his aid, and bade him devise some plan to rescue her. Armed with a handful of poppies, Mercury approached Argus, and offered to while away the time by telling him tales.

As Mercury was the prince of story-tellers, this offer was not to be despised, and Argus joyfully accepted; but instead of exerting himself to be entertaining, Mercury droned out such lengthy, uninteresting stories, that Argus soon closed half his eyes in profound sleep. Still talking in the same monotonous way, Mercury softly shook the poppies over the giant's head, until one by one the remaining eyelids closed, and Argus was wrapped in complete slumber.

Then Mercury seized the giant's sword, and with one well-directed blow severed his head from the huge trunk. Only one half of the task was successfully accomplished; and while Mercury was driving the heifer away, Juno discovered his attempt, and promptly sent an enormous gadfly to torment the poor beast, who, goaded to madness by its cruel stings, fled wildly from one country to another, forded streams, and finally plunged into the sea, since called Ionian. After swimming across it, she took refuge in Egypt, where Jupiter restored her to all her girlish loveliness, and where her son Epaphus was born, to be the first king and the founder of Memphis.

> In coming time that hollow of the sea
> Shall bear the name Ionian, and present
> A monument of Io's passage through,
> Unto all mortals.
>
> E. B. Browning

Juno mourned the loss of her faithful Argus most bitterly, and, gathering up his myriad eyes, scattered them over the tail of her favorite bird, the peacock, to have some memento of her faithful servant ever near her.

> From Argus slain a painted peacock grew,
> Fluttering his feathers stain'd with various hue.
>
> MOSCHUS

This story also is an allegory. Io personifies the moon, restlessly wandering from place to place; Argus, the heavens, whose starry eyes keep ceaseless watch over the moon's every movement; Mercury is the rain, whose advent blots out the stars one by one, thus killing Argus, who else was never known to close all his eyes at once.

MERCURY'S OFFICES AND WORSHIP

To Mercury was intrusted the charge of conducting the souls of the departed to Hades, and when occupied in this way he bore the name of Psychopompus, while, when addressed as conductor of Dreams, he was Oneicopompus.

> Gently as a kiss came Death to sever
> From spirit flesh, and to the realm of gloom
> The pallid shades with fearless brow descended
> To Hades, by the winged god attended.
>
> BOYESEN

He was one of the twelve principal gods of Olympus, and was widely worshiped. Temples, altars, and shrines were dedicated to his service throughout the ancient countries. His statues were considered sacred boundary marks, and their removal punished by death. Solemn annual festivals were held in Rome in Mercury's honor in the month of May, and from him received their name of Mercuralia.

Chapter IX

MARS

Mars' Character

M ars (Ares), son of Jupiter and Juno, was the god of war, the personification of the angry clouded sky, and, although but little worshiped in Greece, was one of the principal Roman divinities. He is said to have first seen the light in Thrace, a country noted for its fierce storms and war-loving people.

> Infant Mars, where Thracia's mountains rose,
> Press'd with his hardy limbs th' incrusted snows.
> STATIUS (Elton's tr.)

Never sated with strife and bloodshed, this god preferred the din of battle to all other music, and found no occupation so congenial as the toils and dangers of war. No gentle deeds of kindness were ever expected from him; no loving prayers were ever addressed to him; and the ancients felt no love for him, but, on the contrary, shuddered with terror when his name was mentioned.

Mars was generally represented in a brilliant suit of armor, a plumed helmet on his proud young head, a poised spear in one muscular hand, and a finely wrought shield in the other, showing him ever ready to cope with a foe.

Mars' Attendants

His attendants, or some say his children, sympathized heartily with his quarrelsome tastes, and delighted in following his lead. They were Eris (Discord), Phobos (Alarm), Metus (Fear), Demios (Dread), and Pallor (Terror).

Bellona, or Enyo, goddess of war, also accompanied him, drove his chariot, parried dangerous thrusts, and watched over his general safety. Mars and Bellona were therefore worshiped together in the selfsame temple, and their altars were the only ones ever polluted by human sacrifices.

And to the fire-ey'd maid of smoky war,
All hot and bleeding, will we offer them:
The mailed Mars shall on his altar sit,
Up to the ears in blood.

SHAKESPEARE

STORY OF OTUS AND EPHIALTES

As strife was his favorite element, Mars was very active indeed during the war between the gods and giants, but in his martial ardor he frequently forgot all caution. On one occasion he was obliged to surrender to Otus and Ephialtes,—two giants, who, though but nine years of age, were already of immense stature, since they increased in height at the rate of nine inches each month.

Proud of their victory over the God of War, these giants bore him off in triumph, and bound him fast with iron chains slipped through iron rings. Day and night they kept watch over him; and even when they slept, the rattle of the chains, whenever any one of the gods attempted to set him free, woke them up, and frustrated all efforts to deliver him. During fifteen weary months poor Mars lingered there in durance vile, until Mercury, the prince of thieves, noiselessly and deftly slipped the chains out of the rings, and restored him to freedom.

In revenge for the cruel treatment inflicted by Otus and Ephialtes, Mars prevailed upon Apollo and Diana to use their poisoned arrows, and thus rid the world of these two ugly and useless giants.

THE AREOPAGUS

Of a fiery disposition, Mars was never inclined to forgive an injury; and when Halirrhothius, Neptune's son, dared to carry off his daughter Alcippe, Mars hotly pursued the abductor, and promptly slew him. Neptune, angry at this act of summary justice, cited the God of War to appear before a tribunal held in the open air, on a hill near the newly founded city of Athens.

It was then customary for such cases to be tried at night, in utter darkness, so that the judges might not be influenced by the personal appearance of either plaintiff or defendant; and no rhetoric of any kind was allowed, that their minds might remain quite unbiased. Mars appeared before the judges, simply stated his case, and was acquitted. Since then the hill upon which his trial took place has been called the Areopagus (Ares' Hill) or Mars' Hill, and the judges of the principal court of justice at Athens received the name of Areopagitæ.

Mars' Children

Although such a partisan of strife, Mars was not impervious to softer emotions, and passionately returned the devotion of Venus, who bore him three beautiful children,—Harmonia, Cupid, and Anteros. Mars also fell in love with a beautiful young Vestal named Ilia, a descendant of Æneas, who, in spite of the solemn pledge not to listen to a lover's pleadings until her time of service at the goddess Vesta's altar was accomplished, yielded to Mars' impetuous wooing, and consented to a clandestine union.

Romulus and Remus

Although secretly married, Ilia continued to dwell in the temple until the birth of her twin sons Romulus and Remus. Her parents, hearing she had broken her vows, commanded that she should suffer the prescribed punishment of being buried alive, and that the children should be exposed to the teeth and claws of the wild beasts of the forest. The double sentence was ruthlessly carried out, and the young mother perished; but, contrary to all previsions, the babes survived, and, after having been suckled for a time by a she-wolf, were found and adopted by a shepherd.

Romulus and Remus throve under this man's kind care, and grew up strong and fearless. When they reached manhood, they longed for a wider sphere for their youthful activity, and, leaving the mountain where they had grown up, journeyed out into the world to seek their fortunes. After some time they came to a beautiful hilly country, where they decided to found a great city, the capital of their future realm. Accordingly the brothers began to trace the outline of their city limits, and, in doing so, quarreled over the name of the prospective town.

Blinded by anger, Romulus suddenly raised the tool he held, and struck Remus such a savage blow that he fell to the ground, slain by his brother in a fit of passion. Alone now, Romulus at first vainly tried to pursue his undertaking, but, being soon joined by a number of adventurers as wicked and unscrupulous as he, they combined their forces, and built the celebrated city of Rome.

VENUS DE MILO AND MARS.

Then, with his nurse's wolf-skin girt,
Shall Romulus the line assert,
Invite them to his new raised home,
And call the martial city Rome.
                    VIRGIL (Conington's tr.)

As founder of this city, Romulus was its first king, and ruled the people with such an iron hand that his tyranny eventually became unbearable. The senators, weary of his exactions and arbitrary measures, finally resolved to free themselves of his presence. Taking advantage of an eclipse, which plunged the city in sudden darkness at noonday, and which occurred while all were assembled on the Forum, the magistrates slew Romulus, cut his body into pieces, and hid them under their wide togas.

QUIRINUS

When the light returned, and the terrified and awestruck people, somewhat reassured, looked about them for their king, they were told he had gone, never to return, carried off by the immortal gods, who wished him to share their abode and dignity. The senators further informed the credulous population that Romulus was to be henceforth worshiped as a god under the name of Quirinus, and gave orders for the erection of a temple on one of the seven hills, which since then has been known as Mount Quirinal. Yearly festivals in Romulus' honor were ever after held in Rome, under the name of Quirinalia.

Well pleased with the new city of Rome and its turbulent, lawless citizens, Mars took it under his special protection; and once, when a plague was raging which threatened to destroy all the people, the Romans rushed in a body to his temple, and clamored for a sign of his favor and protection.

THE ANCILE

Even while they prayed, it is said, a shield, Ancile, fell from heaven, and a voice was distinctly hear d to declare that Rome would endure as long as this token of the god's good will was preserved. The very same day the plague ceased its frightful ravages, and the Romans, delighted with the result of their petitions, placed the heavenly shield in one of their principal temples.

Then, in constant dread lest some of their enemies should succeed in stealing it, they caused eleven other shields to be made, so exactly like the heaven-sent Ancile, that none but the guardian priests, the Salii, who kept continual watch over them, could detect the original from the facsimiles. During the month of March, which, owing to its blustery weather, was dedicated to Mars and bore his name, the ancilæ were carried in a procession all through the city, the Salii chanting their rude war songs, and executing intricate war dances.

A Roman general, ere setting out on any warlike expedition, always entered the sanctuary of Mars, touched the sacred shield with the point of his lance, shook the spear in the hand of the god's effigy, and called aloud, "Mars, watch over us!"

WORSHIP OF MARS

A common superstition among the Roman soldiery was, that Mars, under the name of Gradivus, marched in person at the head of their army, and led them on to victory. Mars' principal votaries were therefore the Roman soldiers and youths, whose exercising ground was called, in his honor, the Campus Martius, or Field of Mars. All the laurel crowns bestowed upon victorious generals were deposited at the foot of his statues, and a bull was the customary thank offering after a successful campaign.

> The soldier, from successful camps returning
> With laurel wreath'd, and rich with hostile spoil,
> Severs the bull to Mars.
>
> PRIOR

Chapter X

VULCAN

Vulcan's Fall

Vulcan, or Hephæstus, son of Jupiter and Juno, god of fire and the forge, seldom joined the general council of the gods. His aversion to Olympus was of old standing. He had once been tenderly attached to his mother, had lavished upon her every proof of his affection, and had even tried to console her when she mourned Jupiter's neglect. On one occasion, intending to punish Juno for one of her usual fits of jealousy, Jupiter hung her out of heaven, fast bound by a golden chain; and Vulcan, perceiving her in this plight, tugged at the chain with all his might, drew her up, and was about to set her free, when Jupiter returned, and, in anger at his son's interference in his matrimonial concerns, kicked him out of heaven.

The intervening space between heaven and earth was so great, that Vulcan's fall lasted during one whole day and night, ere he finally touched the summit of Mount Mosychlus, in the Island of Lemnos.

> From morn
> To noon he fell, from noon to dewy eve,
> A summer's day; and with the setting sun
> Dropt from the zenith like a falling star,
> On Lemnos th' Ægean isle.
>
> Milton

Of course, to any one but a god such a terrible fall would have proved fatal; and even Vulcan did not escape entirely unharmed, for he injured one of his legs, which accident left him lame and somewhat deformed for the remainder of his life.

Vulcan's Forge

Now, although Vulcan had risked so much and suffered so greatly in taking his mother's part, she never even made the slightest attempt to ascertain whether he had reached the earth in safety. Hurt by her indifference and ingratitude, Vulcan vowed never again to return to Olympus, and withdrew to the solitudes of Mount Ætna, where he established a great forge in the heart of the mountain, in partnership with the Cyclopes, who helped him manufacture many cunning and useful objects from the metals found in great profusion in the bosom of the earth.

Among these ingenious contrivances were two golden handmaidens gifted with motion, who attended the god wherever he went, and supported his halting footsteps.

> Two golden statues, like in form and look
> To living maidens, aided with firm gait
> The monarch's steps.
>
> HOMER (Bryant's tr.)

The Golden Throne

Vulcan also devised a golden throne with countless hidden springs, which, when unoccupied, did not present an extraordinary appearance; but as soon as any one ventured to make use of it, the springs moved, and, the chair closing around the person seated upon it, frustrated all attempts to rise and escape from its treacherous embrace.

Vulcan dispatched this throne, when completed, to his mother, who, delighted with its beauty and delicate workmanship, proudly seated herself upon it, and found herself a prisoner. In vain she strove to escape, in vain the gods all gallantly rushed to her assistance. Their united strength and skill proved useless against the cunning springs.

Finally Mercury was sent to Vulcan, primed with a most diplomatic request to honor high Olympus with his presence; but all Mercury's eloquence and persuasions failed to induce the god of the forge to leave his sooty abode, and the messenger god was forced to return alone and report the failure of his attempt.

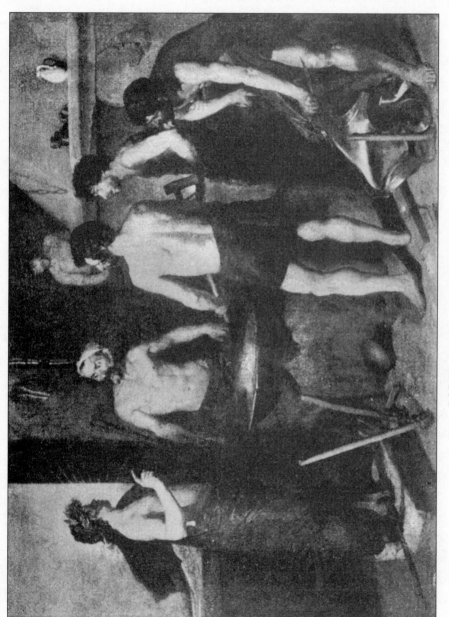

FORGE OF VULCAN. Velasquez.
(Museum, Madrid.)

Then the gods deliberated anew, and decided to send Bacchus, god of wine, hoping his powers of persuasion would prove more effective.

Armed with a flask of his choicest vintage, Bacchus presented himself before Vulcan, and offered him a refreshing draught. Vulcan, predisposed to thirst, and incited to drink by the very nature of his labor, accepted the offered cup, and allowed himself to be beguiled into renewing his potations, until he was quite intoxicated. In this condition, Bacchus led him passive to Olympus, made him release the Queen of Heaven, and urged him to embrace his father and crave forgiveness.

Although restored to favor, Vulcan would not remain permanently in Olympus, but preferred to return to his forge and continue his labors. He undertook, however, the construction of magnificent golden palaces for each of the gods upon the Olympian heights, fashioned their sumptuous furniture from precious metals, and further embellished his work by a rich ornamentation of precious stones.

> Then to their starry domes the gods depart,
> The shining monuments of Vulcan's art:
> Jove on his couch reclin'd his awful head,
> And Juno slumber'd on the golden bed.
>
> HOMER (Pope's tr.)

Aided by the Cyclopes, Vulcan manufactured Jupiter's weapons, the dread thunderbolts, whose frightful power none could withstand, and Cupid's love-inspiring darts.

VULCAN'S LOVES

Vulcan, in spite of his deformity, extreme ugliness, and well-known aversion to any home but his sooty forge, was none the less prone to fall in love with the various goddesses. He first wooed Minerva, who, having sworn never to marry, contemptuously dismissed his suit. To console Vulcan for this rebuff, and at the same time punish the Goddess of Beauty, who, according to some mythologists, had refused even his addresses, Jupiter bestowed upon him the fair hand of Venus, and sent her and her mischievous train of Loves and Graces to reside in the dark caves of Mount Ætna.

Amused by all the strange sights and sounds, the goddess at first seemed quite contented; but after a time Vulcan's gloomy abode lost all its attractions: so she forsook her ill-favored husband, and went in search of another, more congenial mate.

Some time after, Vulcan married one of the Graces, who, however, seems to have also soon wearied of his society, for she deserted him.

Vulcan's children were mostly monsters, such as Cacus, Periphetes, Cercyon, etc., all of whom play an important part in heroic mythology. He is also the reputed father of Servius Tullius, sixth king of Rome, by a slave Ocrisia, whom he was wont to visit in the guise of a bright flame, which played harmlessly about her.

Vulcan was worshiped by all blacksmiths and artisans, who recognized him as their special patron, and venerated him accordingly.

> Those who labor
> The sweaty forge, who edge the crooked scythe,
> Bend stubborn steel, and harden gleaming armor,
> Acknowledge Vulcan's aid.
>
> PRIOR

Great festivals, the Vulcanalia and the Hephæstia, were celebrated in honor of this god, who is generally represented as a short, muscular man, with one leg shorter than the other, a workman's cap on his curly locks, a short upper garment, and a smith's tools in his hand.

Chapter XI

NEPTUNE

When Jupiter assigned to each of his brothers a separate portion of the universe, he decreed that Neptune, or Poseidon, should govern all the waters upon the face of the earth, and be sole monarch of the ocean.

> Neptune, the mighty marine god, I sing;
> Earth's mover, and the fruitless ocean's king.
> That Helicon and th' Ægean deeps dost hold.
> O thou earth-shaker; thy command, twofold
> The gods have sorted; making thee of horses
> The awful tamer, and of naval forces
> The sure preserver. Hail, O Saturn's birth!
> Whose graceful green hair circles all the earth.
> Bear a benign mind; and thy helpful hand
> Lend all, submitted to thy dread command.
>
> HOMER (Chapman's tr.)

Before this new ruler made his appearance, the Titan Oceanus had wielded the scepter of the sea; and regretfully he now resigned it to his youthful supplanter, whom he nevertheless admired sincerely, and described in glowing colors to his brothers.

Have ye beheld the young God of the Seas,
My dispossessor? Have ye seen his face?
Have ye beheld his chariot, foam'd along
By noble winged creatures he hath made?
I saw him on the calmed waters scud,
With such a glow of beauty in his eyes,
That it enforc'd me to bid sad farewell
To all my empire.

KEATS

NEPTUNE'S EXILE

Neptune, the personification as well as the god of the sea, was of an exceedingly encroaching disposition. Dissatisfied with the portion allotted him, he once conspired to dethrone Jupiter; but, unfortunately for the success of his undertaking, his plot was discovered before he could put it into execution, and Jupiter, in punishment for his temerity, exiled him to earth. There he was condemned to build the walls of Troy for Laomedon, king of that city, who, in return, promised a handsome compensation.

Apollo, also banished from heaven at that time, volunteered to aid Neptune by playing on his lyre, and moving the stones by the power of sweet sounds. The task satisfactorily ended, Laomedon, an avaricious and dishonest king, refused the promised guerdon, whereupon Neptune created a terrible monster, which came upon the shore, devoured the inhabitants, devastated everything within his reach, and inspired all with great terror.

A great serpent from the deep,
Lifting his horrible head above their homes,
Devoured the children.

LEWIS MORRIS

To save themselves from the awful death which threatened them all, the Trojans consulted an oracle, who advised the sacrifice of a beautiful virgin, and promised the monster would disappear as soon as he had devoured the appointed victim.

FOUNTAIN OF NEPTUNE. Bologna.
(Bologna.)

Story of Hesione

A young girl was therefore chosen by lot, led down to the seashore, and chained by the priest's own hands to a slimy rock. As soon as her mourning friends had forsaken her, the hideous serpent came out of his lair in the waves, and devoured her; then he vanished, and nothing more was heard of him for a whole year, at the end of which time he reappeared, and resumed his former depredations, which were only checked by the sacrifice of a second virgin.

Year after year, however, he returned, and year after year a fair girl was doomed to perish, until finally the lot fell upon Hesione, the king's only daughter. He could not bear the thought of the terrible fate awaiting her, and tried every means in his power to save her. As a last resort he sent heralds to publish far and wide that the king would give a great reward to any man who would dare attack and succeed in slaying the monster.

Hercules, on his return from the scene of one of his stupendous labors, heard the proclamation, and, with no other weapon than the oaken club he generally carried, slew the monster just as he was about to drag poor Hesione down into his slimy cave. Laomedon was, of course, overjoyed at the monster's death, but, true to his nature, again refused the promised reward, and by his dishonesty incurred the hatred and contempt of this hero also. Some time after, having finished his time of servitude with Eurystheus, Hercules, aided by a chosen band of adventurers, came to Troy to punish him for his perfidy. The city was stormed and taken, the king slain, and his wife and children carried to Greece as captives. There Hesione became the bride of Telamon; while her brother Podarces, later known as Priam, was redeemed by his people and made King of Troy.

Laomedon's failure to pay his just debts was the primary cause of the enmity which Apollo and Neptune displayed towards the Trojans during their famous war with the Greeks.

Neptune's Contests

Their term of exile ended, the gods were reinstated in their exalted positions, and hastened to resume their former occupations; but, in spite of the severe lesson just received, Neptune was not yet cured of his grasping tendencies. Not long after his return from Troy, he quarreled with Minerva for the possession of the then recently founded city of Athens, then nameless, and entered into the memorable contest in which he was signally defeated. He also disputed the sovereignty of TrŒzene with Minerva, and that of Corinth with Apollo. In the latter instance, the disputants having chosen Briareus as umpire, the prize was awarded to him as the most powerful of all the gods except Jupiter.

NEPTUNE'S POWER

As god of the sea, Neptune did not generally remain in Olympus, but dwelt way down in the coral caves of his kingdom, over which he ruled with resistless sway. By one word he could stir up or calm the wildest storm, and cause the billows to roar with fury or subside into peaceful ripples.

> He spake, and round about him called the clouds
> And roused the ocean,—wielding in his hand
> The trident,—summoned all the hurricanes
> Of all the winds, and covered earth and sky
> At once with mists, while from above the night
> Fell suddenly.
>
> HOMER (Bryant's tr.)

The rivers, fountains, lakes, and seas were not only subject to his rule, but he could also cause terrible earthquakes at will, and, when he pleased, raise islands from the deep, as he did when Latona entreated him to shelter her from Juno's persecutions.

Neptune is said to have loved the goddess Ceres, and to have followed her during her prolonged search for her daughter, Proserpina. Annoyed by his persistent wooing, the goddess, to escape him, assumed the form of a mare; but the God of the Sea, not at all deceived by this stratagem, straightway assumed the form of a horse, in which guise he contentedly trotted after her and renewed his attentions.

NEPTUNE'S WIVES

The offspring of this equine pair was Arion, a wonderful winged steed, gifted with the power of speech, whose early education was intrusted to the Nereides. They trained him to draw his father's chariot over the waves with incredible rapidity, and parted with him regretfully when he was given to Copreus, Pelops' son. This marvelous horse passed successively into Hercules' and Adrastus' hands; and the latter won all the chariot races, thanks to his fleetness.

On another occasion, Neptune, having fallen deeply in love with a maiden named Theophane, and fearful lest some one of her numerous suitors should find favor in her eyes before he had time to urge his wooing, suddenly changed her into a sheep, and conveyed her to the Island of Crumissa, where he assumed the guise of a ram, and, in this metamorphosed condition, carried on his courtship, which eventually proved successful. The offspring of this union was the golden-fleeced ram which bore Phryxus in safety to the Colchian shores, and whose pelt was the goal of the Argonautic expedition.

Neptune also loved and married Medusa in the days of her youth and beauty, and when some drops of blood fell from her severed head into the salt sea foam, he produced from them the graceful winged steed Pegasus.

Neptune is also said to be the father of the giants Otus and Ephialtes, of Neleus, Pelias, and Polyphemus.

Amphitrite

The Queen of the Ocean, Neptune's own true and lawful wife, was a Nereid, one of the fifty daughters of Doris and Nereus,—the personification of the calm and sunlit aspect of the sea. Her name was Amphitrite, or Salacia. At first she was in great awe of her distinguished suitor, and in her fear fled at his approach, leaving him no chance to admire any of her charms, except the grace and celerity with which she managed to flit, or rather glide, out of his sight.

> Along the deep
> With beauteous ankles, Amphitrite glides.
> Hesiod (Elton's tr.)

This conduct grieved Neptune so sorely, that he sent a dolphin to plead his cause, and persuade the fair nymph to share his throne. The messenger, carefully instructed beforehand, carried out the directions with such skill, that Amphitrite formally consented to become Neptune's wife.

The King of the Deep was so overjoyed at these good tidings, that he transferred the dolphin to the sky, where he forms a well-known constellation. Neptune and Amphitrite in due time became the happy parents of several children, among whom the most celebrated is Triton, whose body was half man and half fish, and who gave his name to all his male descendants.

Story of Idas and Marpessa

Like all other gods, Neptune took a lively interest in men's affairs, and sometimes interfered in their behalf. On one occasion, for instance, he even lent his beautiful chariot to a youth by the name of Idas, who, loving a maiden dearly, and unable to win her father's consent to their union, had resolved to kidnap her. Marpessa, for such was the lady's name, allowed herself to be carried off without protest; and the lovers were blissfully speeding along in Neptune's chariot, when her father, Evenus, perceiving their escape, started in pursuit of them. In spite of the most strenuous efforts, he could not overtake the fleeing pair, and in his anger plunged into a river, where he was drowned, and which from him received the name of Evenus.

Idas and Marpessa were just congratulating themselves upon their narrow escape, when suddenly Apollo appeared before them, and, checking their steeds, declared he loved the maiden too, and would not tamely yield her up to a rival.

This was quite equivalent to a challenge; and Idas, stepping down from the chariot, was about to engage in the fight, when suddenly out of a clear sky a thunderbolt came crashing down to earth, and an imperious voice was heard to declare that the quarrel could be settled by Marpessa only, and that she should freely choose the suitor she preferred as husband.

The maiden glanced at both her lovers, and quickly reviewed their respective attractions. Remembering that Apollo, being immortal, would retain all his youthful bloom when her more ephemeral beauty had vanished, and that he would then probably cease to love her, she held out her hand to Idas, declaring she preferred to link her fate to that of a mortal, who would grow old when she did, and love her as long as they both lived. This choice was approved by Jupiter; and the lovers, after reaching a place of safety, returned the wondrous chariot to Neptune, with many grateful thanks for his timely aid.

FATHER NILE. (Vatican, Rome.)

NEPTUNE'S ATTENDANTS

All the Nereides, Tritons, and lesser sea divinities formed a part of Neptune and Amphitrite's train, and followed closely when they rode forth to survey their kingdom.

Neptune had, besides this, many subordinates, whose duty it was to look after various seas, lakes, rivers, fountains, etc., confided to their special care. In harmony with their occupations, these divinities were either hoary river gods (such as Father Nile), slender youths, beautiful maidens, or little babbling children. They seldom left the cool waves of their appointed dwellings, and strove to win Neptune's approbation mostly by the zeal they showed in the discharge of their various duties.

Proteus, too, another inferior deity, had the care of the flocks of the deep, and he always attended Neptune when it was safe to leave his great herds of sea calves to bask on the sunny shores.

> In ages past old Proteus, with his droves
> Of sea calves, sought the mountains and the groves.
>
> COWPER

PROTEUS

In common with all the other gods, Proteus enjoyed the gift of prophecy, and had the power to assume any shape he pleased. The former gift he was wont to exercise very reluctantly; and when mortals wished to consult him, he would change his form with bewildering rapidity, and, unless they clung to him through all his changes, they could obtain no answer to their questions.

> ~Shouting [we] seize the god: our force t' evade,
> His various arts he soon r esumes in aid:
> A lion now, he curls a surgy mane;
> Sudden, our hands a spotted pard restrain;
> Then, arm'd with tusks, and lightning in his eyes,
> A boar's obscener shape the god belies:
> On spiry volumes, there, a dragon rides;
> Here, from our strict embrace a stream he glides;
> And last, sublime, his stately growth he rears,
> A tree, and well-dissembled foliage wears.
>
> HOMER (Pope's tr.)

But if these manifestations proved unavailing to drive his would-be hearers away, the god answered every question circumstantially.

Amphitrite, Neptune's wife,—generally represented as a beautiful nude nymph, crowned with seaweed, and reclining in a pearl-shell chariot drawn by dolphins, or sea-horses,—was worshiped with her husband.

WORSHIP OF NEPTUNE

Neptune, majestic and middle-aged, with long, flowing hair and beard, wearing a seaweed crown, and brandishing a trident, or three-pronged fork, was widely worshiped throughout Greece and Italy, and had countless shrines. His principal votaries were the seamen and horse trainers, who often bespoke his aid.

> Hail, Neptune, greatest of the gods!
> Thou ruler of the salt sea floods;
> Thou with the deep and dark-green hair,
> That dost the golden trident bear;
> Thou that, with either arm outspread,
> Embosomest the earth we tread:
> Thine are the beasts with fin and scales,
> That round thy chariot, as it sails,
> Plunging and tumbling, fast and free,
> All reckless follow o'er the sea.
>
> ARION

Many large temples were dedicated exclusively to the worship of Neptune, and games were frequently celebrated in his honor. The most noted of all were undoubtedly the Isthmian Games,—a national festival, held every four years at Corinth, on the isthmus of the same name. Hither people came from all points of the compass, and all parts of the then known world, either to witness or to take part in the noted wrestling, boxing, and racing matches, or in the musical and poetical contests.

Chapter XII

PLUTO

Pluto (Dis, Hades, Orcus, Aïdoneus), son of Cronus and Rhea, received as his share of the world the supervision of the Infernal Regions, situated beneath the earth, and was also appointed god of the dead and of riches, for all precious metals are buried deep in the bosom of the earth.

> Blinded Plutus, didst thou dwell
> Nor in land nor fathomed sea,
> But only in the depths of hell,—
> God of riches! Safe from thee
> Man himself might happy be.
>
> TIMOCREON OF RHODES

This god inspired all men with a great fear. They never spoke of him without trembling, and fervently prayed that they might never see his face; for, when he appeared on the surface of the earth, it was only in search of some victim to drag down into his dismal abode, or to make sure there was no crevice through which a sunbeam might glide to brighten its gloom and dispel its shadows. Whenever the stern god set out on one of these expeditions, he rode in a chariot drawn by four coal-black steeds; and, if any obstacle presented itself to impede his progress, he struck it with his two-pronged fork, the emblem of his power, and the obstacle was immediately removed. It was on one of these occasions that Pluto kidnapped Proserpina, the fair goddess of vegetation, daughter of Ceres, whom he set on his throne in Hades, and crowned his queen.

WORSHIP OF PLUTO

Pluto is always represented as a stern, dark, bearded man, with tightly closed lips, a crown on his head, a scepter and a key in hand, to show how carefully he guards those who enter his domains, and how vain are their hopes to effect their escape. No temples were dedicated to him, and statues of this god are very rare. Human sacrifices were sometimes offered on his altars; and at his festivals, held every hundred years, and thence called Secular Games, none but black animals were slain.

HADES

His kingdom, generally called Hades, was very difficult of access. According to Roman traditions, it could only be entered at Avernus, but the Greeks asserted that there was another entrance near the Promontory of Tænarum. Both nations agreed, however, in saying that it was an almost impossible feat to get out again if one were rash enough to venture in.

> To the shades you go a down-hill, easy way;
> But to return and re-enjoy the day,
> This is a work, a labor!
>
> VIRGIL

To prevent all mortals from entering, and all spirits from escaping, Pluto placed a huge three-headed dog, called Cerberus, to guard the gate.

> There in state old Cerberus sate,
> A three-headed dog, as cruel as Fate,
> Guarding the entrance early and late.
>
> SAXE

From thence a long subterranean passage, through which shadowy spirits glided incessantly, led to the throne room, where Pluto and Proserpina sat in state, clad in their sable robes. From the foot of this throne flowed the rivers which channeled the Lower World. One, the Cocytus, rolled salt waves, composed of naught but the tears flowing continually from the eyes of the criminals condemned to hard labor in Tartarus, the portion of Hades reserved for the exclusive use of the wicked.

> Cocytus, named of lamentation loud
> Heard on the rueful stream.
>
> HOMER

RIVERS OF HADES

To separate this section from the remainder of his realm, Pluto surrounded it with the Phlegethon, a river of fire; while the Acheron, a black and deep stream, was to be passed by all souls ere they reached Pluto's throne and heard his decree. The current of this river was so swift, that even the boldest swimmer could not pass over; and, as there was no bridge, all the spirits were obliged to rely upon the aid of Charon, an aged boatman, who plied the only available skiff—a leaky, worm-eaten punt—from shore to shore. Neither would he allow any soul to enter his bark, unless he was first given a small coin, called the obolus, the ferryman's fare, which the ancients carefully laid under the tongue of the dead, that they might pass on to Pluto without delay. Charon's leaky boat no sooner touched the shore than a host of eager spirits pressed forward to claim a place. The cruel boatman repulsed them roughly, and brandished his oars, while he leisurely selected those he would next ferry across the stream.

> The shiv'ring army stands,
> And press for passage with extended hands.
> Now these, now those, the surly boatman bore;
> The rest he drove to distance from the shore.
>
> VIRGIL (Dryden's tr.)

All those who could not produce the required obolus were obliged to wait one hundred years, at the end of which time Charon reluctantly ferried them over free of charge.

There was also in Hades the sacred river Styx, by whose waters the gods swore their most irrevocable oaths; and the blessed Lethe, whose waters had the power to make one forget all unpleasant things, thus preparing the good for a state of endless bliss in the Elysian Fields.

> Lethe, the river of oblivion, rolls
> Her wat'ry labrinth, whereof who drinks,
> Forthwith his former state and being forgets,
> Forgets both joy and grief, pleasure and pain.
>
> MILTON

THE JUDGES

Near Pluto's throne were seated the three judges of Hades, Minos, Rhadamanthus, and Æacus, whose duty it was to question all newly arrived souls, to sort out the confused mass of good and bad thoughts and actions, and place them in the scales of Themis, the blindfolded, impartial goddess of justice, who bore a trenchant sword to indicate that her decrees would be mercilessly enforced. If the good outweighed the evil, the spirit was led to the Elysian Fields; but if, on the contrary, the evil prevailed, the spirit was condemned to suffer in the fires of Tartarus.

> Where his decrees
> The guilty soul within the burning gates
> Of Tartarus compel, or send the good
> To inhabit, with eternal health and peace,
> The valley of Elysium.
>
> AKENSIDE

THE FURIES

The guilty souls were always intrusted to the three snake-locked Furies (Erinnyes, or Eumenides), who drove them with their stinging lashes to the gates of Tartarus. These deities, who were sisters, and children of Acheron and Nyx, were distin-

THE FURIES. A Study for the Masque of Cupid.
Burne-Jones.

THE THREE FATES. Thumann.

guished by the individual names of Alecto, Tisiphone, and Megæra, and with
Nemesis, goddess of revenge, were noted for their hard hearts and the merciless
manner in which they hurried the ghosts intrusted to their care over the fiery
flood of the Phlegethon, and through the brazen gates of their future place of
incessant torment.

> There rolls swift Phlegethon, with thund'ring sound,
> His broken rocks, and whirls his surges round.
> On mighty columns rais'd sublime are hung
> The massy gates, impenetrably strong.
> In vain would men, in vain would gods essay,
> To hew the beams of adamant away.
> Here rose an iron tow'r: before the gate,
> By night and day, a wakeful Fury sate,
> The pale Tisiphone; a robe she wore,
> With all the pomp of horror, dy'd in gore.
>
> VIRGIL (C. Pitt's tr.)

THE FATES

The three Fates (MŒræ, Parcæ), sisters, also sat near Pluto's throne. Clotho, the
youngest, spun the thread of life, in which the bright and dark lines were inter-
mingled. Lachesis, the second, twisted it; and under her fingers it was now strong,
now weak.

> Twist ye, twine ye! even so,
> Mingle shades of joy and woe,
> Hope, and fear, and peace, and strife,
> In the thread of human life.
>
> SCOTT

Atropos, the third sister, armed with a huge pair of shears, remorselessly cut
short the thread of life,—an intimation that another soul would ere long find its
way down into the dark kingdom of Hades.

TARTARUS

When the gates of Tartarus turned on their hinges to receive the newcomer, a chorus of cries, groans, and imprecations from within fell upon his ear, mingled with the whistling of the whips incessantly plied by retributive deities.

> What sounds were heard,
> What scenes appeared,
> O'er all the dreary coasts!
>   Dreadful gleams,
>   Dismal screams,
>   Fires that glow,
>   Shrieks of woe,
>   Sullen moans,
>   Hollow groans,
> And cries of tortured ghosts.
>
> ADDISON

THE DANAIDES

Many victims renowned while on earth for their cruelty found here the just punishment of their sins. Attention was first attracted by a group of beautiful maidens, who carried water to fill a bottomless cask. Down to the stream they hastened, a long procession, filled their urns with water, painfully clambered up the steep and slippery bank, and poured their water into the cask; but when, exhausted and ready to faint from fatigue, they paused to rest for a moment, the cutting lash fell upon their bare shoulders, and spurred them on to renewed efforts to complete a task so hopeless that it has become proverbial.

These fair maidens were the Danaides, daughters of Danaus, who had pledged his fifty daughters to the fifty sons of his brother Ægyptus. The marriage preparations were all completed, when Danaus suddenly remembered an ancient prophecy which had quite escaped his memory, and which foretold that he would perish by the hand of his son-in-law.

It was now too late to prevent the marriages, so, calling his daughters aside, he told them what the oracle had said, and, giving them each a sharp dagger, bade them slay their husbands on their wedding night. The marriages were celebrated, as was customary, with mirth, dance, and song; and the revelry continued until late at night, when, the guests having departed, the newly married couples retired. But as soon as Danaus' daughters were quite certain their husbands were fast asleep, they produced their daggers and slew their mates.

> Danaus arm'd each daughter's hand
> To stain with blood the bridal bed.
>
> EURIPIDES (Potter's tr.)

One of the brides only, Hypermnestra, loved her husband too dearly to obey her father's command, and, when morning broke, only forty-nine of Ægyptus' sons were found lifeless. The sole survivor, Lynceus, to avenge his brothers' death, slew Danaus, thus fulfilling the ominous prophecy; while the gods, incensed by the Danaides' heartlessness, sent them to Hades, where they were compelled to fill the bottomless cask.

TANTALUS

Tartarus also detained within its brazen portals a cruel king named Tantalus (the father of Niobe), who, while on earth, had starved and ill-treated his subjects, insulted the immortal gods, and on one occasion had even dared to cook and serve up to them his own son Pelops. Most of the gods were immediately aware of the deception practiced upon them, and refused the new dish; but Ceres, who was very melancholy on account of the recent loss of her daughter, paid no heed to what was offered her, and in a fit of absent-mindedness ate part of the lad's shoulder.

The gods in pity restored the youth to life, and Ceres replaced the missing shoulder with one of ivory or of gold. Driven away from his kingdom, which was seized by the King of Troy, Pelops took refuge in Greece, where he ruled the extensive peninsula, the Peloponnesus, which still bears his name.

To punish the inhuman Tantalus, the gods then sent him to Tartarus, where he stood up to his chin in a stream of pure water, tormented with thirst; for, whenever he stooped to drink, the waters fled from his parched lips. Over his head hung a branch of luscious fruit. His hunger was as intolerable as his thirst; but, whenever he clutched at the fruit, the branch swung upward, and eluded his eager grasp.

> Above, beneath, around his hapless head,
> Trees of all kinds delicious fruitage spread.
> The fruit he strives to seize; but blasts arise,
> Toss it on high, and whirl it to the skies.
>
> HOMER (Pope's tr.)

This singular punishment inflicted upon Tantalus gave rise to the expression "to tantalize."

SISYPHUS

Another criminal was Sisyphus, who, while king of Corinth, had misused his power, had robbed and killed travelers, and even deceived the gods. His reprehensible conduct was punished in Tartarus, where he was condemned to roll a huge stone to the top of a very steep hill; and just as he reached the summit, and fancied his task done, the rock would slip from his grasp and roll to the foot of the hill, thus obliging him to renew all his exertions.

> With many a weary step, and many a groan,
> Up the high hill he heaves a huge round stone;
> The huge round stone, resulting with a bound,
> Thunders impetuous down, and smokes along the ground.
> Again the restless orb his toil renews,
> Dust mounts in clouds, and sweat descends in dews.
>
> HOMER (Pope's tr.)

SALMONEUS

Salmoneus, another king, had vainly tried to make his subjects believe he was Jupiter. To that effect, he had once driven over a brazen bridge to imitate the roll of thunder, and, to simulate the thunderbolts, had thrown lighted torches down upon the multitude, purposely assembled below.

> Th' audacious wretch four fiery coursers drew:
> He wav'd a torch aloft, and, madly vain,
> Sought godlike worship from a servile train.
> Ambitious fool, with horny hoofs to pass
> O'er hollow arches of resounding brass,
> To rival thunder in its rapid course,
> And imitate inimitable force!
>
> VIRGIL (Dryden's tr.)

This insolent parody so incensed Jupiter, that he grasped one of his deadliest thunderbolts, brandished it aloft for a moment, and then hurled it with vindictive force at the arrogant king. In Tartarus, Salmoneus was placed beneath an overhanging rock, which momentarily threatened to fall, and crush him under its mass.

> He was doomed to sit under a huge stone,
> Which the father of the gods
> Kept over his head suspended.
> Thus he sat In continual dread of its downfall,
> And lost to every comfort.
>
> PINDAR

TITYUS

Still farther on was the recumbent form of Tityus, a giant whose body covered nine acres of ground. He had dared offer an insult to Juno, and in punishment was chained like Prometheus, while a vulture feasted on his liver.

There Tityus was to see, who took his birth
From heav'n, his nursing from the foodful earth:
Here his gigantic limbs, with large embrace,
Infold nine acres of infernal space.
A rav'nous vulture in his open side
Her crooked beak and cruel talons try'd:
Still for the growing liver digg'd his breast,
The growing liver still supply'd the feast.

> VIRGIL (Dryden's tr.)

IXION

Here in Tartarus, too, was Ixion, king of the Lapithæ, who had been given the hand of Dia in marriage on condition that he would give her father a stipulated sum of money in exchange, but who, as soon as the maiden was his, refused to keep his promise. The father-in-law was an avaricious man, and clamored so loudly for his money, that Ixion, to be rid of his importunities, slew him. Such an act of violence could not be overlooked by the gods: so Jupiter summoned Ixion to appear before him and state his case.

Ixion pleaded so skillfully, that Jupiter was about to declare him acquitted, when he suddenly caught him making love to Juno, which offense seemed so unpardonable, that he sent him to Tartarus, where he was bound to a constantly revolving wheel of fire.

Proud Ixion (doom'd to feel
The tortures of the eternal wheel,
Bound by the hand of angry Jove)
Received the due rewards of impious love.

> SOPHOCLES (Francklin's tr.)

ELYSIAN FIELDS

Far out of sight and hearing of the pitiful sounds which so constantly rose out of Tartarus, were the Elysian Fields, lighted by a sun and moon of their own, decked with the most fragrant and beautiful of flowers, and provided with every charm that nature or art could supply. No storms or wintry winds ever came to rob these fields of their springlike beauty; and here the blessed spent eternity, in pleasant communion with the friends they had loved on earth.

> Patriots who perished for their country's rights,
> Or nobly triumphed in the fields of fight:
> There holy priests and sacred poets stood,
> Who sang with all the raptures of a god:
> Worthies whose lives by useful arts refined;
> With those who leave a deathless name behind,
> Friends of the world, and fathers of mankind.

Chapter XIII

BACCHUS

Among all the mortal maidens honored by the love of Jupiter, king of the gods, none was more attractive than Semele, daughter of Cadmus and Harmonia.

> For Semele was molded in the form
> Of elegance; the beauty of her race
> Shone in her forehead.
>
> NONNUS (Elton's tr.)

STORY OF SEMELE

Although conscious of these superior attractions, Semele was excessively coy, and it was only with the greatest difficulty that Jupiter, disguised as a mortal, could urge his love suit. When he had at last obtained a hearing, he told her who he was, calculating upon the effect which such a revelation must necessarily produce.

He was not mistaken in his previsions, for Semele, proud of having attracted the greatest among the gods, no longer offered any resistance, and consented to their union. Their love grew and prospered, and Jupiter came down from Olympus as often as possible to enjoy the society of his beloved. His frequent absences finally aroused Juno's suspicions, and, as usual, she spared no pains to discover what powerful charm could draw him from her side. After a few days she knew all, and straightway determined to have her revenge, and punish her fickle spouse. To accomplish this successfully, she assumed the face and form of Beroe, Semele's old nurse, and thus entered the young princess's apartment quite unsuspected.

Old Beroe's decrepit shape she wears,
>   Her wrinkled visage, and her hoary hairs;
>   Whilst in her trembling gait she totters on,
>   And learns to tattle in the nurse's tone.
>   OVID (Addison's tr.)

There she immediately entered into conversation with her supposed nursling, artfully extracted a complete confession, heard with suppressed rage how long Jupiter had wooed ere he had finally won the maiden's consent, and received a rapturous and minute catalogue of all his personal charms and a synopsis of all they had both said.

The false nurse listened with apparent sympathy; but in reality she was furious, and, to put an end to it all, asked Semele if she were quite sure he was king of the gods, as he asserted, and whether he visited her in all the pomp of his regal apparel. The maiden shamefacedly replied that he was wont to visit her in the guise of a mortal only; whereupon Beroe, with feigned indignation, told her nursling he must either be a vile impostor, or else that he did not love her as dearly as he loved Juno, in whose presence he seldom appeared except in godlike array.

With artful words she so worked upon the guileless nature of her rival, that, when Jupiter next came, the maiden used all her blandishments to extort from him a solemn oath to grant any request she chose to make. A lover is not very likely to weigh his words under such circumstances, and Jupiter took the most solemn of all the oaths to gratify her whim.

>   "Bear me witness, Earth, and ye, broad Heavens
>   Above us, and ye, waters of the Styx,
>   That flow beneath us, mightiest oath of all,
>   And most revered by the blessed gods!"
>   HOMER (Bryant's tr.)

The promise won, the delighted Semele bade her lover speedily return to Olympus, don his own majestic form and apparel, and hasten back to her side, surrounded by all his heavenly pomp, and armed with his dreaded thunderbolts. Jupiter, horrified at this imprudent request, implored her to ask something else, and release him from a promise fraught with such danger to her; but all in vain. Semele, like many another fair lady, enjoyed having her own way, and fairly forced him to obey.

Jupiter returned to Olympus, modified his costume as much as possible, dimmed his glory wherever he could, and chose the feeblest of all his bolts, for well he knew no mere mortal could endure the shock of his full glory. Then, mounted on a pale flash of lightning, he darted back to Semele.

> To keep his promise he ascends, and shrouds
> His awful brow in whirlwinds and in clouds;
> Whilst all around, in terrible array,
> His thunders rattle, and his lightnings play.
> And yet, the dazzling luster to abate,
> He set not out in all his pomp and state,
> Clad in the mildest lightning of the skies,
> And arm'd with thunder of the smallest size:
> Not those huge bolts, by which the giants slain,
> Lay overthrown on the Phlegrean plain.
> 'Twas of a lesser mold, and lighter weight;
> They call it thunder of a second-rate.
> For the rough Cyclops, who by Jove's command
> Temper'd the bolt and turn'd it to his hand,
> Work'd up less flame and fury in its make,
> And quench'd it sooner in the standing lake.
> Thus dreadfully adorn'd, with horror bright,
> Th' illustrious god, descending from his height,
> Came rushing on her in a storm of light.
>   OVID (Addison's tr.)

But, although so much milder than usual, this apparition was more than poor Semele's human nerves could bear, and she dropped to the floor in a swoon at the first glimpse of her lover. Oblivious of all but her alarming condition, Jupiter sprang to her side; but the lightning which played about his head set fire to the whole palace, which was reduced to ashes.

BIRTH OF BACCHUS

Semele herself perished, burned to death; and the only person in all the building who escaped uninjured was Bacchus (Liber, Dionysus), the infant son of Jupiter and Semele, who was saved by his father's powerful hand. Jupiter was at first inconsolable at the death of Semele; and, to testify to all mortals how fondly he had loved her, he brought her spirit up to heaven, where he raised her to the rank of a deity.

> Semele of the flowing hair,
> Who died in Thunder's crashing flame,
> To deified existence came.
>
> HOMER

The infant Bacchus was first intrusted to the care of his aunt Ino, the second wife of Athamas, King of Thebes, who nursed him as tenderly as if he had been her own child. But all her love could not avail to screen him from the effects of Juno's persistent hatred: so Jupiter, fearing lest some harm might befall his precious son, bade Mercury convey him to the distant home of the Nysiades,—nymphs who guarded him most faithfully.

Juno, not daring to continue her persecutions, wreaked all her anger upon poor Ino and her unhappy household by sending the Fury Tisiphone to goad Athamas to madness. In a fit of deluded frenzy, he pursued his wife and children as if they were wild beasts. One of his sons, Learchus, fell beneath his arrows; and, to escape his murderous fury, Ino plunged headlong into the sea with her second child in her arms. The gods, in pity for her sufferings, changed her into the goddess Leucothea, and her son into a sea deity by the name of Palæmon.

BACCHUS' ATTENDANTS

When still but a youth, Bacchus was appointed god of wine and revelry, and intrusted to the guidance of Silenus, a satyr, half man and half goat, who educated him, and accompanied him on all his travels; for he delighted in roaming all over the world, borne by his followers, or riding in his chariot drawn by wild beasts, while his tutor followed him, mounted on an ass, supported on either side by an attendant.

BACCHUS. (Vatican, Rome.)

And near him rode Silenus on his ass,
Pelted with flowers as he on did pass.

KEATS

Bacchus' train was very large indeed, and composed of men and women, nymphs, fauns, and satyrs, all crowned with ivy leaves, who drank wine,—a drink compounded for their express use out of water and sunshine,—ate grapes, danced and sang, and loudly proclaimed him their chosen leader.

"We follow Bacchus! Bacchus on the wing,
    A conquering!
Bacchus, young Bacchus! good or ill betide,
We dance before him thorough kingdoms wide."

KEATS

The most unruly among his female followers were the Bacchantes, who delighted in revelry, and were in a perpetual state of intoxication as they went with him from land to land, where he taught the people the cultivation of the vine and the art of making wine. He traveled thus, it is said, throughout Greece and Asia Minor, and even ventured as far as India and Ethiopia.

BACCHUS AND THE PIRATES

During these long journeys, Bacchus, as was inevitable, met with many adventures, which have been fertile themes for poetry and art. On one occasion, having strayed away from his followers and lost his way, Bacchus laid himself down upon the sand on the seashore to rest. Some pirates, sailing by, saw the handsome young sleeper, and noiselessly bore him off to their vessel, intending to sell him as a slave in Egypt.

They were already quite far out at sea when the god awoke, and gazed around him in mute wonder at his surroundings. When fully roused, he bade the seamen take him back to land, but they merely replied by laughter and mockery. Their amusement was cut short, however, for the ship came to a sudden standstill; and, when they leaned over the sides to ascertain why their oars could no longer propel it onward, they saw a vine grow out of the sea, and twine its branches and tendrils with lightning-like velocity around oars, mast, and rigging, thus transforming the vessel into a floating arbor. Then a sound of music and revelry greeted their astonished ears, and Bacchus' followers came thronging over the ship's sides, riding on wild beasts, and chanting the praises of their god and of his favorite beverage.

> In chorus we sing of wine, sweet wine,
> Its power benign, and its flavor divine.
> MARTINEZ DE LA ROSA

These extraordinary sights and sounds so bewildered the poor sailors, that they lost all presence of mind, and jumped overboard into the sea, where they were drowned and changed into dolphins.

On another occasion, Silenus, after a great carousal, lost his way in the forest, and helplessly wandered from place to place in search of his companions, until he finally came to the court of Midas, King of Lydia, of ass's ears fame.

THE CURSE OF GOLD

Midas no sooner beheld the red nose and bloated appearance of the wanderer, than he recognized him as Bacchus' tutor, and volunteered to lead him back to his divine pupil. Delighted to see Silenus again, Bacchus promised Midas any reward he wished; whereupon Midas, who was an avaricious old king, fell upon his knees, and humbly besought the god to grant that all he touched might be changed into gold.

> "Give me," says he (nor thought he ask'd too much),
> "That with my body whatsoe'er I touch,
> Changed from the nature which it held of old,
> May be converted into yellow gold."
>
> OVID (Croxall's tr.)

Bacchus immediately signified that his prayer was granted; and Midas, over-joyed at the success of his bold venture, wandered back to his palace, testing his new-won power, which changed all to gold at a mere touch of one of his fingers.

Down from a lowly branch a twig he drew,
The twig straight glitter'd with a golden hue.
He takes a stone, the stone was turn'd to gold:
A clod he touches, and the crumbling mold
Acknowledged soon the great transforming power,
In weight and substance like a mass of ore.
He pluck'd the corn, and straight his grasp appears
Fill'd with a bending tuft of golden ears.
An apple next he takes, and seems to hold
The bright Hesperian vegetable gold:
His hand he careless on a pillar lays,
With shining gold the fluted pillars blaze.

OVID (Croxall's tr.)

The sight of these and many other wonders, wrought by a mere touch, filled his heart with joy; and in his elation he bade his servants prepare a sumptuous feast, and invite all his courtiers to share his merriment. His commands were obeyed with the utmost celerity, and Midas beamed with satisfaction as he took his place at the head of the board, and viewed the choice dishes and wines prepared for his delectation.

Here, too, however, a new revelation awaited him; for cloth, plate, and cup turned to gold, as did the food and drink as soon as they met his eager lips.

Whose powerful hands the bread no sooner hold,
But all its substance is transform'd to gold:
Up to his mouth he lifts the savory meat,
Which turns to gold as he attempts to eat:
His patron's noble juice of purple hue,
Touch'd by his lips, a gilded cordial grew,
Unfit for drink; and, wondrous to behold,
It trickles from his jaws a fluid gold.
The rich poor fool, confounded with surprise,
Starving in all his various plenty lies.

OVID (Croxall's tr.)

In the midst of plenty, the gnawing pangs of hunger now made themselves felt; and the precious gift, which prevented his allaying them, soon lost all its attractions. With weary feet, Midas now retraced the road he had traveled in his pride a few hours before, again cast himself at Bacchus' feet, and this time implored him to take back the inconvenient gift, which prevented him from satisfying his natural appetites.

His distress seemed so real, that Bacchus bade him go and wash in the Pactolus River, if he would be rid of the power which had so soon turned into a curse. Midas hastened off to the river and plunged in its tide, noting that even its sands all turned to gold beneath his tread; since when,

> Pactolus singeth over golden sands.
>
> GRAY

NAXOS

Bacchus' favorite place of resort was the Island of Naxos, which he visited after every journey. During one of his sojourns there, he discovered a fair maiden lying alone on the sandy shore. Ariadne, for such was the girl's name, had been forsaken there by her lover, Theseus, who had sailed away while she slept. As soon as she awoke, she called her faithless lover; but no answering sound fell upon her ear except the mocking tones of Echo. Her tears flowed freely as she beat her breast in despair; but suddenly her lamentations ceased, as she caught the faint sound of music floating toward her on the summer breeze. Eagerly turning toward the pleasant music, she caught sight of a merry procession, headed by the God of Wine.

> "And as I sat, over the light blue hills
>   There came a noise of revelers: the rills
>   Into the wide stream came of purple hue—
>   'Twas Bacchus and his crew!
>   The earnest trumpet spake, and silver thrills
>   From kissing cymbals made a merry din—
>   'Twas Bacchus and his kin!
>   Like to a moving vintage down they came,
>   Crown'd with green leaves, and faces all on flame;
>   All madly dancing through the pleasant valley."
>
> KEATS

BACCHUS AND ARIADNE

Bacchus, the first to perceive the fair mourner, hastened to her side, and brought all his powers of persuasion into play to console her. His devotion at last induced her to forget her recreant lover, and, after a short courtship, Bacchus won her as a bride.

Their wedding was the gayest ever seen, and the feasting lasted for several days. The bridegroom presented the bride with a crown adorned with seven glittering stars,—an ornament which fitly enhanced her peerless beauty. Shortly after her marriage, however, poor Ariadne sickened and died, leaving a disconsolate widower, who took the crown she had so often worn and flung it up into the air. It rose higher and higher, until the gods fixed it in the sky, where it still forms a brilliant constellation, known as Ariadne's Crown, or Corona.

> And still her sign is seen in heaven,
> And, 'midst the glittering symbols of the sky,
> The starry crown of Ariadne glides.
>
> APOLLONIUS RHODIUS

Bacchus' lightheartedness had all vanished, and he no longer took any pleasure in music, dance, or revelry, until Jupiter, in pity for his bereavement, restored Ariadne to his longing arms, and, to prevent her being again claimed by Death, gave her immortal life.

STORY OF PENTHEUS

When but a short distance from Thebes, Bacchus once sent a herald to Pentheus, the king, to announce his approach, and bespeak a suitable reception and sumptuous entertainment. Rumors of the noise and disorder, which seemed to have been the invariable accompaniment of the god's presence, had already reached Pentheus, who therefore dismissed the herald with an insolent message, purporting that Bacchus had better remain outside of the city gates.

To avenge this insult, Bacchus inspired the Theban women with a species of dementia, which made them rush simultaneously out of the city and join his followers. Then they all clamored for permission to witness the religious rites in his honor, generally called Mysteries, which permission was graciously granted.

MARRIAGE OF BACCHUS AND ARIADNE. Tintoretto.
(Ducal Palace, Venice.)

The king's spies reported all that had occurred, and their accounts made Pentheus long to view the ceremonies in secret. He therefore disguised himself, and hid in a bush near the consecrated place, hoping to see all without being seen; but an inadvertent movement attracted the attention of the already excited Bacchantes, who, led by Agave, the king's own mother, dragged him from his hiding place and tore him limb from limb.

Worship of Bacchus

Bacchus, god of wine, was worshiped throughout the ancient world, and festivals without number were held in his honor. The most noted were the Greater and Lesser Dionysia, the Liberalia, and the Bacchanalia, where the wildest merrymaking and license were freely indulged in by all participants.

> Bacchus, on thee they call, in hymns divine,
> And hang thy statues on the lofty pine:
> Hence plenty every laughing vineyard fills,
> Thro' the deep valleys and the sloping hills;
> Where'er the god inclines his lovely face,
> More luscious fruits the rich plantations grace.
> Then let us Bacchus' praises duly sing,
> And consecrated cakes, and chargers bring,
> Dragg'd by their horns let victim goats expire,
> And roast on hazel spits before the sacred fire.
>
> Come, sacred sire, with luscious clusters crown'd,
> Here all the riches of thy reign abound;
> Each field replete with blushing autumn glows,
> And in deep tides for thee the foaming vintage flows.
>
> VIRGIL (Warton's tr.)

Bacchus is generally represented as a handsome youth, crowned with ivy or grape leaves and clusters, bearing the thyrsus, an ivy-circled wand, as scepter, and riding in a chariot drawn by panthers or leopards.

Chapter XIV

CERES AND PROSERPINA

CERES AND PROSERPINA

Ceres (Demeter), daughter of Cronus and Rhea, and one of Jupiter's numerous consorts, was goddess of agriculture and civilization. Her manifold cares were shared by her daughter, Proserpina (Cora, Pherephatta, Persephone), the goddess of vegetation. Whenever her duties permitted, this fair young goddess hastened off to the Island of Sicily, her favorite place of resort, where she wandered about all day long, attended by a merry girlish train, gathering flowers, on the green slopes of Mount Ætna, and danced with the nymphs in the beautiful plain of Enna.

One day, weary of labor, Proserpina called these fair playmates to join her and spend a merry day gathering flowers.

> And one fair morn—
> Not all the ages blot it—on the side
> Of Ætna we were straying. There was then
> Summer nor winter, springtide nor the time
> Of harvest, but the soft unfailing sun
> Shone always, and the sowing time was one
> With reaping.
>
> LEWIS MORRIS

PLUTO KIDNAPS PROSERPINA

The maidens sang merry lays as they wound their long garlands; and their joyous voices and ripples of silvery laughter attracted the attention of Pluto, just then driving past in his dark chariot drawn by four fiery coal-black steeds. To ascertain whence these sounds proceeded, the god stepped out of his car, and cautiously peeped through the thick foliage.

He saw Proserpina sitting on a mossy bank, almost buried in many-hued blossoms, her laughing companions picturesquely grouped around her. One glance sufficed to convince Pluto of her loveliness and grace, and to make him feel that his happiness depended on the possession of this bright young creature.

Long ere this, he had tried to persuade one after another of the goddesses to share his gloomy throne; but one and all had refused the honor, and declined to accompany him to a land where the sun never shone, the birds never sang, and the flowers never bloomed. Hurt and disappointed by these rebuffs, Pluto had finally registered a solemn vow never to go wooing again; and so, instead of gently inviting Proserpina to become his queen, he resolved to kidnap her.

Straight through the bushes he strode, direct to the spot where she was seated. The noise of crackling branches and hasty footsteps made the assembled maidens swiftly turn. One glance sufficed to identify the intruder, for none but he could boast of such a dark, lowering countenance; and all exclaimed in mingled wonder and terror at his unwonted presence in those sunlit regions.

> 'Tis he, 'tis he: he comes to us
> From the depths of Tartarus.
> For what of evil doth he roam
> From his red and gloomy home,
> In the center of the world,
> Where the sinful dead are hurled?
> Mark him as he moves along,
> Drawn by horses black and strong,
> Such as may belong to Night
> Ere she takes her morning flight.
> Now the chariot stops: the god
> On our grassy world hath trod:
> Like a Titan steppeth he,
> Yet full of his divinity.
> On his mighty shoulders lie
> Raven locks, and in his eye
> A cruel beauty, such as none
> Of us may wisely look upon.
>
> BARRY CORNWALL

ABDUCTION OF PROSERPINA. Schobelt.

Frightened by his impetuous approach, the trembling nymphs first crowded around Proserpina, who, in her astonishment and trepidation, dropped all her pretty flowers and stood motionless among them. Her uncertainty as to his purpose was only momentary, for, catching her in his brawny arms ere she could make an attempt to escape, he bore her off to his chariot, in spite of prayers and struggles, and drove away as fast as his fleet steeds could carry him.

He was soon out of hearing of the wild cries and lamentations of the nymphs, who vainly pursued him, and tried to overtake their beloved mistress. Afraid lest Ceres should come and force him to relinquish his new-won treasure, Pluto drove faster and faster, nor paused for an instant until he reached the banks of the Cyane River, whose waters, at his approach, began to seethe and roar in a menacing fashion, and spread themselves as much as possible, to check him in his flight.

Pluto quickly perceived that to attempt to cross the river in his chariot would be madness, while by retracing his footsteps he ran the risk of meeting Ceres, and being forced to relinquish his prize. He therefore decided to have recourse to other means, and, seizing his terrible two-pronged fork, struck the earth such a mighty blow, that a great crevice opened under his feet, through which horses and chariot plunged down into the darkness of the Lower World.

Proserpina turned her weeping eyes to catch a parting glimpse of the fair earth she was leaving, and then, with a fond thought of her anxious mother, who, when evening came, would vainly seek her child in all her favorite haunts, she quickly flung her girdle into the Cyane, and called to the water nymph to carry it to Ceres.

Elated by the complete success of his bold venture, and no longer fearful of immediate pursuit, the happy god strained his fair captive to his breast, pressed kisses on her fresh young cheeks, and tried to calm her terrors, as the black steeds rushed faster and faster along the dark passage, nor paused until they reached the foot of their master's throne.

> Pleased as he grasps her in his iron arms,
> Frights with soft sighs, with tender words alarms.
> DARWIN

CERES' SEARCH

In the mean while the sun had sunk below the Sicilian horizon; and Ceres, returning from the fields of fast-ripening grain to her own dwelling, sought for the missing Proserpina, of whom no trace could be found except the scattered flowers. Hither and thither the mother wandered, calling her daughter, and wondering where she could be, and why she did not come bounding to meet her. As time passed, and still Proserpina did not appear, Ceres' heart beat fast with apprehension, and the tears coursed down her cheeks as she rushed about from place to place, calling her daughter.

> What ails her that she comes not home?
> Demeter seeks her far and wide,
> And gloomy-browed doth ceaseless roam
> From many a morn till eventide.
> "My life, immortal though it be,
> Is naught!" she cries, "for want of thee,
> Persephone—Persephone!"
>
> INGELOW

Night came, and Ceres, kindling a torch at the volcanic fires of Mount Ætna, continued her search. Day dawned, and still the mother called, awakening the morning echoes with her longing cries for her child. Her daily duties were all neglected. The rain no longer refreshed the drooping flowers, the grain was parched by the ardent rays of the sun, and the grass all perished, while Ceres roamed over hill and dale in search of Proserpina.

Weary at last of her hopeless quest, the goddess seated herself by the wayside, near the city of Eleusis, and gave way to her overwhelming grief.

> Long was thine anxious search
> For lovely Proserpine, nor didst thou break
> Thy mournful fast, till the far-fam'd Eleusis
> Received thee wandering.
>
> ORPHIC HYMN

Ceres and Triptolemus

To avoid recognition, she had assumed the appearance of an aged crone; and as she sat there by the wayside, in tears, she attracted the compassionate inquiries of the daughters of Celeus, king of the country. Having heard her bewail the loss of her child, they entreated her to come to the palace, and, knowing nothing could so well soothe a breaking heart, offered her the charge of their infant brother Triptolemus.

Ceres, touched by their ready sympathy, accepted the offer; and when she arrived at the palace, the royal heir was intrusted to her care. Tenderly the goddess kissed the puny child's little pinched face; and at her touch the child became rosy and well, to the unbounded astonishment of the royal family and all the court.

In the night, while Ceres sat alone with her charge, it occurred to her that she might confer a still greater blessing upon him, that of immortality: so she anointed his limbs with nectar, murmured a powerful charm, and placed him upon the red-hot coals, to consume all the perishable elements left in his body.

The queen, Metaneira, who had thought it somewhat imprudent to leave the child thus alone with a stranger, now stole noiselessly into the apartment, and with a wild shriek rushed to the fire and snatched her child out of the flames, pressed him anxiously to her breast, and, after ascertaining that he was quite unharmed, turned to vent her indignation upon the careless nurse; but the aged beggar woman had vanished, and in her stead she confronted the radiant Goddess of Agriculture.

> From her fragrant robes
> A lovely scent was scattered, and afar
> Shone light emitted from her skin divine,
> And yellow locks upon her shoulders waved;
> White as from lightning, all the house was filled
> With splendor.
>
> HOMERIC HYMN

With a gentle reproof to the queen for her untimely interference, Ceres explained what she fain would have done, and vanished, to continue her wanderings in other lands. She finally returned to Italy; and, while wandering along

CERES.
(Vatican, Rome.)

the river banks one day, the waters suddenly cast a glittering object at her feet. Stooping hastily to ascertain what it might be, she recognized the girdle her daughter had worn when she had parted from her in Sicily.

Joyfully she embraced the token, and, thinking she must now be upon Proserpina's track, hastened on until she came to a crystal fountain, by whose side she sat down to rest. Her eyes were heavy with the combined effect of tears, fatigue, and oppressive heat, and she was about to lose all consciousness of her trouble in sleep, when the murmur of the fountain increased, until she fancied it was talking; not as mortals do, but in its own silvery accents.

ARETHUSA AND ALPHEUS

The goddess was not mistaken; for a few minutes later she could distinguish words, and heard the fountain entreat her to listen, if she would hear what had befallen her child. The fountain then went on to tell how she had not always been a mere stream, but was once a nymph, called Arethusa, in Diana's train, and how, overcome by the heat, she had once sought a cool stream wherein she might bathe her heated limbs.

She soon found one, the Alpheus River, and selected a spot where the trees hung over the limpid waters, where the sand on the bottom was fine and even, and where no mortal eyes could see her as she threw aside her sandals and outer garments. She was enjoying the refreshing sensation of the water rippling around her hot limbs, and was reveling in the complete solitude, when suddenly the river, until now as smooth as a mirror, was ruffled by waves, which crept nearer and nearer to the startled nymph, until in affright she sprang out of the water.

Then a voice—the voice of the river god Alpheus—was heard, calling to her in pleading accents to stay her flight and lend an ear to his wooing; but when the impetuous god, instead of waiting for an answer to his suit, rose up out of the water and rushed to clasp her in his arms, she turned and fled in great terror. She fled, but he pursued. Over hill and dale, through forest and field, Arethusa ran, still closely followed by her too ardent lover, until, exhausted, she paused for breath, crying aloud to Diana to come to her rescue.

Her prayer was answered. A moment later she was enveloped in a thick mist and transformed into a fountain. Alpheus could no longer see her, but wandered about, bewailing her disappearance, and calling her in passionate accents.

A NYMPH. Kray.

> "O Arethusa, peerless nymph! why fear
> Such tenderness as mine? Great Dian, why,
> Why didst thou hear her prayer? Oh that I
> Were rippling round her dainty fairness now,
> Circling about her waist, and striving how
> To entice her to a dive! then stealing in
> Between her luscious lips and eyelids thin."
>
> KEATS

The misty cloud in which Arethusa had been enveloped by Diana's protecting care was soon blown away by a mischievous breath from Zephyrus; and Alpheus, who was still hovering near there, suddenly beholding a fountain where none had ever existed before, surmised what had happened. Changing himself into an impetuous torrent, he rushed to join his beloved, who sprang out of her mossy bed, and hurried on over sticks and stones, until Diana, seeing her new plight, opened a crevice, through which she glided away from the bright sunlight she loved so well into the depths of Pluto's realm.

While gliding there in the gloom, Arethusa had caught a glimpse of Proserpina on her sable throne, beside the stern-browed Pluto. She could not, however, pause to inquire how she came there, but hurried on breathlessly, until another crevice offered her the means of returning to the upper world, and seeing once more the blue sky and sun on the Sicilian plains.

The monotonous murmur of the fountain now subsided again into its usual undertone; and Ceres, knowing where to seek her daughter, was about to depart, when she heard the sudden rush and roar of a large body of water. She immediately turned, and beheld the torrent Alpheus, who, after a disconsolate search underground for the lost Arethusa, had found a crevice, through which he passed to join his beloved on the Sicilian plains.

> Alpheus, Elis' stream, they say,
> Beneath the seas here found his way,
> And now his waters interfuse
> With thine, O fountain Arethuse,
>   Beneath Sicilian skies.
>
> VIRGIL (Conington's tr.)

In spite of her previous efforts to escape him, Arethusa must still have been very glad to see him once more, for Ceres heard her murmur contentedly as she sank into his arms and listened to his louder tones of rapturous love.

Maidens in Greece were wont to throw fresh garlands into the Alpheus River; and it was said the selfsame flowers, carried away by his current, soon reappeared in the Sicilian fountain, carried there as love offerings by the enamored river.

> O my beloved, how divinely sweet
> Is the pure joy when kindred spirits meet!
> Like him, the river god, whose waters flow,
> With love their only light, through caves below,
> Wafting in triumph all the flowery braids
> And festal rings, with which Olympic maids
> Have decked his current, an offering meet
> To lay at Arethusa's shining feet.
> Think when at last he meets his fountain bride
> What perfect love must thrill the blended tide!
> And lost in each, till mingling into one,
> Their lot the same for shadow or for sun,
> A type of true love, to the deep they run.
>
> MOORE

CERES' MOURNING

Now, although poor Ceres had ascertained where to find her missing daughter, her grief was not at all diminished, for she felt convinced that Pluto would never willingly relinquish her. She therefore withdrew into a dark cave to mourn unseen, and still further neglected her wonted duties.

Famine threatened to visit the people, and they prayed and clamored for her aid; but, absorbed in grief, she paid no heed to their distress, and vowed that nothing on earth should grow, with her permission, as long as her daughter was detained in Hades. In despair at this frightful state of affairs, the people then besought Jupiter to pity the sufferings they endured, and to allow Proserpina to revisit the upper world once more.

Arise, and set the maiden free;
Why should the world such sorrow dree
By reason of Persephone?

INGELOW

As soon as she became aware of this petition, Ceres hastened to Olympus, to join her supplications to the cries which rose from all parts of the earth; until Jupiter, wearied by these importunities, consented to Proserpina's return, upon condition, however, that she had not touched any food during the whole time of her sojourn in the Infernal Regions.

Last, Zeus himself,
Pitying the evil that was done, sent forth
His messenger beyond the western rim
To fetch me back to earth.

LEWIS MORRIS

THE POMEGRANATE SEEDS

Ceres in person hastened to her daughter's new abode, and was about to lead her away in spite of Pluto, when a spirit, Ascalaphus, suddenly declared that the queen had partaken of some pomegranate seeds that very day. Proserpina could not refute the charge, and Jupiter decreed that for every seed she had eaten she should spend one month of every year in her husband's gloomy kingdom.

Thus it came about that Proserpina was condemned to spend one half the year in Hades, and could linger on the bright earth only for six months at a time.

Mercury was chosen to lead her to and from Hades; and, whenever he brought her out of her gloomy prison, the skies became blue and sunny, the grass sprang fresh and green beneath her elastic tread, the flowers bloomed along her way, the birds trilled forth their merry lays, and all was joy and brightness.

And when, in springtime, with sweet-smelling flowers
Of various kinds the earth doth bloom, thou'lt come
From gloomy darkness back—a mighty joy
To gods and mortal men.

HOMERIC HYMN

PROSERPINA'S RETURN

Ceres, happy once more in the possession of her beloved daughter, cheerfully and diligently attended to all her duties, and blessed the earth with plenty; but when the six months were over, and the skies wept and all nature mourned Proserpina's departure, she again returned to her cave, whence no entreaties could draw her.

As for the merry, happy-natured Proserpina, the moment Hades' portals closed behind her, she became pale and melancholy; and none would have dreamed the playful, flower-crowned Goddess of Vegetation was identical with the sad-faced, sable-vested Queen of Hades (now called Hecate), who held a pomegranate in one hand, and a torch in the other. Proserpina, like Adonis, was the personification of vegetation, visibly prosperous during the six favorable months of the year, and lurking hidden under the cold ground during the remainder of the time.

WORSHIP OF CERES

Many beautiful temples were dedicated to Ceres and Proserpina in Greece and Italy, where yearly festivals, the Thesmophoria and the Cerealia, were celebrated with great pomp.

> To Ceres chief her annual rites be paid,
> On the green turf, beneath a fragrant shade,
> When winter ends, and spring serenely shines,
> Then fat the lambs, then mellow are the wines,
> Then sweet are slumbers on the flowery ground,
> Then with thick shades are lofty mountains crown'd.
> Let all the hinds bend low at Ceres' shrine;
> Mix honey sweet, for her, with milk and mellow wine;
> Thrice lead the victim the new fruits around,
> And Ceres call, and choral hymns resound:
> Presume not, swains, the ripen'd grain to reap,
> Till crown'd with oak in antic dance ye leap,
> Invoking Ceres, and in solemn lays,
> Exalt your rural queen's immortal praise.
>
> VIRGIL (C. Pitt's tr.)

To commemorate her long search for her daughter, Ceres returned to Eleusis, taught her former nursling, Triptolemus, the various secrets of agriculture, and gave him her chariot, bidding him travel everywhere, and teach the people how to plow, sow, and reap; and then she instituted the Eleusinia, festivals held in honor of her daughter and herself at Eleusis.

Triptolemus did not fail to carry out the goddess's instructions, and journeyed far and wide, until he finally reached the court of Lyncus, King of Scythia, where the false monarch would have treacherously slain him had not Ceres by timely interference prevented the execution of his base purpose by changing the traitor into a lynx, the emblem of perfidy.

Ceres was generally represented as a fair, matronly woman, clad in flowing draperies, sometimes crowned with wheat ears, and bearing a sheaf of grain and a sickle, or with a plow and a horn of plenty disgorging its wealth of fruit and flowers at her feet. Groves were frequently dedicated to her; and any mortal rash enough to lay the ax on one of these sacred trees was sure to incur the goddess's wrath, as is proved by the story of Erisichthon.

STORY OF ERISICHTHON

This man was evidently a freethinker, and, to show his contempt for the superstitious veneration paid to Ceres' trees, took his ax and cut down one of her sacred oaks. At his first blow, blood began to flow from the tree; but, undeterred by the phenomenon or the entreaties of the bystanders, Erisichthon continued. Finally, annoyed by the importunities of the spectators, he turned and slew one or two, and then completed his sacrilege.

Ceres, incensed by his insolence and cruelty, devised a terrible chastisement for the unfortunate man, and sent Famine to gnaw his vitals, and torment him night and day. The wretch, tortured by a hunger which no amount of food could allay, disposed of all his property to obtain the means of procuring nourishment; but his monstrous appetite continued, and, as he had but one daughter left, he sold her as a slave to obtain food.

The girl's master left her alone for a moment upon the seashore, and, in answer to her prayer, Neptune delivered her from servitude by changing her into a fisherman. When the master returned and found his slave gone, he questioned the fisherman, and, not obtaining any satisfactory information, departed. Neptune then restored the maiden to her own form, and let her return home; but, as her father sold her again, the god was obliged to interfere once more in her behalf, until at last Erisichthon, deprived of means to procure food, devoured himself.

CERES AND STELLIO

Another anecdote illustrating Ceres' power is told about a lad, Stellio, who made fun of the goddess when she was journeying, on account of the haste with which she disposed of a bowl of gruel offered by some charitable person. To punish the boy for his rudeness, Ceres flung the remainder of her gruel into his face, and changed him into a lizard.

Chapter XV

VESTA

Worship of Vesta

Vesta, or Hestia, daughter of Cronus and Rhea, goddess of fire and of the family hearth, and guardian angel of mankind, was worshiped principally throughout Italy, although she also had shrines in Greece and Asia Minor.

The family hearth in ancient times possessed a far different signification from what it does now, and was considered the family altar, for there the father of the family was wont to offer up his daily prayers and sacrifices. "As, according to the old heathen custom, all men were regarded as enemies unless by a special compact they had been made friends, so Vesta presided especially over true and faithful dealing"; and she was therefore generally represented as pure and undefiled.

A beautiful circular temple in Rome was dedicated to Vesta's service; and here the Palladium of Troy was supposed to be preserved, together with the goddess's sacred fire, originally kindled by the rays of the sun.

This fire—an emblem of the flame of life, which the ancients fancied was kept burning within each human breast by Vesta, the life-giver—was kept constantly burning, and never allowed to go out for want of fuel or timely care. Its flames were also intended to represent the purity of the goddess, who, although wooed by many lovers,—among whom Apollo and Neptune can justly claim the precedence,—remained always a virgin.

The Romans fancied that her worship had been introduced in Italy by Æneas, their famous ancestor, who brought thither his home gods, and who, according to tradition, selected the first Vestal Virgins.

Vestal Virgins

The second king of Rome, Numa Pompilius, built a beautiful temple, and instituted various religious ceremonies, in honor of Vesta. The loveliest and noblest among the Roman maidens were chosen to serve this goddess, and were known

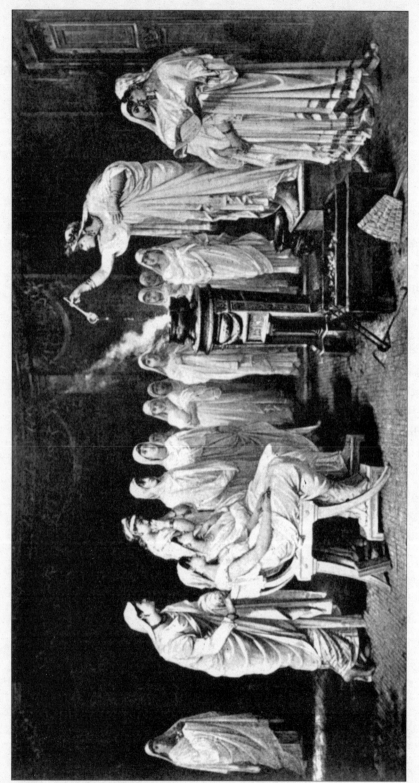

SCHOOL OF THE VESTAL VIRGINS. Le Roux.

as Vestals, or Vestal Virgins. Admitted into the temple at the early age of six, they were compelled to serve ten years in fitting themselves to fulfill the duties they would be called upon to perform during the next decade as priestesses and guardians of the sacred fire. The last ten years were spent in instructing the novices; and, when their thirty-years' service was ended, they were at liberty either to continue in the temple, where they were treated with the greatest respect, or to leave it, and even marry, if such were their pleasure.

During their time of servitude, they were expected to keep their vows of chastity and fidelity to their patroness, and to maintain her sacred fire, under penalty of being buried alive in a vaulted chamber, fashioned for this express purpose by Numa Pompilius' order. In turn, each of the priestesses watched the fire, renewed the fuel, and fanned the flame, nor lost sight of it night or day; for the Romans considered the extinction of this sacred flame the precursor of some great public calamity.

The Vestals were, however, so pure and vigilant, that during one thousand years only eighteen failed to keep their vows satisfactorily, and suffered punishment. The Vestal Tuccia was accused of breach of faith, but, as proof of her purity, was given power to carry water in a sieve from the Tiber to the temple.

In return for the signal services the Vestals rendered to the state by maintaining this sacred fire, they enjoyed many privileges: among others, that of being preceded by a lictor with fasces when they walked abroad; of occupying the seats of honor in public ceremonies and festivities; of being buried within the city limits (a privilege granted to but very few); and of obtaining the pardon of criminals whom they met by accident on their way to the place of execution. Loved and greatly honored by all, the Vestals have become types of all things pure and lovely in woman.

> By these her trembling fires,
> Like Vesta's, ever burning; and, like hers,
> Sacred to thoughts immaculate and pure.
>   YOUNG

The Vestal Virgins were further distinguished by a vesture of pure white linen, with a purple border and a wide purple mantle. In time of war or danger they were answerable for the preservation of the sacred fire, which they were allowed

THE VESTAL TUCCIA. Le Roux.

to remove to any place of safety; and on several occasions they therefore carried it out of Rome and down the Tiber, lest it should fall into the enemy's hands.

The Vestals continued their office until the reign of Theodosius the Great, who, being converted to Christianity A.D. 380, abolished the worship of Vesta, dispersed the Vestals, and extinguished the sacred fire.

FESTIVALS

Vesta's services were held with great pomp; and her festivals, the Vestalia, were among the most beautiful and popular in Rome. Statues of this goddess—generally representing a woman of majestic beauty, clad in long robes, holding a lighted torch or lamp in one hand and a votive bowl in the other—were carried through the main streets of the city on all solemn occasions.

In public processions the Vestals had the privilege of carrying their sacred fire; while the Roman matrons, glad to swell their ranks, followed them, barefooted, chanting the praises of the good goddess Vesta.

> And from the temple brings
> Dread Vesta, with her holy things,
> Her awful fillets, and the fire
> Whose sacred embers ne'er expire.
> VIRGIL (Conington's tr.)

On these occasions great banquets were prepared before each house, all daily toil was suspended, the millstones were decked with flowers, and the very asses wont to turn them were covered with garlands and led in the processions.

Among the Romans, Vesta was not the only goddess invoked on the family hearth, for she shared that place of honor with the Lares, Manes, and Penates, who all enjoyed special veneration and sacrifices.

LARES, MANES, AND PENATES

The Lares, quite unknown to the Greeks, were two in number, the children of Mercury and Lara, a naiad famous for her beauty as well as for her extreme loquacity, which no one could check. Tradition relates that this fair maiden talked from morning till night, and told all she knew. Upon one occasion she incurred Jupiter's wrath by relating to Juno a conversation she had overheard between him and one of his numerous ladyloves.

To punish her, and at the same time prevent further tale-bearing, the king of the gods cut off Lara's tongue, and, summoning Mercury, bade him lead her down to Hades to linger there forever. But on the way to the dismal abode of the dead, the messenger god fell in love with his fair charge, who, being now effectually cured of her sole fault, was irresistibly charming; and, instead of obeying Jupiter, he made love to her, and by pantomime obtained her consent to their union. She bore him two children, who from her were called Lares, and to whom the Romans always paid divine honors, reserving special places for them on the family hearth, for they were supposed to preside over houses and families. Their statues resembled monkeys covered with the skins of dogs; while at their feet a barking dog, the symbol of their care and vigilance, was always represented.

The Manes—a name generally applied to souls when separated from the body—were also reckoned among the Roman divinities, and the illustrious ancestors of different families were often worshiped under this name.

As for the Penates, they presided over the houses and domestic affairs. Each head of a household was wont to choose his own Penates, whom he then invoked as his special patrons. The statues of the Penates were of clay, wax, ivory, silver, or gold, according to the wealth of the family whose hearth they graced, and the offerings generally made to them were a small part of each meal.

Upon removing from one house to another or from one place to another, it was customary for the head of the family to remove his household gods also, and establish them suitably before he thought of his own or his family's comfort, and in return for this kindly care the Penates blessed him with peace and prosperity.

Chapter XVI

JANUS

J anus, god of the past, present, and future, of gates, entrances, war, and peace, and patron of all beginnings, although one of the most important of all the Roman divinities, was entirely unknown to the Greeks.

According to some mythologists, he was the son of Apollo; and, although born in Thessaly, he early in life came to Italy, where he founded a city on the Tiber, to which he gave the name Janiculum. Here he was joined by the exiled Saturn, with whom he generously shared his throne. Together they civilized the wild inhabitants of Italy, and blessed them with such prosperity that their reign has often been called the Age of Gold.

> Saturn fled before victorious Jove,
> Driven down and banish'd from the realms above.
> He, by just laws, embodied all the train,
> Who roam'd the hills, and drew them to the plain;
> There fixed, and Latium called the new abode,
> Whose friendly shores concealed the latent god.
> These realms, in peace, the monarch long controlled,
> And blessed the nations with an age of gold.
>
> VIRGIL (C. Pitt's tr.)

JANUS' TWO FACES

Janus is generally represented with two faces, turned in opposite directions, because he was acquainted with the past and future as well as with the present, and because he is considered an emblem of the sun, which opens the day at its rising, and closes the day at its setting.

In some statues he is represented with one white-haired and bearded face, and the other quite youthful in appearance, while others represent him with three and even four heads.

> Janus am I; oldest of potentates;
>   Forward I look, and backward, and below
> I count, as god of avenues and gates,
>   The years that through my portals come and go.
>
> I block the roads and drift the fields with snow;
>   I chase the wild-fowl from the frozen fen;
> My frosts congeal the rivers in their flow;
>   My fires light up the hearths and hearts of men.
>   LONGFELLOW

The commencement of every new year, month, and day was held sacred to Janus, and at that time special sacrifices and prayers were offered up at his shrines. He also presided over all gates and avenues, and through him alone prayers were supposed to reach the immortal gods: therefore in all religious ceremonies his name was always the first invoked. From this circumstance he often appears with a key in his right hand, and a rod in his left; or, when he presides over the year, he holds the number 300 in one hand, and 65 in the other.

WORSHIP OF JANUS

He was also supposed to watch over peace and war, and had numerous temples throughout all Italy. One very celebrated temple was called Janus Quadrifons, because it was perfectly square. On each side of the building there was one door and three windows. These apertures were all symbolical,—the doors of the four seasons, and the windows of the twelve months, of the year.

In times of war the temple gates were opened wide, for the people, being in need of aid and comfort, were all anxious to enter and present their offerings; but when peace reigned, the doors were immediately closed, for the god's intercession was no longer necessary. The Romans, however, were such a belligerent people, that the temple gates were closed but thrice in more than seven centuries, and then only for a very short period.

Festivals in honor of Janus were celebrated on the first day of the new year; and one month bore the god's name, and was considered sacred to him. It was customary for friends and relatives to exchange calls, good wishes, and gifts on the first day of this month,—a Roman custom in force to this day.

ANCIENT DIVISIONS OF TIME

Janus is not the only one among the Greek and Latin divinities whose name has been given to a part of the year or week; for in Latin the names of the days are *dies Solis* (Sun day), *dies Lunæ* (Moon day), *dies Martis* (Mars' day), *dies Mercurii* (Mercury's day), *dies Jovis* (Jove's day), *dies Veneris* (Venus' day), *dies Saturni* (Saturn's day); Latin names which are still in use in legislative and judiciary acts, while in English the common nomenclature is derived from the names of the corresponding Saxon divinities.

Chapter XVII

SOMNUS AND MORS

CAVE OF SLEEP

After leaving the joyless regions of Pluto's realm, and following the even course of the Lethe River, the ancients fancied one reached a large cave in a remote and quiet valley. This cave was the dwelling of Somnus (or Hupnos), god of sleep, and of his twin brother Mors (or Thanatos), god of death; and both were sons of the Goddess of Night, who had once ruled the whole universe. Near the entrance of the cave, shadowy forms kept constant watch, gently shaking great bunches of poppies, and, with finger to lips, enjoining silence on all who ventured near. These forms were the genii of sleep and death, represented in art as crowned with poppies or amaranths, and sometimes holding a funeral urn or a reversed torch.

SOMNUS AND MORPHEUS

The cave was divided into chambers, each one darker and more silent than the one which preceded it. In one of the inner rooms, which was all draped with sable curtains, stood a downy couch, upon which reclined the monarch of sleep. His garments were also black, but all strewn with golden stars. He wore a crown of poppies on his head, and held a goblet full of poppy juice in his languid hand. His drowsy head was supported by Morpheus, his prime minister, who watched incessantly over his prolonged slumbers, and hindered any one from troubling his repose.

Deep in a cavern dwells the drowsy god:
Whose gloomy mansion nor the rising sun,
Nor setting, visits, nor the lightsome noon:
But lazy vapors round the region fly,
Perpetual twilight, and a doubtful sky;
No crowing cock does there his wings display,
Nor with his horny bill provoke the day:
Nor watchful dogs, nor the more wakeful geese,
Disturb with nightly noise the sacred peace:
Nor beast of nature, nor the tame, are nigh,
Nor trees with tempest rock'd, nor human cry;
But safe repose, without an air of breath,
Dwells here, and a dumb quiet next to death.

    An arm of Lethe, with a gentle flow,
Arising upwards from the rock below,
The palace moats, and o'er the pebbles creeps,
And with soft murmurs calls the coming sleeps;
Around its entry nodding poppies grow,
And all cool simples that sweet rest bestow;
Night from the plants their sleepy virtue drains,
And passing, sheds it on the silent plains:
No door there was the unguarded house to keep,
On creaking hinges turn'd to break his sleep.

    But in the gloomy court was rais'd a bed,
Stuff'd with black plumes, and on an ebon sted:
Black was the covering too, where lay the god,
And slept supine, his limbs display'd abroad.
About his head fantastic visions fly,
Which various images of things supply,
And mock their forms; the leaves on trees not more,
Nor bearded ears in fields, nor sands upon the shore.

                        OVID (Dryden's tr.)

GENIUS OF DEATH. Canova.
(Tomb of Clement XIII, St. Peter's, Rome.)

Dreams and Nightmares

All around the bed and over it hovered throngs of exquisite spirits, the Dreams, who stooped to whisper their pleasant messages in his ear; while in the distant corners of the apartment lurked the hideous Nightmares. The Dreams were often dispatched to earth under Mercury's charge, to visit mortals.

Two gates led out of the valley of sleep,—one of ivory, and the other of horn. The Dreams which passed through the glittering gates of ivory were delusive, while those which passed through the homely gate of horn were destined to come true in the course of time.

> Of dreams, O stranger, some are meaningless
> And idle, and can never be fulfilled.
> Two portals are there for their shadowy shapes,
> Of ivory one, and one of horn. The dreams
> That come through the carved ivory deceive
> With promises that never are made good;
> But those which pass the doors of polished horn,
> And are beheld of men, are ever true.
>
> HOMER (Bryant's tr.)

Dreams were also frequently sent through the gates of horn to prepare mortals for misfortunes, as in the case of Halcyone.

Story of Ceyx and Halcyone

Ceyx, King of Thessaly, was once forced to part from his beloved wife, Halcyone, to travel off to Delphi to consult the oracle. With many tears this loving couple parted, and Halcyone watched the lessening sail until it had quite vanished from sight; then she returned to her palace to pray for her husband's safe return. But, alas! the gods had decreed they should never meet again on earth; and, even while Halcyone prayed, a tempest arose which wrecked Ceyx's vessel, and caused him and all his crew to perish in the seething waves.

Day after day the queen hastened down to the seashore, followed by her attendants, to watch for the returning sails of her husband's vessel; and night after night she lay on her couch, anxiously expecting the morrow, which she ever fancied would prove auspicious. The gods, seeing her anxiety, and wishing to prepare her to receive the news of his death, and especially to view with some composure his corpse, which they had decided should be washed ashore, sent a Dream to visit her.

After assuming the face and form of Ceyx, the Dream glided away through the gate of horn, hastened to Halcyone's bedside, and whispered that her husband was dead, and that his body was even now being cast up on the smooth, sandy beach by the salt sea waves. With a wild cry of terror and grief, Halcyone awoke, and hastened to the seashore to convince herself that the dream had been false; but she had no sooner reached the beach, than the waves washed her husband's corpse to her feet.

To endure life without him seemed too great a task for poor Halcyone, who immediately cast herself into the sea, to perish beside him. Touched by grief so real and intense, the gods changed both bodies into birds, since known as Halcyon birds, and decreed they should ever live on the waters. These birds were said to build their nests and hatch their young on the heaving billows, and to utter shrill cries of warning to the seamen whenever a storm threatened, bidding them prepare for the blast, and hasten to shelter in port, if they would not encounter the mournful fate of poor Ceyx.

MORS

Mors, god of death, occupied one of the corners of Somnus' cave. He was a hideous, cadaverous-looking deity, clad in a winding sheet, and held an hourglass and a scythe in his hand. His hollow eyes were fixed upon the sands of time; and when they had run out, he knew some life was about to end, and sallied forth, scythe in hand, to mow down his prey with relentless joy.

Needless to say, this cruel deity was viewed by the ancients with fear and dislike, and no homage was offered him.

These two divinities were, however, but of slight importance in the general scheme of ancient mythology, in which Proserpina was generally regarded as the emblem of death, and they were therefore more like local divinities. The Lacedæmonians paid the most heed to them, and invariably placed their statues side by side.

MORPHEUS

As for Morpheus, the son as well as the prime minister of Somnus, he was also called the god of sleep, and mortals were wont to intercede for his good offices. He is generally represented as a sleeping child of great corpulence, and with wings. Morpheus held a vase in one hand, and poppies in the other, which he gently shook to induce a state of drowsiness,—according to him, the acme of bliss.

Chapter XVIII

ÆOLUS

Not very far away from the quiet realm of Somnus and Mors, but on the surface of the earth, were the Æolian Islands, now known as the Lipari Islands, where Æolus, god of the storm and winds, governed a very unruly and turbulent population.

ÆOLUS' CHILDREN

He is said to have received his royal dignity from the fair hands of Juno, and he was therefore specially eager to obey all her behests. He is commonly reputed to have married Aurora, or Eos, who gave him six sons: i.e., Boreas, the north wind; Corus, the northwest wind; Aquilo, the west wind; Notus, the southwest wind; Eurus, the east wind; and lastly, Zephyrus, the gentle and lovable south wind, whose mission it was to announce to mortals the return of ever-welcome spring.

Æolus' five elder sons were of a noisy, roving, mischievous, turbulent disposition, and peace and quiet were utterly impossible to them. To prevent their causing serious disasters, he therefore ruled them with a very strict hand, kept them very closely confined in a great cave, and let them loose only one at a time, to stretch their limbs and take a little exercise.

> Æolus in a cavern vast
> With bolt and barrier fetters fast
> Rebellious storm and howling blast.
> They with the rock's reverberant roar
> Chafe blustering round their prison door:
> He, throned on high, the scepter sways,
> Controls their moods, their wrath allays.
>
> VIRGIL (Conington's tr.)

Although very unruly indeed, the winds always obeyed their father's voice, and at his command, however reluctant, returned to their gloomy prison, where they expended their impotent rage in trying to shake its strong walls.

According to his own mood, or in conformity with the gods' request, Æolus either sent the gentler winds to play among the flowers, or, recalling them, let the fiercest of all his children free, with orders to pile up the waves mountain-high, lash them to foam, tear the sails of all the vessels at sea, break their masts, uproot the trees, tear the roofs off the houses, etc.,—in short, to do all the harm they possibly could.

> Now rising all at once, and unconfin'd,
> From every quarter roars the rushing wind:
> First, from the wide Atlantic Ocean's bed,
> Tempestuous Corus rears his dreadful head,
> Th' obedient deep his potent breath controls,
> And, mountain-high, the foamy flood he rolls;
> Him the Northeast encountering fierce, defied,
> And back rebuffeted the yielding tide.
> The curling surges loud conflicting meet,
> Dash their proud heads, and bellow as they beat;
> While piercing Boreas, from the Scythian strand,
> Plows up the waves and scoops the lowest sand.
> Nor Eurus then, I ween, was left to dwell,
> Nor showery Notus in th' Æolian cell,
> But each from every side, his power to boast,
> Ranged his proud forces to defend the coast.
>
> LUCAN

Æolus, king of the winds, shared with Dædalus the honor of inventing the sails which propel the ships so swiftly over the tide. It was he, too, who, according to Homer, bound all his children but one in a leather bag, which he gave to Ulysses when the latter visited Æolia. Thanks to this gift, Ulysses reached the shores of Ithaca, and would have landed in safety, had not his men, in view of port, untied the sack to investigate its contents, and thus set free the angry winds, who stirred up the most frightful tempest in mythic annals.

TEMPLE OF ÆOLUS

The ancients, and especially the Athenians, paid particular attention to the winds, to whom they dedicated a temple, which is still extant, and generally known as the Tower of the Winds, or the Temple of Æolus. This temple is hexagonal, and on each side a flying figure of one of the winds is represented.

Eurus, the east wind, was generally depicted "as a young man flying with great impetuosity, and often appearing in a playful and wanton humor." Notus, or Auster, the southwest wind, "appeared generally as an old man, with gray hair, a gloomy countenance, a head covered with clouds, a sable vesture, and dusky wings," for he was considered the dispenser of rain and of all sudden and heavy showers. Zephyrus, mild and gentle, had a lapful of flowers, and, according to the Athenian belief, was wedded to Flora, with whom he was perfectly happy, and visited every land in turn. Corus, the northwest wind, drove clouds of snow before him; while Aquilo, dreadful in appearance, caused cold shivers to run down one's back at his mere sight. Boreas, rough and shivering too, was the father of rain, snow, hail, and tempests, and was therefore generally represented as veiled in impenetrable clouds. His favorite place of abode was in the Hyperborean Mountains, from whence he sallied forth on wild raids. During one of these excursions he carried off Orithyia, who always fled at his approach. But all her fleetness could not save her: she was overtaken, and borne away to the inaccessible regions of snow and ice, where he detained her, and made her his wife. She became the mother of Zetes and Calais,—who took part in the Argonautic expedition, and drove away the Harpies,—and of two daughters, Cleopatra and Chione.

On another occasion, Boreas, having changed himself into a horse and united himself to the mares of Dardanus, King of Troy, became the father of twelve steeds so swift that none could overtake them.

Chapter XIX

HERCULES

Unto this thy son it shall be given,
With his broad heart to win his way to heaven;
Twelve labors shall he work; and all accurst
And brutal things o'erthrow, brute men the worst;
And in Trachinia shall the funeral pyre
Purge his mortalities away with fire;
And he shall mount amid the stars, and be
Acknowledg'd kin to those who envied thee,
And sent these den-born shapes to crush his destiny.

THEOCRITUS (Hunt's tr.)

The ancients were not content to worship the gods only, but also offered up sacrifices to a few mortals, who, by their heroic deeds and virtuous lives, had won both admiration and respect. Foremost among these heroes—generally designated by the title of demigods—is Hercules (Heracles, Alcides), son of Jupiter and Alcmene, a mortal princess.

JUNO PERSECUTES HERCULES

As soon as the tidings of Hercules' birth reached Olympus, Juno began to plot how to destroy her rival's child. Two colossal serpents with poisonous fangs were therefore dispatched by her orders to attack the babe in its cradle. The monsters crept along noiselessly, entered the palace unseen, twined themselves around the cradle, and were about to crush the child to death in their folds, when, to the utter astonishment of the helpless attendants, little Hercules caught them fast by the neck in each tiny hand and strangled them, thus giving the first proof of the marvelous strength which was to make him famous.

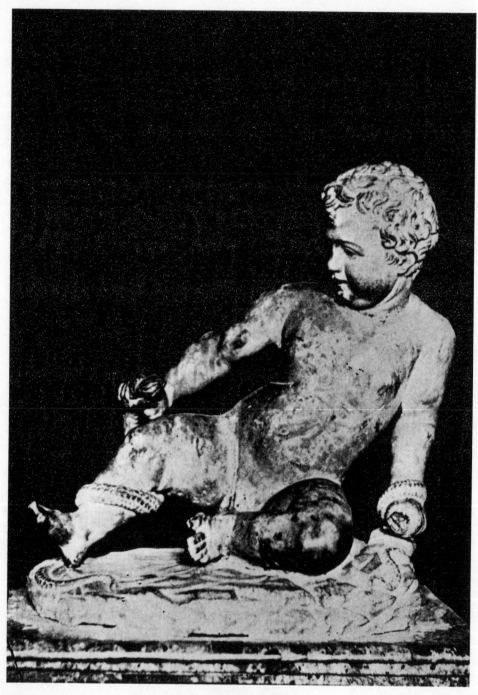

HERCULES AN INFANT.
(Louvre, Paris.)

First two dread Snakes at Juno's vengeful nod
Climb'd round the cradle of the sleeping God;
Waked by the shrilling hiss, and rustling sound,
And shrieks of fair attendants trembling round,
Their gasping throats with clenching hands he holds;
And Death untwists their convoluted folds.

DARWIN

When Juno perceived how easily Hercules had escaped from the danger which threatened him, she deemed it useless to make another attempt to take his life, but decided to vex his proud spirit by inflicting many petty annoyances, and to prevent his enjoying any lasting peace or happiness.

To achieve this purpose, she first extorted from Jupiter a decree that condemned Hercules to serve his cousin Eurystheus—a mean and cowardly prince who ruled over the kingdom of Argos—for a certain number of years.

Hercules' education was carefully attended to by Chiron, a learned Centaur, who taught him how to use all the different weapons, and trained him in all kinds of athletic sports. The years passed by happily and swiftly, until at last the time came when Hercules' education was completed, and the whole world lay before him, full of pleasant possibilities, and rich with many attractions.

HERCULES' CHOICE

The youthful hero, dismissed by his instructor, now set out to seek his fortunes. He had not gone very far, however, before he met two beautiful women, who immediately entered into conversation with him, and drew from him a confession that he was in search of adventures. The women, Arete (Virtue) and Kakia (Vice), each offered to be his guide, but bade him choose which he preferred to follow.

Kakia, to induce him to follow her guidance, promised riches, ease, consideration, and love; while Arete, a modest maiden, warned him that in her wake he would be obliged to wage incessant war against evil, to endure hardships without number, and spend his days in toil and poverty.

Silently Hercules pondered for a while over these two so dissimilar offers, and then, mindful of his tutor's oft-repeated instructions, rose from his seat by the wayside, and, turning to Arete, declared himself ready to obey any command she might choose to give him.

> Young Hercules with firm disdain
> Braved the soft smiles of Pleasure's harlot train;
> To valiant toils his forceful limbs assign'd,
> And gave to Virtue all his mighty mind.
>
> DARWIN

Courageously he then trod along the rough and thorny path she pointed out, and patiently performed the various tasks she assigned him, delivering the oppressed, defending the weak, and redressing all wrongs.

HERCULES' MADNESS

In reward for these good actions he received the hand of Megara, daughter of Creon, King of Thebes, in marriage, and by her had three children, whom he tenderly loved. But Juno was not at all satisfied to see him leading such a peaceful and prosperous life, and to interrupt its even course drove the hero mad.

In a fit of delirium he threw his offspring into the fire, and, we are told, slew his dearly beloved wife. Then only he recovered his senses, and suffered agonies of sorrow and remorse for the terrible crimes he had unwittingly committed. In his grief he withdrew to the mountain solitudes, where he would probably have lingered all the remainder of his life, had not Mercury come to get him, and announced that he was to serve Eurystheus, King of Argos, for a twelvemonth.

HERCULES IN SERVITUDE

The messenger god then offered to lead him to his appointed taskmaster. But when Hercules learned he was doomed to be a slave, he fell into such a passion, that he nearly lost his reason again; and instead of killing noxious beasts, and winning the people's blessings by his deeds of kindness, he wandered about stupidly and aimlessly, until he finally perceived how vain was his attempt to struggle against fate, and urged by his chosen adviser, Arete, voluntarily offered his services to Eurystheus, who informed him that he must accomplish twelve great labors ere he could again be free.

NEMEAN LION

Eager to begin the appointed tasks, Hercules set out first to find and destroy a monstrous lion, whose den was in the Nemean Forest. Far and wide, throughout the whole neighborhood, this monster committed his depredations, carrying off cattle and sheep, men, women, and children, to devour at his ease. All warned Hercules of the danger and difficulty of the undertaking, described the failure of countless previous attempts to slay the monster, and prophesied that he would never return alive. The hero would not be dissuaded, but entered the forest, tracked the lion to his den, grasped him by the throat, and strangled him as he had strangled the snakes in his infancy. He then skinned the monster, whose shaggy pelt became his favorite covering.

> So from Nemea's den Alcides strode,
> The lion's yellow spoil around his shoulders flow'd.
> FLACCUS (Elton's tr.)

HYDRA OF LERNA

On his return to Argos to report the successful termination of his first task, Hercules was told to repair to the marshes of Lerna, where lurked a seven-headed serpent, the Hydra, and put an end to its career of rapacity, for this snake devoured man and beast. Armed with a great sword, Hercules succeeded in cutting off one of the seven heads; but he had no sooner done so, than, to his dismay, he saw seven other heads suddenly spring from the bleeding stump. To prevent a repetition of this unpleasant miracle, Hercules bade his friend Iolaus, who had accompanied him thither to view his prowess, take a lighted brand and sear the wounds as soon as inflicted. Thanks to this wise plan, the monster was finally slain, although a friendly crab sent by Juno to defend Hydra continually pinched Hercules' feet. The hero, angry at this intervention, crushed the crab, which, however, received its reward, for the Queen of Heaven placed it in the sky as the constellation of

Cancer (the Crab). The country was thus freed from its long state of thraldom; but, before leaving the scene of his second labor, Hercules dipped his arrows in the Hydra's venomous blood, knowing well that any wound they inflicted, however slight, would be sure to prove fatal.

STAG OF CERYNEA

The third task appointed by Eurystheus was the capture of the golden-horned, brazen-footed stag of Cerynea, whose fleetness was such that he seemed scarcely to touch the ground. Hercules was obliged to pursue this animal for many a weary mile before he could overtake him; and he only managed the capture by driving him into a deep snowdrift, in a distant northern land, from which he extricated him, and carried him home in triumph.

ERYMANTHIAN BOAR

The same success crowned his fourth labor, the capture of the wild boar of Erymanthus in Arcadia. Attacked by the Centaurs during the performance of this labor, Hercules turned his deadly arrows upon them, and accidentally wounded his beloved tutor Chiron, who was coming to settle the dispute. Vainly the hero applied every healing herb. The wound was mortal, and Chiron died; but in reward for his good offices the gods transferred him to the sky, where he is known as the constellation Sagittarius.

AUGEAN STABLES

Hercules was next sent to Augeas, King of Elis, who had immense droves of cattle. The stables usually occupied by these animals were in an incredibly filthy state, as they had not been cleaned in years; and now Hercules was given the task to remove the accumulated filth, and make a complete purification of the premises.

Close by these stables rushed a torrent, or rather a river, the Alpheus. Hercules, with one glance, saw the use he could make of this rushing stream, which he dammed and turned aside from its course, so that the waters passed directly through the stables, carrying away all impurities, and finally washing them perfectly clean.

FARNESE HERCULES.
(National Museum, Naples.)

Nothing else
Could clean the Augean stables.
WORDSWORTH

When Hercules saw that the work of purification was thoroughly accomplished, he guided the stream back to its original bed, and returned home to announce that the fifth labor was accomplished. The fabulous filth of the Augean stables, and the radical methods employed for their cleansing, have given rise to proverbial expressions still in current use.

CRETAN BULL

Hercules next journeyed off to Crete to accomplish his sixth task, the capture of a mad bull given by Neptune to Minos, king of the island. The god had sent the animal with directions that he should be offered up in sacrifice; but Minos, charmed with his unusual size and beauty, resolved to keep him, and substituted a bull from his own herds for the religious ceremony.

Angry at seeing his express command so wantonly disobeyed, Neptune maddened the bull, which rushed wildly all over the island, causing great damage. This was the animal that Hercules, with his usual strength and skill, caught and bound fast, thus finishing the sixth task.

DIOMEDES' STEEDS

He then hastened on to Thrace, where Diomedes, the king, kept some fine coursers, which were fed on human flesh. In order to obtain a sufficient supply of fresh meat for his horses, Diomedes had decreed that all strangers who ventured into his kingdom should be seized, and, when sufficiently fat, executed, and served up in his horses' mangers. To punish Diomedes for this long-continued barbarity, Hercules fed him to his own horses, which were then led off to Eurystheus, as a token that the seventh labor was done.

Hippolyte's Girdle

Now, at the court of Eurystheus was his beautiful daughter, Admete, a vain princess, who delighted in dress and jewels, and who was never happier than when she obtained some new ornament or article of apparel. One day Admete heard a traveler describe a girdle worn by Hippolyte, queen of the Amazons, and was immediately seized by the desire to possess the ornament.

She imparted this wish to Eurystheus, who, delighted to gratify her as long as he could do so without taking any personal risk or trouble, sent Hercules in quest of the coveted jewel. The journey to the land of the Amazons—a fierce, warlike nation of women—was long and dangerous; but Hercules traveled on undaunted, nor paused, except when his services were needed in furthering some good work for mortals, until he reached their land, presented himself before their queen, and boldly explained the cause of his presence. Hippolyte listened to his explanation and request with queenly condescension, promised to consider the matter, and in the mean while bade him feast and rest in her palace.

Hercules would have succeeded in this undertaking without any trouble, had not Juno suddenly remembered his existence, and resolved to continue her never entirely forgotten persecutions. In the guise of an Amazon, she mingled among the women, and artfully spread the report that Hercules had really come to kidnap their queen, and that the pretended quest of the girdle was a mere excuse, and only intended to distract their attention from his real purpose. The Amazons yielded implicit belief to these rumors, flew to arms, and surrounded their queen.

> The Amazons array their ranks,
> In painted arms of radiant sheen
> Around Hippolyte the queen.
>
> Virgil (Conington's tr.)

The assembled force then attacked Hercules, who met their onslaught single-handed, defeated them, and finally bore away the prize he had risked so much to obtain. It was on his homeward journey from this expedition that he saved Hesione, Laomedon's daughter, from the jaws of the sea monster who was about to devour her, as he had devoured many a fair Trojan maid before her.

MOUNTED AMAZON GOING TO THE CHASE. Thorwaldsen. (Copenhagen.)

Stymphalian Birds

Eurystheus, well pleased with the manner in which Hercules had accomplished eight out of the twelve tasks, bade him now go forth and slay the dangerous, brazen-clawed birds which hovered over the stagnant waters of Lake Stymphalus. The poisoned arrows now served him in good stead, and enabled him to put a speedy end to the whole flock.

> His arrows slew
> The monsters hov'ring fell Stymphalus round.
>
> Catullus

Cattle of Geryones

Hercules was next told to capture the divine cattle of Geryones, a giant of Erythea. On his way home with this marvelous herd, Hercules paused on Mount Aventine, where, during the night, the loathsome giant Cacus stole some of his cows. To punish him for this theft, Hercules forced his way into his cave, attacked him, and, after a memorable encounter, slew him. The animals were soon after delivered into the hands of Eurystheus, who then sent Hercules in search of the Golden Apples of the Hesperides.

Hesperian Apples

This commission sadly perplexed Hercules, for he did not know in what portion of the world he would find these apples, which had been given to Juno as a wedding present, and which she had intrusted to the care of the Hesperides, daughters of Hesperus, god of the West. After numerous journeys and many inquiries, Hercules discovered that these maidens had carried these apples off to Africa, hung them on a tree in their garden, and placed the dragon Ladon at its foot to guard their treasures night and day. Unfortunately, no one could tell Hercules in what part of Africa the garden of the Hesperides might be situated: so he set out at a venture, determined to travel about until he gained some information. On his way he met with many adventures, and saw many strange sights. For instance, he first met the nymphs of the Eridanus River, and, questioning them about the golden apples, was told to consult old Nereus, god of the sea, who would probably be able to give him some information on the subject.

Hercules, having surprised this aged divinity while asleep on the seashore, held him fast, in spite of the multitudinous transformations he underwent in the vain hope of frightening his would-be interlocutor away. In answer to Hercules' question, he finally very reluctantly bade him seek Prometheus, who alone would be able to direct him aright.

In obedience to this advice, Hercules went to the Caucasian Mountains, where, on the brink of a mighty precipice, he found Prometheus, still bound with adamantine chains, and still a prey to the ravenous vulture. To spring up the mountain side, kill the cruel bird, snap the adamantine chains, and set free the benefactor of all mankind, was the work of but a few minutes for such a hero as Hercules; and, in gratitude for the deliverance he had so long sought in vain, Prometheus directed Hercules to his brother Atlas, telling him he would be sure to know where the apples could be found.

PYGMIES

Hercules wended his way to Africa, where Atlas dwelt, and on his way passed through the land of a diminutive race of men, called Pygmies, who were so small that they lived in constant dread of their neighbors, so much larger and stronger than they, and of the cranes, which passed over their country in great flocks, and sometimes alighted to devour their harvests.

To guard against these constant inroads, the Pygmies finally accepted the services of Antæus, a giant son of Gæa, who generously offered to defend them against all their enemies. When these little people, therefore, saw Hercules' mighty form looming up in the dim distance, they called aloud for fear, and bade Antæus go forth and kill the new invader, who, they wrongly fancied, had evil designs against them.

Proud of his strength, Antæus went to meet Hercules, and defied him. A fierce struggle was the immediate result of this challenge, and, as the combatants were of equal size and strength, the victory seemed very uncertain. At last Hercules felt his great strength begin to fail, and noticed that every time his adversary touched the ground he seemed to renew his vigor. He therefore resolved to try and win by strategy, and, watching his opportunity, seized Antæus round the waist, raised him from the ground, and held him aloft in his powerful embrace.

The giant struggled with all his might to get free; but Hercules held him fast, and felt him grow weaker and weaker, now that he was no longer sustained by his mother Earth, from whom he derived all his strength, until at last his struggles ceased, and he hung limp and lifeless in Hercules' crushing embrace.

> Lifts proud Antæus from his mother-plains,
> And with strong grasp the struggling giant strains;
> Back falls his fainting head and clammy hair,
> Writhe his weak limbs, and flits his life in air.
>
> DARWIN

ATLAS

Now that the gigantic defender of the Pygmies no longer blocked his way, Hercules traveled onward in search of Atlas, whom he finally found supporting the heavens on his broad shoulders. Atlas listened attentively to all Hercules had to say, declared he knew where the apples could be found, and promised to get them if the hero would only relieve him of his burden for a little while. Glad to accomplish his purpose so easily, Hercules allowed the burden of the heavens to be transferred to his shoulders, and Atlas hastened off to fulfill his part of the agreement.

From afar the giant saw the golden fruit glittering in the sunshine. Stealthily he drew near, entered the gardens, slew the dragon in his sleep, plucked the apples, and returned unmolested to the place where he had left Hercules. But his steps became slower and slower; and as he neared the hero, he could not help thinking with horror of the burden he must so soon resume, and bear for centuries, perhaps, without relief.

This thought oppressed him. Freedom was so sweet, that he resolved to keep it, and, coolly stepping up to Hercules, announced that he would carry the golden apples to Eurystheus, and leave him to support the heavens in his stead. Feigning a satisfaction which he was very far from feeling, Hercules acquiesced, but detained Atlas for a moment, asking him to hold the heavens until he could place a cushion on his shoulders. Good-natured, as giants proverbially are, Atlas threw the apples on the grass beside him, and assumed the incumbent weight; but Hercules, instead of preparing to resume it, picked up the apples, leaving Atlas alone, in the same plight as he had found him, there to remain until some more compassionate hero should come and set him free.

> There Atlas, son of great Iapetus,
> With head inclined and ever-during arms,
> Sustains the spacious heavens.
>
> HESIOD

It was during the course of one of his mighty labors, that Hercules, with one wrench of his powerful arm, tore a cleft in the mountains, and allowed the waters of the Sea to flow into Oceanus; and ever since, the rocks on either side of the Strait of Gibraltar have borne the name of Hercules' Pillars.

The twelfth and last task appointed by Eurystheus was the most difficult of all to perform. Hercules was commanded to descend into Hades and bring up the dog Cerberus, securely bound.

> But for the last, to Pluto's drear abode
> Through the dark jaws of Tænarus he went,
> To drag the triple-headed dog to light.
>
> EURIPIDES (Potter's tr.)

This command, like all the others, was speedily obeyed; but Eurystheus was so terrified at the aspect of the triple-headed dog, from the foam of whose dripping jaws the nightshade sprang, that he took refuge in a huge jar, and refused to come out until Hercules had carried the monster back to his cave.

OLYMPIAN GAMES

The twelve appointed labors were finished; the time of bondage was ended; and Hercules, a free man, could wander at his own sweet will, and enjoy the happiness of freedom. A roaming existence had, from force of habit, become a necessity: so the hero first journeyed to Olympia, where he instituted games to be celebrated every fifth year in honor of Jupiter, his father. Thence he wandered from place to place, doing good, and came to the house of Admetus, where he was surprised to find all the court in mourning.

His sympathetic inquiries soon brought forth a full account of Alcestis' sacrifice of her own life to insure the immortality of her husband. The hero's heart was touched by the king's loneliness; and he again braved the terrors of Hades, and brought Alcestis back from the grave, and restored her to her husband's arms.

Hercules took a prominent part in many heroic enterprises. Among others, he joined in the Argonautic expedition, in the battle between the Centaurs and Lapithæ, in the war of the gods and giants, and in the first siege of Troy, which proved successful.

HERCULES AND OMPHALE

But the hero, although so lately escaped from servitude, was soon obliged to return into bondage; for in a fit of anger he slew a man, and was condemned by the assembled gods to serve Omphale, Queen of Lydia, for a certain lapse of time.

No great deeds were now required of Hercules, whose strength was derided by his new mistress, and who, governing him easily by his admiration for her, made him submit to occupations unworthy of a man, and, while he was busy spinning, decked herself in his lion's skin, and brandished his renowned club.

> His lion spoils the laughing Fair demands,
> And gives the distaff to his awkward hands.
>
> DARWIN

However unworthy these effeminate tasks may seem for such a hero, they proved very agreeable indeed to Hercules, who, having fallen in love with his new mistress, seemed to wish nothing better than to remain her slave forever, and end his days in idleness and pleasure. Great labors were awaiting his mighty arm, however; and the gods, at the appointed time, freed him from his bondage to the Lydian queen, and bade him go forth and do all the good in his power.

HERCULES AT THE FEET OF OMPHALE. Gleyre.

Hercules and Deianeira

In the course of his wanderings, Hercules next met Deianeira, daughter of Œneus, and, having fallen in love with her, expressed a desire to marry her. But unfortunately another suitor, the river god Achelous, had already won the father's consent.

> Achelous came,
> The river god, to ask a father's voice,
> And snatched me to his arms.
> Sophocles (Francklin's tr.)

So sure was this suitor of his attractions, that he did not even deem it necessary to secure the maiden's good graces; and when Hercules made known his love, she immediately promised to marry him, if he would only free her from the lover her father would fain force upon her. Delighted to be able to win his bride and punish his rival at the same time, Hercules challenged Achelous; and now began a wrestling match, the fame of which has come down to us through all the intervening centuries.

Achelous was an opponent worthy of Hercules, and, besides, took advantage of his power to change his form at will, further to perplex and harass the sturdy hero. At last he assumed the shape of a bull, and with lowered horns rushed toward Hercules, intending to toss him aside. The hero, skillfully avoiding his first onset, seized him by one of his great thickset horns, and held it so firmly that all the bull's efforts to free himself from his powerful grasp were vain, until the horn broke.

The Goddess of Plenty, the Attican Fortuna, a witness of this strange combat, appropriated the broken horn, stuffed her treasures in its hollow, and was so well pleased with the effect, that she decreed it should henceforth be one of her attributes. The fight, only temporarily suspended, was now resumed with redoubled ardor, for each of the lovers was intent upon winning the hand of the fair Deianeira.

FORTUNA.
(Vatican, Rome.)

> Warm, and more warm the conflict grows:
> Dire was the noise of rattling bows,
> Of front to front opposed, and hand to hand:
> Deep was the animated strife
> For love, for conquest, and for life.
>
>   SOPHOCLES (Francklin's tr.)

The victory, though long uncertain, finally rested with Hercules, who triumphantly departed with his hard-won bride, for his destiny would not permit him to tarry long in any place. Instead of wandering alone now, with none to cheer or sympathize, Hercules had Deianeira ever at his side; and after many days they came to the river Evenus, whose usually shallow and peaceful waters were swollen and turbid, for violent rainstorms had recently swept over that portion of the country.

STORY OF NESSUS

Hercules paused for a moment to contemplate the stream, and glanced about for some safe mode to transport Deianeira across. While he was thus considering, a Centaur by the name of Nessus came to his assistance, and proposed to carry the fair young bride to the other shore in complete safety, if she would but consent to mount upon his broad back.

> The hoary centaur, who was wont for hire
> To bear the traveler o'er the rapid flood
> Of deep Evenus: not with oars or sail
> He stemm'd the torrent, but with nervous arm
> Opposed and pass'd it; me, when first a bride,
> I left my father's hospitable roof
> With my Alcides, in his arms he bore
> Athwart the current.
>
>   SOPHOCLES (Francklin's tr.)

Hercules, only too glad to avail himself of the Centaur's kind offer of assistance, quickly helped Deianeira to mount, saw them descend into the water, and

HERCULES AND CENTAUR. Bologna.
(Florence.)

prepared to follow, holding his bow and arrows aloft in one hand, and breasting the waves with the other.

Now, the Centaur Nessus did not often have the good fortune to carry such a pretty passenger as Deianeira over the river, and as he swam he made up his mind to gallop off with her as soon as he reached the opposite shore. All his strength and energy, therefore, were called into requisition; and when he reached the shore, instead of pausing to allow his fair burden to dismount, he set off as fast as he could run.

Nessus' Robe

A loud shriek from Deianeira attracted Hercules' attention, and a second later one of his poisoned arrows had brought the would-be ravisher to the ground, pierced through the heart. With dying accents the Centaur Nessus professed repentance, and bade Deianeira take his robe,—but slightly stained with the blood which gushed from the wound inflicted by the poisoned arrow,—and keep it carefully, for it had magic power; and if she ever found her husband's love waning, he assured her, that, could she but induce him to put it on, all his early affection would revive, as pure and fervent as during their honeymoon.

> "Take
> This white robe. It is costly. See, my blood
> Has stained it but a little. I did wrong:
> I know it, and repent me. If there come
> A time when he grows cold—for all the race
> Of heroes wander, nor can any love
> Fix theirs for long—take it and wrap him in it,
> And he shall love again."

LEWIS MORRIS

Deianeira gratefully accepted the proffered gift, and promised to treasure it up carefully, although she sincerely hoped she would never be called upon to make use of it. Years passed by. Hercules often left Deianeira to deliver the oppressed and relieve the suffering, for people came from great distances to ask for his aid; and although his absences were sometimes prolonged, he always returned to her side, as loving as ever, and she had no cause for complaint. Finally duty took him back to the court of Eurytus, where he beheld Iole, whom he had seen and loved in the beginning of his career, but whom he had been obliged to leave to fulfill his arduous tasks. She was still young and charming, and his first glance into her sweet face rekindled all his former passion. Day after day he lingered by her side, forgetful of duty, Deianeira, and all but his first dream of love and happiness. When absent, Deianeira was wont to hear rumors of his heroic achievements; but on this occasion the only report which reached her ear was that he had returned to his allegiance to his first love, and this roused her jealousy, so long dormant.

DEIANEIRA'S JEALOUSY

Finally she heard that Hercules was wending his way homeward again, and her heart bounded with joy, but only to sink more heavily when told that he was accompanied by Iole and a numerous train. Then she remembered the long-forgotten gift of the Centaur. With trembling hands she sought the glittering robe, gave it to a messenger, and bade him hasten to meet Hercules, and prevail upon him to wear it for his triumphant return. The messenger, Lichas, hastened to do her bidding, and Deianeira waited with fast-beating heart for the success of her venture.

> I only wish the charm may be of power
> To win Alcides from this virgin's love,
> And bring him back to Deianeira's arms.
> SOPHOCLES (Francklin's tr.)

Lichas acquitted himself faithfully of his errand; and Hercules, viewing the costly garment, and anxious to appear to his best advantage before the bright eyes of Iole, immediately donned the richly embroidered robe.

HERCULES' DEATH

He had no sooner put it on, than the Centaur's poisoned blood began its deadly work. First he experienced a burning, stinging sensation, which ran like fire through every vein. Vainly he tried to tear off the fatal garment. It clung to his limbs, and the poison ate its way into his flesh, until the pain was greater than he could bear.

In his rage at the trick which had been played upon him, he seized Lichas—the unfortunate bearer of the poisoned robe—by the foot, and flung him from the heights of Mount Œta down into the sea, where he perished.

> And Lichas from the top of Œta threw
> Into th' Euboic Sea.
>
> MILTON

Then, resolved to end these unendurable torments by a death worthy of his whole life, Hercules called his servants, and bade them build his funeral pyre on the mountain peak; but they, in tears, refused to obey, for they could not bear the thought of parting with their beloved master. Commands and entreaties alike failed to move them: so Hercules climbed up the mountain side alone, tore up the huge oaks by their roots, flung them one upon the other until he had raised a mighty pile, upon which he stretched his colossal, pain-racked limbs, and bade his friend Philoctetes set fire to the stupendous mass.

At first Philoctetes also refused to do his bidding; but, bribed by the promise of the world-renowned poisoned arrows, he finally consented to do as Hercules wished, and the red flames rose higher and higher, the wood crackled and burned, and the hero was soon enveloped in sheets of flame, which purged him from all mortality.

Then Jupiter came down from his glorious abode, caught the noble soul in his mighty arms, and bore it off to Olympus, there to dwell in happiness forever with Hebe, the fair goddess of youth, whose hand was given him in marriage.

> Till the god, the earthly part forsaken,
> From the man in flames asunder taken,
> Drank the heavenly ethers' purer breath.
> Joyous in the new, unwonted lightness,
> Earth's dark, heavy burden lost in death.
> High Olympus gives harmonious greeting
> To the hall where reigns his sire adored;
> Youth's bright goddess, with a blush at meeting,
> Gives the nectar to her lord.
>
> SCHILLER (S. G. B.'s tr.)

Worship of Hercules

Hercules, the special divinity of athletic sports and of strength, was principally worshiped by young men. He is generally represented in art as a tall, powerfully built man, with a small, bearded head, a lion's skin carelessly thrown over his shoulder, and leaning upon a massive club.

> Great Alcides, stooping with his toil,
> Rests on his club.
>
> POPE

It is said that some of the games celebrated at Olympia were held in his honor, although originally instituted by him in honor of Jupiter, his father. The Nemean Games, celebrated in the forest of Nemea, the scene of his first great labor, were the principal games held in Greece in commemoration of his noble deeds and early death.

Chapter XX

PERSEUS

Acrisius and Danae

The life of Acrisius, King of Argos, had been a burden to him ever since the unfortunate day when an oracle had predicted that he would be killed by his grandson. Until then the king had been very fond of his only child, Danae, and until then, too, had thought with pride of the time when he would bestow her hand in marriage upon the noblest of all who came to woo.

Now his plans were all changed, and his only wish was to keep her unmated,— a somewhat difficult task, for the maiden was very fair, and Acrisius knew that the wily God of Love would endeavor to find some way to outwit him and bring his plans to naught. After much thought, Acrisius decided to lock Danae up in a brazen tower, around which he stationed guards to prevent any one from even approaching the captive princess.

But, although safely concealed from the eyes of men, Danae was plainly seen by the everlasting gods; and Jupiter, looking down from Olympus, beheld her in all her loveliness and in all her loneliness. She was seated on top of her brazen tower, her eyes wistfully turned toward the city, where girls of her age enjoyed freedom, and were allowed to marry when they pleased.

The Shower of Gold

Jupiter, pitying her isolation and admiring her beauty, resolved to go down and converse with her for a little while. To avoid being seen, he changed himself into a golden shower, and gently dropped down on the turret beside her, where his presence and spirited conversation soon won the maiden's heart.

> Danae, in a brazen tower
> Where no love was, loved a shower.
> SHELLEY

This first successful visit was frequently repeated, and Danae no longer felt lonely and deserted, for Jupiter spent most of his time with her, pursuing his courtship most diligently, and finally winning her to a secret marriage, to which no one offered the slightest objection, as no one suspected his visits, which he continued quite unmolested.

BIRTH OF PERSEUS

But one morning the guards rushed in terror to Acrisius' palace to announce that Danae, his daughter, had given birth to a son, who, on account of his beauty, was called Perseus. The king no sooner learned this astonishing news, than he flew into a great rage, vowed that mother and child should perish, and dispatched the guards to fetch the unfortunate victims.

Acrisius, however, was not cruel enough to stain his own hands with his child's blood, or to witness her execution: so he ordered that she should be placed in an empty cask with her helpless infant, and exposed to the fury of the waves. These orders were speedily executed; and Danae's heart sank with terror when she felt the cask buffeted about by the great waves far out of sight of land, and out of all reach of help. Clasping her babe close to her bosom, she fervently prayed the gods to watch over them both, and bring them in safety to some hospitable shore.

> When round the well-fram'd ark the blowing blast
> Roar'd, and the heaving whirlpools of the deep
> With rough'ning surge seem'd threatening to o'erturn
> The wide-tost vessel, not with tearless cheeks
> The mother round her infant gently twined
> Her tender arm, and cried, "Ah me! my child!
> What sufferings I endure! thou sleep'st the while,
> Inhaling in thy milky-breathing breast
> The balm of slumber."
>
> SIMONIDES (Elton's tr.)

Danae at Seriphus

Her piteous prayer was evidently heard, for, after much tossing, the cask was finally washed ashore on the Island of Seriphus, where Polydectes, the king, kindly received mother and child. Here Perseus, the golden-haired, grew to manhood, and here made his first appearance in games and combats.

In the mean while, Polydectes had fallen in love with Danae, and expressed his desire to marry her; but Danae did not return his affections, and would not consent. Angry at her persistent refusal of his proposals, Polydectes wished to compel her to obey, and thereby incurred the wrath of young Perseus, who loudly declared that none should dare force his mother as long as he were there to defend her. This boast did not at all allay the monarch's wrath; and, hoping to get rid of the young boaster, he bade him go forth and slay Medusa, if he wished to convince people that his bravery was real.

The Gorgons

This Medusa was one of the three Gorgons. Her sisters, Euryale and Stheno, although immortal, had never had any claims to beauty; but Medusa, when only a girl, had been considered very handsome indeed. Her home, in a land where the sun never shone, was very distasteful to her, so she entreated Minerva to let her go and visit the beautiful sunny south.

But when Minerva refused to grant her wish, she reviled the goddess, and declared that nothing but a conviction that mortals would no longer consider her beautiful if they but once beheld Medusa, could have prompted this denial. This presumptuous remark so incensed Minerva, that, to punish her for her vanity, she changed her beautiful curling locks into hissing, writhing serpents, and decreed that one glance into her still beautiful face would suffice to change the beholder into stone.

Fatal Beauty! thou didst seem
The phantom of some fearful dream.
Extremes of horror and of love
Alternate o'er our senses move,
As, rapt and spellbound, we survey
The horrid coils which round thee play,
And mark thy wild, enduring smile,
Lit by no mortal fire the while,
Formed to attract all eyes to thee,
And yet their withering blight to be;
Thy power mysterious to congeal
And from life's blood its warmth to steal,
To petrify the mortal clay
In its first gleam of wild dismay,
Is a dread gift to one like thee,
Cursed with a hateful destiny.

MRS. ST. JOHN

PERSEUS' QUEST

The gods, who had carefully watched over Perseus through his childhood and youth, now decided to lend him their aid, so that he might successfully accomplish the great task of slaying Medusa. Pluto lent him a magic helmet, which made the wearer invisible at will; Mercury attached his own winged sandals to the youth's heels, to endow him with great rapidity of flight; while Minerva armed him with her own mirror-like shield, the dreadful Ægis.

Minerva thus to Perseus lent her shield;
Secure of conquest, sent him to the field:
The hero acted what the queen ordain'd,
So was his fame complete.

PRIOR

THE GRÆÆ

Thus equipped, Perseus flew northward until he came to the land of perpetual darkness, the home of the Grææ, three horrible sisters, who possessed but one eye and one tooth, which they handed about and used in turn, and who were the only living beings cognizant of the place where Medusa dwelt.

Invisible by virtue of his magic helmet, Perseus drew near the cave without fear of detection, and intercepted the eye while on its way from one sister to another. As soon as it was safe in his possession, he spoke to them, promising to restore it if they would only give him accurate directions for finding Medusa. The sisters, eager to recover the treasured eye, immediately gave the desired information; and Perseus, having honorably fulfilled his share of the contract, departed in search of Medusa.

DEATH OF MEDUSA

Perseus at last perceived the Gorgons' home in the dim distance; and, as he was fully aware of Medusa's petrifying proclivities, he advanced very cautiously, holding his shield before him at such an angle that all surrounding objects were clearly reflected on its smooth, mirrorlike surface.

He thus discovered Medusa asleep, raised his sword, and, without looking at anything but her mirrored form, severed her head from her body, seized it in one hand, and, holding it persistently behind his back, flew away in great haste, lest the two remaining Gorgons should fall upon him and attempt to avenge their sister's death.

BIRTH OF SNAKES

Perseus then swiftly winged his way over land and sea, carefully holding his ghastly trophy behind him; and as he flew, Medusa's blood trickled down on the hot African sand, where it gave birth to a race of poisonous reptiles destined to infest the region in future ages, and cause the death of many an adventurous explorer. The drops which fell into the sea were utilized by Neptune, who created from them the famous winged steed called Pegasus.

PERSEUS. Cellini.
(Loggia dé Lanzi, Florence.)

And the life drops from thy head
On Libyan sands, by Perseus shed,
Sprang a scourging race from thee—
Fell types of artful mystery.

MRS. ST. JOHN

The return journey was long and wearisome, and on his way the hero had many adventures. Once, when flying high above a mountainous country, he caught a glimpse of Atlas, his pale face turned up to the heavens, whose weight he had patiently borne for many a long year,—a burden which seemed all the more grievous after the short taste of freedom he had enjoyed while Hercules stood in his place,—

Supporting on his shoulders the vast pillar
Of Heaven and Earth, a weight of cumbrous grasp.

ÆSCHYLUS (Potter's tr.)

ATLAS PETRIFIED

When Atlas saw Perseus flying toward him, hope revived, for he remembered that Fate had decreed that it was this hero who was to slay the Gorgon; and he thought, that, if he could but once gaze upon her stony face, he would be free from pain and weariness forever. As soon as the hero was within hearing, Atlas therefore addressed him as follows:—

"Hasten now, Perseus, and let me look upon the Gorgon's face, for the agony of my labor is well-nigh greater than I can bear." So Perseus hearkened unto the word of Atlas, and he unveiled before him the dead face of Medusa. Eagerly he gazed for a moment on the changeless countenance, as though beneath the blackness of great horror he yet saw the wreck of her ancient beauty and pitied her for her hopeless woe. But in an instant the straining eyes were stiff and cold; and it seemed to Perseus, as he rose again into the pale yellow air, that the gray hairs which streamed from the giant's head were like the snow which rests on the peak of a great mountain, and that in place of the trembling limbs he saw only the rents and clefts on a rough hillside.

Thus the mere sight of Medusa changed Atlas into the rugged mountains which have since borne his name; and, as their summits are lost in the clouds, the ancients supposed they sustained the full weight of the heavenly vault.

STORY OF ANDROMEDA

Thence Perseus flew on until he reached the seashore, where a strange sight greeted him. Away down on the "rock-bound coast," so near the foaming billows that their spray continually dashed over her fair limbs, a lovely maiden was chained fast to an overhanging rock. This maiden was the Princess Andromeda. To atone for the vanity of her mother, Cassiopeia, who claimed she was fairer than any of the sea nymphs, she had been exposed there as prey for a terrible sea monster sent to devastate the homes along the coast.

An oracle, when consulted, declared that the monster would not depart until Andromeda was sacrificed to his fury; and Perseus could even now perceive the receding procession which had solemnly accompanied her to the appointed place of sacrifice, and chained her fast.

At the same time, too, he saw the waters below the maiden lashed to foam by the monster's tail, and the scales of his hideous body slowly rising up out of the water. Fascinated by this horrible sight, the maiden's eyes were fixed on the monster. She did not see the rapid approach of her deliverer, who, dauntless, drew his sword from its scabbard, and, swooping down, attacked the monster, cheered by the shouts of the people, who had seen him, and now rushed back to witness the slaying of their foe.

> On the hills a shout
> Of joy, and on the rocks the ring of mail;
> And while the hungry serpent's gloating eyes
> Were fixed on me, a knight in casque of gold
> And blazing shield, who with his flashing blade
> Fell on the monster. Long the conflict raged,
> Till all the rocks were red with blood and slime,
> And yet my champion from those horrible jaws
> And dreadful coils was scathless.
>
> LEWIS MORRIS

Of course, this fierce struggle could have but one conclusion; and when Perseus had slain the monster, freed Andromeda from her chains, and restored her to the arms of her overjoyed parents, they immediately offered any reward he might be pleased to claim. When he, therefore, expressed a desire to marry the maiden he had so bravely rescued, they gladly gave him her hand, although in early youth the princess had been promised to her uncle Phineus.

PHINEUS PETRIFIED

Preparations for the marriage were immediately begun; and the former suitor, who had been too cowardly to venture a single blow to deliver her from the monster, prepared to fight the rival who was about to carry off his promised bride. Unbidden he came to the marriage feast with a number of armed followers, and was about to carry off Andromeda, when Perseus suddenly bade his adherents stand behind him, unveiled the Medusa head, and, turning its baleful face toward Phineus and his followers, changed them all into stone.

The interrupted marriage feast was now resumed; and when it was over, Perseus took his bride to Seriphus. There, hearing that Polydectes had dared to ill treat his mother because she still refused to accede to his wishes and become his wife, he changed the importunate king into a rock by showing him his Medusa trophy, gave the kingdom to the king's brother, and, accompanied by wife and mother, returned to his native land. The borrowed helmet, sandals, and shield were all duly restored to their respective owners, and the Medusa head was given to Minerva in token of gratitude for her help. Greatly pleased with this gift, the goddess set it in the center of her terrible Ægis, where it retained all its petrifying power, and served her in many a fight.

RETURN TO ARGOS

Arrived at Argos, Perseus discovered that a usurper had claimed his grandfather's throne. To hurl the unlawful claimant from his exalted seat, and compel him to make full restitution and atonement, was but a trifle for the hero who had conquered Medusa; and Acrisius, now old and weak, was taken from the prison where he languished, and restored to his wonted honors, by the very youth he had been taught to fear.

PERSEUS AND ANDROMEDA. Coypel.

But the gods' decree was always sure to be fulfilled sooner or later; and one day, when Perseus was playing quoits, he accidentally killed his grandfather. To remain at Argos, haunted by the memory of this involuntary crime, was too painful for him: so he exchanged his kingdom for another, that of Mycenæ, which he ruled wisely and well. When Perseus died, after a long and glorious reign, the gods, who had always loved him, placed him among the stars, where he can still be seen, with his wife Andromeda, and mother-in-law Cassiopeia.

Chapter XXI

THESEUS

When yet but a very young man, Ægeus, King of Athens, journeyed off to TrŒzene, where he fell in love with and married a pretty young princess by the name of Æthra. For some reason, which mythologists do not make known, the king was forced to return alone to Athens; but ere he departed he concealed his sword and sandals beneath a stone, bidding his wife remember, that, as soon as the strength of their son Theseus permitted, he must raise the rock, appropriate sword and sandals, and come and join him in Athens, where he should be introduced to the people as his son and heir. These instructions given, Ægeus bade a fond farewell to his wife and infant son, and returned home.

As the years passed by, they brought strength, beauty, and wisdom to Theseus, whose fame began to be published abroad. At last Æthra deemed him strong enough to raise the rock beneath which his father's trusty weapon lay; and, conducting him to the spot where it was, she told him the whole story, and bade him try his strength.

Theseus immediately obeyed. With a mighty effort he raised the rock, and, to his great satisfaction, found the sword and sandals in a perfect state of preservation. Sword in hand, he then set out for Athens,—a long and dangerous journey. He proceeded slowly and cautiously, for he knew that many dangers lurked along his pathway, and that ere he reached his father's city he would have to encounter both giants and monsters, who would strive to bar his way.

PERIPHETES

He was not at all mistaken in his previsions; for TrŒzene was scarcely lost to sight ere he came across the giant Periphetes, son of Vulcan, who stood in the road and attacked with a huge club, whose blows were generally fatal, all who strove to pass.

Adroitly evading the giant's first onslaught, Theseus plunged his sword deep into his huge side ere he could renew the attack, and brought him lifeless to the ground.

Sinis

Theseus then disarmed his fallen foe, and, retaining the club for future use, continued his journey in peace, until he came to the Isthmus of Corinth, where two adventures awaited him. The first was with a cruel giant named Sinis, nick-named The Pine-bender, whose usual practice was to bend some huge pine until its top touched the ground, and call to any unsuspecting passer-by to seize it and lend him a helping hand for a moment. Then, as soon as the innocent stranger had complied with his request, he would suddenly let go the pine, which, freed from his gigantic grasp, sprang back to its upright position, and hurled the unfortunate traveler way up in the air, to be dashed to pieces against the rocky mountain side.

Theseus, who had already heard of the giant's stratagem, skillfully eluded the danger, and finally caused Sinis to perish by the same cruel death which he had dealt out to so many others.

Sciron

In one place the Isthmus of Corinth was exceedingly narrow, and the only prac-ticable pathway led along a rocky ledge, guarded by a robber named Sciron, who forced all who tried to pass him to wash his feet. While the traveler was thus engaged, and knelt in the narrow pathway to do his bidding, he would suddenly raise his foot, kick him over the side, and hurl him down into the sea below, where a huge tortoise was ever waiting with gaping jaws to devour the victims.

Instead of yielding to Sciron's exactions, Theseus drew his sword, and by his determined bearing so terrified the robber, that he offered him a free passage. This offer, however, did not satisfy Theseus, who said he would sheathe his sword only on condition that Sciron performed for him the menial office he had imposed upon so many others. Sciron dared not refuse, and obeyed in fear and trembling; but he was doomed never to molest any one again, for Theseus kicked him over the preci-pice, into the breakers, where the tortoise feasted upon his remains with as keen a relish as upon former victims.

CERCYON AND PROCRUSTES

After disposing of another world-renowned robber, Cercyon (The Wrestler), Theseus encountered Procrustes (The Stretcher), a cruel giant, who, under pretext of entertainment, deluded travelers into entering his home, where he had two beds of very different dimensions,—one unusually short, the other unusually long. If the unfortunate traveler were a short man, he was put to bed in the long bedstead, and his limbs were pulled out of joint to make him fit it; but if, on the contrary, he were tall, he was assigned the short bed, and the superfluous length of limb was lopped off under the selfsame pretext. Taking Procrustes quite unawares, Theseus gave him a faint idea of the sufferings he had inflicted upon others by making him try each bed in turn, and then, to avoid his continuing these evil practices, put an end to his wretched existence.

Theseus successfully accomplished a few more exploits of a similar character, and finally reached Athens, where he found that his fame had preceded him.

> In days of old, there liv'd of mighty fame,
> A valiant prince, and Theseus was his name:
> A chief, who more in feats of arms excell'd,
> The rising nor the setting sun beheld.
>
> MORRIS

MEDEA'S DRAUGHT

The first tidings that there reached his ear were that Ægeus had just married Medea, the enchantress; but, although these tidings were very unwelcome, he hastened on to his father's court, to make himself known, and receive the welcome promised so many years before. Medea, seated by Ægeus' side, no sooner saw the young stranger draw near, than she knew him, and foresaw that he had come to demand his rights. To prevent his making known claims which might interfere with the prospects of her future offspring, she hastily mixed a deadly poison in a cup, which she filled with fragrant wine, and bade Ægeus offer it to the stranger.

The monarch was about to execute her apparently hospitable purpose, when his eye suddenly rested upon the sword at Theseus' side, which he immediately recognized. One swift glance into the youth's open face convinced him that Æthra's son stood before him, and he eagerly stretched out his arms to clasp him to his heart. This sudden movement upset the goblet, and the poisonous contents, falling upon a dog lying at the king's feet, caused his almost instantaneous death. Seeing her crime discovered and Theseus recognized, Medea quickly mounted her magic dragon car, and fled to Media, whence she never returned.

TRIBUTE TO THE MINOTAUR

One day, some time after his arrival at Athens, Theseus heard a sound of weeping and great lamentation throughout all the city, and in reply to his wondering inquiries was told, that ever since an unfortunate war between the Cretans and Athenians, the latter, who had been vanquished, were obliged to pay a yearly tribute of seven youths and as many maidens, destined to serve as food for the Minotaur. Further questions evolved the fact that the Minotaur was a hideous monster, the property of Minos, King of Crete, who kept it in an intricate labyrinth, constructed for that express purpose by Dædalus, the far-famed architect.

> There lived and flourished long ago, in famous Athens town,
> One Dædalus, a carpenter of genius and renown;
> ('Twas he who with an augur taught mechanics how to bore,—
> An art which the philosophers monopolized before.)
>
> SAXE

DÆDALUS AND ICARUS

This labyrinth was so very intricate, that those who entered could not find their way out; and even Dædalus and his son Icarus, after many days' attempt, found they could not leave it. Rather than remain imprisoned forever, Dædalus then manufactured wings for himself and for his son, and determined to make use of them to effect his escape.

> Now Dædalus, the carpenter, had made a pair of wings,
> Contrived of wood and feathers and a cunning set of springs,
> By means of which the wearer could ascend to any height,
> And sail about among the clouds as easy as a kite.
>
> SAXE

DÆDALUS AND ICARUS. Vien.

After repeated cautions to his son not to venture too high, lest the sun's heat should melt the wax fixing the feathers to the frame, Dædalus bade Icarus don his plumage and fly to a country where they would be free, promising to follow him thither very shortly.

> "My Icarus!" he says; "I warn thee fly
> Along the middle track: nor low, nor high;
> If low, thy plumes may flag with ocean's spray;
> If high, the sun may dart his fiery ray."
>
>   OVID (Elton's tr.)

Delighted with this new mode of travel, Icarus flew swiftly along. Little by little he forgot the danger and his father's caution, and rose up higher and higher, until he could bask in the direct rays of the ardent sun. The heat, which seemed so grateful after his chilly flight, soon softened and melted the wax on his wings; and Icarus, no longer supported by the light feathers, sank down faster and faster, until he fell into the sea, where he was drowned, and which, in memory of him, bears the name of Icarian to this day.

These varied details kindled Theseus' love of adventure, and still further strengthened him in his sudden resolve to join the mournful convoy, try his strength against the awful Minotaur, and, if possible, save his country from further similar exactions.

> While Attica thus groan'd, with ills opprest;
> His country's wrongs inflam'd brave Theseus' breast;
> Instant his gen'rous soul resolv'd to save
> Cecrops' great offspring from a timeless grave.
>
>   CATULLUS

Even his father's tears and entreaties were powerless to move him from his purpose, and, the hour having come, he embarked upon the black-sailed vessel which was to bear the yearly tribute to Crete, promising to change the black sails for snowy white ones if he were fortunate enough to return victorious.

TALUS

Favorable winds soon wafted the galley to distant Crete, and as they sailed along the coast, searching for the harbor, they were challenged by the brazen giant Talus, who walked daily thrice around the whole island, killing, by contact with his red-hot body, all who had no business to land on that coast. Knowing, however, that the black-sailed galley brought a fresh supply of youths and maidens for the terrible Minotaur, Talus let it pass unharmed; and the victims were brought into the presence of Minos, who personally inspected each new freight-load, to make sure he was not being cheated by the Athenians.

ARIADNE'S CLEW

At the monarch's side stood his fair daughter Ariadne, whose tender heart was filled with compassion when she beheld the frail maidens and gallant youths about to perish by such a loathsome death. Theseus, by right of his birth, claimed the precedence, and proffered a request to be the first victim,—a request which the king granted with a sardonic smile, ere he returned unmoved to his interrupted feast.

Unnoticed by all, Ariadne slipped out of the palace, and, under cover of the darkness, entered the prison where Theseus was confined. There she tremblingly offered him a ball of twine and a sharp sword, bidding him tie one end of the twine to the entrance of the labyrinth, and keep the other in his hand as a clew to find the way out again should the sword enable him to kill the dreaded Minotaur. In token of gratitude for this timely assistance, Theseus solemnly promised Ariadne to take her with him to Athens as his bride, were he only successful in his undertaking.

At dawn the next day Theseus was conducted to the entrance of the labyrinth, and there left to await the tender mercies of the Minotaur. Like all heroes, he preferred to meet any danger rather than remain inactive: so, mindful of Ariadne's instructions, he fastened his twine to the entrance, and then boldly penetrated into the intricate ways of the labyrinth, where many whitening bones plainly revealed the fate of all who had preceded him.

Theseus and the Minotaur

He had not gone very far before he encountered the Minotaur,—a creature more hideous than fancy can paint,—and he was obliged to use all his skill and ingenuity to avoid falling a prey to the monster's appetite, and all his strength to lay him low at last.

The Minotaur slain, Theseus hastily retraced his footsteps.

> And the slender clew,
> Prepar'd in secret by th' enamor'd maid,
> Thro' the curv'd labyrinth his steps convey'd.
>
> Catullus

Theseus' Escape

Arrived at the place where his ship rode at anchor, he found his companions and Ariadne awaiting him, and, springing on board, bade the sailors weigh anchor as quickly as possible. They were almost out of reach of the Cretan shores, when Talus came into view, and, perceiving that his master's prisoners were about to escape, leaned forward to catch the vessel by its rigging. Theseus, seeing this, sprang forward, and dealt the giant such a blow, that he lost his balance and fell into the deep sea, where he was drowned, and where thermal springs still bear witness to the heat of his brazen body.

Ariadne Forsaken

The returning vessel, favored by wind and tide, made but one port, Naxos; and here youths and maidens landed to view the beautiful island. Ariadne strayed apart, and threw herself down upon the ground to rest, where, before she was aware of it, sleep overtook her. Now, although very brave, Theseus was not very constant. He had already grown weary of Ariadne's love; and, when he saw her thus asleep, he basely summoned his companions, embarked with them, and set sail, leaving her alone upon the island, where Bacchus soon came to console her for the loss of her faithless lover.

ARIADNE. Rae.

THESEUS' PUNISHMENT

Theseus, having committed a deed heinous in the eyes of gods and men, was doomed to suffer just punishment. In his preoccupation he entirely forgot his promise to change the black sails for white; and Ægeus, from Attica's rocky shore, seeing the sable sails when the vessel was yet far from land, immediately concluded that his son was dead, and in his grief cast himself into the sea since known as the Ægean, where he perished.

> As from a mountain's snowy top are driv'n
> The rolling clouds, by the rude blasts of heav'n;
> So from the mem'ry of lost Theseus fled
> Those dictates, which before his reason sway'd:
> But now his father from the ramparts' height,
> All bath'd in tears, directs his eager sight;
> O'er the wide sea, distended by the gale,
> He spies, with dread amaze, the lurid sail.
>
> CATULLUS

THESEUS' REIGN AND MARRIAGE

Theseus, on entering the city, heard of his father's death; and when he realized that it had been caused by his carelessness, he was overwhelmed with grief and remorse. All the cares of royalty and the wise measures he introduced for the happiness of his people could not divert his mind from this terrible catastrophe: so he finally resolved to resign his authority and set out again in search of adventures, which might help him forget his woes. He therefore made an excursion into the land of the Amazons, where Hercules had preceded him, and whence he brought back Hippolyte, whom he married. Theseus was now very happy indeed, and soon all his hopes were crowned by the birth of a son, whom he called Hippolytus. Shortly after this joyful event, the Amazons invaded his country under pretext of rescuing their kidnapped queen, and in the battle which ensued Hippolyte was accidentally wounded by an arrow, and breathed her last in Theseus' arms.

Theseus next set out with an Athenian army to fight Pirithous, king of the Lapithæ, who had dared to declare war; but when the armies were face to face, the two chiefs, seized with a sudden liking for each other, simultaneously cast down their weapons, and, falling on each other's necks, embraced, and swore an eternal friendship.

Centaurs and Lapithæ

To show his devotion to this newly won friend, Theseus consented to accompany him to the court of Adrastus, King of Argos, and witness his marriage to Hippodamia, daughter of the king. Many guests were, of course, present to witness the marriage ceremony, among others Hercules and a number of the Centaurs. The latter, struck with admiration for the bride's unusual beauty, made an attempt to kidnap her, which was frustrated by the Lapithæ, seconded by Theseus and Hercules. The terrible struggle which ensued between the conflicting parties has ever been a favorite subject in art, and is popularly known as the "Battle between the Centaurs and Lapithæ."

Theseus in Hades

The hotly contested bride did not, however, enjoy a very long life, and Pirithous soon found himself, like Theseus, a disconsolate widower. To avoid similar bereavement in future, they both resolved to secure goddesses, who, being immortal, would share their thrones forever. Aided by Pirithous, Theseus carried off Helen, the daughter of Jupiter, and, as she was still but a child, intrusted her to the care of his mother, Æthra, until she attained a suitable age for matrimony. Then, in return for Pirithous' kind offices, he accompanied him to Hades, where they intended to carry off Proserpina.

While they were thus engaged, Helen's twin brothers, Castor and Pollux, came to Athens, delivered her from captivity, and carried her home in triumph. As for Theseus and Pirithous, their treacherous intention was soon discovered by Pluto, who set the first on an enchanted rock, from which he could not descend unassisted, and bound the second to the constantly revolving wheel of his father, Ixion.

When Hercules was in Hades in search of Cerberus, he delivered Theseus from his unpleasant position, and thus enabled him to return to his own home, where he now expected to spend the remainder of his life in peace.

THESEUS. Canova.
(Volksgarten, Vienna.)

Phædra and Hippolytus

Although somewhat aged by this time, Theseus was still anxious to marry, and looked about him for a wife to cheer his loneliness. Suddenly he remembered that Ariadne's younger sister, Phædra, must be a charming young princess, and sent an embassy to obtain her hand in marriage. The embassy proved successful, and Phædra came to Athens; but, young and extremely beautiful, she was not at all delighted with her aged husband, and, instead of falling in love with him, bestowed all her affections upon his son, Hippolytus, a virtuous youth, who utterly refused to listen to her proposals to elope. In her anger at finding her advances scorned, Phædra went to Theseus and accused Hippolytus of attempting to kidnap her. Theseus, greatly incensed at what he deemed his son's dishonorable behavior, implored Neptune to punish the youth, who was even then riding in his chariot close by the shore. In answer to this prayer, a great wave suddenly arose, dashed over the chariot, and drowned the young charioteer, whose lifeless corpse was finally flung ashore at Phædra's feet. When the unfortunate queen saw the result of her false accusations, she confessed her crime, and, in her remorse and despair, hung herself.

Death of Theseus

As for Theseus, soured by these repeated misfortunes, he grew so stern and tyrannical, that he gradually alienated his people's affections, until at last they hated him, and banished him to the Island of Scyros, where, in obedience to a secret order, Lycomedes, the king, treacherously slew him by hurling him from the top of a steep cliff into the sea. As usual, when too late, the Athenians repented of their ingratitude, and in a fit of tardy remorse deified this hero, and built a magnificent temple on the Acropolis in his honor. This building, now used as a museum, contains many relics of Greek art. Theseus' bones were piously brought back, and inhumed in Athens, where he was long worshiped as a demigod.

Chapter XXII

JASON

At Iolcus, in Thessaly, there once reigned a virtuous king, Æson, with his good wife, Alcimede. Their happiness, however, was soon disturbed by Pelias, the king's brother, who, aided by an armed host, took forcible possession of the throne. Æson and Alcimede, in fear of their lives, were forced to resort to a hasty and secret flight, taking with them their only son, Jason.

The king and queen soon found a place of refuge, but, afraid lest their hiding place should be discovered and they should all be slain by the cruel Pelias, they intrusted their son to the Centaur Chiron, revealing to him alone the secret of the child's birth, and bidding him train him up to avenge their wrongs.

Chiron discharged his duties most faithfully, trained the young prince with great care, and soon made him the wisest and most skillful of his pupils. The years spent by Jason in the diligent acquisition of knowledge, strength, and skill, passed very quickly; and at last the time came when Chiron made known to him the secret of his birth, and the story of the wrongs inflicted by Pelias, the usurper, upon his unfortunate parents.

Jason's Vow

This tale aroused the young prince's anger, and made him solemnly vow to punish his uncle, or perish in the attempt. Chiron encouraged him to start, and in parting bade him remember that Pelias alone had injured him, but that all the rest of the human race were entitled to any aid he could bestow. Jason listened respectfully to his tutor's last instructions; then, girding his sword and putting on his sandals, he set out on his journey to Iolcus.

It was early in the spring, and the young man had not gone very far before he came to a stream, which, owing to the usual freshets of the season, was almost impassable. Jason, however, quite undaunted by the rushing, foaming waters, was about to attempt the crossing, when he saw an aged woman not far from him, gazing in helpless despair at the waters she could not cross.

Naturally kind-hearted and helpful, and, besides that, mindful of Chiron's last recommendation, Jason offered the old woman his assistance, proposing to carry her across on his back if she would but lend him her staff to lean upon. The old woman gladly accepted this offer; and a few moments later, Jason, bending beneath his strange load, was battling with the rapid current.

After many an effort, breathless and almost exhausted, Jason reached the opposite bank, and, after depositing his burden there, scrambled up beside her, casting a rueful glance at the torrent, which had wrenched off one of his golden sandals. He was about to part from the old dame with a kindly farewell, when she was suddenly transformed into a large, handsome, imperious-looking woman, whom, owing to the peacock by her side, he immediately recognized as Juno, queen of heaven. He bent low before her, and claimed her aid and protection, which she graciously promised ere she vanished from his sight.

With eager steps Jason now pressed onward, nor paused until he came in view of his native city. As he drew near, he noticed an unusual concourse of people, and upon inquiry discovered that Pelias was celebrating a festival in honor of the immortal gods. Up the steep ascent leading to the temple Jason hastened, and pressed on to the innermost circle of spectators, until he stood in full view of his enemy Pelias, who, unconscious of coming evil, continued offering the sacrifice.

THE ONE SANDAL

At last the ceremony was completed, and the king cast an arrogant glance over the assembled people. His eyes suddenly fell upon Jason's naked foot, and he grew pale with horror as there flashed into his memory the recollection of an ancient oracle, warning him to beware of the man who appeared before him wearing but one sandal. Pelias tremblingly bade the guards bring forth the uninvited stranger. His orders were obeyed; and Jason, confronting his uncle boldly, summoned him to make a full restitution of the power he had so unjustly seized.

PHRYXUS AND HELLE

To surrender power and wealth and return to obscurity was not to be thought of; but Pelias artfully concealed his displeasure, and told his nephew that they would discuss the matter and come to an amicable understanding after the banquet, which was already spread and awaiting their presence. During the festive meal, bards sang of all the heroic deeds accomplished by great men; and Pelias, by judicious flattery, stimulated Jason to attempt similar feats. At last the musicians recited the story of Phryxus and Helle, the son and daughter of Athamas and Nephele, who, to escape the cruel treatment of their stepmother, Ino, mounted a winged, golden-fleeced ram sent by Neptune to transport them to Colchis.

The ram flew over land and sea; but Helle, frightened at the sight of the waves tossing far beneath her, suddenly lost her hold on the golden fleece, and tumbled off the ram's back into a portion of the sea since known as the Hellespont,

> Where beauteous Helle found a watery grave.
>
> MELEAGER

Phryxus, more fortunate than his sister, reached Colchis in safety, and in gratitude to the gods sacrificed the ram they had sent to deliver him, and hung its golden fleece on a tree, near which he stationed a dragon to guard it night and day. The bards then went on to relate that the glittering trophy still hung there, awaiting a hand bold enough to slay the dragon and bear it off.

THE GOLDEN FLEECE

This tale and his liberal potations greatly excited the youth Jason; and Pelias, perceiving it, hypocritically regretted his inability to win the golden fleece, and softly insinuated that young men of the present generation were not brave enough to risk their lives in such a glorious cause. The usurper's crafty remarks had the desired effect; for Jason suddenly sprang from his seat, and vowed he would go in quest of the golden fleece. Pelias, quite certain that the rash youth would lose his life in the attempt, and thus cause no more trouble, with much difficulty restrained all expressions of joy, and dared him to make the attempt.

With terror struck, lest by young Jason's hand
His crown should be rent from him, Pelias sought
By machinations dark to slay his foe.
From Colchis' realm to bring the golden fleece
He charged the youth.

ORPHIC ARGONAUTICS

THE SPEAKING OAK

When Jason, sobered and refreshed by a long night's rest, perceived how foolish had been his vow, he would fain have recalled it; but, mindful of Chiron's teachings ever to be true to his word, he resolved to depart for Colchis. To secure Juno's assistance, he began by visiting her shrine at Dodona, where the oracle, a Speaking Oak, assured him of the goddess's good will and efficacious protection. Next the Speaking Oak bade him cut off one of its own mighty limbs, and carve from it a figurehead for the swift-sailing vessel which Minerva, at Juno's request, would build for his use from pine trees grown on Mount Pelion.

THE ARGO AND CREW

Jason, having finished his figurehead, found that it too had the gift of speech, and that it would occasionally vouchsafe sage counsel in the direction of his affairs. When quite completed, Jason called his vessel the Argo (swift-sailing), and speedily collected a crew of heroes as brave as himself, among whom were Hercules, Castor, Pollux, Peleus, Admetus, Theseus, and Orpheus, who were all glad to undertake the perilous journey to lands unknown. To speed them on their way, Juno then bargained with Æolus for favorable winds, and forbade any tempest which might work them harm.

Then with a whistling breeze did Juno fill the sail,
And Argo, self-impell'd, shot swift before the gale.

ONOMACRITUS (Elton's tr.)

Story of Hylas

On several occasions the heroes landed, either to renew their stock of provisions or to recruit their strength, but in general every delay brought them some misfortune. Once Hercules, having landed with a youth named Hylas to cut wood for new oars, bade the youth go to a neighboring spring and draw a pitcher of water to quench the thirst produced by his exertions. The youth promptly departed; but as he bent over the fountain, the nymphs, enamored with his beauty, drew him down into their moist abode to keep them company. Hercules, after vainly waiting for Hylas' return, went in search of him, but could find no trace of him, and, in his grief and disappointment at the death of his young friend, refused to continue the expedition, and, deserting the Argonauts, made his way home alone and on foot.

Phineus and the Harpies

On another occasion, when Jason visited Phineus, the blind king of Thrace, he heard that this monarch's life was imbittered by the Harpies, vile monsters, part woman, part bird, who ate or befouled all the food placed before him, and never let him eat a mouthful in peace. Having repeated this tale to his companions, the two sons of Boreas, who were also in the Argo, begged permission to drive them away. Jason could not refuse their request; and the two youths, with drawn swords, pursued the Harpies to the Strophades Islands, where the birds promised to remain.

Jason, sailing on in the mean while, was attacked by a flock of brazen-feathered birds, which rained their sharp plumage down upon the Argonauts, wounding many of them sorely. The captain of the expedition, seeing weapons were of no avail against these foes, consulted the figurehead, and, in obedience to its directions, clashed his arms against his shield, until, terrified by the din, the brazen-feathered birds flew rapidly away, uttering discordant cries of terror.

The Symplegades

Some time during the course of their journey the Argonauts came to the Symplegades,—floating rocks which continually crashed together, and ground to powder all objects caught between them. Jason knew he was obliged to pass between these rocks or give up the expedition: so, calculating that the speed of his vessel was equal to that of a dove on the wing, he sent one out before him. The dove flew safely between the rocks, losing only one of its tail feathers as they again clashed together. Watching his opportunity, therefore, Jason bade his men row swiftly. The Argo darted through the opening, and, when the rocks again came into contact, they merely grazed the rudder. As a vessel had passed between them unharmed, their power for evil left them, and they were chained fast to the bottom of the sea, near the mouth of the Bosporus, where they remained immovable like any other rocks.

ARRIVAL AT COLCHIS

The Argonauts, after other adventures far too numerous to recount in detail, reached the Colchian shores, and presented themselves before Æetes, the king, to whom they made known their errand. Loath to part with his golden treasure, Æetes declared, that, before Jason could obtain the fleece, he must catch and harness two wild, fire-breathing bulls dedicated to Vulcan, and make use of them to plow a stony piece of ground sacred to Mars. This done, he must sow the field with some dragon's teeth, as Cadmus had done, conquer the giants which would spring up, and, last of all, slay the guardian dragon, or the fleece would never be his.

MEDEA'S AID

One of these tasks would have sufficed to dismay many a brave youth; but Jason was of the dauntless kind, and merely hastened down to his vessel to ask the figurehead how he had better proceed. On his way to the seashore he met the king's daughter, Medea, a beautiful young sorceress, who had been charmed by his modest but firm bearing, and who was quite ready to bring her magic to his aid if he would but promise to marry her. Jason, susceptible to her attractions, and free from any conflicting ties, readily agreed to her proposal, and, carrying out her directions, caught and harnessed the fiery bulls, plowed the field, and sowed it with the dragon's teeth.

JASON AND THE DRAGON. Salvator Rosa.

And how he yoked the bulls, whose breathings fiery glow'd,
And with the dragons' teeth the furrow'd acres sow'd.

ONOMACRITUS (Elton's tr.)

But when he saw glittering spears and helmets grow out of the ground, and beheld the close ranks of giants in full armor, he was filled with dismay, and would have fled had it been possible. However, aware that such a performance would insure his ruin, he stood his ground, and, when the phalanx was quite near him, threw a handful of dust full in the giants' faces. Blinded with the sand, the giants attacked one another, and in a short time were exterminated.

They, like swift dogs,
Ranging in fierceness, on each other turn'd
Tumultuous battle. On their mother earth
By their own spears they sank; like pines, or oaks,
Strew'd by a whirlwind in the mountain dale.

APOLLONIUS RHODIUS (Elton's tr.)

THE FLEECE CAPTURED

Accompanied by Medea, Jason next hastened to the tree where the dragon kept guard over his treasure. An opiate prepared by Medea's magic skill soon made the dragon forget his charge in a profound sleep, and enabled Jason to draw near enough to sever his frightful head from his hideous trunk. Jason then tore the coveted fleece from the branch where it had hung for many a year, and bore it in triumph to the Argo.

Exulting Jason grasped the shining hide,
His last of labors, and his envied pride.
Slow from the groaning branch the fleece was rent.

FLACCUS (Elton's tr.)

His companions, who had made ready for a hasty departure, were already seated at their oars; and, as soon as he had embarked with Medea and her attendants, the Argo shot out of the Colchian harbor.

MEDEA. Sichel.

How softly stole from home the luckless-wedded maid,
Through darkness of the night, in linen robe array'd;
By Fate to Argo led, and urged by soft desire,
Nor yet regarding aught her father's furious ire.

ONOMACRITUS (Elton's tr.)

When morning dawned and Æetes awoke, he heard that the dragon was slain, the fleece stolen, his daughter gone, and the Grecian ship far out of sight. No time was lost in useless wailing, but a vessel was hurriedly launched and manned, and the king in person set out in pursuit of the fugitives, who had, moreover, taken his most precious treasure, his only son and heir, Absyrtus. Although the Colchian men were good sailors and skillful rowers, they did not catch sight of the Argo until they came near the mouth of the Danube, and Æetes wildly called to his daughter to return to her home and to her father.

"Stay thy rash flight! and, from the distant main,—
For oh! thou canst, my daughter,—turn again.
Whither depart? the vessel backward steer;
Thy friends, thy still fond father, wait thee here."

FLACCUS (Elton's tr.)

DEATH OF ABSYRTUS

But Medea had no wish to be torn away from Jason's arms, and, instead of listening to her father's entreaties, urged the Argonauts to redoubled efforts. Little by little the distance between the two vessels grew less; the Colchian rowers were gaining upon the Greek; and Medea saw, that, unless she found means to delay her father, he would overtake her and compel her to return. With her own hands she therefore slew her little brother, Absyrtus, and cut his body into pieces, which she dropped over the side of the vessel one by one. Æetes, a helpless witness of this cruel, awful deed, piously collected his son's remains, and, in pausing to do so, lost sight of the Argo, and all hope of recovering his unnatural daughter: so he returned sadly to Colchis, where he buried his son's remains with due solemnity.

Pelias Dethroned

In the mean while, Pelias had reigned contentedly over Thessaly, confident that Jason would never return. Imagine his dismay, therefore, when he heard that the Argo had arrived, bearing Jason, now the proud possessor of the renowned golden fleece. Ere he could take measures to maintain his usurped authority, Jason appeared, and compelled him to resign the throne in favor of the rightful king, Æson.

Unfortunately, Æson was now so old and decrepit, that power had no charms for him: so Jason begged Medea to use her magic in his behalf, and restore him to the vigor and beauty of his early manhood. To gratify Jason, Medea called all her magic into play, and by some mysterious process restored Æson to all his former youth, strength, activity, and grace.

> Medea's spells dispersed the weight of years,
> And Æson stood a youth 'mid youthful peers.
>
> WORDSWORTH

The Magic Recipe

As soon as Pelias' daughters heard of this miraculous transformation, they hastened to Medea and implored her to give them the recipe, that they might rejuvenate their father also. The sorceress maliciously bade them cut their father's body into small pieces, and boil them in a caldron with certain herbs, declaring that, if the directions were carefully carried out, the result would be satisfactory; but, when the too credulous maidens carried out these instructions, they only slew the father whom they had so dearly loved.

Days and years now passed happily and uneventfully for Jason and Medea; but at last their affection for each other cooled, and Jason fell in love with Glauce, or Creusa. Frantic with jealousy, Medea prepared and sent the maiden a magic robe, which she no sooner donned than she was seized with terrible convulsions, in which she died. Medea, still full of resentment against Jason, then slew her own children, and, mounting her dragon car, departed, leaving a message for Jason, purporting that the Argo would yet cause his death.

Death of Jason

Jason, a victim of remorse and despair, now led a weary and sorrowful life, and every day he wandered down to the shore, where he sat under the shade of the Argo's hulk, which was slowly rotting away. One day, while he was sitting there musing over his youthful adventures and Medea's strange prophecy, a sudden gale detached a beam, which, falling on his head, fractured his skull and caused instantaneous death.

The Argonautic expedition is emblematic of the first long maritime voyage undertaken by the Greeks for commercial purposes; while the golden fleece which Jason brought back from Colchis is but a symbol of the untold riches they found in the East, and brought back to their own native land.

Chapter XXIII

THE CALYDONIAN HUNT

BIRTH OF MELEAGER

Œneus and Althæa, King and Queen of Calydon, in Ætolia, were very happy in the possession of a little son, Meleager, only a few days old, until they heard that the Fates had decreed the child should live only as long as the brand then smoking and crackling on the hearth. The parents were motionless with grief, until Althæa, with true mother's wit, snatched the brand from the fire, plunged it into an earthen jar filled with water, quenched the flames which were consuming it, and, carefully laying it aside, announced her intention to keep it forever.

Meleager, thus saved from an untimely death by his mother's presence of mind, grew up a brave and handsome youth, and joined the Argonautic expedition. While he was absent, his father omitted the yearly sacrifice to Diana, who, enraged at his neglect, sent a monstrous boar to devour his subjects and devastate his realm. Meleager, on his return, gathered together all the brave men of the country, and instituted a great hunt, whose main object was the capture or death of the obnoxious boar.

THE HUNTERS

Jason, Nestor, Peleus, Admetus, Theseus, Pirithous, and many other noted heroes, came at his call; but the attention of all the spectators was specially attracted by Castor and Pollux, and by the fair Atalanta, daughter of Iasius, King of Arcadia. This princess had led a very adventurous life; for when but a babe, her father, disappointed to see a daughter instead of the longed-for son, had exposed her on Mount Parthenium to the fury of the wild beasts. Some hunters, passing there shortly after this, found the babe fearlessly nursing from a she-bear, and in compassion carried her home, where they trained her to love the chase.

The grand Calydonian Hunt was headed by Meleager and Atalanta, who were very fond of each other, and who boldly led the rest in pursuit of the boar. From one end of the Calydonian forest to the other the boar fled, closely pursued by the hunt, and was at last brought to bay by Atalanta, who succeeded in dealing him a mortal wound. But even in his dying struggles the boar would have killed her, had not Meleager come to her rescue and given him his deathblow.

MELEAGER SLAYS HIS UNCLES

All the hunt now gathered around the boar's corpse, and watched Meleager take its spoil, which he gallantly bestowed upon Atalanta. Althæa's two brothers were present at the hunt; and, as they wished to possess the skin, they bitterly reproved their nephew on their way home for giving it to a stranger. They added taunts to this reproof, which so angered Meleager, that, in a sudden fit of passion, he slew them both. When Althæa saw her brothers' corpses, and heard that they had been slain by her son, she vowed to avenge their death, drew the carefully cherished brand from its hiding place, and threw it upon the fire burning brightly on her hearth. When the last bit of the precious wood crumbled away into ashes, Meleager died. All Althæa's affection for her son returned when his lifeless corpse was brought to her, and in her despair she committed suicide.

ATALANTA'S RACE

In the mean while, Atalanta, proud of her skill and of her spoil, had returned to her father's court, where, no other heir having appeared, she was joyfully received, and entreated to marry. Many suitors came to woo the fair princess, but most of them refrained from pressing their suit when they heard what conditions were imposed upon all who would obtain her hand; for Atalanta disapproved of marriage, and, anxious to keep her freedom, decreed that she should marry only on condition that her suitor would beat her in a foot race. If he were beaten, however, he must pay for his defeat by forfeiting his life.

THE GOLDEN APPLES

In spite of these barbarous terms, a few youths had tried to outrun her; but they failed, and their lifeless heads were exposed on the racing ground to deter all other suitors. Undaunted by these ghastly trophies, Hippomenes, or Milanion, once came to

ATALANTA'S RACE. Poynter.

Atalanta and expressed a desire to race with her. This youth had previously obtained Venus' protection, and concealed under his garment her gift of three golden apples. Atalanta prepared for her race as usual, and, as usual, passed her rival; but just as she did so, one of the golden apples rolled at her feet. For a moment she paused, then stooped and picked it up ere she resumed the race. Her adversary had passed her and won some advance; but she soon overtook him, when a second golden apple caused a second delay. She was about to reach the goal first, as usual, when a third golden treasure tempted her to pause, and enabled Hippomenes to win the race.

> Hippomenes turns her astray
> By the golden illusions he flings on her way.
> MOORE

Atalanta could now no longer refuse to marry, and her nuptials were soon celebrated. In his happiness at having won such a peerless bride, Hippomenes forgot to pay the promised thanks to Venus, for which offense he and his wife were severely punished by being transformed into a pair of lions, and doomed to drag Cybele's car.

CASTOR AND POLLUX

The twin brothers Castor and Pollux, the Dioscuri, or Gemini, who had greatly distinguished themselves by their daring in the Calydonian Hunt, were made the deities of boxing, wrestling, and all equestrian exercises.

> Leda's sons I'll sound,
> Illustrious twins, that are
> For wrestling this, and for the race renown'd.
> HORACE

One of these twins, Castor, was a mortal, and in a combat with the sons of Aphareus was slain. Pollux, who was immortal, then implored Jupiter to allow him to die also, that he might not be parted from his brother,—a proof of brotherly affection which so touched the father of the gods, that he permitted Castor to return to life on condition that Pollux would spend half his time in Hades.

Later on, satisfied that even this sacrifice was none too great for their fraternal love, he translated them both to the skies, where they form a bright constellation, one of the signs of the zodiac. Castor and Pollux are generally represented as handsome youths, mounted on snowy chargers.

> So like they were, no mortal
>   Might one from other know:
> White as snow their armor was:
>   Their steeds were white as snow.
>   MACAULAY

Their appearance under certain circumstances foretold success in war, and the Romans believed that they fought at the head of their legions at the celebrated battle of Lake Regillus. Their name was also given to meteors, sometimes seen at sea, which attach themselves like balls of fire to the masts of ships,—a sure sign, according to the sailors, of fine weather and an auspicious journey.

> Safe comes the ship to haven,
>   Through billows and through gales,
> If once the Great Twin Brethren
>   Sit shining on the sails.
>   MACAULAY

Festivals celebrated in honor of these twin brethren, and called the Dioscuria, were held in many places, but specially in Sparta, their birthplace, where they had world-renowned wrestling matches.

Chapter XXIV

ŒDIPUS

Laius and Jocasta, King and Queen of Thebes, in BŒotia, were greatly delighted at the birth of a little son. In their joy they sent for the priests of Apollo, and bade them foretell the glorious deeds their heir would perform; but all their joy was turned to grief when told that the child was destined to kill his father, marry his mother, and bring great misfortunes upon his native city.

> Laius once,
> Not from Apollo, but his priests, receiv'd
> An oracle, which said, it was decreed
> He should be slain by his own son.
>
> SOPHOCLES (Francklin's tr.)

To prevent the fulfillment of this dreadful prophecy, Laius bade a servant carry the new-born child out of the city, and end its feeble little life. The king's mandate was obeyed only in part; for the servant, instead of killing the child, hung it up by its ankles to a tree in a remote place, and left it there to perish from hunger and exposure if it were spared by the wild beasts.

When he returned, none questioned how he had performed the appointed task, but all sighed with relief to think that the prophecy could never be accomplished. The child, however, was not dead, as all supposed. A shepherd in quest of a stray lamb had heard his cries, delivered him from his painful position, and carried him to Polybus, King of Corinth, who, lacking an heir of his own, gladly adopted the little stranger. The Queen of Corinth and her handmaidens hastened with tender concern to bathe the swollen ankles, and called the babe Œdipus (swollen-footed).

Years passed by. The young prince grew up in total ignorance of the unfortunate circumstances under which he had made his first appearance at court, until one day at a banquet one of his companions, heated by drink, began to quarrel with him, and taunted him about his origin, declaring that those whom he had been accustomed to call parents were in no way related to him.

> A drunken rev'ler at a feast proclaim'd
> That I was only the supposed son
> Of Corinth's king.
>
> SOPHOCLES (Francklin's tr.)

ŒDIPUS CONSULTS THE ORACLE

These words, coupled with a few meaning glances hastily exchanged by the guests, excited Œdipus' suspicions, and made him question the queen, who, afraid lest he might do himself an injury in the first moment of his despair if the truth were revealed to him, had recourse to prevarication, and quieted him by the assurance that he was her beloved son.

Something in her manner, however, left a lingering doubt in Œdipus' mind, and made him resolve to consult the oracle of Delphi, whose words he knew would reveal the exact truth. He therefore went to this shrine; but, as usual, the oracle answered somewhat ambiguously, and merely warned him that fate had decreed he should kill his father, marry his mother, and cause great woes to his native city.

>   I felt
> A secret anguish, and unknown to them
> Sought out the Pythian oracle; in vain;
> Touching my parents, nothing could I learn;
> But dreadful were the mis'ries it denounc'd
> Against me; 'twas my fate, Apollo said,
> To wed my mother, to produce a race
> Accursed and abhorr'd; and last, to slay
> My father.
>
> SOPHOCLES (Francklin's tr.)

ŒDIPUS LEAVES CORINTH

What! kill Polybus, who had ever been such an indulgent father, and marry the queen, whom he revered as his mother! Never! Rather than perpetrate these awful crimes, and bring destruction upon the people of Corinth, whom he loved, he would wander away over the face of the earth, and never see city or parents again.

> Lest I should e'er fulfill the dire prediction,
> Instant I fled from Corinth, by the stars
> Guiding my hapless journey.
>
> SOPHOCLES (Francklin's tr.)

But his heart was filled with intense bitterness, and as he journeyed he did not cease to curse the fate which drove him away from home. After some time, he came to three crossroads; and while he stood there, deliberating which direction to take, a chariot, wherein an aged man was seated, came rapidly toward him.

DEATH OF LAIUS

The herald who preceded it haughtily called to the youth to stand aside and make way for his master; but Œdipus, who, as Polybus' heir, was accustomed to be treated with deference, resented the commanding tone, and refused to obey. Incensed at what seemed unparalleled impudence, the herald struck the youth, who, retaliating, stretched his assailant lifeless at his feet.

This affray attracted the attention of the master and other servants. They immediately attacked the murderer, who slew them all, thus unconsciously accomplishing the first part of the prophecy; for the aged man was Laius, his father, journeying *incognito* from Thebes to Delphi, where he wished to consult the oracle.

Œdipus then leisurely pursued his way until he came to the gates of Thebes, where he found the whole city in an uproar, "because the king had been found lifeless by the roadside, with all his attendants slain beside him, presumably the work of a band of highway robbers or assassins."

He fell

By strangers, murdered, for so fame reports,

By robbers in the place where three ways meet.

SOPHOCLES (FRANCKLIN'S TR.)

Of course, Œdipus did not connect the murder of such a great personage as the King of Thebes by an unknown band of robbers, with the death he had dealt to an arrogant old man, and he therefore composedly inquired what the second calamity alluded to might be.

THE SPHINX

With lowered voices, as if afraid of being overheard, the Thebans described the woman's head, bird's wings and claws, and lion's body, which were the outward presentment of a terrible monster called the Sphinx, which had taken up its station without the city gates beside the highway, and would allow none to pass in or out without propounding a difficult riddle. Then, if any hesitated to give the required answer, or failed to give it correctly, they were mercilessly devoured by the terrible Sphinx, which no one dared attack or could drive away.

While listening to these tidings, Œdipus saw a herald pass along the street, proclaiming that the throne and the queen's hand would be the reward of any man who dared encounter the Sphinx, and was fortunate enough to free the country of its terrible presence.

THE RIDDLE

As Œdipus attached no special value to the life made desolate by the oracle's predictions, he resolved to slay the dreaded monster, and, with that purpose in view, advanced slowly, sword in hand, along the road where lurked the Sphinx. He soon found the monster, which from afar propounded the following enigma, warning him, at the same time, that he forfeited his life if he failed to give the right answer:—

Tell me, what animal is that

Which has four feet at morning bright,

Has two at noon, and three at night?

PRIOR

ŒDIPUS AND THE SPHINX. Ingres.
(Louvre, Paris.)

Œdipus was not devoid of intelligence, by any manner of means, and soon concluded that the animal could only be man, who in infancy, when too weak to stand, creeps along on hands and knees, in manhood walks erect, and in old age supports his tottering steps with a staff.

Œdipus Marries His Mother

This reply, evidently as correct as unexpected, was received by the Sphinx with a hoarse cry of disappointment and rage as it turned to fly; but ere it could effect its purpose, it was stayed by Œdipus, who drove it at his sword's point over the edge of a neighboring precipice, where it was killed. On his return to the city, Œdipus was received with cries of joy, placed on a chariot, crowned King of Thebes, and married to his own mother, Jocasta, unwittingly fulfilling the second fearful clause of the prophecy.

The Plague

A number of happy and moderately uneventful years now passed by, and Œdipus became the father of two manly sons, Eteocles and Polynices, and two beautiful daughters, Ismene and Antigone; but prosperity was not doomed to favor him long.

Just when he fancied himself most happy, and looked forward to a peaceful old age, a terrible scourge visited Thebes, causing the death of many faithful subjects, and filling the hearts of all with great terror. The people now turned to him, beseeching him to aid them, as he had done once before when threatened by the Sphinx; and Œdipus sent messengers to consult the Delphic oracle, who declared the plague would cease only when the former king's murderers had been found and punished.

> The plague, he said, should cease,
> When those who murder'd Laius were discover'd,
> And paid the forfeit of their crime by death,
> Or banishment.
>
> SOPHOCLES (Francklin's tr.)

Messengers were sent in every direction to collect all possible information about the murder committed so long ago, and after a short time they brought unmistakable proofs which convicted Œdipus of the crime. At the same time the guilty servant confessed that he had not killed the child, but had exposed it on a mountain, whence it was carried to Corinth's king.

DEATH OF JOCASTA

The chain of evidence was complete, and now Œdipus discovered that he had involuntarily been guilty of the three crimes to avoid which he had fled from Corinth. The rumor of these dreadful discoveries soon reached Jocasta, who, in her despair at finding herself an accomplice, committed suicide.

Œdipus, apprised of her intention, rushed into her apartment too late to prevent its being carried out, and found her lifeless. This sight was more than the poor monarch could bear, and in his despair he blinded himself with one of her ornaments.

> He pluck'd from off the robe she wore
> A golden buckle that adorn'd her side,
> And buried in his eyes the sharpen'd point,
> Crying, he ne'er again would look on her,
> Never would see his crimes or mis'ries more,
> Or those whom guiltless he could ne'er behold,
> Or those to whom he now must sue for aid.
>   SOPHOCLES (Francklin's tr.)

DEATH OF ŒDIPUS

Penniless, blind, and on foot, he then left the scene of his awful crimes, accompanied by his daughter Antigone, the only one who loved him still, and who was ready to guide his uncertain footsteps wherever he wished to go. After many days of weary wandering, father and daughter reached Colonus, where grew a mighty forest sacred to the avenging deities, the Furies, or Eumenides.

Here Œdipus expressed his desire to remain, and, after bidding his faithful daughter an affectionate farewell, he groped his way into the dark forest alone.

The wind rose, the lightning flashed, the thunder pealed; but although, as soon as the storm was over, a search was made for Œdipus, no trace of him was ever found, and the ancients fancied that the Furies had dragged him down to Hades to receive the punishment of all his crimes.

ETEOCLES AND POLYNICES

Antigone, no longer needed by her unhappy father, slowly wended her way back to Thebes, where she found that the plague had ceased, but that her brothers had quarreled about the succession to the throne. A compromise was finally decided upon, whereby it was decreed that Eteocles, the elder son, should reign one year, and at the end of that period resign the throne to Polynices for an equal space of time, both brothers thus exercising the royal authority in turn. This arrangement seemed satisfactory to Eteocles; but when, at the end of the first year, Polynices returned from his travels in foreign lands to claim the scepter, Eteocles refused to relinquish it, and, making use of his power, drove the claimant away.

> Thou seest me banish'd from my native land,
> Unjustly banish'd, for no other crime
> But that I strove to keep the throne of Thebes,
> By birthright mine, from him who drove me thence,
> The young Eteocles: not his the claim
> By justice, nor to me his fame in arms
> Superior; but by soft, persuasive arts
> He won the rebel city to his love.
>
> SOPHOCLES (Francklin's tr.)

THE SEVEN CHIEFS BEFORE THEBES

Polynices' nature was not one to endure such a slight patiently; and he hastened off to Argos, where he persuaded Adrastus, the king, to give him his daughter in marriage, and aid him to recover his inheritance. True to his promise, Adrastus soon equipped a large army, which was led by seven determined and renowned chiefs, ready to risk all in the attempt, and either win or perish.

Seven valiant leaders march
To Thebes, resolved to conquer or to die.
SOPHOCLES (Francklin's tr.)

Their bravery was of no avail, however, for Thebes was well fortified and defended; and after a seven-years' siege they found themselves no nearer their goal than at the beginning of the war. Weary of the monotony of this quarrel, the conflicting armies finally decreed that the difference should be settled by a duel between the inimical brothers, who no sooner found themselves face to face, than they rushed upon each other with such animosity that both fell.

By order of Jocasta's father, Creon, the corpse of Eteocles received all the honors of a Greek burial, while that of Polynices was left on the plain, a prey to the birds and wild beasts.

Polynices' wretched carcass lies
Unburied, unlamented, left expos'd
A feast for hungry vultures on the plain.
SOPHOCLES (Francklin's tr.)

ANTIGONE'S DEVOTION

Then a proclamation was issued, that, if any dared bury the body of the fallen prince, he would incur the penalty of being buried alive. Heedless of this injunction and Ismene's prayers to refrain from endangering her own life, Antigone dug a grave for her brother's remains, and, unaided, fulfilled the various customary funeral rites. Her task was almost completed, when the guards discovered her, and dragged her into the presence of Creon, who, although she was a relative and the promised wife of his son Hæmon, condemned her to death.

Let her be carried instant to the cave,
And leave her there alone, to live, or die;
Her blood rests not on us: but she no longer
Shall breathe on earth.
SOPHOCLES (Francklin's tr.)

ANTIGONE AND ISMENE. Teschendorf.

Antigone and Hæmon

Hæmon pleaded passionately for her life; but, when he saw his prayers were vain, he ran to the place where Antigone was confined, sprang into her narrow cell, wound his arms closely around her, and refused to leave her. There they were walled in; Antigone's sufferings were cut mercifully short by asphyxiation; and, when Hæmon saw she was no more, he, in utter despair, thrust his dagger into his side, and perished too.

> On himself bent all his wrath,
> Full in his side the weapon fix'd, but still,
> Whilst life remain'd, on the soft bosom hung
> Of the dear maid, and his last spirit breath'd
> O'er her pale cheek, discolor'd with his blood.
> Thus lay the wretched pair in death united,
> And celebrate their nuptials in the tomb.
>
> SOPHOCLES (Francklin's tr.)

Ismene, the last of Œdipus' unfortunate race, died of grief, and thus the prophecy was fully accomplished. The Theban war was not, however, entirely ended, for, when both brothers fell, the two armies flew to attack each other; and such was their courage, that many fell, and only one of the seven chiefs returned to Argos. There he patiently waited until the children of these brave captains were old enough to bear arms, and then proposed to them to attack Thebes and avenge their fathers' death.

The Epigoni (or those who come after), as these youths are collectively designated, received this proposal with rapture; and Thebes, again besieged, fell into their hands, and was duly sacked, burned, and destroyed, as the Delphic oracle had foretold so many years before.

Chapter XXV

BELLEROPHON

Bellerophon, a brave young prince, the grandson of Sisyphus, King of Corinth, had the great misfortune to kill his own brother while hunting in the forest. His grief was, of course, intense; and the horror he felt for the place where the catastrophe had occurred, added to his fear lest he should incur judicial punishment for his involuntary crime, made him flee to the court of Argos, where he took refuge with PrŒtus, the king, who was also his kinsman.

ANTEIA'S TREACHERY

He had not sojourned there very long, before Anteia, the queen, fell in love with him; and although her husband, PrŒtus, treated her with the utmost kindness, she made up her mind to desert him, and tried to induce Bellerophon to elope with her. Too honest to betray a man who had treated him as a friend, the young prince refused to listen to the queen's proposals. His refusal was to cost him dear, however; for, when Anteia saw that the youth would never yield to her wishes, she became very angry indeed, sought her husband, and accused the young stranger of crimes he had never even dreamed of committing.

PrŒtus, indignant at what he deemed deep treachery on the part of an honored guest, yet reluctant to punish him with his own hand as he deserved, sent Bellerophon to Iobates, King of Lycia, with a sealed message bidding him put the bearer to death.

Quite unconscious of the purport of this letter, Bellerophon traveled gayly onward, and presented himself before Iobates, who received him very hospitably, and, without inquiring his name or errand, entertained him royally for many days. After some time, Bellerophon suddenly remembered the sealed message intrusted to his care, and hastened to deliver it to Iobates, with many apologies for his forgetfulness.

The Chimæra

With blanched cheeks and every outward sign of horror, the king read the missive, and then fell into a deep reverie. He did not like to take a stranger's life, and still could not refuse to comply with PrŒtus' urgent request: so, after much thought, he decided to send Bellerophon to attack the Chimæra, a terrible monster with a lion's head, a goat's body, and a dragon's tail.

> Dire Chimæra's conquest was enjoin'd;
> A mingled monster, of no mortal kind;
> Behind, a dragon's fiery tail was spread;
> A goat's rough body bore a lion's head;
> Her pitchy nostrils flaky flames expire;
> Her gaping throat emits infernal fire.
>
> HOMER (Pope's tr.)

His principal motive in choosing this difficult task was, that, although many brave men had set forth to slay the monster, none had ever returned, for one and all had perished in the attempt.

Although very courageous, Bellerophon's heart beat fast with fear when told what great deed he must accomplish; and he left Iobates' palace very sorrowfully, for he dearly loved the king's fair daughter, Philonoe, and was afraid he would never see her again.

Minerva's Advice

While thus inwardly bewailing the ill luck which had so persistently dogged his footsteps, Bellerophon suddenly saw Minerva appear before him in all her splendor, and heard her inquire in gentle tones the cause of his too evident dejection. He had no sooner apprised her of the difficult task appointed him, than she promised him her aid, and before she vanished gave him a beautiful golden bridle, which she bade him use to control Pegasus.

Bridle in hand, Bellerophon stood pondering her words, and gradually remembered that Pegasus was a wonderful winged steed, born from the blood which fell into the foam of the sea from Medusa's severed head. This horse, as white as snow, and gifted with immortal life as well as incredible speed, was the

CHIMÆRA. (Egyptian Museum, Florence.)

favorite mount of Apollo and the Muses, who delighted in taking aërial flights on his broad back; and Bellerophon knew that from time to time he came down to earth to drink of the cool waters of the Hippocrene (a fountain which had bubbled forth where his hoofs first touched the earth), or to visit the equally limpid spring of Pirene, near Corinth.

Pegasus Bridled

Bellerophon now proceeded to the latter fountain, where, after lingering many days in the vain hope of catching even a glimpse of the winged steed, he finally beheld him sailing downward in wide curves, like a bird of prey. From his place of concealment in a neighboring thicket, Bellerophon watched his opportunity, and, while the winged steed was grazing, he boldly vaulted upon his back.

Pegasus, who had never before been ridden by a mortal, reared and pranced, and flew up to dizzy heights; but all his efforts failed to unseat the brave rider, who, biding his time, finally thrust Minerva's golden bit between his teeth, and immediately he became gentle and tractable. Mounted upon this incomparable steed, Bellerophon now went in search of the winged monster Chimæra, who had given birth to the Nemean lion and to the riddle-loving Sphinx.

Chimæra Slain

From an unclouded sky Bellerophon and Pegasus swooped suddenly and unexpectedly down upon the terrible Chimæra, whose fiery breath and great strength were of no avail; for after a protracted struggle Bellerophon and Pegasus were victorious, and the monster lay lifeless upon the blood-soaked ground.

This mighty deed of valor accomplished, Bellerophon returned to Iobates, to report the success of his undertaking; and, although the king was heartily glad to know the Chimæra was no more, he was very sorry to see Bellerophon safe and sound, and tried to devise some other plan to get rid of him.

He therefore sent him to fight the Amazons; but the hero, aided by the gods, defeated these warlike women also, and returned to Lycia, where, after escaping from an ambush posted by the king for his destruction, he again appeared victorious at court.

These repeated and narrow escapes from certain death convinced Iobates that the youth was under the special protection of the gods; and this induced the king not only to forego further attempts to slay him, but also to bestow upon the young hero his daughter's hand in marriage.

BELLEROPHON'S FALL

Bellerophon, having now attained his dearest wishes, might have settled down in peace; but his head had been utterly turned by the many lofty flights he had taken upon Pegasus' back, and, encouraged by the fulsome flattery of his courtiers, he finally fancied himself the equal of the immortal gods, and wished to join them in their celestial abode.

Summoning his faithful Pegasus once more, he rose higher and higher, and would probably have reached Olympus' heights, had not Jupiter sent a gadfly, which stung poor Pegasus so cruelly, that he shied viciously, and flung his too confident rider far down to the earth below.

> Bold Bellerophon (so Jove decreed
> In wrath) fell headlong from the fields of air.
>
> WORDSWORTH

This fall, which would doubtless have killed any one but a mythological hero, merely deprived Bellerophon of his eyesight; and ever after he groped his way disconsolately, thinking of the happy days when he rode along the paths of air, and gazed upon the beautiful earth at his feet.

Bellerophon, mounted upon Pegasus, winging his flight through the air or fighting the Chimæra, is a favorite subject in sculpture and painting, which has frequently been treated by ancient artists, a few of whose most noted works are still extant in various museums.

This story, like many others, is merely a sun myth, in which Bellerophon, the orb of day, rides across the sky on Pegasus, the fleecy white clouds, and slays Chimæra, the dread monster of darkness, which he alone can overcome. Driven from home early in life, Bellerophon wanders throughout the world like his brilliant prototype, and, like it, ends his career in total darkness.

Chapter XXVI

MINOR DIVINITIES

NAIADES AND OREADES

According to the ancients' belief, every mountain, valley, plain, lake, river, grove, and sea was provided with some lesser deity, whose special duty was assigned by the powerful gods of Olympus. These were, for instance, the Naiades, beautiful water nymphs, who dwelt in the limpid depths of the fountains, and were considered local patrons of poetry and song.

The Oreades, or mountain nymphs, were supposed to linger in the mountain solitudes, and guide weary travelers safely through their rocky mazes.

> Mark how the climbing Oreads
> Beckon thee to their Arcades!
> EMERSON

NAPÆÆ AND DRYADES

As for the Napææ, they preferred to linger in the valleys, which were kept green and fruitful by their watchful care, in which task they were ably seconded by the Dryades, the nymphs of vegetation.

The very trees in the forest and along the roadside were supposed to be each under the protection of a special divinity called Hamadryad, said to live and die with the tree intrusted to her care.

> When the Fate of Death is drawing near,
> First wither on the earth the beauteous trees,
> The bark around them wastes, the branches fall,
> And the nymph's soul, at the same moment, leaves
> The sun's fair light.
>
> HOMER

STORY OF DRYOPE

A sweet and touching story was told by the ancients of a mortal who was changed into a Hamadryad. This young girl, whose name was Dryope, was a beautiful young princess, the daughter of Baucis, so bright and clever, that all who knew her loved her dearly. Of course, as soon as she was old enough to think of marriage, a host of suitors asked her hand, each eager to win for his bride one so beautiful and gifted.

> No nymph of all Œchalia could compare,
> For beauteous form, with Dryope the fair.
>
> OVID (Pope's tr.)

Fully aware of the importance of making a wise choice, Dryope took her time, and finally decided to marry Andræmon, a worthy young prince, who possessed every charm calculated to win a fair girl's heart. The young people were duly married, and daily rejoiced in their happiness, which seemed almost too great for earth, when they became the parents of a charming little son.

Every day Dryope carried the child along the banks of a little lake close by the palace, where bloomed a profusion of gay-colored flowers.

> A lake there was, with shelving banks around,
> Whose verdant summit fragrant myrtles crown'd.
> Those shades, unknowing of the Fates, she sought,
> And to the Naiads flowery garlands brought;
> Her smiling babe (a pleasing charge) she press'd
> Between her arms.
>
> OVID (Pope's tr.)

One day, while wandering there as usual, accompanied by her sister, she saw a lotus blossom, and pointed it out to her little son. He no sooner saw the brilliant flower, than he stretched out his little hands. To please him, the fond mother plucked it and gave it to him.

She had scarcely done so, when she noticed drops of blood trickling from the broken stem; and while she stood there, speechless with wonder, a voice was heard accusing her of having slain Lotis, a nymph, who, to escape the pursuit of Priapus, god of the shade, had assumed the guise of a flower.

> Lotis the nymph (if rural tales be true),
> As from Priapus' lawless love she flew,
> Forsook her form; and fixing here became
> A flowery plant, which still preserves her name.
>
> OVID (Pope's tr.)

Recovering from her first speechless terror, Dryope turned to flee, with a pitiful cry of compassion on her pale lips, but, to her astonishment, she could not leave the spot: her feet seemed rooted to the ground. She cast a rapid glance downward to ascertain what could so impede her progress, and noticed the rough bark of a tree growing with fearful rapidity all around her.

Higher and higher it rose, from her knees to her waist, and still it crept upward, in spite of her frantic attempts to tear it away from her shapely limbs. In despair she raised her trembling hands and arms to heaven to implore aid; but, ere the words were spoken, her arms were transformed into twisted branches, and her hands were filled with leaves.

Nothing human now remained of poor Dryope except her sweet, tear-stained face; but this too would soon vanish under the all-involving bark. She therefore took hasty leave of her father, sister, husband, and son, who, attracted by her first cry, had rushed to give her all the assistance in their power. The last words were quickly spoken, but none too soon, for the bark closed over the soft lips and hid the lovely features from view.

> She ceased at once to speak, and ceased to be,
> And all the nymph was lost within the tree:
> Yet latent life through her new branches reign'd,
> And long the plant a human heat retain'd.
>
> OVID (Pope's tr.)

One of Dryope's last requests had been that her child might often play beneath her shady branches; and when the passing winds rustled through her leaves, the ancients said it was "Dryope's lone lulling of her child."

SATYRS AND PAN

The male divinities of the woods, which were also very numerous, were mostly Satyrs,—curious beings with a man's body and a goat's legs, hair, and horns. They were all passionately fond of music and revelry, and were wont to indulge in dancing at all times and in all places. The most famous among all the Satyrs was Silenus, Bacchus' tutor; and Pan, or Consentes, god of the shepherds, and the personification of nature. The latter was the reputed son of Mercury and a charming young nymph named Penelope; and we are told, that, when his mother first beheld him, she was aghast, for he was the most homely as well as the most extraordinary little creature she had ever seen. His body was all covered with goat's hair, and his feet and ears were also those of a goat.

Amused at the sight of this grotesque little divinity, Mercury carried him off to Olympus, where all the gods turned him into ridicule. Pan was widely worshiped in olden times, however; and the ancients not only decked his altars with flowers, but sang his praises, and celebrated festivals in his honor.

> He is great and he is just,
> He is ever good, and must
> Be honored. Daffodillies,
> Roses, pinks, and loved lilies,
> Let us fling, while we sing,
> Ever Holy! Ever Holy!
> Ever honored! Ever young!
> The great Pan is ever sung!
>
> BEAUMONT AND FLETCHER

STORY OF SYRINX

Pan was equally devoted to music, the dance, and pretty nymphs. He saw one of the nymphs, Syrinx, whom he immediately loved; but unfortunately for him, she, frightened at his appearance, fled. Exasperated by her persistent avoidance of him, Pan once pursued and was about to overtake her, when she paused, and implored Gæa to protect her. The prayer was scarcely ended, when she found herself changed into a clump of reeds, which the panting lover embraced, thinking he had caught the maiden, who had stood in that very spot a few moments before.

His deception and disappointment were so severe, that they wrung from him a prolonged sigh, which, passing through the rustling reeds, produced plaintive tones. Pan, seeing Syrinx had gone forever, took seven pieces of the reed, of unequal lengths, bound them together, and fashioned from them a musical instrument, which was called by the name of the fair nymph.

> Fair, trembling Syrinx fled
> Arcadian Pan, with such a fearful dread.
> Poor nymph!—poor Pan!—how he did weep to find
> Naught but a lovely sighing of the wind
> Along the reedy stream; a half-heard strain
> Full of sweet desolation—balmy pain.
>
> KEATS

Pan was supposed to delight in slyly overtaking belated travelers and inspiring them with sudden and unfounded fears,—from him called "panic." He is generally represented with a syrinx and shepherd's crook, and a pine garland around his misshapen head.

SILVAN DEITIES

The Romans also worshiped three other divinities of nature entirely unknown to the Greeks; i.e., Silvanus, Faunus, and Fauna, the latter's wife, who had charge over the woods and plants. Priapus, god of the shade, was also a rural deity, but his worship was only known along the shores of the Hellespont.

FLORA AND ZEPHYRUS

The fairest among all the lesser gods was doubtless Flora, goddess of flowers, who married Zephyrus, the gentle god of the south wind, and wandered happily with him from place to place, scattering her favors with lavish generosity. She was principally worshiped by young girls, and the only offerings ever seen on her altars were fruits and garlands of beautiful flowers. Her festivals, generally celebrated in the month of May, were called the Floralia.

> Crowds of nymphs,
> Soft voiced, and young, and gay,
> In woven baskets bringing ears of corn,
> Roses and pinks and violets to adorn
> The shrine of Flora in her early May.
>
> KEATS

VERTUMNUS AND POMONA

Vertumnus and Pomona were the special divinities of the garden and orchard. They are represented with pruning knives and shears, gardening implements, and fruits and flowers. Pomona was very coy indeed, and had no desire to marry. Vertumnus, enamored of her charms, did his best to make her change her mind, but she would not even listen to his pleadings.

At last the lover had recourse to stratagem, disguised himself as an aged crone, entered Pomona's garden, and inquired how it happened that such a very charming young woman should remain so long unmarried. Then, having received a mocking answer, he began to argue with her, and finally extracted an avowal, that, among all the suitors, one alone was worthy of her love, Vertumnus. Vertumnus seized the favorable opportunity, revealed himself, and clasped her to his breast. Pomona, perceiving that she had hopelessly betrayed herself, no longer refused to wed, but allowed him to share her labors, and help her turn the luscious fruit to ripen in the autumn sunshine.

SEA DEITIES

The lesser divinities of the sea were almost as numerous as those of the land, and included the lovely Oceanides and Nereides, together with their male companions the Tritons, who generally formed Neptune's regal train.

"A FAVORABLE OPPORTUNITY." Thumann.
(Vertumnus and Pomona.)

Story of Glaucus

One of the lesser sea gods, Glaucus, was once a poor fisherman, who earned his daily bread by selling the fish he caught in his nets. On one occasion he made an extra fine haul, and threw his net full of fish down upon a certain kind of grass, which the flapping fish immediately nibbled, and, as if endowed with extraordinary powers, bounded back into the waves and swam away.

Greatly surprised at this occurrence, Glaucus began chewing a few blades of this peculiar grass, and immediately felt an insane desire to plunge into the sea,—a desire which soon became so intense, that he could no longer resist it, but dived down into the water. The mere contact with the salt waves sufficed to change his nature; and swimming about comfortably in the element, where he now found himself perfectly at home, he began to explore the depths of the sea.

> "I plung'd for life or death. To interknit
> One's senses with so dense a breathing stuff
> Might seem a work of pain; so not enough
> Can I admire how crystal-smooth it felt,
> And buoyant round my limbs. At first I dwelt
> Whole days and days in sheer astonishment;
> Forgetful utterly of self-intent;
> Moving but with the mighty ebb and flow.
> Then, like a new fledg'd bird that first doth show
> His spreaded feathers to the morrow chill,
> I try'd in fear the pinions of my will.
> 'Twas freedom! and at once I visited
> The ceaseless wonders of this ocean-bed."
>
>   Keats

Glaucus was worshiped most particularly by the fishermen and boatmen, whose vessels he was supposed to guard from evil, and whose nets were often filled to overflow through his intervention.

Chapter XXVII

THE TROJAN WAR

Jupiter, father of the gods, once fell deeply in love with a beautiful sea nymph named Thetis, the daughter of Nereus and Doris,—

> Thetis of the silver feet, and child
> Of the gray Ancient of the Deep.
>   HOMER (Bryant's tr.)

JUPITER AND THETIS

He was very anxious indeed to marry her, but, before taking such an important step, deemed it prudent to consult the Fates, who alone could inform him whether this union would be for his happiness or not. It was very fortunate for him that he did so, for the three sisters told him that Thetis was destined to be the mother of a son who would far outshine his father.

Jupiter carefully pondered this reply, and concluded to renounce the marriage rather than run any risk of being forced to surrender his power to one greater than he. Thetis' hand he then decreed should be given in marriage to Peleus, King of Athens, who had loved her faithfully, and had long sued in vain.

Thetis, however, was not at all anxious to accept the hand of a mere mortal after having enjoyed the attention of the gods (for Neptune also had wooed her), and demurred, until Jupiter promised his own and the gods' attendance at the marriage feast. The prospect of this signal honor reconciled the maiden, and the wedding preparations were made in the coral caves of her father, Nereus, beneath the foam-crested waves.

Thither, mindful of his promise, came Jupiter, with all the gods of Olympus.

> Then, with his Queen, the Father of the gods
> Came down from high Olympus' bright abodes;
> Came down, with all th' attending deities.
>
> CATULLUS

The guests took their seats, and pledged the bride and groom in brimming cups of wine,—Bacchus' wedding gift to Thetis. All was joy and merriment, when an uninvited guest suddenly appeared in the banquet-hall. All present immediately recognized Eris, or Discordia, goddess of discord, whose snaky locks, sour looks, and violent temper had caused her to be omitted from the wedding list,—

> The Abominable, that uninvited came
> Into the fair Peleian banquet-hall.
>
> TENNYSON

THE APPLE OF DISCORD

This omission angered her, and made her determine to have her revenge by troubling the harmony which evidently reigned among all the guests. For a moment she stood beside the bountiful board, then threw upon it a golden apple, and, exhaling over the assembly her poisoned breath, she vanished. The general attention was, of course, turned upon the golden fruit, whereon the inscription "To the fairest" was clearly traced.

All the ladies were at first inclined to contend for the prize; but little by little all the claimants withdrew except Juno, Minerva, and Venus, who hotly disputed for its possession. Juno declared that the queen of the gods, in her majesty and power, surely had the best right; Minerva, that the beauty of wisdom and knowledge far surpassed external charms; and Venus smiled, and archly requested to be informed who might assert greater claims than the goddess of beauty.

The dispute grew more and more bitter, and the irate goddesses called upon the guests to award the prize to the most deserving; but the guests, one and all, refused to act as umpires, for the apple could be given to but one, and the two others would be sure to vent their anger and disappointment upon the judge who passed over their charms in favor of a third. The final decision was therefore referred to Paris, who, although performing the lowly duties of a shepherd, was the son of Priam and Hecuba, King and Queen of Troy.

When but a babe, Paris had been exposed on a mountain to perish, because an oracle had predicted that he would cause the death of his family and the downfall of his native city. Although thus cruelly treated, he had not perished, but had been adopted by a shepherd, who made him follow his own calling.

PARIS AND ŒNONE

When Paris reached manhood, he was a very handsome and attractive young man, and won the love of Œnone, a beautiful nymph to whom he was secretly united. Their happiness, however, was but fleeting, for the Fates had decreed that Paris' love for the fair Œnone would soon die.

> The Fate,
> That rules the will of Jove, had spun the days
> Of Paris and Œnone.
> QUINTUS SMYRNÆUS (Elton's tr.)

JUDGMENT OF PARIS

Instead of lingering by the fair nymph's side, Paris wandered off to a lonely mountain top, where the three goddesses sought him to judge their quarrel. Minerva, in glittering armor, first appeared before his dazzled eyes, and proffered the bribe of extensive wisdom if he would but give her the preference.

Juno, queen of heaven, next appeared in royal robes and insignia, and whispered that he should have great wealth and unlimited power were he only to award the prize to her.

> She to Paris made
> Proffer of royal power, ample rule
> Unquestion'd, overflowing revenue
> Wherewith to embellish state, "from many a vale
> And river-sunder'd champaign clothed with corn,
> Or labor'd mine undrainable of ore.
> Honor," she said, "and homage, tax and toll,
> From many an inland town and haven large,
> Mast-throng'd beneath her shadowing citadel
> In glassy bays among her tallest towers."
>
> TENNYSON

But all Minerva's and Juno's charms and bribes were forgotten when Venus, in her magic cestus, appeared before the judge. This artful simplicity was the result of much thought, for we are told that

> Venus oft with anxious care
> Adjusted twice a single hair.
>
> COWPER

Then, trembling lest her efforts should prove vain, she gently drew near the youth, and softly promised him a bride as fair as herself, in return for the coveted golden apple.

Won either by her superior attractions or by her alluring bribe, Paris no longer hesitated, but placed the prize in her extended palm.

> Ere yet her speech was finished, he consign'd
> To her soft hand the fruit of burnished rind;
> And foam-born Venus grasp'd the graceful meed,
> Of war, of evil war, the quickening seed.
>
> COLUTHUS (Elton's tr.)

This act of partiality, of course, called down upon him the wrath and hatred of Juno and Minerva, who, biding their time, watched for a suitable opportunity to

PARIS. (Vatican, Rome.)

avenge themselves; while Venus, triumphant, and anxious to redeem her promise, directed Paris to return to Troy, make himself known to his parents,—who, the goddess promised, would welcome him warmly,—and obtain from them a fleet in which he might sail to Greece.

In obedience to these instructions, Paris ruthlessly abandoned the fair and faithful Œnone, and, joining a band of youthful shepherds, went to Troy, under pretext of witnessing a solemn festival. There he took part in the athletic games, distinguished himself, and attracted the attention of his sister Cassandra.

PARIS' RETURN TO TROY

This princess was noted for her beauty, and it is said had even been wooed by Apollo, who, hoping to win her favor, bestowed upon her the gift of prophecy. For some reason the god's suit had not prospered; and, as he could not take back the power conferred, he annulled it by making her hearers refuse to credit her words.

Cassandra immediately called her parents' attention to the extraordinary likeness Paris bore to her other brothers; and then, breaking out into a prophetic strain, she foretold that he would bring destruction upon his native city. Priam and Hecuba, scorning her prophecy, joyfully received their long-lost son, lovingly compelled him to take up his abode in their palace, and promised to atone for their past neglect by granting his every wish.

PARIS SAILS FOR GREECE

Still advised by Venus, Paris soon expressed a desire to sail for Greece, under the pretext of rescuing Hesione, his father's sister, whom Hercules had carried off, after besieging Troy. He was promptly provided with several well-manned galleys, and soon after appeared at the court of Menelaus, King of Sparta, whose young wife, Helen, was the most beautiful woman of her time, if we are to believe the testimony of her contemporaries.

Full threescore girls, in sportive flight we stray'd,
Like youths anointing, where along the glade
The baths of cool Eurotas limpid play'd.
But none, of all, with Helen might compare,
Nor one seem'd faultless of the fairest fair.
As morn, with vermeil visage, looks from high,
When solemn night has vanish'd suddenly;
When winter melts, and frees the frozen hours,
And spring's green bough is gemm'd with silvery flowers:
So bloom'd the virgin Helen in our eyes,
With full voluptuous limbs, and towering size:
In shape, in height, in stately presence fair,
Straight as a furrow gliding from the share;
A cypress of the gardens, spiring high,
A courser in the cars of Thessaly.
So rose-complexion'd Helen charm'd the sight;
Our Sparta's grace, our glory, and delight.

THEOCRITUS (Elton's tr.)

HELEN'S SUITORS

A daughter of Jupiter and Leda (whom Jove had courted in the guise of a snow-white swan), Helen had many suitors who ardently strove to win her favor. The noblest, bravest, and best came to woo and hoped to win; but all were left in suspense, as the maiden did not show any preference, and refused to make known her choice.

Tyndareus, Helen's stepfather, thinking the rejected suitors might attempt to steal her away from any husband she selected, proposed that all the candidates for her hand should take a solemn oath, binding themselves to respect the marital rights of the favored suitor, and help him regain possession of his wife should any one venture to kidnap her.

This was cause
To Tyndarus her father of much doubt,
To give, or not to give her, and how best
To make good fortune his: at length this thought
Occurr'd, that each to each the wooers give
Their oath, and plight their hands, and on the flames
Pour the libations, and with solemn vows
Bind their firm faith that him, who should obtain
The virgin for his bride, they all would aid;
If any dar'd to seize and bear her off,
And drive by force her husband from her bed,
All would unite in arms, and lay his town,
Greek or Barbaric, level with the ground.

EURIPIDES (Potter's tr.)

All agreed to this proposal, the oath was taken, and Helen, whose delibera-
tions had come to an end, bestowed her hand upon Menelaus, King of Sparta.

ABDUCTION OF HELEN

On his arrival at Sparta, in Lacedæmonia, Paris was received with graceful hospitality by Menelaus and Helen. He had not sojourned there many days, however,
before the king was called away from home, and departed, confiding to his wife the
care of entertaining his princely guest. During his absence, Paris, urged by Venus,
courted Helen so successfully, that she finally consented to elope with him, and
allowed herself to be borne away in triumph to Troy.

Then from her husband's stranger-sheltering home
He tempted Helen o'er the ocean foam.

COLUTHUS (Elton's tr.)

ABDUCTION OF HELEN. Deutsch.

PREPARATIONS FOR WAR

Menelaus, on his return from Crete, discovered his guest's treachery, and swore never to rest satisfied until he had recovered his truant wife, and punished her seducer. Messengers were sent in haste in every direction, to summon Helen's former suitors to keep their oath, and join Menelaus at Aulis with men and weapons. All came promptly at his call except Ulysses, King of Ithaca, who, to console himself for Helen's refusal of his suit, had married her cousin, Penelope, and had now no dearer wish than to linger by her side and admire his infant son, Telemachus.

ULYSSES FEIGNS MADNESS

In the presence of the messenger Palamedes, Ulysses feigned insanity, hoping thereby to elude the tedious journey to Troy; but the messenger was not so easily duped, and cleverly determined to ascertain the truth by stratagem. One day, therefore, when the king was plowing the seashore with an ox and horse harnessed together, and sowing this strange field with salt, Palamedes placed the babe Telemachus in the furrow, directly in front of the plow, and marked how skillfully Ulysses turned his ill-assorted team aside to avoid harming his heir. This action sufficed to prove to Palamedes that the king had not lost all control of his senses, and enabled him to force Ulysses to obey Menelaus' summons.

AGAMEMNON MADE CHIEF

At Aulis the assembled army with unanimous consent elected Agamemnon, Menelaus' brother, chief of the expedition, which numbered, among many others, Nestor, noted for his wise counsel; Ajax, gigantic in strength and courage; and Diomedes, the renowned warrior.

The troops were assembled, the vessels freighted; but before they departed, the chiefs considered it expedient to consult an oracle, to ascertain whether their expedition was destined to succeed. In a somewhat veiled and ambiguous manner, they received answer that Troy could never be taken without the aid of the son of Peleus and Thetis, Achilles, of whom the Fates had predicted that he would surpass his father in greatness.

ACHILLES' EARLY LIFE

Thetis loved this only child so dearly, that when he was but a babe, she had carried him to the banks of the Styx, whose waters had the magic power of rendering all the parts they touched invulnerable. Premising that her son would be a great warrior, and thus exposed to great danger, she plunged him wholly into the tide with the exception of one heel, by which she held him, and then returned home.

Some time after, an oracle foretold that Achilles would die beneath the walls of Troy from a wound in his heel, the only vulnerable part of his body. With many tears Thetis vowed that her son should never leave her to encounter such a fate, and intrusted the care of his education to the Centaur Chiron, who had taught all the greatest heroes in turn.

From this instructor Achilles learned the arts of war, wrestling, poetry, music, and song,—all, in short, that an accomplished Greek warrior was expected to know,—and, when his studies were finished, returned to his father's court to gladden his fond mother's heart by his presence.

Thetis' joy was all turned to grief, however, when rumors of the war imminent between Greece and Troy came to her ears. She knew her son would soon be summoned, and, to prevent his going, sent him off to the court of Lycomedes, where, under some pretext, he was prevailed upon to assume a disguise and mingle with the king's daughters and their handmaidens.

One messenger after another was dispatched to summon Achilles to join the fleet at Aulis, but one after another returned without having seen him, or being able to ascertain where he was hiding. The Greeks, however anxious to depart, dared not sail without him. They were in despair, until Ulysses, the wily, proposed a plan, and offered to carry it out.

> Ulysses, man of many arts,
> Son of Laertes, reared in Ithaca,
> That rugged isle, and skilled in every form
> Of shrewd device and action wisely planned.
>
> HOMER (Bryant's tr.)

Ulysses Discovers Achilles

Arrayed in peddler's garb, with a pack upon his shoulders, Ulysses entered Lycomedes' palace, where he shrewdly suspected Achilles was concealed, and offered his wares for sale. The maidens selected trinkets; but one of them, closely veiled, seized a weapon concealed among the ornaments, and brandished it with such skill, that Ulysses saw through the assumed disguise, explained his presence and purpose, and by his eloquence persuaded the young Achilles to accompany him to Aulis.

The Greeks were now ready to embark; but no favorable wind came to swell the sails, which day after day hung limp and motionless against the tall masts of their vessels.

> The troops
> Collected and imbodied, here we sit
> Inactive, and from Aulis wish to sail
> In vain.
>
> Euripides (Potter's tr.)

Sacrifice of Iphigenia

Calchas, the soothsayer of the expedition, was again consulted, to discover how they might best win the favor of the gods; and the reply given purported that no favorable wind would blow until Iphigenia, daughter of Agamemnon, was offered up in sacrifice to appease the everlasting gods.

Many other propitiatory methods were tried; but as they all proved ineffective, Agamemnon, urged by his companions, sent for his daughter, feigning that he wished to celebrate her nuptials with Achilles before his departure.

> I wrote, I seal'd
> A letter to my wife, that she should send
> Her daughter, to Achilles as a bride
> Affianc'd.
>
> Euripides (Potter's tr.)

Iphigenia came to her father secretly delighted at being the chosen bride of such a hero; but, instead of being led to the hymeneal altar, she was dragged to the place of sacrifice, where the priest, with uplifted knife, was about to end her sufferings, when Diana suddenly appeared, snatched her up in a cloud, and left in her stead a deer, which was duly sacrificed, while Iphigenia was borne in safety to Tauris, where she became a priestess in one of the goddess's temples.

ARRIVAL AT TROY

The gods were now propitious, and the wind slowly rose, filled the sails of the waiting vessels, and wafted them swiftly and steadily over the sea to the Trojan shores, where an army stood ready to prevent the Greek troops from disembarking. The invaders were eager to land to measure their strength against the Trojans; yet all hesitated to leave the ships, for an oracle had foretold that the first warrior who attempted to land would meet with instant death.

> "The Delphic oracle foretold
> That the first Greek who touched the Trojan strand
> Should die."
>
> WORDSWORTH

PROTESILAUS AND LAODAMIA

Protesilaus, a brave chief, seeing his comrades' irresolution, and animated by a spirit of self-sacrifice, sprang boldly ashore, and perished, slain by the enemy, as soon as his foot had touched the foreign soil. When the tidings of his death reached his beloved wife, Laodamia, whom he had left in Thessaly, they well-nigh broke her heart; and in her despair she entreated the gods to let her die, or allow her to see her lord once more, were it but for a moment. Her appeal was so touching, that the gods could not refuse to hear it, and bade Mercury conduct her husband's shade back to earth, to tarry with her for three hours' time.

"Such grace hath crowned thy prayer,
Laodamia! that at Jove's command
Thy husband walks the paths of upper air:
He comes to tarry with thee three hours' space;
Accept the gift, behold him face to face!"

WORDSWORTH

With an inarticulate cry of joy, Laodamia beheld the beloved countenance of Protesilaus once more, and from his own lips heard the detailed account of his early death. The three hours passed all too quickly in delicious intercourse; and when Mercury reappeared to lead him back to Hades, the loving wife, unable to endure a second parting, died of grief.

The same grave, it is said, was the resting place of this united pair, and kind-hearted nymphs planted elm trees over their remains. These trees grew "until they were high enough to command a view of Troy, and then withered away, while fresh branches sprang from the roots."

Upon the side
Of Hellespont (such faith was entertained)
A knot of spiry trees for ages grew
From out the tomb of him for whom she died;
And ever, when such stature they had gained
That Ilium's walls were subject to their view,
The trees' tall summits withered at the sight;
A constant interchange of growth and blight!

WORDSWORTH

Hostilities had now begun, and the war between the conflicting hosts was waged with equal courage and skill. During nine long years of uninterrupted strife, the Greeks' efforts to enter Troy, or Ilium, as it was also called, were vain, as were also the Trojans' attempts to force the foe to leave their shores. This memorable struggle is the theme of many poems. The oldest and most renowned of all, the *Iliad*, begins with the story of the tenth and last year's events.

CHRYSEIS AND BRISEIS

Among a number of captives taken in a skirmish by the Hellenic troops, were two beautiful maidens, Chryseis, daughter of Chryses, priest of Apollo, and Briseis. The prisoners were, as usual, allotted to various chiefs, and Agamemnon received the priest's daughter as reward for his bravery, while Achilles triumphantly led to his tent the equally fair Briseis.

When Chryses heard that his child had fallen into the hands of the enemy, he hastened to Agamemnon's tent to offer a rich ransom for her recovery; but the aged father's entreaties were all unheeded, and he was dismissed with many heartless taunts. Exasperated by this cruel treatment, he raised his hands to heaven, and implored Apollo to avenge the insults he had received by sending down upon the Greeks all manner of evil. This prayer was no sooner heard than answered, by the sun god's sending a terrible plague to decimate the enemy's troops.

> The aged man indignantly withdrew;
> And PhŒbus—for the priest was dear to him—
> Granted his prayer, and sent among the Greeks
> A deadly shaft. The people of the camp
> Were perishing in heaps.
>
> HOMER (Bryant's tr.)

The Greeks, in terror, now consulted an oracle to know why this calamity had come upon them, and how they might check the progress of the deadly disease which was so rapidly reducing their forces. They were told that the plague would never cease until Agamemnon surrendered his captive, and thus disarmed Apollo's wrath, which had been kindled by his rude refusal to comply with the aged priest's request.

All the Greek chiefs, assembled in council, decided to send Achilles to Agamemnon to apprise him of their wish that he should set Chryseis free,—a wish which he immediately consented to grant, if Briseis were given him in exchange.

The plague was raging throughout the camp; the cries of the sufferers rent the air; many had already succumbed to the scourge, and all were threatened with an inglorious death. Achilles, mindful of all this, and anxious to save his beloved companions, consented to comply with this unreasonable request; but at the same time he swore, that, if Agamemnon really took his captive away, he would not strike another blow.

Chryseis was immediately consigned to the care of a herald, who led her back to her aged father's arms. Ready to forgive all, now that his child was restored to him, Chryses implored Apollo to stay his hand, and the plague instantly ceased.

As for Agamemnon, he sent his slaves to Achilles' tent to lead away Briseis; and the hero, true to his promise, laid aside his armor, determined to fight no more.

> The great Achilles, swift of foot, remained
> Within his ships, indignant for the sake
> Of the fair-haired Briseis.
> HOMER (Bryant's tr.)

ACHILLES' WRATH

Thetis, hearing of the wanton insult offered her son, left her coral caves, ascended to Olympus, cast herself at Jupiter's feet, and with many tears tremulously prayed he would avenge Achilles and make the Greeks fail in all their attempts as long as her son's wrath remained unappeased.

Jupiter, touched by her beauty and distress, frowned until the very firmament shook, and swore to make the Greeks rue the day they left their native shores,

> To give Achilles honor and to cause
> Myriads of Greeks to perish by their fleet.
> HOMER (Bryant's tr.)

AGAMEMNON MISLED

In consequence of a treacherous dream purposely sent by Jupiter to delude him, Agamemnon again assembled his troops, and proposed a new onslaught upon the Trojan forces. But when the army was drawn up in battle array, Hector, the eldest son of Priam, and therefore leader of his army, stepping forward, proposed that the prolonged quarrel should be definitely settled by a single combat between Paris and Menelaus.

> Hector then stood forth and said:
> "Hearken, ye Trojans and ye nobly-armed
> Achaians, to what Paris says by me.
> He bids the Trojans and the Greeks lay down
> Their shining arms upon the teeming earth,
> And he and Menelaus, loved of Mars,
> Will strive in single combat, on the ground
> Between the hosts, for Helen and her wealth;
> And he who shall o'ercome, and prove himself
> The better warrior, to his home shall bear
> The treasure and the woman, while the rest
> Shall frame a solemn covenant of peace."
>
> HOMER (Bryant's tr.)

MENELAUS AND PARIS FIGHT

This proposal having been received favorably, Menelaus and Paris soon engaged in a duel, which was witnessed by both armies, by Helen and Priam from the Trojan walls, and by the everlasting gods from the wooded heights of Mount Ida; but in the very midst of the fight, Venus, seeing her favorite about to succumb, suddenly snatched him away from the battlefield, and bore him unseen to his chamber, where he was joined by Helen, who bitterly reproached him for his cowardly flight.

Indignant at this interference on Venus' part, the gods decreed that the war should be renewed; and Minerva, assuming the form of a Trojan warrior, aimed an arrow at Menelaus, who was vainly seeking his vanished opponent. This act of treachery was the signal for a general call to arms and a renewal of hostilities. Countless deeds of valor were now performed by the heroes on both sides, and also by the gods, who mingled in the ranks and even fought against each other, until recalled by Jupiter, and forbidden to fight any more.

PARTING OF HECTOR AND ANDROMACHE. Maignan.

HECTOR AND ANDROMACHE

For a little while fortune seemed to favor the Greeks; and Hector, hastening back to Troy, bade his mother go to the temple with all her women, and endeavor by her prayers and gifts to propitiate Minerva and obtain her aid. Then he hastened off in search of his wife Andromache and little son Astyanax, whom he wished to embrace once more before rushing out to battle and possible death.

He found his palace deserted, and, upon questioning the women, heard that his wife had gone to the Scæan Gate, where he now drove as fast as his noble steeds could drag him. There, at the gate, took place the parting scene, which has deservedly been called the most pathetic in all the *Iliad*, in which Andromache vainly tried to detain her husband within the walls, while Hector gently reproved her, and demonstrated that his duty called him out upon the field of battle, where he must hold his own if he would not see the city taken, the Trojans slain, and the women, including his mother and beloved Andromache, borne away into bitter captivity.

Andromache
Pressed to his side meanwhile, and, all in tears,
Clung to his hand, and, thus beginning, said:—
   "Too brave! thy valor yet will cause thy death.
Thou hast no pity on thy tender child,
Nor me, unhappy one, who soon must be
Thy widow. All the Greeks will rush on thee
To take thy life. A happier lot were mine,
If I must lose thee, to go down to earth,
For I shall have no hope when thou art gone,—
Nothing but sorrow. Father have I none,
And no dear mother.

*   *   *   *   *   *

> Hector, thou
> Art father and dear mother now to me,
> And brother and my youthful spouse besides.
> In pity keep within the fortress here,
> Nor make thy child an orphan nor thy wife
> A widow."
>   Then answered Hector, great in war: "All this
> I bear in mind, dear wife; but I should stand
> Ashamed before the men and long-robed dames
> Of Troy, were I to keep aloof and shun
> The conflict, coward-like."
>   HOMER (Bryant's tr.)

Then he stretched out his arms for his infant son, who, however, shrank back affrighted at the sight of his brilliant helmet and nodding plumes, and would not go to him until he had set the gleaming headdress aside. After a passionate prayer for his little heir's future welfare, Hector gave the child back to Andromache, and, with a last farewell embrace, sprang into his chariot and drove away.

> "Sorrow not thus, beloved one, for me.
> No living man can send me to the shades
> Before my time; no man of woman born,
> Coward or brave, can shun his destiny.
> But go thou home, and tend thy labors there,—
> The web, the distaff,—and command thy maids
> To speed the work. The cares of war pertain
> To all men born in Troy, and most to me."
>   HOMER (Bryant's tr.)

GREEKS REPELLED

Paris, ashamed now of his former flight, soon joined his brother upon the battle-field, and together they performed many deeds of valor. The time had now come when Jupiter was about to redeem the promise given to Thetis, for little by little the Greeks were forced to yield before the might of the Trojans, who, stimulated by their partial success, and fired by Hector's example, performed miracles of valor, and finally drove their assailants into their intrenchments.

Death and defeat now dogged the very footsteps of the Greek forces, who were driven, inch by inch, away from the walls, ever nearer the place where their vessels rode at anchor. They now ardently longed for the assistance of Achilles, whose mere presence, in days gone by, had filled the Trojan hearts with terror; but the hero, although Briseis had been returned unmolested, paid no heed to their entreaties for aid, and remained a sullen and indifferent spectator of their flight, while the Trojans began to set fire to some of the vessels of their fleet.

> The goddess-born Achilles, swift of foot,
> Beside his ships still brooded o'er his wrath,
> Nor came to counsel with the illustrious chiefs,
> Nor to the war, but suffered idleness
> To eat his heart away; for well he loved
> Clamor and combat.
>
> HOMER (Bryant's tr.)

Discouraged by all these reverses, in spite of their brave resistance, the Greeks, in despair, concluded that the gods had entirely forsaken them, and beat a hasty and ignominious retreat to the shore, closely followed by the enemy, who uttered loud cries of triumph.

PATROCLUS DONS ACHILLES' ARMOR

Patroclus, Achilles' intimate friend, then hastened to the hero's side to inform him of his comrades' flight, and implore him once more to rescue them from inevitable death. But Achilles, summoning all his pride to his assistance, did not waver in his resolve. Suddenly Patroclus remembered that the mere sight of Achilles' armor might suffice to arrest the enemy's advance and produce a diversion in favor of the Greeks: so he asked permission to wear it and lead the Myrmidons, Achilles' trusty followers, into the fray.

> Send me at least into the war,
> And let me lead thy Myrmidons, that thus
> The Greeks may have some gleam of hope. And give
> The armor from thy shoulders. I will wear
> Thy mail, and then the Trojans, at the sight,
> May think I am Achilles, and may pause
> From fighting, and the warlike sons of Greece,
> Tired as they are, may breathe once more, and gain
> A respite from the conflict.
>
> HOMER (Bryant's tr.)

Achilles had sworn, it is true, not to return to the scene of strife, but was quite willing to lend men and arms, if they might be of any use, and immediately placed them at his friend's disposal. Hastily Patroclus donned the glittering armor, called aloud to the Myrmidons to follow his lead, and rushed forth to encounter the enemy.

DEATH OF PATROCLUS

The Trojans paused in dismay, thinking Achilles had come, and were about to take flight, when all at once they discovered the fraud. With renewed courage, they opposed the Greek onslaught. Many heroes bit the dust in this encounter, among others Sarpedon, the son of Jupiter and Europa,—whose remains were borne away from the battlefield by the twin divinities Sleep and Death,—ere Hector, son of Priam, and chief among the Trojan warriors, challenged Patroclus to single combat. Needless to say, the two closed in deadly battle, and fought with equal valor, until Patroclus, already exhausted by his previous efforts, and betrayed by the gods, finally succumbed.

> The hero fell
> With clashing mail, and all the Greeks beheld
> His fall with grief.
>
> HOMER (Bryant's tr.)

With a loud cry of victory, Hector wrenched the armor off the mangled corpse, and quickly withdrew to array himself in the brilliant spoils. The tidings of Patroclus' fall spread rapidly all through the Grecian camp, and reached Achilles, who wept aloud when he heard that his beloved friend, who had left him but a short time before full of life and energy, was now no more. So noisily did the hero mourn his loss, that Thetis, in the quiet ocean depths, heard his groans, and rushed to his side to ascertain their cause.

ACHILLES' GRIEF

Into his mother's sympathetic ear Achilles poured the whole story of his grief and loss, while she gently strove to turn his thoughts aside from the sad event, and arouse an interest for some pursuit less dangerous than war. All her efforts were vain, however; for Achilles' soul thirsted for revenge, and he repeatedly swore he would go forth and slay his friend's murderer.

> No wish
> Have I to live, or to concern myself
> In men's affairs, save this: that Hector first,
> Pierced by my spear, shall yield his life, and pay
> The debt of vengeance for Patroclus slain.
> HOMER (Bryant's tr.)

Then, in sudden dread lest Hector should fall by another's hand, or withdraw from the battlefield and thus escape his vengeance, Achilles would have rushed from his tent unarmed; but his mother prevailed upon him to wait until the morrow, when she promised to bring him a full suit of armor from Vulcan's own hand. Rapidly Thetis then traversed the wide space which separates the coast of Asia Minor from Mount Ætna, where Vulcan labored at his forge.

> She found him there
> Sweating and toiling, and with busy hand
> Plying the bellows.
> HOMER (Bryant's tr.)

ACHILLES' ARMOR

Arrived before him, she breathlessly made known her errand, and the god promised that the arms should be ready within the given time, and immediately set to work to fashion them. By his skillful hands the marvelous weapons were forged; and when the first streak of light appeared above the horizon, he consigned them to Thetis, who hastened back to her son's tent, where she found him still bewailing the loss of Patroclus.

During Thetis' absence, messengers had come to Achilles' tent to warn him that Patroclus' body was still in the enemy's hands, and to implore him to come and rescue the precious corpse. Mindful of his promise to his mother, Achilles still refused to fight, but, springing upon the rampart, uttered his mighty war-cry, the sound of which filled the enemy's hearts with terror, and made them yield to the well-directed onslaught of Ajax and Diomedes, who finally succeeded in recovering the body, which they then reverently bore to Achilles' tent.

To console Achilles for his friend's death, Thetis exhibited the glorious armor she had just obtained, helped him put it on, and then bade him go forth and conquer.

> "Leave we the dead, my son, since it hath pleased
> The gods that he should fall; and now receive
> This sumptuous armor, forged by Vulcan's hand,
> Beautiful, such as no man ever wore."
>
> HOMER (Bryant's tr.)

DEATH OF HECTOR

Thus armed, mounted in his chariot drawn by his favorite steeds, and driven by his faithful charioteer Automedon, Achilles went forth to battle, and finally seeing Hector, whom alone he wished to meet, he rushed upon him with a hoarse cry of rage. The Trojan hero, at the mere sight of the deadly hatred which shone in Achilles' eyes, turned to flee. Achilles pursued him, and taunted him with his cowardice, until Hector turned and fought with all the courage and recklessness of despair.

Their blows fell like hail, a cloud of dust enveloped their struggling forms, and the anxious witnesses only heard the dull thud of the blows and the metallic

THETIS BEARING THE ARMOR OF ACHILLES. Gérard.

clash of the weapons. Suddenly there came a loud cry, then all was still; and when the dust-cloud had blown away, the Trojans from the ramparts, where they had waited in agony for the issue of the fight, beheld Achilles tear the armor from their champion's body, bind the corpse to his chariot, and drive nine times round the city walls, Hector's princely head dragging in the dust. Priam, Hecuba, and Andromache, Hector's beautiful young wife, tearfully watched this ignominious treatment, and finally saw Achilles drive off to the spot where Patroclus' funeral pile was laid, and there abandon the corpse.

Achilles then returned to his tent, where for a long time he continued to mourn his friend's untimely end, refusing to be comforted.

The Gods' Decree

The gods, from their celestial abode, had also witnessed this heartrending scene, and now Jupiter sent Iris to Thetis, and bade her hasten down to Achilles and command him to restore Hector's body to his mourning family. He also directed Mercury to lead Priam, unseen, into Achilles' tent, to claim and bear away his son's desecrated corpse. Thetis, seeking Achilles in his tent, announced the will of Jove:—

>   I am come
>   A messenger from Jove, who bids me say
>   The immortals are offended, and himself
>   The most, that thou shouldst in thy spite detain
>   The corse of Hector at the beaked ships,
>   Refusing its release. Comply thou, then,
>   And take the ransom and restore the dead.
>   HOMER (Bryant's tr.)

Return of Hector's Body

Mercury acquitted himself with his usual dispatch, and soon guided Priam in safety through the Grecian camp to Achilles' tent, where the aged king fell at the hero's feet, humbly pleading for his son's body, and proffering a princely ransom in exchange.

Achilles, no longer able to refuse this entreaty, and touched by a father's tears, consigned Hector's corpse to the old man's care, and promised an armistice of fourteen days, that the funeral rites in both camps might be celebrated with all due pomp and solemnity; and with the burial of Hector the *Iliad* comes to a close.

DEATH OF PENTHESILEA

At the end of the truce the hostilities were renewed, and the Trojans were reinforced by the arrival of Penthesilea, queen of the Amazons, who, with a chosen troop of warrior maidens, came to offer her aid. The brave queen afforded them, however, only temporary relief, as she was slain by Achilles in their very first encounter.

He, too, however, was doomed to die "in the flower of his youth and beauty," and the Fates had almost finished spinning his thread of life. In an early skirmish, while in close pursuit of the Trojans, Thetis' son had once caught sight of Polyxena, daughter of Priam, and had been deeply smitten by her girlish charms. He now vainly tried to make peace between the conflicting nations, hoping that, were the war but ended, he might obtain her hand in marriage.

DEATH OF ACHILLES

His efforts to make peace failed; but at last he prevailed upon Priam to celebrate his betrothal with Polyxena, with the stipulation that the marriage would take place as soon as the war was over. The betrothal ceremony was held without the city gates; and Achilles was just about to part from his blushing betrothed, when Paris, ever treacherous, stole behind him and shot a poisoned arrow into his vulnerable heel, thus slaying the hero who had caused so many brave warriors to bite the dust.

> Thus great Achilles, who had shown his zeal
> In healing wounds, died of a wounded heel.
>
> O. W. HOLMES

His armor—the glorious armor forged by Vulcan—was hotly contested for by Ulysses and Ajax. The former finally obtained the coveted weapons; and Ajax' grief at their loss was so intense, that he became insane, and killed himself in a fit of frenzy, while Polyxena, inconsolable at her betrothed's death, committed suicide on the magnificent tomb erected over his remains on the Trojan plain.

PHILOCTETES' ARROWS

The oracles, silent so long, now announced that Troy could never be taken without the poisoned arrows of Hercules, then in the keeping of Philoctetes. This hero had started with the expedition, but had been put ashore on the Island of Lemnos on account of a wound in his foot, which had become so offensive that none of the ship's company could endure his presence on board.

Ten long years had already elapsed since then, and, although a party of Greeks immediately set out in search of him, they had but little hope of finding him alive. They nevertheless wended their way to the cave where they had deposited him, where, to their unbounded surprise, they still found him. The wound had not healed, but he had managed to exist by killing such game as came within reach of his hand.

> Exposed to the inclement skies,
> Deserted and forlorn he lies;
> No friend or fellow-mourner there,
> To soothe his sorrows, and divide his care;
> Or seek the healing plant, of power to 'suage
> His aching wound, and mitigate its rage.
>   SOPHOCLES (Francklin's tr.)

Incensed by the Greeks' former cruel desertion, no entreaty could now induce Philoctetes to accompany the messengers to Troy, until Hercules appeared to him in a dream, and bade him go without delay, for there he would find Machaon, Æsculapius' son, who was to heal his wound.

DEATH OF PARIS AND ŒNONE

The dream was realized. Philoctetes, whole once more, joined the Greek host, and caused great dismay in the enemy's ranks with his poisoned arrows. One of his deadly missiles even struck Paris, and, as the poison entered his veins, it caused him grievous suffering. Paris then remembered that his first love, Œnone, who knew all remedies and the best modes of applying them, had once told him to send for her should he ever be wounded. He therefore sent for Œnone; but she, justly offended by the base desertion and long neglect of her lover, refused her aid, and let him die in torture. When he was dead, Œnone repented of this decision; and when the flames of his funeral pyre rose around him, she rushed into their midst, and was burned to death on his corpse.

> But when she gain'd the broader vale and saw
> The ring of faces redden'd by the flames
> Infolding that dark body which had lain
> Of old in her embrace, paused—and then ask'd
> Falteringly, "Who lies on yonder pyre?"
> But every man was mute for reverence.
> Then moving quickly forward till the heat
> Smote on her brow, she lifted up a voice
> Of shrill command, "Who burns upon the pyre?"
> Whereon their oldest and their boldest said,
> "He, whom thou would'st not heal!" and all at once
> The morning light of happy marriage broke,
> Thro' all the clouded years of widowhood,
> And muffling up her comely head, and crying
> "Husband!" she leapt upon the funeral pile,
> And mixt herself with him and past in fire.
>
>   TENNYSON

THE PALLADIUM

Two of Priam's sons had already expired, and yet Troy had not fallen into the hands of the Greeks, who now heard another prophecy, to the effect that Troy could never be taken as long as the Palladium—a sacred statue of Minerva, said to have fallen from heaven—remained within its walls. So Ulysses and Diomedes in disguise effected an entrance into the city one night, and after many difficulties succeeded in escaping with the precious image.

THE WOODEN HORSE

Men and chiefs, impatient of further delay, now joyfully hailed Ulysses' proposal to take the city by stratagem. They therefore secretly built a colossal wooden horse, within whose hollow sides a number of brave warriors might lie concealed. The main army feigned weariness of the endless enterprise, and embarked, leaving the horse as a pretended offering to Neptune; while Sinon, a shrewd slave, remained to persuade the Trojans to drag the horse within their gates and keep him there, a lasting monument of their hard-won triumph.

To the unbounded joy of the long-besieged Trojans, the Greek fleet then sailed away, until the Island of Tenedos hid the ships from view. All the inhabitants of Troy poured out of the city to view the wooden horse, and question Sinon, who pretended to have great cause of complaint against the Greeks, and strongly advised them to secure their last offering to Neptune.

The Trojans hailed this idea with rapture; but Laocoon, Neptune's priest, implored them to leave the horse alone, lest they should bring untold evil upon their heads.

> "Wretched countrymen," he cries,
> "What monstrous madness blinds your eyes?
>
> *   *   *   *   *   *
>
> Perchance—who knows?—these planks of deal
> A Grecian ambuscade conceal,
> Or 'tis a pile to o'erlook the town,
> And pour from high invaders down,
> Or fraud lurks somewhere to destroy:
> Mistrust, mistrust it, men of Troy!"
>
> VIRGIL (Conington's tr.)

DEATH OF LAOCOON

Deaf to all warnings and entreaties, they dragged the colossal image into the very heart of their city, tearing down a portion of their ramparts to allow its passage, while Laocoon hastened down to the shore to offer sacrifice to the gods. As he stood there by the improvised altar, with one of his sons on either side to assist him

LAOCOON.
(Vatican, Rome.)

in his office, two huge serpents came out of the sea, coiled themselves around him and his sons, and crushed and bit them to death.

> Unswerving they
> Toward Laocoon hold their way;
> First round his two young sons they wreathe,
> And grind their limbs with savage teeth:
> Then, as with arms he comes to aid,
> The wretched father they invade
> And twine in giant folds: twice round
> His stalwart waist their spires are wound,
> Twice round his neck, while over all
> Their heads and crests tower high and tall.
> He strains his strength their knots to tear,
> While gore and slime his fillets smear,
> And to the unregardful skies
> Sends up his agonizing cries.
>   VIRGIL (Conington's tr.)

The awestruck witnesses of this terrible scene, of course, declared that the gods resented his interference concerning the wooden horse, and had justly punished the sacrilegious hand which had dared strike it with a spear, merely to demonstrate, that, being hollow, it might contain an armed band. Ever since then, Laocoon and his sons' struggle with the serpents has been a favorite subject for poets and artists.

FALL OF TROY

In the mean while, the Greeks had been hiding behind Tenedos; but when night came on, they returned to the site of their ten-years' encampment, and were let into the city by Sinon, who also released their companions from their prison within the wooden horse. Although taken by surprise, the city guards made desperate attempts to repel the Greeks; but it was now too late, for the enemy had already broken into houses and palaces, and were killing, pillaging, and burning all in their way.

The melancholy years,
The miserable melancholy years,
Crept onward till the midnight terror came,
And by the glare of burning streets I saw
Palace and temple reel in ruin and fall,
And the long-baffled legions, bursting in
Through gate and bastion, blunted sword and spear
With unresisted slaughter.

LEWIS MORRIS

The royal family, even, was not exempt from the general massacre; and the aged Priam, who lived to see his last son perish before his eyes, finally found relief in death.

RETURN OF THE GREEKS

Their object accomplished, the Greeks immediately sailed for home, their vessels heavily laden with plunder and slaves. But the homeward journey was not as joyful as might have been expected; and many, after escaping from the enemy's hands, perished in the waves, or found death lying in wait for them by their own fireside.

Menelaus, with his wife Helen, who, in spite of the added ten years, retained all her youthful beauty, were detained in Egypt by contrary winds, sent to punish them for omitting the usual sacrifice to the gods. He at last consulted Proteus, who revealed how the wrath of the gods could best be allayed, and how favorable winds could be secured to waft him home.

As for Agamemnon, leader of the Greeks, he returned to Argos only to be murdered by his wife Clytæmnestra and her paramour Ægisthus.

"Ægisthus, bent upon my death,
Plotted against me with my guilty wife,
And bade me to his house, and slew me there,
Even at the banquet."

HOMER (Bryant's tr.)

Then, mortally afraid lest Orestes, Agamemnon's son, should avenge his father's death, Ægisthus prepared to slay him too; but Electra, the boy's sister, discovering this intention, helped him to escape, and placed him under the fatherly protection of Strophius, King of Phocis, whose son, Pylades, became his inseparable friend. In fact, their devotion to each other was so great, that it has become proverbial in every tongue.

Electra had not forgotten her father's base murder, although years had elapsed since it occurred; and when Orestes had attained manhood, she bade him come and punish those who had committed the crime. Orestes came, slew Ægisthus and Clytæmnestra, and then, terrified at what he had done, took flight, but only to be pursued by the Furies and Nemesis, goddess of revenge, sent by the gods to punish him for taking justice into his own hands.

Arrived at Delphi, Orestes consulted the oracle, and learned that his crime would be forgiven if he brought a statue of Diana in Tauris back to Greece. The young prince hastened thither, accompanied by the ever-faithful Pylades, who never left his side; and there, in a temple, he found his long-lost sister Iphigenia, who helped him obtain the image he sought, and accompanied him back to his native land, where Nemesis left him forever.

Chapter XXVIII

ADVENTURES OF ULYSSES

The Greek chiefs, on their return from Troy, were, as we have seen, all more or less visited by the wrath of the gods; but none of them endured as many hardships as Ulysses (Odysseus), King of Ithaca, the hero of Homer's world-renowned epic the *Odyssey*. During ten long years he roamed the seas, driven away from his native land by adverse winds, sailing about from place to place, losing his ships and companions, until at last the gods allowed him to return home. His marvelous adventures and numerous mishaps during these ten years form the theme of the *Odyssey*, which is about as follows.

Siege of Ismarus

After leaving Troy in ruins, Ulysses embarked with his men and spoils, and, favored by a good wind, soon came within sight of Ismarus, the home of the worthy and wealthy Ciconians. To increase the riches he was carrying home, he proposed to his army to land and storm the city,—a proposal which was enthusiastically received and immediately carried out.

But when the men collected near the fleet, instead of embarking as Ulysses urged them to do, they began to drink the rich wine, to roast oxen whole, and to indulge in games and revelry. While they were thus employed and entirely off their guard, the neighbors and allies of the Ciconians came upon them unawares, and put many to death.

The Greeks, although taken by surprise, fought bravely; but it was only when the sun was fast sinking, that they finally embarked, and left the fatal Ciconian shores.

Onward we sailed, lamenting bitterly
Our comrades slain, yet happy to escape
From death ourselves.

HOMER (Bryant's tr.)

THE LOTUS-EATERS

A hurricane soon arose. The flying clouds blotted the stars from view. The vessels, with broken masts and torn sails, were driven far out of their course, and, after ten days, reached the land of the Lotophagi or Lotus-eaters,—a people whose sole food consisted of lotus fruit and blossoms.

Three of Ulysses' best men were sent ashore to reconnoiter; but they had not gone very far before they met the natives, seated under their favorite trees, banqueting on their sweet food. These received the strangers hospitably, and made them partake of the lotus blossoms; but no sooner had the three men done so, than all recollection of their waiting companions or distant homes passed from their minds, while a dreamy, lethargic sensation stole over them, and made them long to recline there and feast forever.

Whoever tasted once of that sweet food
Wished not to see his native country more,
Nor give his friends the knowledge of his fate.
And then my messengers desired to dwell
Among the Lotus-eaters, and to feed
Upon the lotus, never to return.

HOMER (Bryant's tr.)

Ulysses impatiently watched for their return; then, seeing they did not appear, feared some evil had befallen them, and set out, with a few well-armed men, to go in search of them. Instead of finding them in chains, as he fully expected, he soon perceived them feasting among the Lotus-eaters. Their eyes had lost all animation, and rested upon him in a vague, dreamy way, which aroused his suspicions. At the same moment some of the Lotus-eaters advanced to invite him and his troop to join in their feast.

Branches they bore of that enchanted stem,
Laden with flower and fruit, whereof they gave
To each, but whoso did receive of them,
And taste, to him the gushing of the wave
Far, far away did seem to mourn and rave
On alien shores; and if his fellow spake,
His voice was thin, as voices from the grave;
And deep asleep he seem'd, yet all awake,
And music in his ears his beating heart did make.

TENNYSON

In peremptory tones Ulysses quickly forbade his men to taste of the magic food, directed them to seize and bind their unwilling comrades, and forcibly take them back to their ships. There the magic effect of the lotus food soon wore away, and the men rowed steadily westward, until they came to the Island of Sicily, then inhabited by the Cyclopes, a rude race of one-eyed giants.

A single ball of sight was fix'd
In their mid-forehead: hence the Cyclops' name:
For that one circular eye was broad infix'd
In the mid-forehead:—strength was theirs, and force,
And craft of curious toil.

HESIOD (Elton's tr.)

The main part of the fleet was stationed at another island not far distant, but Ulysses and twelve companions landed in Sicily in search of food. The prospect was promising, for on the plains and hillsides great flocks of sheep cropped the tender grass; and Ulysses and his followers soon came to a great cave filled with rich stores of milk and cheese. This was the abode of Polyphemus, son of Neptune, the largest and fiercest among the gigantic Cyclopean race. The Greeks' first impulse was to help themselves, since no one was there to say them nay; but they finally decided to await the master's home-coming, and courteously ask his assistance. They had moored their vessel under an overhanging cliff, where no one would be likely to find it, and had therefore no fear lest their means of escape should be cut off.

POLYPHEMUS AND GALATEA

Polyphemus, the ugly giant in whose cave they were waiting, had once seen the charming sea nymph Galatea riding in her pearl-shell chariot drawn by bounding dolphins. Her unsurpassed loveliness made a vivid impression upon him, and he was soon deeply in love with her. He neglected his flocks, shunned his companions, and spent all his time near the seashore, watching for her, and bitterly cursing his fate, which prevented his seeking her in her native element, for the gods had cursed the race of Cyclops with an unconquerable aversion to water. He

> —lov'd
> Not in the little present-making style,
> With baskets of new fruit and pots of roses,
> But with consuming passion. Many a time
> Would his flocks go home by themselves at eve,
> Leaving him wasting by the dark seashore,
> And sunrise would behold him wasting still.
>
> THEOCRITUS (Hunt's tr.)

To induce Galatea to leave the salt sea waves and linger by his side on the white sandy beach, Polyphemus constantly made the most extravagant promises; but the dainty nymph merely laughed at all his professions, and strolled on the shore only when he was sound asleep. Although she made fun of his love, she was not so obdurate to the suit of Acis, a very fascinating young shepherd, who had no need to call her repeatedly; for she always yielded to his first appeal, joyfully joined him, and sat beside him under the shade of some great rock, listening to his tender wooing.

Polyphemus once accidentally came upon them thus, ere they were aware of his proximity. For a moment he glared down upon them; then, seizing a huge rock, he vowed his rival Acis should not live to enjoy the love which was denied him, and hurled it down upon the unsuspecting lovers. Galatea, the goddess, being immortal, escaped unhurt; but poor Acis, her beloved, was crushed to death. The stream of blood from his mangled remains was changed by the gods into an exhaustless stream of limpid water, which ever hastened down to the sea to join Galatea.

TRIUMPH OF GALATEA. Raphael.

ACIS AND GALATEA (Evening). Claude Lorraine.
(St. Petersburg.)

POLYPHEMUS' CAVE

Ulysses and his companions, waiting in the cave, soon felt the ground shake beneath their feet, and saw the sheep throng into the cave and take their usual places; then behind them came the horrible apparition of Polyphemus, who picked up a huge rock and placed it before the opening of the cave, preventing all egress. Ulysses' companions had shrunk with fear into the darkest corners of the cave, whence they watched the giant milk his ewes, dispose of his cheeses, and make his evening meal. But the firelight soon revealed the intruders; and Polyphemus immediately demanded who they were, whence they came, and what they were seeking.

Ulysses, ever wily, replied that his name was No man, that he and his companions were shipwrecked mariners, and that they would fain receive his hospitality. In answer to this statement, the Cyclops stretched forth his huge hand and grasped two of the sailors, whom he proceeded to devour for dessert. Then, his frightful repast being ended, he lay down on the rushes and fell asleep, his loud snores reverberating like thunder through the great cave.

Ulysses silently crept to his side, sword in hand, and was about to kill him, when he suddenly recollected that neither he nor his men could move the rock at the cave's mouth, and that they would never be able to escape. He therefore resolved to have recourse to a stratagem.

When morning came, the giant rose, milked his flock, made his cheese, arranged the vessels, and then, without the least warning, again seized and devoured two of the Greeks. His brawny arm next pushed aside the rock, and he stood beside it with watchful eye, until all his herd had passed out; then, replacing the stone to prevent the escape of his prisoners, he went off to the distant pasture ground.

During his absence, Ulysses and his men devised a cunning plan whereby they hoped to effect their escape, and made all their preparations to insure its complete success. A huge pine club which they found in the cave was duly pointed, hardened in the fire, and set aside for future use.

When the darkness began to fall over the earth, Polyphemus again rolled the stone away to admit his flocks, keeping careful guard upon the Greeks. The sheep all in, he replaced the rock, performed his usual evening duties, and then devoured two of Ulysses' crew.

ULYSSES BLINDS POLYPHEMUS

When this part of the evening meal was over, Ulysses drew near and offered him a leather flask full of heady wine, which the giant took down at a gulp, little suspecting its effect. Very soon he sank into a deep drunken sleep; and then the men, at a sign from Ulysses, heated the point of the huge club and put out his sole eye, in spite of his frightful cries and execrations, which soon attracted the attention of the other Cyclopes.

They thronged without the cave, clamoring to know who was hurting him. "No man!" replied the Cyclops, howling with pain, "No man!" which answer convinced his would-be helpers that he needed no assistance, and made them disperse.

> "If no man does thee violence, and thou
> Art quite alone, reflect that none escape
> Diseases; they are sent by Jove."
>
> HOMER (Bryant's tr.)

ULYSSES' ESCAPE

Deserted by his companions, Polyphemus spent the night in agony; and, when the anxious lowing of his herd roused him at break of day, he fumblingly milked them, and prepared to let them go forth, as usual, in search of their morning meal. To avoid the Greeks escaping, he rolled the stone only partly aside, and allowed the sheep to pass out a few at a time, carefully running his hand over each broad back to make sure that none of the prisoners were mounted upon them.

Ulysses, in the mean while, having observed this maneuver, fastened his companions under the rams, reserving one for his own use, and watched them pass out one after the other undetected. Then, clinging to the wool of the largest ram, he too was slowly dragged out; while Polyphemus petted the ram, and inquired how he came to pass out last of all.

"My favorite ram, how art thou now the last
To leave the cave? It hath not been thy wont
To let the sheep go first, but thou didst come
Earliest to feed among the flowery grass,
Walking with stately strides, and thou wert first
At the fresh stream, and first at eve to seek
The stable; now thou art the last of all.
Grievest thou for thy master, who has lost
His eye, put out by a deceitful wretch
And his vile crew?"

> HOMER (Bryant's tr.)

Ulysses, having thus escaped, sprang to his feet, set his companions free, rushed with them down to the seashore, taking the choice animals on board, and then, when his men had rowed some distance, raised his voice and taunted Polyphemus, revealing at the same time his identity.

"Ha! Cyclops! those whom in thy rocky cave
Thou, in thy brutal fury, hast devoured,
Were friends of one not unexpert in war;
Amply have thy own guilty deeds returned
Upon thee. Cruel one! who didst not fear
To eat the strangers sheltered by thy roof,
Jove and the other gods avenge them thus!

*   *   *   *   *   *

Cyclops, if any man of mortal birth
Note thine unseemly blindness, and inquire
The occasion, tell him that Laertes' son,
Ulysses, the destroyer of walled towns,
Whose home is Ithaca, put out thine eye."

> HOMER (Bryant's tr.)

With a cry of rage, Polyphemus then ran down to the shore, tore up some huge rocks, which he hurled in the direction whence the taunting voice came, and in his rage almost destroyed the Greeks; for one piece of rock fell very near their vessel, and they were forced to redouble their efforts to row out of reach and prevent disaster.

GIFT OF ÆOLUS

The Greeks now sailed on until they reached the Æolian Islands, where dwelt Æolus, king and father of the winds. He had heard of Ulysses' prowess, received him kindly, and at parting gave him a leather bag containing all the contrary winds, which Ulysses was thus at liberty to retain imprisoned until he had safely reached home.

Day and night Ulysses' barks now bounded over the blue waves. On the ninth evening the shores of Ithaca were discerned by the eager eyes on board, and all made their preparations for landing early the next morning. For the first time since he had left the Æolian shores, Ulysses now indulged in sleep; and while he was lost in oblivion his sailors opened the leather bag, intending to rob their master of a portion of his treasure, for they imagined that Æolus had given him much gold.

The bag was no sooner opened, than the contrary winds, weary and cramped with their uncomfortable position, sprang out with a rush and a roar, and in a few moments stirred up a terrible storm, which tore the ships from their anchors, and soon drove them far out to sea.

After untold suffering, the Greeks landed again upon the Æolian Isle, and Ulysses sought the king, to beseech his aid once more; but this time the god received him coldly, and bade him depart, as his cruelty to Polyphemus had awakened the gods' wrath.

> "Hence with thee! Leave our island instantly,
> Vilest of living men! It may not be
> That I receive or aid as he departs
> One who is hated by the blessed gods,—
> And thou art hated by the gods. Away!"
>
> HOMER (Bryant's tr.)

THE LÆSTRYGONIANS

Sorrowfully now the Greeks embarked; but, instead of being hurried along by favorable winds, they were obliged to row against wind and waves, and only after many days came to the land of the Læstrygonians, where fresh losses awaited them. These people were cannibals, who were in the habit of slaying all the strangers who visited their shores, to satisfy their horrible appetites. When they saw the vessels enter their harbor, they sunk some of them by casting huge rocks at them from their tall cliffs, and speared and devoured the unfortunate crews.

Ulysses, ever cautious, had lingered without the harbor; and when, from afar, he saw his companions' horrible fate, he bade his men strike the waves with their "sounding oars" and escape.

CIRCE, THE ENCHANTRESS

The Greeks went on again until they came to Æǣa, an island inhabited by the golden-haired enchantress Circe, sister of Æetes, and aunt of Medea. Here Ulysses' crew was divided into two parties, one of which, led by Eurylochus, set out to explore the island, while the other, headed by Ulysses, remained to guard the ships. Through a dense forest, peopled with strangely gentle wild beasts, Eurylochus led his force, until they came in sight of the beautiful palace home of Circe. From afar they could hear her sweet voice raised in song, as she wove a beautiful web for her own adornment: so they pressed eagerly on, and entered the palace hall, Eurylochus alone lingering on the porch, fearing lest some fraud might suddenly be revealed.

Circe received her self-invited guests most graciously, seated them on tapestry-covered couches, and bade her numerous handmaidens speedily set before them all manner of good cheer,—an order which was immediately carried out. The men feasted greedily, for they had fasted for many days, and Circe watched them with ill-concealed disgust. Suddenly she started from her seat, waved her wand over their heads, and bade them assume the form of swine (which obscene animals their gluttony suggested), and hie them to their sties.

Then instantly
She touched them with a wand, and shut them up
In sties, transformed to swine in head and voice,
Bristles and shape, though still the human mind
Remained to them. Thus sorrowing they were driven
Into their cells, where Circe flung to them
Acorns of oak and ilex, and the fruit
Of cornel, such as nourish wallowing swine.

HOMER (Bryant's tr.)

Eurylochus, meanwhile, vainly awaited their return, and finally resolved to go back alone to the ships and report what had happened. Sword in hand, Ulysses then set out alone to rescue his comrades; but he had not gone far before he met a youth,—Mercury in disguise,—who warned him not to approach any nearer Circe, and told him of his companions' transformation.

ULYSSES AND CIRCE

As Ulysses would not be dissuaded from his purpose, Mercury gave him some moly, an herb warranted to preserve him from Circe's magic spells, and sundry important directions, which were all duly listened to and observed.

Pressing onward, Ulysses reached the palace, entered the banquet room, drank Circe's mixture, which was rendered ineffective by the moly's power, and, when she waved her wand over his head and bade him join his fellows, drew his sword and rushed upon her, threatening to take her life if she did not immediately restore his friends to their human forms, and promise to do them no further harm.

Circe, terrified at the threat, agreed to comply with all his demands; and in a few moments Ulysses was again surrounded by his companions, who were touchingly grateful for their rescue. Circe now prepared a second feast, and entertained them all so well, that Ulysses lingered there for one whole year.

CIRCE AND THE FRIENDS OF ULYSSES. Rivière.

> And there from day to day
> We lingered a full year, and banqueted
> Nobly on plenteous meats and delicate wines.
>
> HOMER (Bryant's tr.)

ULYSSES VISITS CIMMERIA

At the end of that time, Ulysses' companions began to long for their own homes, and prevailed upon their chief to leave the fair enchantress Circe. At first she was loath to let him go; but, seeing that her efforts to detain him longer would be of no avail, she bade him seek the Cimmerian shores, and there consult the seer Tiresias. This land, which lay on the confines of Pluto's dark realm, was inhabited by shadows, the spirits of the dead, condemned to sojourn there a while ere they were admitted into Hades.

Ulysses embarked, and, according to Circe's directions, let his vessel drift along until its prow grated on a pebbly beach, where he landed. Then, walking straight before him, he came to a spot whence he could hear the roar of the Phlegethon as it joined the Acheron, and here he dug a trench with his sword.

The trench finished, he killed two black victims, furnished by Circe, and made their blood flow into the trench. Immediately all the spirits crowded about him, eager to drink the fresh blood; but Ulysses, with drawn sword, forced them back, until at last Tiresias, the blind seer, approached.

He was allowed to stoop down and drink; and, as soon as he had done so, he recovered the power of human speech, and warned Ulysses of the many trials still awaiting him. Then, his prophecy concluded, he vanished; but Ulysses lingered a little longer to allow his mother to drink some blood, and explain how she came to be here in the spirit land.

Many others came and conversed with him; but at last he was forced to depart, and return to Æææa, where he lingered to perform the funeral rites for Elpenor,— one of his followers, a youth who had fallen asleep on one of the palace turrets, and by an inadvertent movement had fallen to the ground, where he had been found dead.

THE SIRENS

These obsequies over, the Greeks, favored by a fresh wind, left Circe's isle, and sailed along until they drew near the rocky ledge where the Sirens had their abode. These maidens were wont to sit on the rocks and sing entrancing songs, which allured the mariners until they turned aside from their course, and their vessels were dashed to pieces on the rocks.

According to Circe's advice, Ulysses bade his men bind him fast to the mast, disregard his cries and gestures of command, and keep on their course until the dangerous rocks were lost to view; but, before he allowed them to execute these orders, he stopped their ears with melted wax, so they could not hear a sound, for he alone could hear the Sirens' song and live.

The men then bound him hand and foot to the mast, returned to their oars, and rowed steadily on. Soon the Sirens' melody fell upon Ulysses' charmed ears; but, although he commanded and implored his men to set him free and alter their course, they kept steadily on until no sound of the magic song could reach them, when they once more set their leader free.

CHARYBDIS AND SCYLLA

Now, although this danger had been safely passed, Ulysses was troubled in spirit, for he knew he would soon be obliged to steer his course between two dread monsters, Charybdis and Scylla, who lay so close together, that, while striving to avoid one, it was almost impossible not to fall an easy prey to the other.

Charybdis' den lay under a rock crowned with a single wild fig tree; and three times daily she ingulfed the surrounding waters, drawing even large galleys into her capacious jaws.

As for Scylla, she too dwelt in a cave, whence her six ugly heads protruded to devour any prey that came within reach.

> No mariner can boast
> That he has passed by Scylla with a crew
> Unharmed; she snatches from the deck, and bears
> Away in each grim mouth, a living man.
> HOMER (Bryant's tr.)

SIREN. (Acropolis Museum, Athens.)

This selfsame Scylla, once a lovely maiden, had won the heart of the sea god Glaucus, but coquettishly tormented him until he implored Circe to give him some love potion strong enough to compel her love.

Circe, who had long nursed a secret passion for Glaucus, was angry at him, and jealous of her rival, and, instead of a love potion, prepared a loathsome drug, which she bade him pour into the water where Scylla was wont to bathe. Glaucus faithfully did as she commanded; but when Scylla plunged into the water, her body, and not her feelings, changed, and she became a loathsome monster, a terror to gods and men.

When in sight of the fig tree, Ulysses, cased in armor, stood on the prow to attack Scylla should she attempt to seize one of his crew. The sound of the rushing waters whirling around Charybdis made all on board tremble with fear, and the pilot steered nearer still to dread Scylla's den.

Suddenly a piercing cry was heard, as the monster seized six of the men and devoured them. The rest passed on unharmed; but since then, in speaking of conflicting dangers, it has been customary to use the expression, "falling from Charybdis into Scylla."

CATTLE OF THE SUN

Only too glad to effect an escape at any price, the Greeks again rowed on until they sighted Trinacria, the island of the sun, where Phaetusa and Lampetia watched over the sun god's sacred herds. The men wished to land here to rest; but Ulysses reminded them that Tiresias, the blind seer, had warned them to avoid it, lest by slaying any of the sacred animals they should incur divine wrath.

The men, however, worn out with the toil of many days' rowing, entreated so piteously to be allowed to rest, voluntarily pledging themselves to be content with their own provisions and not to slay a single animal, that Ulysses reluctantly yielded to their entreaties, and all went ashore.

After they had duly rested, they were still detained by unfavorable winds, until all their provisions were exhausted, and the few birds and fishes they managed to secure no longer sufficed to still the pangs of hunger.

Led by Eurylochus, some of the men, during one of Ulysses' temporary absences, caught and slew some of the sun god's cattle. To the general amazement and terror, the meat lowed while roasting on the spit, and the empty skins moved and crawled as if alive. All these sounds and sights could not, however, deter the sailors, who were bound to have a good feast, which they kept up for seven days, ere Ulysses could make them leave the Trinacrian shores.

In the mean while, Lampetia had hastened to Apollo to apprise him of the crime committed by Ulysses' men. In anger he appeared before the assembled gods and demanded amends, threatening to withdraw the light of his countenance if he were not properly indemnified. Jupiter, to appease his hot anger, immediately promised that all the offenders should perish.

> "Still shine, O Sun! among the deathless gods
> And mortal men, upon the nourishing earth.
> Soon will I cleave, with a white thunderbolt,
> Their galley in the midst of the black sea!"
>
> HOMER (Bryant's tr.)

This promise he immediately fulfilled by drowning all except Ulysses, who alone had not partaken of the sacred flesh, and who, after clinging to the rudder for nine long days, a plaything for the wind and waves, was washed ashore on the Island of Ogygia, where the fair sea nymph Calypso had taken up her abode.

ULYSSES AND CALYPSO

There he was kindly and most hospitably entertained during eight long years; but he could not depart, as he had no vessel or crew to bear him away. At last Minerva, who had always befriended him, prevailed upon Jupiter to allow him to return to Ithaca. Mercury was sent to Ogygia to bid Calypso furnish all things necessary for his comfort, and aid in the construction of a huge raft, whereon our hero found himself afloat after many years of reluctant lingering on the land.

All seemed well now; but Neptune suddenly became aware that his old enemy, the torturer of Polyphemus, was about to escape from his clutches. With one blow of his trident he stirred up one of those sudden tempests whose fury nothing can withstand, shattered Ulysses' raft, and buffeted him about on the waves, until the goddess Leucothea, seeing his distress, helped him to reach the Phæacian shore.

NAUSICAA AND ULYSSES

Too weary to think of aught but rest, Ulysses dragged himself into a neighboring wood, where he fell asleep on a bed of dry leaves. While he was thus resting, Minerva visited Nausicaa, daughter of Alcinous, King of the Phæacians, in a dream, and bade her go down to the shore and wash her linen robes in readiness for her wedding day, which the goddess assured her was near at hand. Nausicaa obeyed, and drove with her maidens down to the shore, where, after their labors were duly finished, they all indulged in a game of ball, with the usual accompaniment of shrill cries and much laughter. Their cries awoke Ulysses, who came on the scene just in time to save their ball from the waves, and claimed Nausicaa's protection for a shipwrecked mariner.

She graciously permitted him to follow her to her father's palace, and presented him to Alcinous and Arete, who bade him welcome, and invited him to join in the games then taking place. He did so, and displayed such strength and skill that his identity was revealed. Alcinous then promised to send him safely home in a Phæacian bark, which reached Ithaca in safety, and deposited Ulysses, asleep, on his native shore.

THE PETRIFIED SHIP

When Neptune discovered that the Phæacians had outwitted him, he was so angry that he changed the returning vessel into a rock, which blocked the harbor and put an end to further maritime excursions on their part.

> He drew near
> And smote it with his open palm, and made
> The ship a rock, fast rooted in the bed
> Of the deep sea.
>
> HOMER (Bryant's tr.)

ULYSSES' RETURN TO ITHACA

Disguised as a beggar by Minerva's kindly care, Ulysses sought the lowly dwelling of Eumæus, his swineherd, and from him learned all he wished to know about his wife and son. He heard that Penelope was fairly besieged with suitors, who were even now feasting and reveling in his palace, whence they refused to depart until she had made choice of a second husband; and also that Telemachus, now a young man, indignant and displeased with the suitors' conduct, and guided and accompanied by his tutor Mentor, had set out in search of the father whom he could not believe dead.

Mentor was Minerva in disguise, who guided the young man to the courts of Nestor and Menelaus, and finally in a dream bade him return to Ithaca, where he would find the parent he sought. The young prince immediately obeyed, and landed near Eumæus' hut, escaping a clever ambuscade posted by the suitors at the entrance of the port.

Minerva now permitted the father and son to recognize each other, in spite of their twenty years' separation, and together they planned how best to punish the insolent suitors. They finally agreed that Telemachus should return to the palace and make no mention of his father's return; while Ulysses, still in the guise of a beggar, should enter his home and claim the usual hospitality.

All was executed as they had planned. No one recognized the long-expected hero in the miserable old beggar—no one save his aged nurse Euryclea, and his faithful old dog Argus, who died for joy at his long-lost master's feet.

> While over Argus the black night of death
> Came suddenly as soon as he had seen
> Ulysses, absent now for twenty years.
>   HOMER (Bryant's tr.)

PENELOPE'S WEB

Penelope, hearing that a stranger was within her gates, sent for him, to inquire whether he knew aught of her husband. She too failed to pierce his disguise, and languidly continued a piece of work which she cleverly used to baffle her suitors; for once, when urged to marry, she had replied that she would do so as soon as her work was finished.

PENELOPE.
(Vatican, Rome.)

As she was a diligent worker, the suitors expected soon to hear her decision, little knowing that she raveled at night all the web so carefully woven during the day.

> Three full years
> She practiced thus, and by the fraud deceived
> The Grecian youths.
>
> HOMER (Bryant's tr.)

ULYSSES' BOW

At last the subterfuge was discovered, and the unfortunate Penelope was forced to finish her work; but ere it was quite done, she found another expedient to postpone her choice of a husband. She brought Ulysses' bow, and announced that she would marry the man who could bend it and send an arrow through twelve rings which she pointed out.

> "I bring to you
> The mighty bow that great Ulysses bore.
> Whoe'er among you he may be whose hand
> Shall bend this bow, and send through these twelve rings
> An arrow, him I follow hence, and leave
> This beautiful abode of my young years,
> With all its plenty,—though its memory,
> I think, will haunt me even in my dreams."
>
> HOMER (Bryant's tr.)

DEATH OF THE SUITORS

The suitors all vainly strove to bend the mighty bow, which was then seized by the disguised Ulysses, while the youths laughed aloud in scorn, until Telemachus bade them let the old man try his strength. To the amazement of all, Ulysses easily performed the required feat; and then, turning his aim toward Antinous, the handsomest and most treacherous of all the suitors, he pierced his heart.

A scene of wild commotion ensued, in which Ulysses, Telemachus, Eumæus, and Minerva disguised as Mentor, opposed and slew all the wooers. Penelope, unconscious of all this bloodshed, slept in her room, until she was gently awakened by Euryclea, who announced the return of her long-absent husband.

> "Awake, Penelope, dear child, and see
> With thine own eyes what thou hast pined for long.
> Ulysses has returned; thy lord is here,
> Though late, and he has slain the arrogant crew
> Of suitors, who disgraced his house, and made
> His wealth a spoil, and dared insult his son."
>
> HOMER (Bryant's tr.)

But Penelope had too long believed her husband dead to credit this marvelous news; and it was only after Ulysses had given her an infallible proof of his identity, by telling her a secret which was shared by her alone, that she received him.

ULYSSES' LAST JOURNEY

Ulysses was now safe at home, after twenty years of warfare and adventure, and at first greatly enjoyed the quiet and peace of his home life; but after a while these tame joys grew wearisome, and he decided to renew his wanderings. He therefore prepared a fleet, and sailed "out into the West," whence he never returned. The Greeks, however, averred that he had gone in search of the Isles of the Blest, where he dwelt in perfect peace, and enjoyed the constant society of heroes as brave and renowned as himself.

"Come, my friends,
'Tis not too late to seek a newer world.
Push off, and sitting well in order smite
The sounding furrows; for my purpose holds
To sail beyond the sunset, and the baths
Of all the western stars, until I die.
It may be that the gulfs will wash us down:
It may be we shall touch the Happy Isles,
And see the great Achilles, whom we knew.
Tho' much is taken, much abides: and tho'
We are not now that strength which in old days
Moved earth and heaven; that which we are, we are;
One equal temper of heroic hearts,
Made weak by time and fate, but strong in will
To strive, to seek, to find, and not to yield."

TENNYSON

Chapter XXIX

ADVENTURES OF ÆNEAS

You have already heard how the Greeks entered the city of Troy in the dead of night, massacred the inhabitants, and set fire to the beautiful buildings which had been the king's pride and delight. Now you shall hear how Virgil relates the escape of some of the Trojans from general destruction.

Unconscious of coming danger, Æneas, son of Venus and Anchises, lay fast asleep in his palace; but the gods had not doomed him to perish, and sent the shade of Hector to warn him in a dream to arise, leave the city, and fly to some distant land.

> "Ah, goddess-born," he warns me, "fly!
> Escape these flames: Greece holds the walls;
> Proud Ilium from her summit falls.
> Think not of king's or country's claims:
> Country and king, alas! are names:
> Could Troy be saved by hands of men,
> This hand had saved her then, e'en then.
> The gods of her domestic shrines
> That country to your care consigns:
> Receive them now, to share your fate:
> Provide them mansions strong and great,
> The city's walls, which Heaven has willed
> Beyond the seas you yet shall build."
>
> VIRGIL (Conington's tr.)

Æneas Goes to Save Priam

Awakened at last by the ever-increasing tumult without, Æneas seized his arms and hastened forth, attended by many of his fellow-citizens, to ascertain the cause of the great uproar. A few minutes later he discovered that the Greek army had entered the town, and was even now killing, plundering, and burning without mercy. The men were all slain, but the fairest women were dragged away to be sold as slaves in Greece; and among them Æneas beheld in the hands of Agamemnon's soldiers the unfortunate daughter of Priam, Cassandra, whom the gods had endowed with prophetic powers, but whom no one would heed.

Æneas, seeing ere long that there was no hope of saving the doomed city, quickly disguised himself in a Greek armor which he tore from the corpse of one of his foes, and rushed on to the palace, hoping to save the aged king, who, at the first alarm, had seized his weapons, determined to fight to the very last.

Hecuba, his wife, was clinging to him, imploring him to remain, when suddenly Polites, their son, rushed into their presence, closely followed by Pyrrhus, or Neoptolemus, son of Achilles, who thrust his sword into the youth, and then murdered Priam also.

> So Priam's fortunes closed at last:
> So passed he, seeing as he passed
> His Troy in flames, his royal tower
> Laid low in dust by hostile power,
> Who once o'er land and peoples proud
> Sat, while before him Asia bowed:
> Now on the shore behold him dead,
> A nameless trunk, a trunkless head.
>
> VIRGIL (Conington's tr.)

Æneas, who arrived just too late to hinder this frightful catastrophe, now suddenly remembered that a similar fate awaited his aged father Anchises, his wife Creusa, and little son Iulus, who were at home without any protector near them. The hero therefore madly cut his way through the foe, and rushed through the once magnificent palace, which was now stripped of its rarest treasures and desecrated by an enemy's tread.

VENUS APPEARS TO ÆNEAS

There, in one of the abandoned halls, he saw Helen, the fair cause of all this war and bloodshed,—who, after Paris' death, had married Deiphobus, his brother,—and for a moment he determined to take her life; but ere he could do so, Venus, his mother, stayed his hand, and bade him remember that the immortal gods had long ago decreed that the city should fall, and that Helen was merely the pretext used to induce the rival nations to fly to arms.

Further to convince him of the truth of her assertions, she enabled him to see what was hidden from mortal eyes: i.e., Neptune, Minerva, Juno, and Jupiter even, fighting and leveling the walls with mighty blows. She then vehemently implored her son to leave this scene of carnage, and fly, with his family and followers, to some safe place without the city, whence he could embark, and sail away to a more fortunate land; and her entreaties finally prevailed.

ANCHISES' ESCAPE

Æneas rushed home and bade his father prepare to leave Troy; but Anchises obstinately refused to leave his post, until he saw a bright flame hover for a moment above his grandson's head, which sign he interpreted as an omen that his race should endure. He no longer resisted; and, as he was too weak to walk, Æneas bade him hold the Lares and Penates, and, taking him on his back, carried him off, while with one hand he led his little son, and bade Creusa closely follow him.

> "Come, mount my shoulders, dear my sire:
> Such load my strength shall never tire.
> Now, whether fortune smiles or lowers,
> One risk, one safety shall be ours.
> My son shall journey at my side,
> My wife her steps by mine shall guide,
> At distance safe."
>
> VIRGIL (Conington's tr.)

CREUSA'S GHOST

A trysting place near a ruined temple had already been appointed for his servants, and thither Æneas turned his steps. When he arrived there, he found many awaiting him, and counted them carefully to make sure none were missing. All were there except Creusa, his beloved young wife; and he retraced his steps with anxious haste, hoping to find her still alive. But on the threshold of his once happy home he met her disembodied spirit, and heard her bid him seek the banks of the Tiber, where a beautiful young bride would comfort him for her loss. This speech ended, Creusa's ghost vanished, and Æneas sadly returned to the ruined temple, where he found many fugitives ready to follow him wherever he went, and eager to obey his every command. Their preparations for departure were speedily completed, the sails unfurled, and the little exiled band soon lost sight of the shores of Troy.

> Weeping I quit the port, the shore,
> The plains where Ilium stood before,
> And homeless launch upon the main,
> Son, friends, and home gods in my train.
>
> VIRGIL (Conington's tr.)

ARRIVAL IN THRACE

Although they had escaped from burning Troy and the swords of the Greeks, their trials had only just begun. After many days' sailing, they landed in Thrace, viewed the country, decided to settle there, and began to trace the foundations of a new city, which they decided to call the Æneadæ, in honor of their leader.

Their next care was to offer a sacrifice to the gods; but when Æneas, with due ceremony, cut down a sapling, he was startled to see blood flow from its severed stem. At the same time a mysterious voice was heard, bidding him forbear, for his former friend Polydorus, sent to Thrace to conceal some treasures, had been murdered there by an avaricious king, and this grove of trees had sprouted from the spear handles driven into his unhappy breast.

DELOS AND CRETE

After paying the customary funeral rites to appease the soul of his unfortunate friend, Æneas easily prevailed upon his followers to leave these inhospitable shores and seek another resting place. They rowed over the briny deep until they came to Delos, where they stopped to consult the oracle, who bade them seek the cradle of their race, and settle there.

> "Stout Dardan hearts, the realm of earth
> Where first your nation sprang to birth,
> That realm shall now receive you back:
> Go, seek your ancient mother's track.
> There shall Æneas' house, renewed
> For ages, rule a world subdued."
>
> VIRGIL (Conington's tr.)

This obscure command left them uncertain what course to pursue, until the aged Anchises remembered that one of his ancestors, Teucer, had once reigned in Crete. Thither they sailed, and hoped to settle; but a terrible pestilence came upon them, and decimated their already sparse ranks.

ÆNEAS' VISION

One night Æneas had a vision, in which his household gods bade him seek the Italian or Hesperian shores; and when, on waking, he imparted this advice to Anchises, the latter remembered a long-forgotten prophecy of Cassandra, purporting that they would settle there, and also that Dardanus, their first progenitor, was reported to have come from thence.

There is a land, by Greece of old
Surnamed Hesperia, rich its mold,
    Its children brave and free:
Œnotrians were its settlers: fame
Now gives the race its leader's name,
    And calls it Italy.
Here Dardanus was born, our king,
And old Iasius, whence we spring:
    Here our authentic seat.

                    VIRGIL (Conington's tr.)

CELÆNO, THE HARPY

Ere many days Æneas and his trusty followers were once more afloat, and forced to battle with fierce storms sent by Juno to hinder their advance. Exhausted, they landed on the Strophades Islands, where they proposed to recruit their strength by a hearty meal; but no sooner was their table spread, than the meats were devoured and destroyed by the loathsome Harpies. A terrible prophecy uttered by Celæno, one of these monsters,—half woman and half bird,—made them embark again in great haste, and row on until they came to Epirus, where they again effected a landing. In this country they met the sorrowing Andromache, Hector's widow, the slave of King Helenus, who entertained them royally and sent them on their way again, with many kindly cautions to beware of the Cyclopes and avoid Charybdis and Scylla by circumnavigating the whole island of Sicily.

RESCUE OF ACHEMENIDES

This advice was duly followed by Æneas, who, while rounding one of the promontories of the island, saw and rescued Achemenides, one of Ulysses' companions, accidentally left behind when they escaped from the rage of Polyphemus, the Cyclops. This giant now came down to the shore, and was regarded with unconcealed horror by the Trojans, who rowed away in haste. Soon after, Æneas moored his ships in the harbors of Sicania and Drepanum, and while there lost his aged father Anchises.

> There
> I lose my stay in every care,
> My sire Anchises!
> VIRGIL (Conington's tr.)

Juno, in the mean while, had not been idle, and gloated over the dangers she had forced the unhappy Trojans to encounter during the seven years which had already elapsed since they first sailed from Troy. She was not yet weary of persecuting them, however; and as soon as she saw them once more afloat, she hurried off to Æolus, and bade him let loose his fiercest children, and scatter the fleet by a terrible storm.

> "O Æolus! since the Sire of all
> Has made the wind obey thy call
> To raise or lay the foam,
> A race I hate now plows the sea,
> Transporting Troy to Italy
> And home gods reft of home:
> Lash thou thy winds, their ships submerge,
> Or toss them weltering o'er the surge."
> VIRGIL (Conington's tr.)

THE TEMPEST

This request was immediately granted. The vessels, tossed hither and thither, lost sight of each other. Some were stranded, some sank, and still the tempest raged on with unabated fury, and death stared the unhappy Trojans in the face. The commotion on the deep finally aroused Neptune, who came to the surface just in time to see all the misfortunes which had overwhelmed Æneas. He imperiously sent the winds away, and lent a helping hand to float the stranded ships once more.

"Back to your master instant flee,
And tell him, not to him but me
The imperial trident of the sea
Fell by the lot's award."

VIRGIL (Conington's tr.)

The Trojans, grateful for his timely aid, and reassured by the calm which now reigned supreme, steered for the nearest port, where they anchored their seven vessels, all that now remained of their once large fleet.

ARRIVAL IN LIBYA

Æneas and Achates, his faithful friend, immediately set out to view the land, and ere long encountered Venus, disguised as a mortal, who informed them that they had landed upon the Libyan coast, which was under the sway of Dido, a fugitive from Tyre. Dido's husband, Sychæus, King of Tyre, the possessor of untold riches, had been murdered by Pygmalion, his brother-in-law; but the queen was kept in complete ignorance of this crime, until visited in a dream by the shade of Sychæus, which bade her fly with his treasures, whose place of concealment she alone knew.

Dido obeyed the ghost's commands, and, accompanied by a number of faithful subjects, landed on the Libyan coast, where she entreated the inhabitants to sell her as much land as an ox-hide would inclose. This seemingly modest request was immediately granted; but the Libyans regretted their compliance when they saw the ox-hide cut up into tiny strips, which inclosed a considerable tract of land, the site of Dido's beautiful capital, Carthage.

ÆNEAS AND DIDO

Thither Venus advised her son to proceed and claim the queen's protection. Æneas and Achates obediently hastened onward, and entered the town unseen, for Venus had enveloped them both in a mist. Their attention was first attracted by the festive appearance of the people assembled together, and by the beauty of the queen, giving audience to some of their companions, who had miraculously escaped from the waves.

These men spoke to the queen of their renowned chief, whose fame had already reached her ear; and she gladly promised to send out a search party to discover him, and aid him if necessary.

> "I will send
> And search the coast from end to end,
> If haply, wandering up and down,
> He bide in woodland or in town."
>
> VIRGIL (Conington's tr.)

At these gracious words, Æneas stepped forward, the mist vanished, and he stood before the queen in all his manly beauty.

Dido then led her guests to the banquet hall, where they recounted their adventures by land and sea, while partaking of the viands and wines set before them. At this feast, Cupid, at Venus' request, assumed the face and form of Iulus, Æneas' young son, and, reclining on the queen's bosom, secretly thrust one of his darts into her heart, and made her fall in love with Æneas.

Day after day now passed in revelry and pleasure, and still Æneas lingered by Dido's side, forgetful of the new kingdom he was destined to found. One whole year passed thus; and the gods, impatient of delay, finally sent Mercury to remind Æneas of his duty.

To avoid Dido's tears and recriminations, the hero kept his preparations for departure a complete secret, and finally set sail while she was wrapt in slumber. When she awoke and looked out of her palace window, it was only to see the last vessel sink beneath the horizon.

DEATH OF DIDO

Concealing her grief, and pretending an anger she did not feel, she bade her servants make a funeral pyre, and place upon it all the objects Æneas had used during his sojourn in her palace; then, on top of it all, she set an effigy of her false lover, set fire to the pyre, sprang into the midst of the flames, and there stabbed herself.

ÆNEAS AT THE COURT OF DIDO. Guerin.

"Yet let me die: thus, thus I go
Exulting to the shades below.
Let the false Dardan feel the blaze
That burns me pouring on his gaze,
And bear along, to cheer his way,
The funeral presage of to-day."
VIRGIL (Conington's tr.)

From the mast of his vessel Æneas saw the rising column of smoke, and his heart sank within him; for he suspected its fatal import, and honestly mourned the death of the beautiful queen.

FUNERAL GAMES

The Trojans sailed onward until the threatening clouds made them take refuge in the Sicanian port, where they celebrated the usual games to commemorate Anchises' death, which had occurred there just one year previous. While the men were engaged in the customary naval, foot, and horse races, boxing, wrestling, and archery matches, the women gathered together, and, instigated by Juno, began to bewail the hard lot which compelled them to encounter again the perils of the sea. Their discontent ultimately reached such a pitch that they set fire to the vessels. When Æneas heard of this new misfortune, he rushed down to the shore, tore his costly festal garments, and cried to Heaven for assistance in this his time of direst need.

"Dread Sire, if Ilium's lorn estate
Deserve not yet thine utter hate,
If still thine ancient faithfulness
Give heed to mortals in distress,
Oh, let the fleet escape the flame!
Oh, save from death Troy's dying name!"
VIRGIL (Conington's tr.)

Apparition of Anchises

This prayer was instantly answered by a sudden severe shower, which quenched the devouring flames. Soon after this miracle, Anchises appeared to Æneas, and bade him leave the women, children, and aged men in Sicily, and travel on to Cumæ, where he was to consult the Sibyl, visit the Infernal Regions, and there receive further advice from him.

> First seek the halls of Dis below,
> Pass deep Avernus' vale, and meet
> Your father in his own retreat.
> VIRGIL (Conington's tr.)

Æneas again dutifully obeyed; but when Venus saw him afloat once more, she hastened to Neptune, and bade him watch over her unfortunate son. Neptune listened very graciously to her appeal, and promised to take but one of all the many lives intrusted to his care. That one was Æneas' pilot, Palinurus, who, falling asleep at the helm, fell overboard and was drowned.

The Cumæan Sibyl

As for the fleet, it reached the Cumæan shore in safety; and Æneas hastened off to the Sibyl's cave, made known his wish to visit Hades, and entreated her to serve as his guide in that perilous journey. She consented, but at the same time informed him that he must first obtain a golden twig, which grew in a dark forest.

> None may reach the shades without
> The passport of that golden sprout.
> VIRGIL (Conington's tr.)

Almost despairing, Æneas now prayed for assistance; for how could he find a tiny golden sprig in the midst of the dense forest foliage without the gods' aid? In answer to this appeal, Venus, ever mindful of her son, sent two of her snowy doves to lead the way and alight on the tree, where Æneas readily found the object of his search.

CUMÆAN SIBYL. Domenichino.
(Borghese Gallery, Rome.)

Armed with this branch as key, he and the Sibyl boldly entered the Lower Regions, where all the ghastly sights and sounds we have already described met them on every side. Charon quickly ferried them over the Acheron, on whose bank they saw the wandering shade of Palinurus, who had no obolus to pay his way across, and that of Dido, with a gaping wound in her breast.

They did not pause, however, until they reached the Elysian Fields, where they found Anchises, gravely considering among the unborn souls those who were destined to animate his race and make it illustrious in the future. These he carefully pointed out to Æneas, foretelling their future achievements, and called by name Romulus, Brutus, Camillus, the Gracchi, Cæsar,—in fact, all the heroes of Roman history.

> Anchises showed Æneas, in long line,
> The illustrious shades of those who were to shine
> One day the glory of the Italian shore.
>
> TOMAS DE IRIARTE

ARRIVAL IN LATIUM

After a prolonged conversation with his father, Æneas returned to his companions, and led them to the mouth of the Tiber, whose course they followed until they reached Latium, where their wanderings were to cease. Latinus, king of the country, received them hospitably, and promised the hand of his daughter Lavinia in marriage to Æneas.

Lavinia was very beautiful, and had already had many suitors, among whom Turnus, a neighboring prince, boasted of the most exalted rank. The queen, Amata, specially favored this youth's suit; and the king would gladly have received him for a son-in-law, had he not twice been warned by the gods to reserve his daughter for a foreign prince, who had now appeared.

In spite of all the years which had elapsed since Paris scorned her attractions and bribes, Juno had not yet forgotten her hatred of the Trojan race, and, afraid lest her enemy's course should now prove too smooth, she sent Alecto, the Fury, down upon earth to stir up war, and goad Amata to madness. The Fury executed both commands, and Amata fled to the woods, where she concealed her daughter Lavinia, to keep her safe for Turnus, whom she preferred to Æneas.

WAR WITH THE LATINS

As Iulus and some companions had unfortunately wounded the pet stag of Silvia, daughter of the head shepherd, a brawl ensued, which, fomented by Alecto, soon developed into a bloody war. Hostilities having thus begun, Turnus, with the various Latin chiefs, immediately besought Latinus to open the gates of Janus' temple. He refused; but Juno, afraid lest even now her plans might be set at naught, came down from Olympus, and with her own hand flung wide the brazen doors. This unexpected apparition kindled a general ardor; new troops enlisted; and even Camilla, the Volscian warrior-maiden, came to proffer her aid to Turnus.

> Last marches forth for Latium's sake
> Camilla fair, the Volscian maid,
> A troop of horsemen in her wake
> In pomp of gleaming steel arrayed;
> Stern warrior queen!
> VIRGIL (Conington's tr.)

STORY OF CAMILLA

When but a babe in arms, Camilla had been carried off by her father, as he fled before the Volscian troops. When he came to the Amasenus River, he found his pursuers close at his heels. Tying his infant daughter to his spear, he hurled her to the opposite bank, which, thanks to Diana's aid, she reached unharmed, while her father plunged into the waves to join her. In his gratitude to find her safe, he dedicated her to Diana, who trained her to love the chase and all manly pursuits.

Surprised to see Latinus' friendly offers of hospitality so suddenly withdrawn, Æneas made rapid preparations for war, and sailed farther up the Tiber to secure the aid of Evander, king of the Tuscans, the hereditary foe of the Latins. This monarch, too old to lead his troops in person, nevertheless promised his aid, and sent his beloved son Pallas in his stead to command the troops he supplied.

Nisus and Euryalus

Juno, still implacable, had in the mean while sent Iris to apprise Turnus of Æneas' departure, and to urge him to set fire to the remainder of the fleet,—a suggestion which Turnus joyfully obeyed. The Trojans, headed by young Iulus, Æneas' son, defended themselves with their usual courage; but, seeing the enemy would soon overpower them, they dispatched Nisus and Euryalus, two of their number, to warn Æneas of their danger, and entreat him to hasten up with his reënforcements. These unfortunate youths passed through the camp unseen, but farther on fell into the hands of a troop of Volscian horsemen, who cruelly put them to death, and then hurried with the Rutules to lend assistance to Turnus. Next some of the Trojan vessels were fired by the enemy; but, instead of being consumed by the flames, they were changed into water nymphs by the intervention of the gods, and, sailing down the Tiber, met Æneas, and warned him to hasten to his son's rescue.

> His vessels change their guise,
> And each and all as Nereids rise.
>
> Virgil

The Armor

In the mean while, Venus, who befriended the Trojans, had sought Vulcan's detested abode, and had prevailed upon him to forge a beautiful armor for Æneas. On the shield, which is minutely described in one of the books of Virgil's celebrated epic poem, the Æneid, were depicted many of the stirring scenes in the lives of the future descendants of Æneas, the heroes of Roman history. As soon as this armor was completed, Venus brought it to her son, who donned it with visible pleasure, and, encouraged by his mother's words, prepared to meet the Latins and hold his own.

Venus and Juno were not the only deities interested in the coming struggle; for all the gods, having watched Æneas' career, were anxious about his fate. Seeing this, and fearful lest their interference should still further endanger the hero whom he favored, Jupiter assembled the gods on high Olympus, and sternly forbade their taking any active part in the coming strife, under penalty of his severe displeasure.

ÆNEAS' ARRIVAL

Æneas and his Tuscan allies arrived on the battle scene just in time to give the necessary support to the almost exhausted Trojans; and now the fight raged more fiercely than ever, and prodigies of valor were accomplished on both sides, until finally young Pallas fell, slain by Turnus. When aware of the death of this promising young prince, Æneas' heart was filled with grief, for he could imagine the sorrow of the aged Evander when he saw his son's corpse brought home for burial; and he then and there registered a solemn vow to avenge Pallas' death by slaying Turnus, and immediately hastened forth to keep his word.

JUNO'S TREACHERY

In the mean while, Juno, suspecting what his purpose would be, and afraid to allow Turnus to encounter such a formidable antagonist as Æneas, had determined to lure her favorite away from the field. To compass this, she assumed the form of Æneas, challenged Turnus, and, as soon as he began the fight, fled toward the river, and took refuge on one of the vessels, closely pursued by him. No sooner did she see the Rutule chief safe on board, than she loosed the vessel from its moorings, and allowed it to drift down the stream, bearing Turnus away from the scene of battle. Aware now of the delusion practiced, Turnus raved, and accused the gods, and then eagerly watched for an opportunity to land, and make his way, alone and on foot, back to the scene of conflict.

ÆNEAS' PROWESS

During Turnus' involuntary absence, Æneas had ranged all over the battlefield in search of him, and had encountered and slain many warriors, among others Lausus and his aged father Mezentius, two allies of Latinus, who had specially distinguished themselves by their great valor. The dead and dying covered the field, when Latinus, weary of bloodshed, summoned a council, and again vainly tried to make peace. But his efforts were of no avail. The war was renewed more fiercely than ever; and in the next encounter, Camilla, the brave Volscian maiden, fell at last, breathing a fervent entreaty that Turnus should hasten to the succor of his despairing people if he would not see them all slain and the town in the hands of the Trojans.

"Go: my last charge to Turnus tell,
  To haste with succor, and repel
  The Trojans from the town—farewell."
                                   VIRGIL (Conington's tr.)

ÆNEAS' WOUND

Shortly after her death, in the very midst of the fray, Æneas suddenly felt himself wounded by an arrow sent by some mysterious hand. He hastened to seek the aid of the leech Iapis; but, in spite of his ministrations, the barb could not be removed nor the wound dressed, until Venus brought a magic herb, which instantly healed the hero, and enabled him to return to the fight with unabated strength and energy.

The tide was now decidedly turning in favor of the Trojans; for Amata, the Latin queen, sorry for her ill-advised opposition to her daughter's marriage with Æneas, brought Lavinia home and hung herself in a fit of remorse.

DEATH OF TURNUS

Æneas, appearing once more on the battlefield, finally encountered the long-sought Turnus, who had made his way back, and was now driving about in his chariot, jealously guarded by his sister Juturna, who, the better to watch over his safety, had taken the place of his chariot driver. The two heroes, having met, instantly closed in deadly fight; but, in spite of Turnus' bravery, he was finally obliged to succumb, and sank to the ground, frankly acknowledging himself beaten as he exhaled his last sigh.

"Yours is the victory: Latian bands
  Have seen me stretch imploring hands:
  The bride Lavinia is your own:
  Thus far let foeman's hate be shown."
                                   VIRGIL (Conington's tr.)

ÆNEAS' PROGENY

With the death of Turnus the war came to an end. A lasting peace was made with Latinus; and the brave Trojan hero, whose woes were now over, was united in marriage with Lavinia. In concert with Latinus, he ruled the Latins, and founded a city, which he called Lavinia in honor of his bride, and which became for a time the capital of Latium.

Æneas, as the gods had predicted, became the father of a son named Æneas Silvia, who founded Alba Longa, where his descendants reigned for many a year, and where one of his race, the Vestal Virgin Ilia, after marrying Mars, gave birth to Remus and Romulus, the founders of Rome.

Chapter XXX

ANALYSIS OF MYTHS

*I shall indeed interpret all that I can, but I cannot interpret all
that I should like.*

GRIMM

EARLY THEORIES

In attempting an analysis of the foregoing myths, and an explanation of their origin, it is impossible, in a work of this kind, to do more than give a very superficial idea of the scientific theories of various eminent mythologists, who, on this subject, like doctors, are sure to disagree.

These myths, comprising "the entire intellectual stock of the age to which they belonged," existed as "floating talk among the people" long ere they passed into the literature of the nation; and while to us mythology is merely "an affair of historical or antiquarian study, we must remember that the interpretation of myths was once a thing full of vital interest to men whose moral and religious beliefs were deeply concerned." Received at first with implicit faith, these myths became a stumbling block as civilization advanced. Cultured man recoiled from much of the grossness which had appeared quite natural to his ancestors in a savage state, and made an attempt to find out their primitive meaning, or an explanation which would satisfy his purer taste.

With the latter object in view, the sages and writers of old interpreted all that seemed "silly and senseless" in mythology as physical allegories,—a system subsequently carried to extremes by many heathen philosophers in the vain hope of evading Christian satire.

Learned men have also explained these selfsame myths as historical facts disguised as metaphors, or as moral allegories, which the choice of Hercules undoubtedly is. Euhemerus (316 B.C.) was the pioneer of the former theory, and Bacon an exponent of the latter. Euhemerus' method was exaggerated by his disciples, who declared Zeus was merely a king of Crete; his war with the giants, an attempt to repress a sedition; Danae's shower of gold, the money with which her guards were bribed; Prometheus, a maker of clay images, "whence it was hyperbolically said he created man out of clay"; and Atlas, an astronomer, who was therefore spoken of as supporting the weight of the heavens. This mode of interpretation was carried to such an extreme that it became ridiculous, and the inevitable reaction took place. In the course of time, however, the germ of truth it contained was again brought to light; and very few persons now refuse to believe that some of the heroic myths have some slight historical basis, the "silly and senseless" element being classed as accretions similar to the fabulous tales attached to the indubitably historical name of Charlemagne. During the seventeenth century, some philosophers, incited by "the resemblance between biblical narrative and ancient myths, came to the conclusion that the Bible contained a pure and the myths a distorted form of an original revelation." But within the past century new theories have gradually gained ground: for the philologists have attempted to prove that the myths arose from a "disease of language"; while the anthropologists, basing their theory on comparative mythology, declare "it is man, it is human thought and human language combined, which naturally and necessarily produced the strange conglomerate of ancient fable."

Modern Theories

As these two last-named schools have either successfully confuted or incorporated the theories of all their predecessors, a brief outline of their respective beliefs will not be out of place. While philology compares only the "myths of races which speak languages of the same family" (as will shortly be demonstrated), anthropology resorts to all folklore, and seeks for the origin of myths, not in language, which it considers only as a subordinate cause, but in the "condition of thought through which all races have passed."

Anthropological Theory

The anthropologists, or comparative mythologists, do not deny that during the moderate allowance of two hundred and fifty thousand years, which they allot to the human race on earth, the myths may have spread from a single center, and either by migration, or by slave or wife stealing, or by other natural or accidental methods, may have "wandered all around the globe"; but they principally base their arguments on the fact that just as flint arrowheads are found in all parts of the world, differing but slightly in form and manufacture, so the myths of all nations "resemble each other, because they were formed to meet the same needs, out of the same materials."

They argue that this similarity exists, "not because the people came from the same stock" (which is the philologist's view), "but because they passed through the same savage intellectual condition." By countless examples taken from the folklore of all parts of the earth, they prove that the savage considers himself akin to beasts (generally to the one whose image is used as a tribal or family badge or totem), and "regards even plants, inanimate objects, and the most abstract phenomena, as persons with human parts and passions." To the savage, "sun, moon, and stars are persons, but savage persons"; and, as he believes "many of his own tribe fellows to have the power of assuming the form of animals," he concedes the same privilege and power to sun, moon, and stars, etc. This school further prove that all pre-Christian religions have idols representing beasts, that all mythologies represent the gods as fond of appearing in animal forms, and declare, that, although the Greeks were a thoroughly civilized people, we can still find in their mythology and religion "abundant survivals of savage manners and savage myths." They claim, that, during the myth-making age, the ancestors of the Greeks were about on an intellectual level with the present Australian Bushmen, and that "everything in civilized mythologies which we regard as irrational, seems only part of the accepted and rational order of things to the contemporary savages, and in the past seemed equally rational and natural to savages concerning whom we have historical information." Of course it is difficult, not to say impossible, for civilized man to put himself in the savage's place, and regard things from his point of view. The nearest approach to primitive intelligence which comes under our immediate observation is the working of the minds of small children, who, before they can talk intelligibly, whip the table or chair against which they have bumped their heads, and later on delight in weaving the most extraordinary tales. A little four-year-old seized a book and began to "read a story"; that is to say, to improvise a very improbable and highly colored tale of a pony. Forced to pause from lack of breath, she resumed the thread of her narrative with the words, "Now, this dog"; and, when it was suggested that the story was about a pony, she emphatically replied, "Well, this pony was a dog," and continued. Now, either because she perceived that the transformation had attracted attention, or to satisfy the childish inborn taste for the marvelous, in the course of the next few minutes the pony underwent as many transformations as Proteus, all of which apparently seemed perfectly natural to her. The anthropologists explain the tales of the various transformations of Jupiter and his animal progeny "as in many cases survivals of the totemistic belief in descent from beasts," while the mythologists explain them as "allegories of the fruitful union of heaven and earth, of rain and grain." The former school also declare that the myth of Cupid and Psyche, which has its parallel in stories found in all parts of the world, was invented to explain curious marriage customs (for in some countries it is unlawful for the husband to see his wife's face until after she has given birth to her first child, and in others a wife may not speak her husband's name): the latter school interpret the same myth as a beautiful allegory of the soul and the union of faith and love.

Philological Theory

The philologists' interpretation of myths is not only the most accredited at the present time, but also the most poetical. We therefore give a brief synopsis of their theory, together with an analysis, from their point of view, of the principal myths told at length in the course of this work. According to this school, "myths are the result of a disease of language, as the pearl is the result of a disease of the oyster"; the key to all mythologies lies in language; and the original names of the gods, "ascertained by comparative philology, will be found, as a rule, to denote elemental or physical phenomena," that is, phenomena of the sunshine, the clouds, rain, winds, fire, etc.

To make their process of reasoning plain, it should be explained, that as French, Spanish, and Italian are derived from the Latin, even so Latin, Greek, and Sanskrit have a common source in a much older language; that, even if Latin were entirely lost, the similarity of the word "bridge," for instance (*pons* in Latin), in French (*pont*), in Spanish (*puente*), and in Italian (*ponte*), would justify the conclusion that these terms had their origin in a common language, and that the people who spoke it were familiar with bridges, which they evidently called by some name phonetically the same.

Further to prove their position, they demonstrate the similarity of the most common words in all the languages of the same family, showing (as is the case with the word "father" in the accompanying table) that they undergo but few changes in sixteen different languages.

Sanskrit, *pitri*	Latin, *pater*
Zend, *paitar*	Greek, pronounced *pätair*
Persian, *pader*	Gothic, *vatar*
Erse, *athair*	German, *vater*
Italian, *padre*	Dutch, *fader*
Spanish, *padre*	Danish, *fader*
French, *père*	Swedish, *fader*
Saxon, *fæder*	English, *father*

The most learned of all these philologists argues that during the first or Rhematic period, there existed a tribe in Central Asia which spoke a monosyllabic language, in which lay the germs of the Turanian, Aryan, and Semitic forms of speech. This Rhematic period was followed by the Nomadic or Agglutinative age, when, little by little, the languages "received once for all that peculiar impress of their formative system which we still find in all the dialects and national idioms comprised under the name of Aryan or Semitic"; that is to say, in the Hindoo, Persian, Greek, Roman, Celt, Slav, and Teutonic languages, and in some three thousand kindred dialects.

After the Agglutinative period, and previous to the National era and "the appearance of the first traces of literature," he places "a period represented everywhere by the same characteristic features, called the Mythological or MythopŒic age."

It was during this period that the main part of the vast fund of mythic lore is supposed to have crystallized; for primitive man, knowing nothing whatever of physical laws, cause and effect, and the "necessary regularity of things," yet seeking an explanation of the natural phenomena, described them in the only way possible to him, and attributed to all inanimate objects his own sentiments and passions, fancying them influenced by the same things, in the same way. This tendency to personify or animate everything is universal among savages, who are nothing but men in the primitive state; and "in early philosophy throughout the

world, the sun, moon, and stars are alive, and, as it were, human in their nature."
"Poetry has so far kept alive in our minds the old animative theory of nature, that
it is no great effort in us to fancy the waterspout a huge giant or a sea monster,
and to depict, in what we call appropriate metaphor, its march across the field
of ocean."

As the names of the Greek gods and heroes have in a great measure been
found to correspond with the Sanskrit names of physical things, we have been able
to read some of the first thoughts of primitive man; and "the obvious meaning" of
many words "did much to preserve vestiges of plain sense in classic legend, in spite
of all the efforts of the commentators."

According to the philologists, therefore, these thoughts had already assumed a
definite form in the remote epoch when many nations, now scattered over the face
of the earth, occupied the same country, spoke the same language, and formed but
one people. Of course, "as long as such beings as Heaven or Sun are consciously
talked of in mythic language, the meaning of their legends is open to no question,
and the action ascribed to them will as a rule be natural and appropriate"; but with
the gradual diffusion of this one people to various parts of the earth, the original
meaning of these words was entirely lost, and they came to be looked upon eventually simply as the names of deities or heroes—very much in the way that the word
"good-by" has long survived its original form as a conscious prayer, "God be with
you!" and the word "ostracism" has lost all connection with an oyster shell.

The primitive meaning of a myth died away with the original meaning of a
word; and it is because "the Greek had forgotten that Zeus (Jupiter) meant 'the
bright sky,' that he could make him king" over a company of manlike deities on
Olympus.

We can best explain how the many anomalies occur, and how the myths got so
tangled up together that now it is almost impossible to disentangle them and trace
them back to their original meanings, by comparing their descent through the ages
to the course of a snowball, which, rolling down a mountain side, gathers to itself
snow, earth, rocks, etc., until, in the vast agglomeration of kindred and foreign
substances, the original nucleus is entirely lost to sight.

The fact that there are many different myths to explain the same phenomenon
can readily be accounted for by the old saying, "circumstances alter cases." Thus
the heat of the sun, for example, so beneficial at certain times, may prove baleful
and injurious at others.

The philologists, who believe that all myths (except the imitative myths, of which the tale of Berenice is a fair example) were originally nature myths, have divided them into a few large classes, which include the myths of the sky, the sun, dawn, daylight, night, moon, earth, sea, clouds, fire, wind, and finally those of the underworld and of the demons of drought and darkness.

SKY MYTHS

URANUS

Taking them in the order in which they are presented in this work, we find among the myths of the sky, Uranus, whose name, like that of the old Hindoo god Varuna, is derived from the Sanskrit root *var* ("to veil, conceal, or cover") This god was therefore a personification of the heavens, which are spread out like a veil, and cover all the earth; and we are further told that he hurled the thunder and lightning, his Cyclop children, down from his abode into the abyss called Tartarus.

JUPITER

Zeus (or Jupiter), whose name is the same as the Hindoo Dyaus Pitar, the god and personification of the bright sky or the heavens, has likewise been traced to the Sanskrit root *div* or *dyu*, meaning "to shine"; and there is also a noun *dyu* in that language which means either "sky" or "day." In early times the name was applied to the one God, and was therefore "retained by the Greeks and all other kindred people to express all they felt toward God"; but as the word also meant the visible sky, with its ever-changing aspect, some of the phrases used to describe it came, in the course of time, to denote vile and fickle actions, and apparently inconsistent behavior.

JUNO

The name of Hera (or Juno), the heavenly light, and therefore the complement and consort of the sky, is supposed to be derived from the Sanskrit *soar* ("the bright sky") and *surya* ("the sun"); and all the manifold changes which at first merely denoted the varying atmosphere, by being personified, gradually gave the impression of the jealous, capricious, vengeful person whom poets and writers have taken pleasure in depicting ever since.

ARGUS

Another personification of the sky, this time under the nocturnal and starry aspect, is Argus, whose many bright eyes never closed all at once, but kept constant watch over the moon (Io)—confided to his care by the heavenly light (Juno)—until at last their beams were quenched by the wind and rain (Mercury).

SUN AND DAWN MYTHS

EUROPA

The myths of the sun, from which it is almost impossible to separate those of the dawn, are probably more numerous than any others, and have some main features of resemblance in all cases. The first sun myth mentioned in the course of this work is the story of Europa, in which Europa is "the broad spreading light," born in PhŒnicia (the "purple land of morn"), the child of Telephassa ("she who shines from afar"), carried away from her eastern birthplace by the sky (Jupiter), closely pursued by the sun (her brother Cadmus), who, after passing through many lands, slays a dragon (the usual demon of drought or darkness), and sets (dies) at last without having ever overtaken the light of dawn (Europa).

APOLLO

Apollo, whose name of Helios is pure Greek for "the sun," had therefore not lost all physical significance for the Hellenic race, who worshiped in him the radiant personification of the orb of day. Another of his appellations, PhŒbus ("the lord of life and light"), still further emphasizes his character; and we are informed that he was born of the sky (Jupiter) and of the dark night (Leto), in the "bright land" (Delos), whence he daily starts on his westward journey.

Like all other solar heroes, Apollo is beautiful and golden-haired, radiant and genial, armed with unerring weapons, which he wields for good or evil, as the mood sways him. He is forced to labor, against his will at times, for the benefit of man, as, for instance, when he serves Admetus and Laomedon; and the cattle, by which he evidently sets such store, are the fleecy clouds, pasturing "in the infinite meadows of heaven," whose full udders drop down rain and fatness upon the land, which are stolen away either by the wind (Mercury), or the storm demon (Cacus), or the impious companions of Ulysses, who pay for their sacrilegious temerity with their lives.

CORONIS

The sun's affinity for the dawn is depicted by his love for Coronis, who, however beloved, falls beneath his bright darts; and, as "the sun was regarded naturally as the restorer of life" after the blighting influence of winter and disease, so their offspring (Æsculapius) was naturally supposed to have been endowed with marvelous curative powers.

The sun, for the same reason, was supposed to wage continual warfare against cold, sickness, and disease, and to use his bright beams or arrows against the demon of drought, darkness, or illness (Python), which in some form or other inevitably appears in every solar myth.

DAPHNE

In the story of Daphne, a name derived from *Dahana*, the Sanskrit *dawn*, we find another version of the same story, where the sun, although enamored with the dawn, causes her death. As some mythologists have interpreted it, Daphne is a personification of the morning dew, which vanishes beneath the sun's hot breath, and leaves no trace of its passage except in the luxuriant verdure.

CEPHALUS AND PROCRIS

In Cephalus and Procris the sun again appears, and his unerring spear unwittingly causes the death of his beloved Procris "while she lingers in a thicket (a place where the dew lingers longest)." This interpretation has been further confirmed by philological researches, which prove that the name "Procris" originated from a Sanskrit word meaning "to sprinkle"; and the stories evidently arose from three simple phrases,—"'the sun loves the dew,' 'the morning loves the sun,' and 'the sun kills the dew.'"

Orpheus and Eurydice

In the tale of Orpheus and Eurydice, while some mythologists see in him a personification of the winds, which "tear up trees as they course along, chanting their wild music," others see an emblem of "the morning, with its short-lived beauty." Eurydice, whose name, like that of Europa, comes from a Sanskrit word denoting "the broad spreading flush of the dawn across the sky," is, of course, a personification of that light, slain by "the serpent of darkness at twilight."

Orpheus is also sometimes considered as the sun, plunging into an abyss of darkness, in hopes of overtaking the vanishing dawn, Eurydice; and as the light (Eurydice) reappears opposite the place where he disappeared, but is no more seen after the sun himself has fairly risen, "they say that Orpheus has turned around too soon to look at her, and so was parted from the wife he loved so dearly."

His death in the forest, when his strength had all forsaken him, and his severed head floated down the stream murmuring "Eurydice," may also, perchance, have been intended to represent either the last faint breath of the expiring wind, or the setting of the sun in blood-tinged clouds.

Phaeton

In the story of Phaeton, whose name means "the bright and shining one," a description of the golden palace and car of the sun is given us. We are told that the venturesome young charioteer, by usurping his father's place, causes incalculable mischief, and, in punishment for his mismanagement of the solar steeds (the fleecy white clouds), is hurled from his exalted seat by a thunderbolt launched by the hand of Jupiter.

"This story arose from phrases which spoke of drought as caused by the chariot of Helios, when driven by some one who knew not how to guide his horses; and the smiting of Phaeton by the bolt of Zeus is the ending of the time of drought by a sudden storm of thunder."

ENDYMION

The story of Diana and Endymion has also been interpreted as a sun myth, in which the name "Endymion" refers specially to the dying or setting sun, who sinks to rest on Mount Latmus ("the land of forgetfulness," derived from the same root as "Leto"). Müller, the great authority in philology, tells us, that, in the ancient poetical and proverbial language of Elis, people said, "Selene loves and watches Endymion," instead of saying, "It is getting late"; "Selene embraces Endymion," instead of, "The sun is setting and the moon is rising"; "Selene kisses Endymion into sleep," instead of, "It is night."

These expressions remained long after their real meaning had ceased to be understood; and, as the human mind is generally as anxious for a reason as ready to invent one, a story arose without any conscious effort, that Endymion must have been a young lad loved by a young maiden, Selene.

ADONIS

In the story of Adonis some mythologists find another sun myth, in which Adonis, the short-lived sun, is slain by the boar, the demon of darkness, and passionately mourned by the dawn or twilight (Venus), who utterly refuses to exist without him.

TANTALUS

In the story of Tantalus (the sun), who in time of drought offers to Jupiter the flesh of his own offspring, Pelops (the withered fruits), and in punishment for his impiety is doomed to hunger and torturing thirst, we have again merely a story founded upon an expression used in time of drought, when the sun's heat, becoming too intense, burns up the fruit his fostering rays had produced, and men exclaimed, "Tantalus is slaying and roasting his own child!"

SISYPHUS

In the same way the stone which Sisyphus painfully forced up a steep ascent, only to see it go rolling down and plunge into a dark abyss enveloped in a great cloud of dust, has been interpreted to represent the sun, which is no "sooner pushed up to the zenith, than it rolls down to the horizon."

IXION

The name of Ixion has been identified with the Sanskrit word *Akshanah*, denoting one who is bound to a wheel, and has been proved akin "to the Greek *axón*, the Latin *axis*, and the English *axle*." This whirling wheel of fire is the bright orb of day, to which he was bound by order of Jupiter (the sky) because he dared insult Juno (the queen of the blue air); while Dia, his wife, is the dawn, the counterpart of Europa, Coronis, Daphne, Procris, Eurydice, and Venus, in the foregoing illustrations.

HERCULES

One of the greatest of all the solar heroes is doubtless the demigod Hercules, born at Argos (a word signifying "brightness") from the sky (Jupiter) and the dawn (Alcmene), who, in early infancy, throttles the serpents of darkness, and who, with untiring strength and patience, plods through life, never resting, and always on his journey performing twelve great tasks, interpreted to represent either the twelve signs of the Zodiac, or the twelve months of the solar year, or the twelve hours of daylight.

IOLE

Like Apollo and Cadmus, Hercules is forced to labor for mankind against his will. We see him early in life united to Megara, and, like Tantalus, slaying his own offspring in a sudden fit of madness. He loves and is soon forced to leave Iole, the violet-colored clouds. He performs great deeds, slays innumerable demons of drought and darkness on his way, and visits the enchanted land of the Hesperides,—a symbol of the western sky and clouds at sunset.

DEIANEIRA

The main part of his life is spent with Deianeira ("the destroying spouse"), a personification of the daylight; but toward the end of his career he again encounters Iole, now the beautiful twilight. It is then that Deianeira (the daylight), jealous of her rival's charms, sends him the bloody Nessus robe, which he has no sooner donned, than he tears it from his bleeding limbs, ascends the burning pile, and ends his career in one grand blaze,—the emblem of the sun setting in a framework of flaming crimson clouds.

Like all solar heroes, he too has unerring poisoned weapons ("the word *ios*, 'a spear,' is the same in sound as the word *ios*, 'poison'"), of which he is shorn only at death.

PERSEUS

Perseus also belongs to this category of myths. Danae, his mother, either the earth (*dano* means "burnt earth") or the dawn, a daughter of Acrisius (darkness), is born in Argos (brightness). Loved by Jupiter, the all-embracing sky, she gives birth to the golden-haired Perseus, a personification of the radiant orb of day; and he, like many another solar hero, is cast adrift immediately after his birth, owing to an ominous prophecy that he will slay the darkness from which he originally sprang.

As soon as Perseus attains manhood, he is forced to journey against his will into the distant land of the mists (the Grææ), and conquer the terrible Medusa, "the starlit night, solemn in its beauty, but doomed to die when the sun rises." He accomplishes this by means of his irresistible sword, the piercing rays of the sun, and then passes on to encounter the monster of drought, and to marry Andromeda, another personification of the dawn, the offspring of Celeus and Cassiopeia, who also represent night and darkness.

In company with Andromeda, Perseus, whose name also signifies "the destroyer," revisits his native land, and fulfills the prophecy by slaying Acrisius (the darkness), whence he originally sprang.

THESEUS

In the Athenian solar myth, Theseus is the sun, born of Ægeus (the sea, derived from *aisso*, "to move quickly like the waves") and Æthra (the pure air). He lingers in his birthplace, TrŒzene, until he has acquired strength enough to wield his invincible sword, then journeys onward in search of his father, performing count-less great deeds for the benefit of mankind. He slays the Minotaur, the terrible monster of darkness, and carries off the dawn (Ariadne); whom he is, however, forced to abandon shortly after on the Island of Naxos.

In his subsequent career we find him the involuntary cause of his father's death, then warring against the Centaurs (personifications of the clouds, through which the victorious sun is sometimes forced to fight his way), then again plung-ing for a short space of time into the depths of Tartarus, whence he emerges once more; and finally we see him uniting his fate to Phædra (the twilight), a sister of the beautiful dawn he loved in his youth. He ends his eventful career by being hurled headlong from a cliff into the sea,—an emblem of the sun, which often seems to plunge into the waves at eventide.

ARGONAUTS

In the story of the Argonautic expedition we have Athamas, who marries Nephele (the mist). Their children are Phryxus and Helle (the cold and warm air, or per-sonifications of the clouds), carried off to the far east by the ram—whose golden fleece was but an emblem of the rays of the sun—to enable them to escape from the baleful influence of their stepmother Ino (the broad daylight), who would fain encompass their destruction.

MEDEA

Helle, an emblem of the condensation of vapor, falls from her exalted seat into the sea, where she is lost. The ship Argo "is a symbol of the earth as a parent, which contains in itself the germs of all living things." Its crew is composed mainly of solar heroes, all in quest of the golden fleece (the rays of the sun), which Jason recovers by the aid of Medea (the dawn), after slaying the dragon (the demon of drought). Æetes, Medea's father, is a personification of the darkness, which vainly attempts to recover his children, the dawn and light (?), after they have been borne away by the all-conquering sun.

GLAUCE

Glauce (the broad daylight) next charms Jason; and the poisoned robe which causes her death is woven by Medea, now the evening twilight, who mounts her dragon car and flies to the far east, forsaking her husband (the sun) in his old age, when he is about to sink into the sleep of death.

MELEAGER

Meleager is also a solar hero. After joining the Argonautic expedition, and wandering far and wide, he returns home, slays the boar (or drought fiend), loves, but parts from, Atalanta (the dawn maiden), and is finally slain by his own mother, who casts into the flames the brand upon which his existence depends.

ŒDIPUS

In the Theban solar myth, Laius (derived from the same root as "Leto" and "Latmus") is the emblem of darkness, who, after marrying Jocasta (like Iole, a personification of the violet-tinted clouds of dawn), becomes the father of Œdipus, doomed by fate to be the murderer of his father. Early in life Œdipus is exposed on the barren hillside to perish,—an emblem of the horizontal rays of the rising sun, which seem to lie for a while upon the mountain slopes, ere they rise to begin their journey.

He too, like Cadmus, Apollo, Hercules, Perseus, Theseus, and Jason, is forced to wander far from home, and, after a prolonged journey, encounters and slays Laius (the darkness), from whom he derived his existence, and kills the dread monster of drought, the Sphinx, whose very name means "one who binds fast,"—a creature who had imprisoned the rain in the clouds, and thus caused great distress.

Urged on by unrelenting fate, he marries his own mother, Jocasta, now the violet-tinted twilight, and ends his life amid lightning flashes and rolls of thunder, after being accompanied to the end of his course by Antigone ("the pale light which springs up opposite the sun at his setting"). This story—which at first was merely intended to signify that the sun (Œdipus) must slay the darkness (Laius) and linger for a while beside the violet-colored clouds (Jocasta)—having lost its physical meaning, the Thebans added the tragic sequel, for it seemed but poetic justice that the author of such crimes should receive signal punishment.

EUMENIDES

As the Eumenides, or Erinnyes, were at first merely the searching light of day, from which nothing can be hidden, they came gradually to be considered the detectives and avengers of crime, and were therefore said to take possession of a criminal at the end of his course, and hurry him down into darkness to inflict horrible torments upon him.

BELLEROPHON

In the story of Bellerophon, although the name originally came from *Bellero* (some "power of darkness, drought, winter, or moral evil") and from *phon* or *phontes* (a word derived from the Sanskrit *han-tâ*, "the killer"), the Greeks, having forgotten the signification of the first part of the word, declared this hero was the murderer of Bellero, his brother, for which involuntary crime he was driven from home, and forced to wander about in search of shelter.

We find this hero, although enticed by Anteia (the dawn), virtuously hastening away, then sent against his will to fight the Chimæra (the monster of drought), whom he overcomes, thanks to his weapon and to Pegasus (the clouds), born from the mist of the sea, beneath whose hoofs fresh fountains were wont to spring.

Bellerophon, after many journeys, is finally united to Philonoe, a personification of the twilight, and ends his career by being hurled from the zenith into utter darkness by one of Jupiter's deadly thunderbolts.

"The fall of Bellerophon is the rapid descent of the sun toward evening, and the Alein plain is that broad expanse of somber light through which the sun sometimes seems to travel sullenly and alone to his setting."

TROJAN WAR

In the story of the Trojan war there are several sun myths; for Paris, Menelaus, Agamemnon, and Achilles have equal claims to be considered personifications of the sun. They love Œnone, Helen, Clytæmnestra, Briseis, various impersonations of the dawn, and forsake, or are forsaken by, their ladyloves, whom they meet again at the end of their career: for Paris sees Œnone, and expires with her on the burning pile; Menelaus recovers Helen, with whom he vanishes in the far west; Agamemnon rejoins Clytæmnestra, and dies by her hand in a bloody bath; while Achilles, after a period of sullen gloom, meets with an untimely death shortly after recovering the beautiful Briseis.

Like Perseus and Œdipus, Paris is exposed in early infancy, and lives to fulfill his destiny, and cause, though indirectly, the death of his parents.

In this myth, Helen (the beautiful dawn or twilight), whose name corresponds phonetically with the Sanskrit *Sarama*, born of the sky (Jupiter) and of the night (Leda, derived from the same root as "Leto," "Latmus," and "Laius"), is carried away by Paris, whom some mythologists identify with the Hindoo *Panis* (or "night demons") instead of the sun. In this character he entices away the fickle twilight (Helen) during her husband's temporary absence, and bears her off to the far east, where, after struggling for a while to retain possession of her and her treasures, he is finally forced to relinquish her, and she returns to her husband and her allegiance.

The siege of Troy has thus been interpreted to signify "a repetition of the daily siege of the east by the solar powers, that every evening are robbed of their brightest treasures in the west."

Achilles, like several of his brother heroes, "fights in no quarrel of his own; his wrath is the sun hiding his face behind the clouds; the Myrmidons are his attendant beams, who no longer appear when the sun is hidden; Patroclus is the feeble reflection of the sun's splendor, and stands to him in precisely the same relation as Phaeton to Helios," and, like him, meets with an early death.

ULYSSES

In the story of Ulysses we find a reproduction of the story of Hercules and Perseus: for Ulysses, early in life, after wedding Penelope, is forced to leave her to fight for another; and on his return, although longing to rejoin his morning bride, he cannot turn aside from the course marked out for him. He is detained by Circe (the moon), who weaves airy tissues, and by Calypso (the nymph of darkness); but neither can keep him forever, and he returns home enveloped in an impenetrable disguise, after having visited the Phæacian land (the land of clouds or mists). It is only after he has slain the suitors of Penelope (the weaver of bright evening clouds) that he casts aside his beggar's garb to linger for a short time beside her ere he vanishes in the west.

MINERVA

The greater part of the dawn myths have been explained simultaneously with the sun myths, with which they are inextricably interwoven. One personification of the dawn, however, stands apart. It is Minerva, whose Greek name, Athene, is derived, like Daphne, from the Sanskrit *Dahana*, or *ahana* (meaning "the light of daybreak"), and we are thus enabled to understand why the Greeks described her as sprung from the forehead of Zeus (the heavens). She gradually became the impersonation of the illuminating and knowledge-giving light of the sky; for in Sanskrit the same word also means "to wake" and "to know," while the Latins connected her name of Minerva with *mens*, the same as the Greek *ménos* and the English *mind*.

MOON MYTHS

DIANA, IO, AND CIRCE

In the moon myths the most important personification is first Diana, the horned huntress, "for to the ancients the moon was not a lifeless ball of stones and clods." Diana, like Apollo, her twin brother, was also a child of the sky (Jupiter) and of night (Latona), and, like him, was born in the "bright land" (Delos). She also possessed bright and unerring arrows, and in the course of her nightly journey she looked lovingly down upon the sleeping face of the setting sun (Endymion).

Io and Circe, already mentioned, are also personifications of the moon, and Io's wanderings represent its journeys across the sky.

EARTH MYTHS

GÆA AND RHEA

In the earth myths, beside those already mentioned in connection with the sun myths, we have Gæa and Rhea, the mothers and consorts of the Sky and of Time, who swallows his own children, "the Days, as they come each in order."

CERES AND PROSERPINA

We have also Ceres or Demeter, "the mother of all things," and more particularly of "the maiden" Cora (or Proserpina), whose loss she grievously mourned; for she had been carried away by Pluto to the underworld, whence she could only emerge at the command of Jupiter. During the time of Ceres' mourning, the earth remained barren, and it seemed as though all mortal things must die. But when Proserpina (the spring or vegetation) returned from her sojourn under the ground, people said "that the daughter of the earth was returning in all her beauty; and when summer faded into winter, they said that the beautiful child had been stolen away from her mother by dark beings, who kept her imprisoned beneath the earth." The sorrow of Ceres was therefore merely a poetical way of expressing "the gloom which falls on the earth during the cheerless months of winter."

DANAE AND SEMELE

Danae, as a personification of the earth, was quickened by the golden shower, the light of the morning, which streamed in upon the darkness of the night. Semele has also been interpreted as the earth, the chosen bride of the sky, who brings forth her offspring in the midst of the thunder and lightning of a summer storm.

SEA MYTHS

Oceanus and Neptune

The myths of the sea comprise, of course, Oceanus and Neptune (the earth-shaker), whose name is connected with such words as "potent" and "despot," and whose "green hair circles all the earth." We are further informed that he loves the earth (Ceres), whom he embraces, and that he marries the graceful undulating Amphitrite, whose gliding charms appeal to him. Neptune's palace is beneath the deep waters near Greece, and he is said to ride about his realm in a swift chariot drawn by golden or white maned steeds.

Nereus

Nereus, another personification of the sea, whose name is derived from *nao* ("to flow"), is quite inseparable from his native element, even in the Greeks' conception of him, as are also the Tritons, Oceanides, Nereides, and the alluring Sirens; who, however, have also been viewed as personifications of the winds.

CLOUD MYTHS

Charon

The cloud myths, to which frequent allusion has already been made, comprise not only the cattle of the sun, the Centaurs, Nephele, Phryxus, Helle, and Pegasus, but as, "in primitive Aryan lore, the sky itself was a blue sea, and the clouds were ships sailing over it," so Charon's boat was supposed to be one of these vessels, and the gilded shallop in which the sun daily made his pilgrimage back to the far east, another.

Niobe

As the ancient Aryan had the same word to denote cloud and mountain ("for the piles of vapor on the horizon were so like Alpine ranges"), the cloud and mountain myths are often the same. In the story of Niobe we have one of the cloud myths. According to some mythologists, Niobe herself is a personification of the clouds. Her many children, the mists, are fully as beautiful as Apollo and Diana, by whose bright darts they are ruthlessly slain. Niobe grieves so sorely at their untimely death, that she dissolves in a rain of tears, which turns into hard ice on the mountain summit. According to other authorities, she was a personification of winter, and her tears represented the thaw occasioned by the sunbeams (Apollo's arrows).

FIRE MYTHS

CYCLOPES

The fire myths also form quite a large class, and comprise the Cyclopes (the thunder and lightning), children of Heaven and Earth, whose single blazing eye has been considered an emblem of the sun. They forge the terrible thunderbolts, the weapons of the sky (Jupiter), by means of which he is enabled to triumph over all his enemies, and rule supreme.

TITANS

The Titans are emblems of the subterranean fires and the volcanic forces of nature, which, hidden deep underground, occasionally emerge, heave up great masses of rock, and hurl them about with an accompaniment of deafening roars, while their ponderous tread causes the very earth beneath them to tremble.

PROMETHEUS

In this group we also find Prometheus, whose name has been traced to the Sanskrit *pramantha* (or "fire drill"). Learned men have therefore proved that the "beneficent Titan, who stole fire from heaven and bestowed it upon mankind as the richest of boons," was originally nothing but the lightning ("the celestial drill which churns fire out of the clouds"); but the Greeks had so entirely forgotten this etymological meaning, that they interpreted his name as the "fore-thinker," and considered him endowed with extraordinary prophetic powers.

VULCAN

Vulcan (or Hephæstus), strictly "the brightness of the flame," another fire hero, is represented as very puny at birth, because the flame comes from a tiny spark. His name is derived from the Hindoo *agni*, whence come the Latin *ignis* and the English verb *to ignite*. Vulcan dwells by preference in the heart of volcanoes, where the intense heat keeps the metals in fusion, and so malleable that he can mold them at will; and, as "the association of the heavenly fire with the life-giving forces of nature is very common," the Hindoo Agni was considered the patron of marriage as well as of fire; and the Greeks, to carry out this idea, united their fire god, Hephæstus, to the goddess of marriage, Aphrodite.

VESTA

The Greek Hestia (or Latin Vesta) was also a personification of fire; and, her name having retained its primitive meaning to a great extent, "she continued to the end, as she had been from the beginning, the household altar, the sanctuary of peace and equity, and the source of all happiness and wealth." Her office was not limited merely to the hearths of households and cities, for it was supposed "that in the center of the earth there was a hearth which answered to the hearth placed in the center of the universe."

WIND MYTHS

MERCURY

In the myths of the wind, Mercury (or Hermes) was one of the principal personifications. According to the ancients, he was born of the sky (Jupiter) and the plains (Maia), and after a very few hours' existence assumed gigantic proportions, stole away the cattle of the sun (the clouds), and, after fanning up a great fire in which he consumed some of the herd, glided back into his cradle at dawn. With a low, mocking chuckle at the recollection of the pranks he had played, he sank finally into rest. His name, derived from the Sanskrit *Sarameias*, means "the breeze of a summer morning"; and it is in his capacity of god of the wind that he is supposed to waft away the souls of the dead; for "the ancients held that in the wind were the souls of the dead." Mercury is the "lying, tricksome wind god who invented music," for his music is but "the melody of the winds, which can awaken feelings of joy and sorrow, of regret and yearning, of fear and hope, of vehement gladness and utter despair."

MARS

Another personification of the wind was Mars (or Ares), born of the sky (Jupiter) and of the heavenly light (Juno) in the bleak land of Thrace, rejoicing in din and in the noise of warfare. His nature is further revealed by his inconstancy and capriciousness; and whenever he is overcome, he is noted for his great roar. His name comes from the same root as Maruts, the Indian god, and means the "grinder" or "crusher." It was first applied "to the storms which throw heaven and earth into confusion, and hence the idea of Ares is confined to mere disorder and tumult."

OTUS AND EPHIALTES

Otus and Ephialtes, the gigantic sons of Neptune, were also at first merely personifications of the wind and hurricanes. The name of the latter indicates "one who leaps." Although very short-lived, these giants were supposed to increase rapidly in size, and assume colossal proportions, which inspired the hearts of men and gods with terror, until they saw them finally slain by the unfailing arrows of the sun.

PAN, ÆOLUS, AND THE HARPIES

Pan, Æolus, his numerous progeny, and the Harpies, were also wind divinities who never entirely lost their original character with the Greeks, and were therefore worshiped merely as personifications of the elements.

UNDERWORLD MYTHS

CERBERUS AND PLUTO

The myths of drought, darkness, and of the underworld have sufficiently been dwelt upon as personified by Python, the Hydra, Geryones, the Gorgons, Grææ, Minotaur, Sphinx, Chimæra, etc.; but their main personifications were Cerberus (the grim three-headed guardian of the nether world) and Pluto (or Aïdes), whose name means "the wealth-giver," or "the unseen," who greedily drew all things down into his realm, never to relinquish his grasp upon them.

Such is the physical explanation of the various poetical myths which form the staple of classic literature, and which have been a fount of inspiration for poets and artists of all ages.

GENEALOGICAL TABLE.

NOTE.—Double vertical lines indicate that several generations intervene.

Chaos–*Nyx*
Erebus–*Nyx*

Hemera–*Ether* Charon *Eris* Somnus Mors
Morpheus

Gæa Eros *Gæa*
Uranus–*Gæa*

Pontus
Phorcys

Bellona Stheno Euryale Medusa–Neptune
Pegasus Polyphemus

Harpies Tityus Nereus
Antæus
Typhœus Enceladus
Chimæra
Hydra Cerberus
Nemean Lion *Sphinx*

Oceanus–*Thetis* Cœus–*Phœbe* Iapetus–*Clymene* Hyperion–*Crius* *Themis*–*Ilia* Cronus–*Rhea* Mnemosyne–Jupiter Brontes Steropes Arges Briareus Cottus Gyes

Clio Calliope *Thalia Euterpe Urania Melpomene Terpsichore Polyhymnia Erato*
Hymen Orpheus–*Eurydice*

Mars *Latona*–Jupiter
Dia–Ixion *Coronis*–Apollo–*Diana*
Æsculapius
Machaon *Hygeia*

Aurora–*Eolus* *Parcæ Horæ*
Corus Eurus Notus Aquila Zephyrus–*Flora*
Boreas–*Orithyia*

Vesta Juno–Jupiter Neptune–*Amphitrite* *Ceres*–Jupiter Pluto–*Proserpina* Jupiter–*Io*
Triton *Proserpina* Epaphus
Neptune–*Libya*
Agenor–*Telephassa* Belus

Mars–Venus Vulcan–*Medusa* *Hebe*–Hercules
Cacus Periphetes Cercyon

Anteros Cupid–*Psyche Harmonia*–Cadmus Cilix Phœnix *Europa*–Jupiter
Ino–Athamas–Nephele *Autonoe–Agave–Semele* Polydorus Sarpedon Minos–*Pasiphae*
Aristæus Pentheus Jupiter Rhadamanthus Minos
Actæon Bacchus–*Ariadne*

Danaus Ægyptus
Danaides–50 Sons
Acrisius
Danae–Jupiter
Perseus–*Andromeda*

Pygmalion Dido–Sychæus
Labdacus
Laius–*Jocasta*
Jocasta–Œdipus

Æolus Xuthus
Dorus Ion Achæus
Æolus
Salmoneus Sisyphus
Tyro–Neptune Glaucus
Bellerophon–*Philonoe*

Sthenelus Eurystheus *Admete Œneus–Althæa* Meleager
Electryon Iphicles Hercules–*Deianeira* Hyllus–*Iole*
Alcæus Iolaus
Amphitryon–*Alcmene*–Jupiter

Pirithous–*Hippodamia* *Chione*
Menetius Atlas Hesperus Epimetheus–*Pandora* Prometheus
Hesperides *Pyrrha*–Deucalion
Hellen

Zetus Calais *Cleopatra*

Hippolyte–Theseus–*Phaedra Ariadne*–Bacchus
Hippolytus

Capys–Themis
Anchises–*Venus*
Æneas–*Lavinia–Creusa*
Numitor Iulus
Ilia–Mars
Remus Romulus

Eteocles Polynices *Antigone Ismene*

Tithonus–*Aurora*
Laomedon

Sol
*Pasiphae Circe Æetes Æson Pelias Neleus
Absyrtus Medea*–Jason Nestor

Peneus–*Gæa* Inachus Proteus *Doris–Nereus Metis*–Jupiter
Daphne *Io* *Minerva*

Clymene–Æthra *Calypso Clytie Electra*
Iapetus Atlas Ulysses Jupiter Teucer
Pleiades Dardanus–*Batea*

Mercury–*Penelope*–Ulysses
Pan Telemachus

Iphigenia Electra–Pylades Orestes

Achelous–*Calliope Sirens*

Alpheus–*Arethusa*

Amphitrite–Neptune *Dione*–Jupiter *Arethusa Galatea*–Acis Peleus–*Thetis Clymene*–Apollo
Triton *Venus* Achilles *Heliades* Phaeton

Jupiter–*Antiope–Lycus–Dirce Tantalus*
Zethus Amphion–*Niobe* Pelops
Jupiter–*Leda*–Tyndareus Atreus
Helen Castor Pollux Clytemnestra–Agamemnon Menelaus–*Helen*
Hermione–Pyrrhus

Priam–*Hecuba* *Hesione*–Telamon
Ajax

Hector–*Andromache Paris–Helen Cassandra Polites Polyxena* Deiphobus–*Helen*

INDEX TO POETICAL QUOTATIONS

Addison, 14, 39, 74, 75, 160, 168, 169

Æschylus, 245

Akenside, 156

Apollonius, 118

Apollonius Rhodius, 176, 272

Arion, 152

Aristophanes, 5,

Arnold, Edwin, 103, 104, 105, 107

Arnold, Matthew, 64

Beaumont and Fletcher, 304

Bion, 101, 102

Boyesen, 89, 129

Browning, E. B., 12, 101, 128

Bryant, 31, 32, 48, 86, 138, 147, 208, 309,
    319, 323, 324, 325, 327–328, 329, 330,
    331, 332, 334, 341, 344, 350, 351, 352,
    354, 356, 357, 360, 361, 362, 364, 365

Byron, 38, 82, 85, 108–109

Catullus, 225, 256, 258, 260, 310

Chapman, 143

Coluthus, 312, 316

Conington, 31, 41, 54, 132, 188, 199,
    211, 223, 338, 340, 367, 368, 369, 370,
    371, 372, 373, 374, 375, 377, 378, 381,
    384

Cornwall, Barry, 180

Cowper, 123, 149, 312

Croxall, 173, 174

Darwin, 115, 182, 217, 218, 227, 229

Dryden, 25, 26, 27, 34, 60, 155, 163, 164,
    206

Elton, 2, 3, 11, 19, 23, 35, 42, 102, 127,
    131, 148, 167, 218, 240, 256, 268, 272,
    274, 311, 312, 315, 316, 345

Emerson, 301

Euripides, 161, 228, 316, 320

Eusden, 110

Flaccus, 42, 218, 272, 274

Fletcher, 28

Francklin, 164, 231, 233, 236, 283, 284,
    285, 286, 288, 289, 290, 291, 293, 336

Frere, 5

Goldsmith, 126

Gray, 175

H. H. (Helen Hunt Jackson), 64

Hemans, 51, 90

Hesiod, 3, 11, 19, 23, 148, 228, 345

Holmes, 335, 345

Homer, 13, 29, 31, 32, 48, 86, 138, 140,
    143, 147, 149, 155, 162, 168, 170, 208,
    296, 301, 309, 319, 323, 324, 325,
    327–328, 329, 330, 331, 332, 341, 344,
    350, 351, 352, 354, 356, 357, 360, 361,
    362, 364, 365

Homeric Hymn, 184, 190

Horace, 17, 65, 280

Hunt, 107, 215, 346

Ingelow, 183, 190

Iriarte, Tomas de, 380

Keats, 57, 81, 90, 96, 111,112, 126, 144,
    172, 175, 188, 305, 306, 308

Landon, 105
Longfellow, 78, 91, 99, 202
Lowell, 13, 54, 70, 123
Lucan, 212

Macaulay, 122, 281
Martinez de la Rosa, 173
Melanippides, 63
Meleager, 86, 267
Meredith, Owen, 62
Milton, 69, 137, 156, 237
Moore, 6, 60, 189, 280
Morris, Lewis, 89, 92, 93, 103, 115, 118,
    119, 121, 144, 190, 235, 246, 254, 341
Moschus, 35, 129

Nonnus, 167

Onomacritus, 268, 272, 274
Orphic Argonautics, 268
Orphic Hymn, 183
Ovid, 2, 25, 26, 27, 34, 60, 110, 168, 169,
    173, 174, 206, 256, 302, 303

Pike, 51
Pindar, 7, 163
Pitt, C., 159, 191, 201
Pope, 13, 29, 47, 69, 140, 149, 162, 238,
    296, 302, 303
Potter, 161, 228, 245, 320
Prior, 58, 136, 141, 242, 286

Quintus Smyrnæus, 311

St. John, Mrs. 242, 245
Saxe, 52, 53, 67, 74, 111, 154, 254

Schiller, 113, 237
Scott, 159
S. G. B., 237
Shakespeare, 34, 66, 132
Shelley, 45, 95, 239
Simonides, 240
Somerville, 80
Sophocles, 164, 231, 233, 236, 283, 284,
    285, 286, 288, 289, 290, 291, 293, 336
Southey, 81
Spenser, 49, 73, 96
Statius, 127, 131
Swift, 65

Tennyson, 49, 70, 98, 310, 312, 337, 345,
    366
Theocritus, 215, 315, 346
Timocreon of Rhodes, 153

Virgil, 31, 41, 54, 123, 132, 154, 155, 159,
    163, 164, 178, 188, 191, 199, 201, 211,
    223, 338, 340, 367, 368, 369, 370, 371,
    372, 373, 374, 375, 377, 378, 381, 382,
    384

Warton, 178
Wordsworth, 23, 54, 78, 222, 275, 299,
    321, 322
Worsley, 77

Young, 197

GLOSSARY AND INDEX

AB-SYR´TUS. Son of King Æetes of Colchis, slain by Medea, 274

A-BY´DUS. A city of Asia Minor, the home of Leander, 103–109

A-CHÆ´US. Grandson of Hellen, and ancestor of the Achaians, 28

A-CHA´I-ANS. Inhabitants of the province of Achaia, 28, 325

A-CHA´TES. Friend and inseparable companion of Æneas, 374

ACH-E-LO´US. River in Greece, bearing the name of its god, 231

ACH-E-MEN´I-DES. Ulysses' sailor, rescued from Polyphemus by Æneas, 372

ACH´E-RON
    1. River in Hades, 155
        Ulysses visits, 356
        Æneas crosses, 380
    2. Father of Furies, 156

A-CHIL´LES. Son of Peleus and Thetis, 319–321
    surrenders Briseis, 323, 324
    the Greeks appeal to, 328–329
    slays Hector, 331–334
    death, 335–336
    in Happy Isles, 366
    father of Pyrrhus, 368
    significance, 403

A´CIS. Youth loved by Galatea, and slain by Polyphemus, 346

A-CRIS´I-US. King of Argos, and father of Danae, 208–210
    significance, 399

A-CROP´O-LIS. Hill in Athens, the site of the Parthenon and Theseus' temple, 263

AC-TÆ´ON. Hunter changed to a stag by Diana, 92–93

AD-ME´TE. Daughter of Eurystheus, covets Hippolyte's girdle, 223, 225

AD-ME´TUS. King of Thessaly, served by Apollo, and saved from death by Alcestis, 54–55
    Hercules restores Alcestis to, 229
    one of the Argonauts, 268
    in Calydonian Hunt, 277

A-DO´NIS. Hunter loved by Venus and slain by a boar, 101–103
    significance, 191, 397

A-DRAS´TUS. King of Argos;
    his horse Arion, 147–148
    father of Hippodamia, 261
    sends expedition against Thebes, 291

Æ´A-CUS. One of the three judges of the dead in Hades, 156

Æ-Æ´A. Island inhabited by Circe and visited by Ulysses, 353, 354–356

Æ-E´TES. King of Colchis, father of Medea and Absyrtus, 270, 272
    brother of Circe, 353
    significance, 400–401

Æ-GE´AN SEA. Delos chained in, 52
    Arion borne by dolphins in, 71, 73
    named after Ægeus, 260

Æ-GE´US. King of Athens, father of Theseus, 251, 253–254

drowns himself, 256

significance, 400

Æ´GIS. Shield or breastplate of Minerva
and Jupiter, 47–48

loaned to Perseus, 242

bears Medusa's head, 247

Æ-GIS´THUS. Murderer of
Agamemnon;

slain by Orestes, 342

ÆG´LE. One of the Heliades;

changed to a poplar tree, 77

Æ-GYP´TUS. Brother of Danaus, 160–161

Æ-NE´A-DÆ. City which Æneas
proposed to found in Thrace, 370

Æ-NE´AS. Son of Venus and Anchises, 103

Æneas' descendants, 133

worship introduced into Italy by,
196

hero of Virgil's Æneid, 367–385

Æ-NE´AS SIL´VI-A. Son of Æneas;

founder of Alba Longa, 385

Æ-NE´ID. Virgil's epic poem on the
adventures of Æneas, 382

Æ-O´LI-A. Same as Æolian Islands;

in Asia Minor, near Ægean Sea, 212

Æ-O´LI-AN ISLANDS. The home of
Æolus, god of the winds, 211

supposed to be Lipari Islands, 211

Æ-O´LI-AN RACE. Descendants of
Æolus, son of Hellen, 27

Æ´O-LUS.

1. God of the winds, 211–213

Juno's bargain with, 268

gift to Ulysses, 352

destruction of Æneas' fleet, 373

significance, 409

2. Son of Hellen, founder of the
Æolian race, 27

ÆS-CU-LA´PI-US. Son of Apollo and
Coronis, 53–54

Machaon, son of, 336

significance, 395

Æ´SON. Father of Jason, 265

rejuvenated by Medea, 265

Æ´THER. God of light, 3

dethroned, 7

Æ´THRA. Princess of Trœzene, 251

mother of Theseus, 253–254

Helen intrusted to, 261

significance, 400

ÆT´NA. Volcano in Sicily, 179

the tomb of Enceladus, 14

forge of Vulcan, 138, 140, 331

Ceres' visit to, 183

Æ-TO´LI-A. Country between Epirus
and Locris, 277

AF´RI-CA.

Hercules' visit to, 225, 226

AFTERTHOUGHT. Name given to
Epimetheus, 15

AG-A-MEM´NON. Chief of the
expedition against Troy, 319–327

return of, 341

troops of, 368

significance, 403

A-GA´VE. Mother of Pentheus, 178

infuriated by Bacchus, slays her
son, 178

A-GE´NOR. Father of Europa, Cadmus,
Cilix, Phœnix, 34, 35

AG-LA´IA. One of the Graces;

an attendant of Venus, 96

A-ï´DES. Same as Pluto;
significance, 410

A-ï-DO´NEUS. Same as Pluto, god of the
Infernal Regions, 153

A´JAX. Greek hero in Trojan war, 318
Patroclus' corpse recovered by, 332
insanity of, 335–336

AL´BA LON´GA. City in Italy founded
by Æneas Silvia, 385

AL-CES´TIS. Wife of Admetus;
dies to save his life, 55
restored by Hercules, 229

AL-CI´DES. Same as Hercules, 215
lion skin of, 219
Deianeira accompanies, 231
Deianeira's charm for, 235
pose of, 238

AL-CIM´E-DE. Queen of Iolcus;
mother of Jason, 265

AL-CIN´O-US. Phæacian king,
enables Ulysses to reach Ithaca, 361

AL-CIP´PE. Daughter of Mars;
carried off by Halirrhothius, 132

ALC-ME´NE. Wife of Jupiter, and
mother of Hercules, 18, 215
significance, 398

A-LEC´TO. One of the Furies, 19
sent by Juno to kindle war
between Æneas and the Latins,
381

A-LEC´TRY-ON. Servant of Mars;
changed to a cock, 99

AL-PHE´US.
1. River of Peloponnesus;
dammed to clean Augean
stable, 220

2. The river god who pursued
Arethusa, 186, 188

AL-THÆ´A. Mother of Meleager, 277, 278

AM-AL-THE´A. Goat which nursed
Jupiter, 11

AM-A-SE´NUS. River over which
Metabus flung Camilla, 381

A-MA´TA. Wife of Latinus, 380
driven mad by Alecto, 380
suicide of, 384

AM´A-ZONS. Nation of warlike women;
Hercules visits, 223
Theseus visits, 260
Bellerophon visits, 298
Queen of the, 335

AM-BRO´SI-A. Celestial food used by
the gods, 29
gods deprived of, 74

AM´MON. Temple of Jupiter in Libya, 38

A´MOR. Same as Eros, Cupid, etc.;
god of love, 3
son of Venus and Mars, 99

AM-PHI´ON. Son of Jupiter and Antiope;
musician, 70
King of Thebes, 71

AM-PHI-TRI´TE. Same as Salacia, queen
of the sea;
wife of Neptune, 148, 149, 151
train of, 151
significance, 406

AN-CHI´SES. Husband of Venus, 103
father of Æneas, 367
prophecy recalled by, 371
death of, 372
death anniversary of, 377
Æneas' visit to, 378, 380

AN-CI´LE. Shield of Mars, guarded by the Salii in Rome, 135

AN-DRÆ´MON. Husband of Dryope; saw her changed to a tree, 302–303

AN-DROM´A-CHE. Wife of Hector; parting of Hector and, 327–328 grief of, 334 captivity of, 372

AN-DROM´E-DA. Daughter of Celeus and Cassiopeia; saved by Perseus, 246–247, 249 significance, 399

AN-TÆ´US. Giant son of Gæa; defender of the Pygmies, 226 slain by Hercules, 227

AN-TE´I-A. Wife of Prœtus; accuses Bellerophon falsely, 295 significance, 402

AN´TE-ROS. God of passion, 101 son of Venus and Mars, 103

AN-TIG´O-NE. Daughter of Œdipus and Jocasta; buried alive, 293 significance, 401

AN-TIN´O-US. One of Penelope's suitors; slain by Ulysses, 364

AN-TI´O-PE. Wife of Jupiter; mother of Amphion and Zethus; persecuted by Dirce, 71

A-PHA´RE-US. Father of Castor's murderer, 280

APH-RO-DI´TE. Same as Venus, Dione, etc., 95–122 significance, 408

A-POL´LO. Same as Phœbus, Sol, and Helios, 51–82 god of the sun, music, poetry, and medicine, 44 Diana's brother, 85 Niobe's sons slain by, 88 Mars and Venus seen by, 98 Mercury steals cattle of, 124 giants slain by, 128 walls built by, 144 Marpessa claimed by, 149 Vesta loved by, 179 Janus, son of, 201 oracles of, 283, 284 steed of, 296 Cassandra loved by, 314 Chryses appeals to, 322–324 significance, 394–395, 398, 401, 404, 407

AQ´UI-LO. West wind, son of Æolus and Aurora, 211, 213

A-RACH´NE. Minerva's needlework contest with, 48–49

AR-CA´DI-A. Province of Peloponnesus, 220, 276 Mercury's birthplace, 123

AR´CAS. Son of Jupiter and Callisto; constellation of the Little Bear, 42

A-RE-O-PA-GI´TÆ. Judges of the criminal court of Athens, 133

A-RE-OP´A-GUS. Hill near Athens; site of the Parthenon, 133

A´RES. Same as Mars, 131 significance, 409

A-RE´TE.
   1. Goddess of virtue; takes charge of Hercules, 217–218

2. Wife of Alcinous;
mother of Nausicaa, 361

AR-E-THU´SA. Nymph of Diana;
changed to a fountain, 186,
188–189

AR´GES (Sheet-lightning). A Cyclop;
son of Uranus and Gæa, 8

AR´GO. Vessel in which Jason set sail in
search of the golden fleece, 268–271
significance, 400

AR-GO-NAU´TIC EXPEDITION.
in search of golden fleece, 148
Zetes and Calais in, 213
Hercules in, 229
Meleager in, 277
significance, 400

AR´GO-NAUTS. Name given to Jason
and crew, 268–276
significance, 400

AR´GOS. City in Argolis, dedicated to
Juno, 42, 44
Eurystheus, king of, 217–218
Acrisius, king of, 239
Adrastus, king of, 261
Prœtus, king of, 295
Agamemnon's return to, 341
significance, 398, 399

AR´GUS.
Name of myriad-eyed giant who
watched Io, 127–129
significance, 394
Name of Ulysses' faithful hound,
362

A-RI-AD´NE. Daughter of Minos;
deserted by Theseus, 175–176
marries Bacchus, 175

Theseus aided by, 257–258
significance, 400

A-RI´ON.
1. Winged steed;
the offspring of Neptune and
Ceres, 147
2. Musician;
thrown into the sea by pirates,
saved by a dolphin, 71, 73

AR-IS-TÆ´US. Youth who indirectly
causes Eurydice's death, 66

AR´TE-MIS. Same as Diana, goddess of
the moon and the chase, 85–93

AS-CAL´A-PHUS. Spirit in Hades who
saw Proserpina eat pomegranate
seeds, 190

A´SI-A MI´NOR. West of Asia;
Bacchus' visit to, 172
Vesta's shrine in, 195
Thetis' flight from, 331

AS-KLE´PI-OS. Same as Æsculapius;
son of Apollo and Coronis, 53

AS-TY´A-NAX. Infant son of Hector
and Andromache, 327

AT-A-LAN´TA. Maiden who takes part
in Calydonian Hunt and races with
Milanion or Hippomenes, 277–278, 280
significance, 400

A´TE, or ERIS. Goddess of discord, 131

ATH´A-MAS. King of Thebes;
Ino in madness slain by, 170
father of Phryxus and Helle, 267
significance, 400

A-THE´NE. Same as Minerva, 45
tutelary goddess of Athens, 47
significance, 405

A-THE´NI-ANS. Inhabitants of Athens;
        tribute of, 213
        ingratitude of, 254
ATH´ENS. Minerva's festivals at, 50
        tribunal at, 132
        contest for, 146
        Ægeus, king of, 251
        Theseus' arrival at, 253, 254
        Ariadne elopes to, 257
        Castor and Pollux' visit to, 261
        Theseus, king of, 263
        Peleus, king of, 309
AT´LAS. One of Iapetus' sons, 15
        daughters of, 90
        brother of Prometheus visited by
            Hercules, 226–228
        heavens supported by, 227–228
        Perseus petrifies, 245–246
        significance, 388
AT´RO-POS. One of the Fates;
        cuts the thread of life, 159
AT´TI-CA. Province of Greece;
        Cecrops founds city in, 47
        oppression of, 231
        shores of, 260
AU-GE´AS. King of Elis;
        his stables were cleansed by
            Hercules, 220
AU´LIS. Port in Bœotia, the meeting-
        place of the Greek expedition against
        Troy, 318, 319, 320
AU-RO´RA. Same as Eos, goddess of
        dawn;
        jealousy of, 60
        attendant of Apollo, 75, 99
        Tithonus loved by, 80

Æolus' wife, 211
AUS´TER. Southwest wind, same as
        Notus;
        a son of Æolus and Aurora, 213
AU-TOM´E-DON. Achilles' charioteer, 332
AV´EN-TINE. One of the seven hills on
        which Rome is built, 225
A-VER´NUS. Lake near Naples;
        the entrance to Hades in Italy, 154
        Æneas' visit to, 378

BAB´Y-LON. The home of Pyramus and
        Thisbe, 109
BAC-CHA-NA´LI-A. Festivals in honor
        of Bacchus, 178
BAC-CHAN´TES. Female followers of
        Bacchus, 172, 178
        Orpheus slain by, 70
BAC´CHUS. Same as Dionysus, god of
        wine and revelry;
        Vulcan visited by, 140
        son of Jupiter and Semele, 170–178
        Ariadne rescued by, 176
        tutor of, 304
        gift from, 310
BAU´CIS.
        1. The mortal who showed
            hospitality to Jupiter and
            Mercury, 32, 34
            wife of Philemon, 302
        2. Father of Dryope (changed to a
            tree), 402
BEL-LER´O-PHON. Demigod;
        mounts Pegasus and slays the
            dread Chimæra, 295–299
        significance, 402

BEL-LO´NA. Goddess of war; attendant of Mars, 131

BER-E-NI´CE. Queen whose hair was changed into a comet, 121, 393

BER´O-E. Nurse of Semele, whose form Juno assumes to arouse Semele's jealousy, 167, 168

BI´TON. Brother of Cleobis; draws his mother to the temple, 44

BŒ-O´TI-A. Province in Greece, whose principal city was Thebes, 37

BO´RE-AS. North wind; son of Æolus and Aurora; kidnaps Orithyia, 211–213 sons of, 269

BRASS AGE. Third age of world, 25

BRI-A´RE-US. One of the Centimani; son of Uranus and Gæa, 8 umpire, 147

BRI-SE´IS. Captive of Achilles during Trojan war; claimed by Agamemnon, 323–324, 329 significance, 403

BRON´TES (Thunder). A Cyclop; son of Uranus and Gæa, 8

BRU´TUS. Unborn soul of Roman hero, seen by Anchises in Hades, 380

CA´CUS. Son of Vulcan, 141 giant slain by Hercules on Mount Aventine, 225 significance, 395

CAD´MUS. Brother of Europa; founder of Thebes, 34–35, 37 husband of Harmonia, 99

daughter of, 167 dragon–tooth seed of, 270 significance, 394, 398, 401

CA-DU´CE-US. Wand given to Mercury by Apollo, 124

CÆ´SAR. Unborn soul of Roman hero, seen by Anchises in Hades, 380

CAL´A-IS. Son of Boreas and Orithyia, 213

CAL´CHAS. Soothsayer of the Greeks during the Trojan war, 320

CAL-LI´O-PE. One of the nine Muses, loved by Apollo, 80 mother of Orpheus, 66

CAL-LIS´TO. Maiden loved by Jupiter, changed into a bear by Juno; the Great Bear, 41

CAL´Y-DON. Home of Meleager; site of Calydonian Hunt, 277

CAL-Y-DO´NI-AN HUNT. Organized by Meleager to slay a boar, 277–278

CA-LYP´SO. Nymph who detained Ulysses on Ogygia seven years, 360 significance, 404

CA-MIL´LA. Volscian maiden; fights, and is slain by, Æneas, 381 dedicated to Diana, 383

CA-MIL´LUS. Unborn soul of Roman hero, seen by Anchises in Hades, 380

CAM´PUS MAR´TI-US. Roman exercising grounds sacred to Mars, 136

CAN´CER. Crab which attacked Hercules to defend the Hydra; a constellation, 220

CAP´I-TOL. Temple dedicated to Jupiter in Rome, 38

CAR´THAGE. A city in Africa, built by Dido, visited by Æneas, 374

CAS-SAN´DRA. Daughter of Priam; her prophecies, though true, were always disbelieved, 314
captivity of, 368, 371

CAS-SI-O-PE´IA. Mother of Andromeda, a constellation, 246
significance, 399

CAS´TOR. One of the Dioscuri or Gemini, 280–281
rescue of Helen by, 261
Argonauts joined by, 268
Calydonian Hunt joined by, 277

CAU-CA´SI-AN MOUNTAINS. Same as Caucasus, 18
Prometheus chained to, 226

CE´CROPS. Founder of Athens, 47
descendants of, 256

CE-LÆ´NO. One of the Harpies; frightens Æneas by prophesying harm, 372

CE´LE-US.
1. King of Eleusis; father of Triptolemus, 184
2. Father of Andromeda; significance, 399

CEN´TAURS. Children of Ixion, half man, half horse;
Chiron, 217, 265, 268, 319
Hercules fights, 220
battle of, 229, 261
Nessus, 233, 235
significance, 400, 406

CEN-TIM´A-NI (Hundred-handed). Three sons of Uranus and Gæa, 8

CEPH´A-LUS. Hunter loved by Procris and Aurora, 60–61, 80
significance, 395

CER´BE-RUS. Three-headed dog which guarded the entrance of Hades, 67, 154
Hercules captures, 228, 261
significance, 410

CER´CY-ON. Son of Vulcan, 141
encountered by Theseus, 253

CE-RE-A´LI-A. Festivals in honor of Ceres, goddess of agriculture, 191

CE´RES. Same as Demeter, goddess of agriculture and civilization, 153, 179–193
Cronus disgorges, 12
Psyche consults, 119
Neptune loves, 147
Pelops' shoulder eaten by, 161
significance, 405, 406

CER-Y-NE´A. Town of Achaia, 220

CER-Y-NE´IAN STAG. Stag taken by Hercules, 220
one of his labors, 253

CES´TUS. Venus' magic, love-inspiring girdle, 122, 130

CE´YX. King of Thessaly; shipwrecked, and changed with his wife Halcyone into birds, 208–209

CHA´OS. The first of all divinities, who ruled over confusion, 2
ejection of, 7
daughter of, 47

CHAR´I-TES. The three Graces; attendants of Venus, 96

CHA´RON. The boatman who ferries the souls over Acheron, 155
>Æneas ferried by, 380
>significance, 406

CHA-RYB´DIS. Whirlpool near the coast of Sicily, 357, 359, 372

CHI-MÆ´RA. Monster slain by Bellerophon, 296–299
>significance, 402

CHI´O-NE. Daughter of Boreas and Orithyia, 213

CHI´OS. One of the islands of the Archipelago, 91

CHI´RON. Learned Centaur, 217, 265, 268, 319
>death of, 220

CHRY-SE´IS. Daughter of Chryses; taken by Agamemnon, 323–325

CHRY´SES. Father of Chryseis; priest of Apollo;
>brings a plague on the Greek camp, 323–324

CI-CO´NI-ANS. Inhabitants of Ismarus, visited by Ulysses, 343

CI-LIC´I-A. Province in Asia Minor, between Æolia and Troas, 37

CI´LIX. Brother of Europa; founder of Cilicia, 34–36

CIM-ME´RI-AN SHORES. Land visited by Ulysses to consult Tiresias, 356

CIR´CE. Sister of Æetes;
>sorceress who changes Ulysses' men into swine, 353–359
>significance, 404

CLE´O-BIS. Brother of Biton; a devoted son, 44

CLE-O-PA´TRA. Daughter of Boreas and Orithyia, 213

CLI´O. One of the nine Muses, 78

CLO´THO. One of the Fates;
>she spins the thread of life, 159

CLYM´E-NE.
>1. Wife of Iapetus; an ocean nymph, 15
>2. Nymph loved by Apollo; mother of Phaeton, 73, 77

CLYT-ÆM-NES´TRA. Wife of Agamemnon;
>slain by Orestes, 341–342
>significance, 403

CLYT´I-E. Maiden who loves Apollo, and is changed into a sunflower, 62

CO-CY´TUS. River in Hades, formed of tears of the condemned, 154–155

CŒ´US. One of the Titans; son of Uranus and Gæa, 7

COL´CHI-AN LAND.
>Ram bears Phryxus to, 148
>Argonauts arrive at, 270
>Argonauts depart from, 272
>sailors of, 274

COL´CHIS. Land in Asia ruled by Æetes, where the golden fleece was kept, 267–268
>return from, 274

CO-LO´NUS. Forest sacred to Furies, where Œdipus vanished in a storm, 289

CO-LOS´SUS. Statue of Apollo in the Island of Rhodes, 82

CON-SEN´TES. Same as Pan, god of the universe and of nature, 304

Co´pre-us. Son of Pelops;
    owner of the marvelous horse
        Arion, 148

Co´ra. Same as Proserpina, goddess of
    vegetation, 179
        significance, 405

Cor´inth. City and isthmus between
    Greece proper and the Peloponnesus,
    147, 152, 298
        Sciron at, 152
        Sisyphus, king of, 162, 295
        Polybus, king of, 263

Co-ro´na. Constellation, also known as
    Ariadne's Crown, 176

Co-ro´nis. Maiden loved by Apollo;
    mother of Æsculapius, 52–53
        significance, 398

Co´rus. Northwest wind;
    son of Æolus and Aurora, 211–213

Cor-y-ban´tes. Same as Curetes;
    Rhea's priests, 11

Cot´tus. One of the Centimani;
    son of Uranus and Gæa, 8

Cre´on. Father of Jocasta and of Megara,
    218
        King of Thebes, 291

Cre´tan Bull.
    Hercules captures, 222

Crete. Island home of Minos, 222, 254, 256
    Menelaus' journey to, 318
    Æneas' sojourn in, 371
    Zeus, king of, 388

Cre-u´sa.
    1. Wife of Æneas;
        killed in attempting to fly
            from Troy, 369–370

    2. Same as Glauce;
        maiden loved by Jason, 275

Cri´us. One of the Titans;
    son of Uranus and Gæa, 7

Cro´nus. Same as Saturn; a Titan who
    rules supreme;
        father of Jupiter, 7–12, 13, 15, 23
        daughters of, 41, 178, 195
        son of, 153

Cru´mis-sa. Island where Neptune
    carried Theophane;
        birthplace of the golden-fleeced
            ram, 148

Cu´mæ. Cave where the Sibyl gave her
    prophecies, 378

Cu´pid, or Cu-pi´do. Same as Amor,
    god of love;
        son of Venus and Mars, 99, 133
        growth of, 101
        darts of, 104, 140, 375
        Psyche and, 113, 390

Cu-re´tes. Same as Corybantes;
    Rhea's priests, 11

Cy´a-ne. River which tried to stop Pluto
    when he kidnapped Proserpina, 182

Cyb´e-le. Same as Rhea, goddess of
    the earth, 10
        chariot of, 280

Cy-clo´pes. Three children of Uranus
    and Gæa, 8
        thunderbolts forged by, 12, 54, 138
        Orion visits the, 91
        Vulcan and the, 138, 140
        Island of the, 345, 350
        Æneas warned against, 372
        significance, 407

CY′CLOPS. Polyphemus the, 345–351, 372

CYC′NUS. Intimate friend of Phaeton, 77

CYL-LE′NE. Mountain upon which Mercury was born, 123–124

CYN′THI-A. Same as Diana, goddess of the moon and the chase, 85–93

CYN′THI-US. Name given to Apollo, god of the sun and fine arts, 51

CYP-A-RIS′SUS. Friend of Apollo; turned to a cypress tree, 57

CY′PRUS. Island in the Mediterranean sacred to Venus, 95, 112

CYTH-E-RE′A. Name given to Venus, goddess of beauty, love, and laughter, 95

DÆD′A-LUS. Architect who planned the Cretan Labyrinth, 254, 256
    inventor of sails, 212

DAN′A-E. Maiden visited by Jupiter as a golden shower;
    mother of Perseus, 239–241
    significance, 388, 399, 405

DA-NA′I-DES. Daughters of Danaus, who slay their husbands, 160–161

DAN′A-US. King of Argos;
    father of the fifty Danaides, 160–161

DAN′UBE. River of Europe;
    Medea slays Absyrtus near its mouth, 274

DAPH′NE. Maiden loved by Apollo, and changed into a laurel tree, 58–60
    significance, 395, 398, 404

DAR′DA-NUS. Ancient king of Troy, who gives his name to his race, 371
    mares of, 213

DE-I-A-NEI′RA. Wife of Hercules, 231–236
    causes Hercules' death by using the Nessus robe, 236–237
    significance, 399

DE-IPH′O-BUS. Son of Priam and Hecuba;
    married Helen after the death of Paris, 369

DE′LOS. Floating island;
    birthplace of Apollo and Diana, 52
    shrine of Apollo at, 81, 371
    significance, 394, 404

DEL′PHI. Shrine of Apollo, famed for its oracles, 27, 37, 81
    Ceyx visits, 208
    Œdipus consults oracle at, 284, 285, 288, 293
    Orestes at, 342

DEL′UGE. Caused by Jupiter's wrath, 26
    slime from, 55

DE-ME′TER. Same as Ceres;
    goddess of agriculture, 179, 183
    significance, 405

DE′MI-OS (Dread). Attendant or son of Mars, 131

DES′TI-NY. One of the ancient deities not subjected to Jupiter, 29

DEU-CA′LI-ON. Only male survivor of Deluge;
    father of Hellen, 27–28

DI′A. Maiden loved and deserted by Ixion, king of the Lapithæ, 164
    significance, 398

DI-A´NA. Goddess of the moon and
chase;
    birth of, 52
    nymphs of, 60
    daughter of Jupiter and Latona,
      85–93
    arrows of, 132
    Arethusa protected by, 186
    Œneus neglects, 277
    Iphigenia saved by, 320
    temple of, 342
    Camilla rescued by, 381
    significance, 397, 404, 407

DI´DO. Queen of Tyre and Carthage;
    loved and deserted by Æneas,
      374–375
    Æneas sees, in Hades, 380

DI-O-ME´DES.
    1. Greek hero during Trojan war,
      318
      recovers Patroclus' body, 332
      helps Ulysses secure the
        Palladium, 337
    2. The possessor of horses taken
      by Hercules, 222

DI-O´NE.
    1. Name given to Venus, goddess of
      beauty, love, laughter, etc., 96
    2. Mother of Venus by Jupiter;
      goddess of moisture, 34, 96

DI-O-NYS´I-A. Festivals held in Greece
in honor of Bacchus, 178

DI-O-NYS´US. Same as Bacchus, god of
wine and revelry, 170

DI-OS-CU´RI. Collective name given to
Castor and Pollux, 280

DI-OS-CU´RI-A. Festivals in honor of
Castor and Pollux, 281

DIR´CE. Wife of Lycus;
    bound to a bull by Amphion and
      Zethus, 71

DIS-COR´DI-A, or ERIS. Goddess of
discord, 131
    she appears at Peleus' marriage
      feast, 310

DO-DO´NA. Temple and grove sacred to
Jupiter, 38, 268

DOL´PHIN. Constellation, 52

DO´RI-AN RACE. Descendants of Dorus, 27

DO´RIS. Wife of Nereus, 148, 309

DO´RUS. Son of Hellen;
    ancestor of Dorian race, 27

DREAMS. Spirits in cave of Somnus;
    passed out through gates of ivory
      and horn, 208
    Mercury, leader of, 129

DREP´A-NUM. Land visited by Æneas,
where Anchises died, 372

DRY´A-DES. Plant nymphs, supposed to
watch over vegetation, 301

DRY´O-PE. Princess changed into a tree,
302–303

DULL´NESS. Obscure deity put to flight
by Minerva, 45

EARTH. Æther and Hemera create the, 3
    divisions of the, 5
    realm of the, 15
    the mother of all, 27
    oath by the, 168
    Antæus, son of the, 226
    significance, 497

E´CHO. Nymph who pined for love of
Narcissus;
    answers Cephalus, 61
    changed to a voice, 112–114
    mocks Ariadne, 175
EGG. Earth hatched from a mythical, 5
E´GYPT. Gods take refuge in, 14
    Io takes refuge in, 128
    Menelaus and Helen detained in,
    341
E-LEC´TRA. Daughter of Agamemnon;
    saves Orestes, 342
EL-EU-SIN´I-A. Festivals at Eleusis, in
honor of Ceres and Proserpina, 192
E-LEU´SIS. City in Greece visited by Ceres
during her search for Proserpina, 192
E´LIS. Province of the Peloponnesus;
    Alpheus in, 188
    Augeas, king of, 220
    significance, 397
EL-PE´NOR. Follower of Ulysses;
    dies in Island of Æaea, 356
E-LYS´I-AN FIELDS. Abode of the
blessed in Hades, 156, 165
    Cleobis and Biton conveyed to, 44
    Adonis conveyed to, 102
EN-CEL´A-DUS. Giant defeated by Jupiter;
    buried under Mt. Ætna, 14
EN-DYM´I-ON. Youth loved by Diana,
who carries him to a cave on Mt.
Latmus, 88–90
    significance, 397, 405
EN´NA. Plain in Sicily;
    favorite resort of Proserpina, 179
E-NY´O. Name given to Bellona, goddess
of war, 131

E´OS. Name given to Aurora, goddess
of dawn, 60, 80
    jealousy of, 60
    winds, offspring of, 211
EP´A-PHUS. Son of Jupiter and Io;
    founder of Memphis, 128
EPH´E-SUS. City in Asia Minor sacred to
Diana, 193
EPH-I-AL´TES. Giant son of Neptune;
    brother of Otus, 148
    brother imprisons Mars, 132
    significance, 409
E-PIG´O-NI. Sons of the seven chiefs
who besieged Thebes, 293
EP-I-ME´THEUS (Afterthought). Son of
Iapetus, 15
    husband of Pandora, 19–23, 26
E-PI´RUS. Country visited by Æneas,
who meets Andromache there, 372
ER´A-TO. One of the Muses;
    daughter of Jupiter and
    Mnemosyne, 80
ER´E-BUS. God of darkness, 2
    marries his mother, Night, 3
    progenitor of egg, 5
    dethroned, 7
E-RID´A-NUS. River into which Phaeton
fell from the sun chariot, 77
    Hercules consults nymphs of,
    225
E-RIN´NY-ES. Collective name given to
the Furies, 156
    significance, 402
E´RIS. Same as Discordia, goddess of
discord and strife, 131
    apple cast by, 310

ER-I-SICH´THON. An unbeliever; punished by famine, 192

E´ROS. Same as Cupid, 99
child of Light and Day, 3
arrows of, 3, 104
egg produces, 5
causes man's creation, 15
man's life given by, 16

ER-Y-MAN´THUS. Place where Hercules slew the wild boar, 220

ER-Y-THE´A. Island home of Geryones; visited by Hercules, 225

E-TE´O-CLES. Son of Œdipus and Jocasta, 228
reigns one year, 290
slain by his brother, 291

E-THI-O´PI-A. Country visited by Bacchus, 172

E-THI-O´PI-ANS. Happy race of Africa, south of the river Oceanus; visited by the gods, 6

EU-BŒ´AN or EU-BO´IC SEA. Sea where Hercules cast Lichas, 237

EU-HEM´ER-US. Exponent of the theory of myths, 341

EU-MÆ´US. Swineherd visited by Ulysses on his return to Ithaca, 362
Ulysses aided by, 365

EU-MEN´I-DES. Collective name given to Furies, 156
forest sacred to, 189
significance, 402

EU-PHROS´Y-NE. One of the three Graces or Charites; attendant of Venus, 96

EU-RO´PA. Daughter of Agenor; wife of Jupiter, 34–38
mother of Minos, Rhadamanthus, and Sarpedon, 35,
significance, 394, 396, 398

EU-RO´TAS. River near Sparta, where Helen bathed, 315

EU´RUS. East wind; son of Æolus and Aurora, 211–213

EU-RY´A-LE. One of the three terrible Gorgons, 241

EU-RY´A-LUS. Youth sent with Nisus to warn Æneas that his son was in danger, 382

EU-RY-CLE´A. Nurse of Ulysses; recognizes him after twenty years' absence, 362
Penelope awakened by, 365

EU-RYD´I-CE. Wife of Orpheus, who seeks her in Hades, 66–70
significance, 396, 398

EU-RYL´O-CHUS. Leader of Ulysses' men, 353
escaped Circe's spell, 359
Ulysses' men misled by, 359

EU-RYN´O-ME. Wife of Jupiter; mother of the Graces, 96

EU-RYS´THEUS. Hercules' taskmaster, 136
appointed twelve labors, 217–228

EU´RY-TUS. Iole's father; visited twice by Hercules, 236

EU-TER´PE. One of the Muses; presided over music, 78

EUX´INE SEA. Same as Pontus Euxinus, or the Black Sea, 5

E-VAN´DER. King of Tuscans;
     ally of Æneas, father of Pallas,
        381, 385

E-VE´NUS. Father of Marpessa;
     drowned himself in river of same
        name, 149
     Hercules crosses, 233

FA´MA. Attendant of Jupiter, goddess of
     fame, 31

FATES. Three sisters;
     also known as Mœræ or Parcæ,
        29, 159, 309, 318, 335

FAU´NA. Wife of Faunus;
     a rural divinity of the Romans, 305

FAU´NUS. Rural divinity of the Romans;
     husband of Fauna, 305

FLO´RA. Goddess of flowers, 305
     wife of Zephyrus, 213

FLO-RA´LI-A. Festivals in May in honor
     of Flora, 306

FORETHOUGHT. Name given to
     Prometheus, 15

FOR-TU´NA.
     1. Goddess of fortune;
        an attendant of Jupiter, 31
     2. Goddess of plenty, 231

FO´RUM. Chief place in Rome where
     public matters were discussed, 135

FU´RIES. The Eumenides, or avenging
     deities, 156
        Œdipus punished by, 289
        Orestes pursued by, 342

GÆ´A. Same as Tellus and Terra, 3
     wife of Uranus, 3

     reign of, 7
     conspiracy of, 8
     Typhœus created by, 13
     Enceladus created by, 14
     Antæus, son of, 226
     Syrinx protected by, 304
     significance, 405

GAL-A-TE´A.
     1. Nymph loved by Polyphemus
        and Acis, 346
     2. Statue loved by Pygmalion,
        who prays Venus to give it life,
        112

GAN´Y-MEDE. Trojan prince carried off
     by Jupiter to act as cup-bearer, 32

GE. Same as Gæa, Tellus, Terra, the
     Earth, 3

GEM´I-NI. Same as Dioscuri;
     Castor and Pollux, 280

GE-RY´O-NES. Giant whose cattle are
     taken by Hercules, 225
     significance, 410

GLAU´CE. Maiden loved by Jason;
     slain by Medea, 275
     significance, 401

GLAU´CUS. Fisherman changed to a sea
     god, 308
     lover of Scylla, 359

GOLDEN AGE. First age of the ancient
     world, when all was bliss, 23
     Janus' reign, 201

GOR´GONS. Three sisters, Euryale,
     Stheno, and Medusa, 241–243
        Ægis decorated by head of one
        of, 48
     significance, 410

GRAC´CHI, THE. Unborn souls of
Roman heroes, seen by Anchises in
Hades, 380

GRA´CES. Same as Gratiæ;
the three attendants of Venus,
96, 140

GRA-DI´VUS. Name given to Mars
when leader of armies, 136

GRÆ´Æ. Three sisters with but one eye
and tooth among them, 243
significance, 399, 410

GRA´TI-Æ. Same as Graces, or Charites;
Venus' attendants, 96, 140

GREAT BEAR. Constellation formed by
Callisto, 42

GRE´CI-AN.
Mythology, 15
camp, 331

GREECE.
Highest peak in, 26
alphabet introduced into, 38
nations of, 38
art in, 42
Cecrops comes to, 47
captives taken to, 146, 327
Neptune worshipped in, 152
Pelops takes refuge in, 161
Bacchus' visit to, 172
Paris visits, 195, 314
war between Troy and, 319
Orestes' return to, 342

GREEK DIVINITIES, 29
Panathenæa, 50
fleet, 340

GREEKS.
Departure of, 320

plague visits, 323
defeat of, 328, 329
return of, 340
Agamemnon, chief of, 341
attack Ciconians, 343
Polyphemus visited by, 345–351
Circe visited by, 353
a civilized nation, 389

GY´ES. One of the three Centimani;
son of Uranus and Gæa, 8

HA´DES. The Infernal Region,
kingdom of Pluto, 153–165
Sacred river Styx, 156
Three judges of, 146
Hercules' visit to, 55, 228
Orpheus' visit to, 67, 69–70
Adonis' visit to, 102
Psyche's visit to, 119–121
Mercury conducts souls to, 129, 322
Proserpina's visit to, 189–190
Lara conducted to, 199–200
Theseus' visit to, 261
Pollux in, 280
Œdipus in, 290
Ulysses' visit to, 356
Æneas' visit to, 378

HÆ´MON. Son of Creon;
lover of Antigone, 291

HAL-CY´O-NE. Wife of Ceyx, King of
Thessaly, 208, 209

HAL-IRR-HO´THI-US. Son of Neptune;
slain by Mars, 132

HAM-A-DRY´A-DES. Nymphs who lived
and died with the trees they inhabited,
301, 302

HAR-MO´NI-A. Daughter of Mars and
  Venus, 99, 133
        wife of Cadmus, 38
        mother of Semele, 167
HAR´PIES. Monsters, half woman, half
  bird;
        banished to Strophades Islands,
        269
        Æneas sees, 372
        significance, 409
HEAV´EN. Creation of, 3
        realm of, 15
        Atlas, supporter of, 245
        significance, 392, 407
HE´BE. Goddess of youth;
        cup-bearer of the gods, 31
        daughter of Juno, 42
        wife of Hercules, 237
HE´BRUS. River in which the Bacchantes
  cast Orpheus' remains, 70
HEC´A-TE. Name given to Proserpina
  as Queen of Hades, 191
HEC´TOR. Son of Priam;
        leader of Trojan army, 324–331
        slain by Achilles, 332
        Priam buries, 334
        shade of, 367
        widow of, 372
HEC´U-BA. Wife of Priam;
        mother of Paris and Hector, 311,
        314
        Hector seen by, 334
        captivity of, 368
HEL´EN. Daughter of Jupiter and
  Leda; wife of Menelaus;
        kidnapped by Theseus, 261

        kidnapped by Paris, 314–316
        Paris upbraided by, 325
        return of, 341
        Æneas wishes to slay, 369
        significance, 403
HEL´E-NUS. King of Epirus, whose
  slave Andromache became after the
  death of Hector, 372
HE-LI´A-DES. Sisters of Phaeton;
        changed into trees, 77
HEL´I-CON. Mountain in Greece,
  sacred to Apollo and Muses, 80, 143
HE´LI-OS. Name of Apollo as god of
  the sun, 51, 62
        significance, 394, 396, 403
HEL´LE. Daughter of Athamas and
  Nephele;
        drowned in the Hellespont, 108,
        267
        significance, 400, 406
HEL´LEN. Son of Deucalion;
        ancestor of the Hellenes, 27
HEL-LE´NES. Name given to ancient
  Greeks, 27
HEL´LES-PONT. Name given to the
  strait from Helle, 267, 305, 322
        Leander swims across the,
        103–109
HE-ME´RA (Day). One of the first
  divinities, who rules with Æther
  (Light), 3, 7
HEPH-ÆS-TI´A. Festivals in honor of
  Hephæstus, or Vulcan, 141
HE-PHÆS´TUS. Name given to Vulcan,
  god of the forge, 137
        significance, 408

HE´RA, or HE´RE. Name given to Juno, queen of heaven, and goddess of the atmosphere and of marriage, 41
significance, 393

HER´A-CLES. Same as Hercules; son of Jupiter and Alcmene, 215

HE-RÆ´UM. Town dedicated to the service of Juno, 42

HER´CU-LES. Same as Heracles, god of all athletic games, 215–238
Prometheus delivered by, 18
Hades visited by, 55
Hesione delivered by, 146
Centaurs defeated by, 261
Argonautic expedition joined by, 268
arrows of, 336
apparition of, 336
significance, 387, 398, 401, 404

HER´MES. Same as Mercury, messenger of the gods, 123
significance, 408

HER-MI´O-NE. Same as Harmonia; daughter of Venus and Mars, 99

HE´RO. Maiden loved by Leander, who swam the Hellespont to visit her, 103–109

HE-SI´O-NE. Daughter of Laomedon, 146
rescued from sea monster by Hercules, 223, 314

HES-PE-RI´A. Ancient name of Italy, so called by Æneas, 13, 371

HES-PER´I-DES. Daughters of Hesperus, guardians of golden apples, 225
significance, 398

HES´PE-RUS. God of the West; father of the Hesperides, 225

HES´TI-A. Same as Vesta, goddess of the family hearth, 195
significance, 408

HIM´E-RUS. God of the desire of love; attendant in Venus' numerous train, 98

HIP-PO-CRE´NE. Fountain created by Pegasus, 298

HIP-PO-DA-MI´A. Wife of Pirithous; almost carried off by the Centaurs, 261

HIP-POL´Y-TE. Queen of the Amazons, 223
Theseus' wife, 260

HIP-POL´Y-TUS. Son of Theseus and Hippolyte, 260
loved by Phædra, 263

HIP-POM´E-NES. Same as Milanion; lover of Atalanta, 278

HOPE. The good spirit in Pandora's box; an ancient deity, 22, 23

HO´RÆ. Collective name of the seasons; Venus' attendants, 96

HORN GATE. Gate leading from cave of Somnus to outer world, 208, 209

HOURS. Attendants of Apollo, 75
attendants of Venus, 96, 98

HUNDRED-HANDED, THE. Same as Centimani, 8

HUP´NOS. Same as Somnus, god of sleep, 2–5

HY-A-CIN´THUS. Youth loved by Apollo and Zephyrus; changed to a flower, 57

HY´DRA. Monster serpent slain by Hercules in the swamp of Lerna, 219, 220
 significance, 410

HY-GE´IA. Daughter of Æsculapius; watched over health of man, 54

HY´LAS. Youth loved by Hercules; stolen by the water nymphs, 269

HY´MEN. God of marriage; attendant of Venus, 98

HY-MET´TUS. Mountain in Attica, 80

HYP-ER-BO´RE-AN MOUNTAINS. The mountains separating the land of the Hyperboreans from Thrace, 213

HYP-ER-BO´RE-ANS. People north of Oceanus, a virtuous race, 5

HY-PE´RI-ON. The Titan who had charge of the sun chariot, 7, 10, 12

HYP-ERM-NES´TRA. Daughter of Danaus;
 saves her husband, 161

I-AP´E-TUS. One of the Titans; father of Prometheus, 7, 15, 228

I-A´PIS. Leech consulted by Æneas; cures Æneas with Venus' aid, 384

I-A´SI-US. Same as Iasion; father of Atalanta, 277, 372

IC´A-RUS. Son of Dædalus; fell into the Icarian Sea, 254

I´DA. Mountain in Crete, and near Troy also, 11, 325

I´DAS. A mortal befriended by Neptune; elopes with Marpessa, 149

IL´I-A.
 1. One of the Titanides; daughter of Uranus and Gæa, 7
 2. Priestess of Vesta, wife of Mars; mother of Romulus and Remus, 133, 385

IL´I-AD. Homer's epic poem on the Trojan war, 322, 327, 335

IL´I-UM. Same as Troy whence comes the *Iliad*'s name, 322, 366, 370, 377

IN´A-CHUS. River god (father of Io), 126, 128

INFERNAL REGIONS.
 Judges in the, 35
 Orpheus visits, 67, 69–70
 Adonis visits, 102
 Pluto's realm, 152
 Proserpina's sojourn in, 189–190
 Æneas visits, 378

I´NO. Same as Leucothea; second wife of Athamas;
 daughter of Cadmus and Harmonia, 170, 267
 significance, 400

I´O. Maiden loved by Jupiter; changed into a heifer, 126–129
 significance, 394, 405

I-OB´A-TES. King of Lycia; recipient of the sealed letter carried by Bellerophon, 295, 297–299

I-O-LA´US. Friend of Hercules; helped slay the Hydra, 219

I-OL´CUS. Kingdom of Æson and Jason; usurped by Pelias, 265

I´O-LE. Maiden loved by Hercules, 236
　significance, 398, 399, 401
I´ON. Grandson of Hellen;
　ancestor of Ionian race, 27
I-O´NI-AN RACE. Race descended from
　Ion, grandson of Hellen, 28
I-O´NI-AN SEA. Sea west of Greece,
　named after Io, 128
IPH-I-GE-NI´A. Daughter of
　Agamemnon;
　　sacrificed to Diana, 320, 321
　　Orestes finds, 342
I´RIS (the Rainbow). Attendant of
　Juno, 42, 334, 382
IRON AGE. Fourth and last age
　previous to the Deluge, 25
ISLES OF THE BLEST. Islands west of
　Oceanus, inhabited by the virtuous
　dead, 6, 7
　　Ulysses searches for, 365
IS´MA-RUS. Town in Thrace, spoiled by
　Ulysses, 343
IS-ME´NE. Daughter of Œdipus and
　Jocasta, 288
　　dies of grief, 293
ISTH´MI-AN GAMES. Games held in
　honor of Neptune, at Corinth, every
　four years, 152
IT´A-LY.
　　Saturn retires to, 13, 23
　　Statues of Juno, 42
　　Neptune worshipped in, 152
　　Ceres returns to, 184
　　Janus, king of, 201
ITH´A-CA. Ulysses' island kingdom,
　212, 318, 343, 351

Ulysses arrives in sight of, 352
　Ulysses returns to, 360, 361
　Telemachus returns to, 362
　home of Penelope, 318
I-U´LUS. Æneas' son;
　Æneas saves, 368
　Cupid assumes form of, 375
　stag wounded by, 381
　brave defense by, 382
IVORY GATE. Gate leading from cave
　of Somnus to outer world, 208
IX-I´ON. Criminal in Tartarus;
　bound to wheel of fire, 67, 164, 261
　makes love to Juno, 164
　significance, 398

JA-NIC´U-LUM. City on the Tiber,
　founded by Janus, 208
JA´NUS. God of all beginnings, of
　entrances, gates, etc., 201–203
　opening of temple of, 381
JA´NUS QUAD´RI-FONS. A square
　temple dedicated to Janus, 202
JA´SON. Son of Æson;
　captured the golden fleece, 265–276
　joins the Calydonian Hunt, 277
　significance, 400, 401
JO-CAS´TA. Wife of Laius, 283
　marries Œdipus, her son, 288
　commits suicide, 289
　significance, 401
JOVE. Same as Jupiter, 29
　birth of, 10
　omnipotence, 13
　day of, 203
　Leda courted by, 315

decree of, 334

Ju´no. Birth of, 12

flight of, 14

Jupiter's wife, 34

same as Hera, 41–44

jealousy of, 52, 126–127, 147,
167, 168, 170, 200

Mars, son of, 131

Vulcan, son of, 137

Tityus insults, 163–164

Æolus, servant of, 210

Hercules persecuted by, 215, 216,
223

Jason carries, 266

Jason aided by, 269, 270

contest of Minerva and Venus
with, 310–312

Troy destroyed by, 369

Æneas persecuted by, 372, 373,
377, 381, 382, 383

significance, 393, 394, 398

Ju´pi-ter. Birth of, 10, 11

supremacy of, 12

giants defeated by, 12–13

kingdom divided by, 15

Prometheus punished by, 18

and Pandora, 18–23

Mercury, messenger of, 21, 128

Deluge caused by, 26

same as Jove, 29–39

Juno courted by, 41

Minerva borne by, 45

Latona courted by, 52

Æsculapius slain by, 54

Amphion, son of, 71

Phaeton slain by, 77

Muses, daughters of, 77

Venus, daughter of, 95

Graces, daughters of, 96

Venus borrows thunderbolts of,
103

Mercury, son of, 123

Io courted by, 126–127

Mars, son of, 131

Vulcan, son of, 137

thunderbolts of, 140

Neptune exiled by, 144

Semele courted by, 167–170

Ceres, wife of, 179

Hercules, son of, 215, 216

games in honor of, 229, 238

Hercules saved by, 238

Danae courted by, 239, 240

Helen, daughter of, 261, 315

Bellerophon punished by, 299

Thetis loved by, 309

Thetis seeks, 324

interference of, 324, 369, 382

Sarpedon, son of, 330

Apollo appeased by, 360

significance, 390, 392, 393, 394,
396, 397, 398, 402, 403, 404,
405, 407, 408, 409

Jus´tice. Same as Themis, 34

mother of seasons, 96

Ju-tur´na. Sister and charioteer of
Turnus, 384

Ju-ven´tas. Same as Hebe, goddess of
youth, 31

Ka´kia. Goddess of vice;
tries to mislead Hercules, 217

LAB´Y-RINTH. A maze in Crete, constructed by Dædalus for the Minotaur, 254, 257

LAC-E-DÆ-MO´NI-A. Province in Peloponnesus; capital Sparta, also name of Sparta, 316

LAC-E-DÆ-MO´NI-ANS. Inhabitants of Lacedæmonia, or Sparta, 209

LACH´E-SIS. One of the Fates; twists the thread of life, 159

LA´DON. Dragon which guarded golden apples of Hesperides, 225

LA-ER´TES. Father of Ulysses, 319, 351 Penelope weaves his shroud, 364

LÆS-TRY-GO´NI-ANS. Cannibals visited by Ulysses, 353

LA´IUS. Father of Œdipus, 283 slain by him, 285 significance, 401, 402, 403

LAM-PE´TIA. One of the Heliades, 77 guards the cattle of the sun, 359

LA-OC´O-ON. Trojan priest; crushed to death by two serpents, 338, 340

LA-OD-A-MI´A. Wife of Protesilaus; dies of grief, 321, 322

LA-OM´E-DON. King of Troy, 144, 146 employs Neptune and Apollo to build walls, 223 significance, 395

LAP´I-THÆ. People who dwelt in Thessaly and fought the Centaurs, 229, 260 Ixion, king of, 164 Pirithous, king of, 260

LA´RA. Wife of Mercury; mother of the two Lares, 199

LA´RES. Two tutelary divinities of ancient Roman households, 199, 200 saved by Anchises, 369

LAT´IN. Names of days in, 203

LAT´INS. People of Latinus and Æneas, 382, 385, 404 Æneas fights, 381

LA-TI´NUS. King of Latium, 380 welcomes and then wars against Æneas, 381, 383, 385 Æneas makes peace with, 385

LA´TI-UM. Province of Italy, ruled by Latinus, 380, 381 Æneas comes to, 385

LAT´MUS. Mountain in Asia Minor, where Endymion lies asleep, 89 significance, 391, 401, 403

LA-TO´NA. Same as Leto; wife of Jupiter, 52 mother of Apollo and Diana, 52, 53, 404 boast of, 85 significance, 404

LAU´SUS. Hero slain by Æneas during wars against the Rutules, 383

LA-VIN´I-A. Daughter of Latinus, 380 Æneas' second wife, 384, 385

LE-AN´DER. Youth of Abydus; Hero's lover, who swam the Hellespont, 103–109

LE-AR´CHUS. Son of Athamas and Ino; slain by his father, 170

LE´DA. Mother of Castor and Pollux,

Helen, and Clytæmnestra, 315
   significance, 403
LE´LAPS. The tireless hunting dog
   given by Procris to Cephalus, 60
LEM´NOS. Island in the Grecian
   Archipelago;
      Vulcan landed there, 137
      Philoctetes on, 336
LER´NA. Marsh where the Hydra lay
   concealed, 219
LE´THE. River of forgetfulness, which
   separated the Elysian Fields from
   Hades, 156, 205, 206
LE´TO. Same as Latona;
      mother of Apollo and Diana, 52
      significance, 394, 397, 401, 403
LEU-CO´THE-A. Same as Ino, Athamas'
   wife;
      sea goddess, 170
      Ulysses rescued by, 360
LI´BER. Same as Bacchus, god of wine
   and revelry, 170
LIB-ER-A´LI-A. Festivals in honor of Liber,
   or Bacchus, held in the autumn, 178
LIB´Y-A. Ancient name of Africa;
      coast upon which Æneas landed,
      38, 374
LI´CHAS. Bearer of the Nessus robe;
      slain by Hercules, 236, 237
LIGHT. Same as Æther, 3
LIP´A-RI ISLANDS. Same as Æolian
   Islands, where Ulysses landed, 211
LITTLE BEAR. Arcas changed into the
   constellation of the, 42
LO´TIS. Nymph changed into a lotus
   blossom, 303

LO-TOPH´A-GI. People whose food was
   the lotus;
      the Lotus-eaters, 344
LOVE. Same as Eros, Cupid, etc., 3, 4
      Psyche courted by, 113–122
LOVES. Attendants of Venus, 141
LOWER WORLD.
      Pluto receives scepter, 15
      Adonis leaves, 102
      Pluto conveys Proserpina to, 182
      visited by Æneas, 380
LU´NAE. Same as Diana, 203
LYC´I-A. Land ruled by Iobates,
   who sends Bellerophon to slay the
   Chimæra, 295, 298
LYC-O-ME´DES. King of Scyros;
      treacherously slays Theseus, 263
      shelters Achilles, 319, 320
LY´CUS. Antiope's second husband;
      slain by Amphion and Zethus, 71
LYD´I-A. Kingdom of Midas, in Asia
   Minor, 173, 229
LYN´CEUS. Husband of Hypermnestra,
   who spared his life, 161
LYN´CUS. King of Scythia;
      changed into a lynx by Ceres, 192
LY´RA. Orpheus' lute;
      placed in heavens as a
      constellation, 70

MA-CHA´ON. Celebrated leech;
      son of Æsculapius, 54
      Philoctetes healed by, 336
MA´IA. Goddess of the plains;
      mother of Mercury, 123
      significance, 408

MA´NES. Tutelary divinities of Roman households, with the Lares and Penates, 199

MAR-PES´SA. Daughter of Evenus; marries Idas, 149

MARS. Same as Ares;
son of Jupiter and Juno, 42
Venus courted by, 98–99, 101
god of war, 131–136
day of, 203
descendants of, 385
significance, 409

MAR´SY-AS.
1. Shepherd who enters into competition with Apollo, 63, 64
2. Name of river, 64

MAR´TI-US, CAM´PUS. Roman exercising grounds, 136

MAT-RO-NA´LI-A. Festivals in honor of Juno, in Rome, 44

ME-DE´A. Daughter of Æetes, 270–272
wife of Ægeus, 253, 254
wife of Jason, 272, 274
significance, 400

ME´DI-A. Country in Asia Minor, where Medea took refuge, 254

MED-I-TER-RA´NE-AN. Sea dividing world in two, 5

ME-DU´SA. Gorgon slain by Perseus, whose hair was turned into snakes, 241–243
Neptune marries, 148
Pegasus, offspring of, 296
significance, 399

ME-GÆ´RA. One of the Furies, Eumenides, or Erinnyes, 159

MEG´A-RA. First wife of Hercules, whose three children he burns in his madness, 218
significance, 398

ME-LE-A´GER. Son of Œneus and Althæa; leader of Calydonian Hunt, 277, 278
significance, 401

ME´LI-AN NYMPHS. Nymphs who nursed Jupiter in infancy, 11

MEL-POM´E-NE. One of the Muses; presides over tragedy, 78

MEM´PHIS. Town in Egypt, founded by Epaphus, 128

MEN-E-LA´US. King of Sparta;
husband of Helen of Troy, 314, 316
Paris fights, 325
return of, 341
Telemachus visits, 362
significance, 403

MEN´E-TI-US. One of the four sons of Iapetus and Clymene, 15

MEN´TOR. Name assumed by Minerva to act as a guide for Telemachus, 362, 365

MER-CU-RA´LI-A. Festivals in honor of Mercury, the messenger god, 129

MER´CU-RY. Same as Hermes;
Pandora guided by, 19
Jupiter's ally, 32
Adonis guided by, 102
son of Jupiter and Maia, 123–129
Mars delivered by, 132
Bacchus guarded by, 170
Proserpina guided by, 191
Lara loved by, 199–200
day of, 203

leader of dreams, 208

Perseus helped by, 242

Pan, son of, 304

Protesilaus guided by, 321

Priam led by, 334

Ulysses aided by, 354, 360

Æneas aided by, 375

significance, 394, 395, 408, 409

MER´O-PE. Daughter of Œnopion;
   promised bride of Orion, 91

MET-A-NEI´RA. Wife of Celeus, king
   of Eleusis;
      mother of Triptolemus, 184

ME´TIS. Daughter of Oceanus;
   gives a potion to Cronus,12

ME´TUS. Attendant of Mars;
   god of war and strife, 131

ME-ZEN´TI-US. Father of Lausus;
   slain by Æneas, 383

MI´DAS. King of Lydia, 64, 65
   changed all he touched to gold,
      173–175

MI-LA´NI-ON. Same as Hippomenes;
   husband of Atalanta, 278, 280

MI´LO. Island where statue of Venus
   was found, 122

MI-NER´VA. Same as Athene, goddess
   of wisdom;
      man given soul by, 17
      daughter of Jupiter, 45–50
      flute of, 63
      Vulcan woos, 140
      contest of Neptune and, 146
      Medusa punished by, 241
      Perseus aided by, 242
      gift to, 247

Argo built by, 268

Bellerophon helped by, 296

Juno and Venus dispute with, 310

Ulysses aided by, 360

significance, 404

MIN-ER-VA´LI-A. Festivals in honor of
   Minerva, in Rome, 50

MI´NOS.

   1. King of Crete, 222
         father of Ariadne and
            Phædra, 254, 257

   2. Son of Jupiter and Europa;
         judge in Hades, 32, 156

MIN´O-TAUR. Monster which Minos
   kept in the Labyrinth, 254–258
   significance, 400, 410

MNE-MOS´Y-NE. A Titanide, 7, 12
   goddess of memory, wife of
      Jupiter, mother of the Muses, 78

MŒ´RÆ. The Fates, or Parcæ, who spin,
   twist, and cut the thread of life, 159

MOR´PHEUS. Prime minister of
   Somnus, god of sleep, 205–210

MORS. Same as Thanatos, god of death,
   205–210

MO-SYCH´LUS. Mountain in Lemnos,
   where Vulcan fell from heaven, 137

MU-SAG´E-TES. Apollo's name when he
   led the choir of the Muses, 78

MU´SES, THE NINE. Daughters of
   Jupiter and Mnemosyne, 63, 64, 66,
   78, 80
      mount of the, 298

MY-CE´NÆ. Favorite city of Juno, with
   Sparta and Argos, 42
      Perseus exchanges Argos for, 249

Myr´mi-dons. Achilles' followers;
  led by Patroclus, 329, 330
  significance, 403
Mys´ter-ies. Religious rites celebrated
  in honor of the God of Wine, 176
Myths. Fabulous tales, 387–410

Na-i´a-des. Fountain nymphs subject
  to Neptune, 301, 302
Na-pæ´æ. Valley nymphs, who looked
  after the flocks also, 301
Nar-cis´sus. Youth loved by Echo;
  enamored with his own image,
    110–113
Nau-sic´a-a. Daughter of Alcinous
  and Arete;
    befriends Ulysses, 361
Nax´os. Island visited by Theseus and
  Bacchus, 175, 258
  significance, 400
Nec´tar. Beverage of the gods,
  poured out by Hebe and Ganymede,
  29, 31, 74
Ne´leus. Son of Neptune;
  brother of Pelias, 148
Ne´me-a. Forest in Greece, devastated
  by a lion slain by Hercules, 219
Ne´me-an Games. Games in honor of
  Jupiter and Hercules, 238
Ne´me-an Lion. Monster slain by
  Hercules, 219, 298
Nem´e-sis. Goddess of vengeance, 159
  pursues Orestes, 342
Ne-op-tol´e-mus. Same as Pyrrhus,
  Achilles' son;
    slays Priam, 368

Neph´e-le. Wife of Athamas;
  mother of Phryxus and Helle, 267
  significance, 400, 406
Nep´tune. Same as Poseidon, god of
  the sea, 143–152
  son of Cronus, 12
  kingdom given to, 15
  Deluge controlled by, 26–27
  horse created by, 47
  Delos created by, 52
  walls built by, 55
  Mars punished by, 132
  girl protected by, 192
  Vesta wooed by, 195
  Minos punished by, 222
  Pegasus created by, 243
  Hippolytus slain by, 263
  Thetis wooed by, 309
  Trojans punished by, 338
  Polyphemus, son of, 345
  Ulysses' men slain by, 360, 361
  Æneas saved by, 369, 378
  significance, 406, 409
Ne-re´i-des. Water nymphs;
  daughters of Nereus and Doris,
    95, 147, 148, 151, 306
  significance, 406
Ne´re-us. God of the sea;
  the personification of its pleasant
    aspect, 148, 226
  father of Thetis, 309
  significance, 406
Nes´sus. The Centaur who carries
  Deianeira across the river;
    slain by Hercules, 233, 235
  significance, 399

NES´TOR. Greek hero during Trojan war; noted for wise counsel, 276, 318, 362

NI´CE. Same as Victory; attendant of Jupiter, 31

NIGHT. Same as Nyx or Nox, 2, 5, 47, 205

NIGHTMARES. Attendants of Somnus, crouching in his cave, 208

NI´O-BE. Daughter of Tantalus, whose children are slain by Apollo and Diana, 85–86, 88, 161 significance, 406, 407

NI´SUS. Youth who accompanies Euryalus to summon Æneas back to camp, 382

NO´MAN. Name assumed by Ulysses to mislead Polyphemus, 349, 350

NO´TUS or AUSTER. Southwest wind; son of Æolus and Aurora, 211–213

NOX. Same as Nyx, goddess of night; marries Chaos and Erebus, 2

NU´MA POM-PIL´I-US. Second king of Rome; built Vesta's temple, 195

NYMPHS. Name given to female minor divinities, 301

NY-SI´A-DES. Nymphs who cared for Bacchus, and form a constellation, 170

NYX. Same as Nox, goddess of night; mother of Day and Light, 2, 3, 5, 7, 156

O-CE-AN´I-DES. Daughters of Oceanus; nymphs of the ocean, 15, 95, 306 significance, 406

O-CE´A-NUS.
1. River surrounding the earth, according to ancients, 5, 6, 228
2. One of the Titans; son of Uranus and Gæa, 7, 10, 12, 15, 143, 228 significance, 406

O-CRIS´I-A. A slave, wife of Vulcan; mother of Servius Tullius, 141

O-DYS´SEUS. Same as Ulysses; hero of the *Odyssey*, 343

OD´YS-SEY. Epic poem of Homer on the adventures of Ulysses, 343

ŒD´I-PUS. Son of Laius and Jocasta; King of Thebes, 282–293 significance, 401, 402, 403

Œ´NEUS. Father of Meleager and Deianeira; husband of Althæa, 231, 276

Œ-NO´NE. Wife of Paris, son of Priam; she dies on his funeral pyre, 311, 314, 337 significance, 403

Œ-NO´PI-ON. Father of Merope; blinds Orion, 91

Œ´TA. Mountain on whose summit Hercules builds his funeral pyre, 237

O-GYG´I-A. Island where Calypso detains Ulysses seven years, 360

O-LYM´PI-A. City in Elis noted for its temple and games, 38, 229, 238

O-LYM´PI-AD. Time between Olympian Games, i.e., four years, 38

O-LYM´PI-AN GAMES. Games instituted by Hercules in honor of Jupiter, 38

O-LYM´PUS. Mountain north of Greece; the abode of the gods, 5–14, 17, 19, 29, 41, 45, 48, 60, 67, 74, 86, 88, 92, 102, 105, 112, 121, 124, 127, 129, 137, 140, 147, 167, 168, 169, 237, 239, 301, 304, 309, 310, 324, 381, 382
gods fly from, 14
Prometheus visits, 18
Ganymede transported to, 32
Vulcan expelled from, 138
Ceres visits, 190
Bellerophon storms, 299
significance, 392

OM´PHA-LE. Queen of Lydia; the taskmistress of Hercules, 229

O-NE-I-CO-POM´PUS. Name borne by Mercury as conductor of dreams, 123

OPS. Same as Cybele; name given to Rhea, and also to Ceres, 10

O-RE´A-DES. Mountain nymphs who guided travelers, 301

O-RES´TES. Son of Agamemnon and Clytæmnestra; friend of Pylades, 342

O-RI´ON. Youth loved by Diana, and accidentally slain by her, 90–93

OR-I-THY´I-A. Wife of Boreas; mother of Calais, Zetus, Cleopatra, and Chione, 213

OR´PHEUS. Musician; son of Apollo and Calliope, 66–70, 268
significance, 396

OS´SA. Mountain in Thessaly, upon which the Titans piled Pelion, 13

O´TUS. Giant son of Neptune; slain by Diana and Apollo, 132, 148
significance, 409

PAC-TO´LUS. River in Asia Minor in which Midas washed, to remove his golden plague, 175

PA-LÆ´MON. Son of Athamas and Ino; changed into sea god, 170

PAL-A-ME´DES. Messenger sent to summon Ulysses to war against Troy, 318

PAL-I-NU´RUS. Æneas' pilot; lost at sea off Cape Misenum, 378, 380

PAL-LA´DI-UM. Statue of Minerva, 50 stolen from Troy by Ulysses and Diomedes, 195, 337

PAL´LAS.
1. Name given to Minerva in Athens, 17, 45
2. Son of Evander; slain by Turnus while fighting for Æneas, 381, 383

PAL´LOR. Special attendant of Mars; lover of strife, 131

PAN. Same as Consentes, god of nature and the universe, 64, 65, 119, 304, 305
significance, 409

PAN-ATH-E-NÆ´A. Festivals held in honor of Minerva, 50

PAN-DO´RA. First woman; created in heaven, she brings evil into the world, 19–23, 26

PAR´CÆ. The Fates, or Mœræ;
they spin the thread of destiny, 159

PAR´IS. Son of Priam and Hecuba, 311
judgment of, 311
visits Troy, 314
elopes with Helen, 316, 318
duel with Menelaus, 324–325
in battle, 328
Achilles slain by, 335
death of, 337
significance, 403

PAR-NAS´SUS. Mountain in Greece, 26–28
sacred to Apollo and the Muses, 80

PAR-THE´NI-UM. Mountain upon which
Atalanta was exposed, 277

PAR´THE-NON. Temple dedicated to
Minerva at Athens, 50

PA-TRO´CLUS. Friend of Achilles;
slain by Hector, 329–334
significance, 403

PEG´A-SUS. Steed born from the sea
foam and the blood of Medusa, 148,
243
Bellerophon rides, 296–299
significance, 402, 406

PE´LEUS. Husband of Thetis;
father of Achilles, 268, 277, 309, 318

PE´LI-AS. Uncle of Jason;
brother of Neleus, 148
usurps the throne of Æson,
265–268, 275

PE´LI-ON. A high mountain in
Thessaly, piled upon Ossa by the
giants to reach Olympus, 13, 268

PEL-O-PON-NE´SUS. The peninsula
south of Greece, 38, 161

PE´LOPS. Son of Tantalus;
father of Copreus, 148
gave his name to the
Peloponnesus, 161
significance, 397

PE-NA´TES. Household gods worshiped
in Rome with the Lares, 199, 200
Æneas saves the, 369

PE-NEL´O-PE.
1. Wife of Ulysses, 318
suitors of, 362–365
significance, 404
2. A nymph, the mother of Pan,
304

PE-NE´US.
1. River god; father of Daphne;
changes Daphne into a
laurel, 58
2. Name of a river in Greece, 58

PEN-THE-SI-LE´A. Queen of Amazons;
slain during Trojan war, 335

PEN´THEUS. King of Thebes;
refuses to receive Bacchus, and is
slain, 176, 178

PER-I-PHE´TES. Son of Vulcan, 141
encountered and slain by
Theseus, 251

PER-SEPH´O-NE. Same as Proserpina,
goddess of vegetation, 179, 183, 190

PER´SEUS. Son of Jupiter and Danae;
slays Medusa, 239–249
significance, 399, 401, 403, 404

PET´A-SUS. Name given to the winged
cap worn by Mercury, 126

PHÆ-A´CI-ANS. People who dwelt in
Scheria, and sent Ulysses home, 361

PHÆ´DRA. Daughter of Minos; wife of Theseus, 263
significance, 400

PHA´E-TON. Son of Apollo and Clymene;
drives the sun car, and is slain, 73–78
significance, 396

PHA-E-TU´SA. Sister of Phaeton; one of the Heliades, 77
Apollo's flocks guarded by, 359

PHE-RE-PHAT´TA. Name given to Persephone, or Proserpina, 179

PHID´I-AS. Noted Greek sculptor; made statues of the gods, 38, 39, 50

PHI-LE´MON. Husband of Baucis; changed into an oak, 32, 34

PHIL-OC-TE´TES. Friend of Hercules; receives his arrows, 237, 336

PHI-LON´O-E. Daughter of Iobates; wife of Bellerophon, 296
significance, 402

PHIN´E-US.
1. Rival to Perseus for Andromeda, 247
2. The blind king of Thrace; annoyed by the Harpies, 269

PHLEG´E-THON. One of the rivers of Hades;
a river of fire, 155, 159, 356

PHO´BOS. One of the attendants of Mars, god of war, 131

PHO´CIS. Province in Greece, bounded by Doris, Locris, and the Gulf of Corinth, 342

PHŒ´BE. One of the Titanides, 7, 10
same as Diana, 85–93

PHŒ´BUS. Name given to Apollo, god of the sun and of medicine, 51, 57, 81, 86, 88, 323

PHŒ-NIC´I-A. Province in Asia Minor, named after Phœnix, 37
significance, 394

PHŒ´NIX. Brother of Europa, who gave his name to Phœnicia, 34, 37

PHRYX´US. Son of Athamas and Nephele;
rides on golden-fleeced ram to Colchis, 148, 267
significance, 400, 406

PI-RE´NE. Fountain near Corinth, where Pegasus drinks, 298

PI-RITH´O-US. King of the Lapithæ; friend of Theseus, 260, 261, 277

PLE´IA-DES. Seven of Diana's nymphs; pursued by Orion and changed into stars, 90

PLU´TO. Same as Hades, Dis, Aïdoneus, etc., 153–166
birth of, 12
god of the Infernal Regions, 15, 66, 67
Proserpina kidnapped by, 153–156
Arethusa sees, 186
Ceres visits, 189
Perseus aided by, 242
Theseus punished by, 263
significance, 405, 410

PLU´TUS. Name given to Pluto when invoked as god of wealth, 153

Pod-a-lir´i-us. Son of Æsculapius;
skilled in medicine, 54

Po-dar´ces. Same as Priam, King of
Troy;
slain by Pyrrhus, 146

Po-li´tes. Last of Priam's sons;
slain at his feet by Pyrrhus, 368

Pol´lux. Son of Jupiter and Leda;
brother of Castor, Helen, and
Clytæmnestra, 261, 268, 277,
280, 281

Pol´y-bus. King of Corinth;
adopted Œdipus when forsaken
by the servant, 283, 285

Pol-y-dec´tes. King of Seriphus;
sends Perseus in quest of
Medusa, 241, 247

Pol-y-do´rus. Trojan youth, murdered
in Thrace;
his grave discovered by Æneas, 370

Pol-y-hym´ni-a. Muse of rhetoric;
daughter of Jupiter and
Mnemosyne, 80

Pol-y-ni´ces. Son of Œdipus, 288
slain by Eteocles, 290
buried by Antigone, 291

Pol-y-phe´mus. Giant son of Neptune,
148
Ulysses visits, 345–352
Galatea loved by, 346
blinded by Ulysses, 350
Achemenides escapes from, 360

Po-lyx´e-na. Daughter of Priam;
affianced wife of Achilles, 335

Po-mo´na. Goddess of the orchards;
wife of Vertumnus, 306

Pon´tus. Name given to the sea when
first created, 3, 5

Po-sei´don. Same as Neptune, god of
the sea and of horse trainers, 143

Po´thos. God of the amities of love;
one of the numerous attendants
of Venus, 98

Pri´am. Same as Podarces, 146
King of Troy, 311
Paris received by, 314
duel witnessed by, 321–325
Hector, son of, 325, 330
Hector's death seen by, 334
Mercury leads, 334
Polyxena, daughter of, 335
death of, 341, 368

Pri-a´pus. God of the shade;
pursues the nymph Lotis, 303, 305

Pro´cris. Wife of Cephalus;
slain by his unerring javelin, 60,
61
significance, 395, 396, 398

Pro-crus´tes (The Stretcher).
Encountered and slain by Theseus, 253

Prœ´tus. Husband of Anteia, and
kinsman of Bellerophon, 295, 296

Pro-me´theus (Forethought). Son of
Iapetus, 15–18
man created by, 17
Olympus visited by, 17
chained to Caucasian Mountains,
18
Hercules delivers, 18
Pandora taken to, 21
Deucalion, son of, 26
significance, 388, 407

PRO-SER´PI-NA. Same as Proserpine and Persephone, 179–193

    Orpheus visits, 67

    Adonis welcomed by, 102

    goddess of vegetation, 119

    Pluto kidnaps, 153, 179–180

    emblem of death, 209

    significance, 405

PRO-TES-I-LA´US. First Greek who landed on Trojan coast, 321, 322

PRO´TEUS. Inferior sea divinity;

    shepherd of the deep, 151

    Menelaus consults, 341

    significance, 390

PSY´CHE. Fair princess loved by Cupid;

    the emblem of the soul, 113–122

    significance, 390

PSY-CHO-POM´PUS. Name given to Mercury as leader of souls to Hades, 123, 129

PYG-MA´LI-ON.

    1. Celebrated sculptor, who loves a statue, 112, 113

    2. Brother of Dido;

        murderer of Sychæus, Dido's husband, 374

PYG´MIES. Race of small people in Africa;

    defended by Antæus, 226, 227

PYL´A-DES. Son of Strophius;

    intimate friend of Orestes, 342

PYR´A-MUS. Faithful lover of Thisbe;

    commits suicide, 109, 110

PYR´RHA. Wife of Deucalion;

    the only woman who survives the Flood, 26–28

PYR´RHUS. Same as Neoptolemus, son of Achilles, 368

PYTH´E-US. Surname given to Apollo as python slayer, 51, 57

PYTH´I-A. Name given to Apollo's priestess at Delphi, 81

PYTH´I-AN GAMES. Games celebrated at Delphi every three years, 81

PY´THON. Serpent born of the Deluge slime;

    slain by Apollo, 55, 57

    significance, 395, 410

QUEEN OF HEAVEN. Name given to Juno, 41–44, 127, 140

QUIN-QUA´TRI-A. Festivals in honor of the goddess Minerva, 50

QUIR´I-NAL. One of the seven hills on which Rome is built, 135

QUIR-I-NA´LI-A. Festivals in Rome in honor of Quirinus, 135

QUI-RI´NUS. Name given to Romulus when deified, 135

RE-GIL´LUS. Lake in Italy where occurred the battle in which the Dioscuri were supposed to assist, 281

RE´MUS. Son of Mars and Ilia; twin brother of Romulus, 133, 385

RHAD-A-MAN´THUS. Son of Jupiter and Europa;

    judge in Hades, 35, 156

RHE´A. Female Titan;

    daughter of Uranus and Gæa, 7

    wife of Cronus, 10

Jupiter saved by, 11

Corybantes, priests of, 11

Cronus defeated by, 12

Juno, daughter of, 41

Pluto, son of, 153

Ceres, daughter of, 179

Vesta, daughter of, 195

significance, 405

RHODES. Island in the Mediterranean, where the Colossus stood, 82

ROME. City founded by Romulus;

worship of Juno, 42

worship of Mercury, 129

it comprises seven hills, 133

temple to Vesta in, 195

ROM´U-LUS. Son of Mars and Ilia; founder of Rome, 133, 135, 380, 385

RU´TU-LES. Nation in Italy, governed by Turnus, 382

SA-GIT-TA´RI-US. The constellation formed by Chiron, the Centaur who taught Hercules, 220

SA-LA´CI-A. Same as Amphitrite; wife of Neptune, 148

SA´LI-I. Priests appointed to watch the sacred shields in Rome, 136

SAL-MO´NEUS. King who wished to emulate Jupiter, 163

SAR-PE´DON. Son of Jupiter and Europa, 35

slain during the Trojan war, 330

SAT´URN, or CRONUS. Son of Uranus and Gæa, 8

father of Jupiter, 11

Italy ruled by, 14

husband of Rhea, 15

day of, 203

SA´TYRS. Male divinities of the woods, half man, half goat, 304

SCÆ´AN GATE. Gate which led from Troy to the plain, 327

SCI´RON. Giant encountered by Theseus on the Isthmus of Corinth, 252

SCYL´LA. Sea nymph changed to monster by Circe; she lived under rock of same name, 357, 359

SCY´ROS. Island in the Archipelago, the home of Lycomedes, visited by Achilles and Theseus, 263

SCYTH´I-A. Country north of the Euxine Sea, 192

SEASONS. The four daughters of Jupiter and Themis, 96

SEC´U-LAR GAMES. Games in honor of Pluto every hundred years, 154

SE-LE´NE. Name given to Diana as moon goddess, 85–93

significance, 397

SEM´E-LE. Daughter of Cadmus; wife of Jupiter; mother of Bacchus, 167–170

significance, 405

SE-RI´PHUS. Island where Danae and Perseus were cast ashore, 241, 247

SER´VI-US TUL´LI-US. Sixth king of Rome;

son of Vulcan and Ocrisia, 141

SES´TUS. City opposite Abydus; the home of Hero, 104

SEVEN WONDERS OF THE WORLD, 38–39

SHEET-LIGHTNING. Same as Arges, 8

SIB´YL. Prophetess of Cumæ, who led Æneas down to the infernal Regions, 378, 379

SI-CA´NI-A. Land where Anchises died; visited twice by Æneas, 372, 377

SIC´I-LY. Island home of Polyphemus; visited by Arion, 71
visited by Proserpina, 179
visited by Ulysses, 345
visited by Æneas, 372

SI-LE´NUS. Tutor of Bacchus; generally represented on an ass, 171, 172, 173, 304

SIL-VA´NUS. God of the woods; one of the lesser Roman divinities, 305

SILVER AGE. Second age of the ancient world, 25

SIL´VI-A. Daughter of Latin shepherd; her stag was wounded by Iulus, 381

SI´NIS (The Pine-bender). Giant encountered and slain by Theseus, 252

SI´NON. Greek slave, who advised the Trojans to secure the wooden horse, 338, 340

SIP´Y-LUS. Mountain where stood the statue of Niobe, 86

SI´RENS. Maidens who allured mariners by their wondrous songs, 357
significance, 406

SIR´I-US. Favorite dog of Orion; a constellation, 90, 91

SIS´Y-PHUS. King condemned to roll a rock in Tartarus to the top of a steep hill, 67, 162
significance, 398

SOL. Name frequently given to Apollo as god of the sun, 51

SOM´NUS. God of sleep; the child of Nox, and twin brother of Mors, 207–210

SPAR´TA. Capital of Lacedæmon; favorite city of Juno, 42
home of Menelaus, 314–316

SPHINX. Riddle-giving monster; slain by Œdipus, 286–287, 298
significance, 401, 410

STEL´LI-O. Urchin changed to lizard by Ceres when searching for Proserpina, 193

STER´O-PES (Lightning). One of the Cyclopes; son of Uranus and Gæa, 8

STHE´NO. One of the three Gorgon sisters, immortal, like Euryale, 241

STROPH´A-DES. Islands where the Harpies took refuge when driven from Thrace, 269
Æneas visits the, 372

STRO´PHI-US. Father of Pylades; shelters Orestes, 342

STYM-PHA´LUS. Lake upon whose banks Hercules slew the brazen-clawed birds, 225

STYX. River in Hades, by whose waters the gods swore their most sacred oaths, 32, 69, 74, 156, 168
Achilles bathed in the, 319

SU-A-DE´LA. One of Venus' train of attendants; god of the soft speech of love, 98

Sy-chæ´us. King of Tyre; husband of Dido; murdered by Pygmalion, 374

Sym-pleg´a-des. Floating rocks safely passed by the Argo, 269–270

Sy´rinx. Nymph loved by Pan, and changed into reeds, 304–305

Tæn´a-rum, or Tæn´a-rus. The Greek entrance to Hades on Cimmerian coast, 154

Ta-la´ri-a. Mercury's winged sandals, given by the gods, 126

Ta´lus. Brazen giant; son of Vulcan; the watchman of Minos, 257, 258

Tan´ta-lus. Father of Pelops; condemned to hunger and thirst in Hades, 67, 85, 161
significance, 397, 398

Tar´ta-rus. Abyss under the earth, where the Titans, etc., were confined, 7, 8, 12, 15
Orpheus' music heard in, 67
wicked in, 153–165
significance, 393–400

Tau´ris. Country to which Diana brought Iphigenia, 321
visited by Orestes, 342

Tel´a-mon. Husband of Hesione, the daughter of Laomedon, 146

Te-lem´a-chus. Son of Ulysses and Penelope, 318
adventures of, 362, 364

Tel-e-phas´sa. Wife of Agenor; mother of Europa, 35, 37
significance, 394

Tel´lus. Same as Gæa; name given to Rhea, 3

Ten´e-dos. Island off the coast of Troy, 338, 340

Terp-sich´o-re. Muse of dancing; daughter of Jupiter and Mnemosyne, 78

Ter´ra. Same as Gæa, goddess of the earth, 3

Teu´cer. Ancient king of the Trojans, 371

Tha-li´a.
1. One of the three Graces; daughter of Jupiter and Eurynome, 96
2. One of the nine Muses; Muse of comedy, 78

Than´a-tos. Same as Mors, god of death, 205

Thebes. Capital of Bœotia; founded by Cadmus, 37, 38
Amphion, king of, 71
Cadmus, king of, 99
Athamas, king of, 170
Pentheus, king of, 176
Œdipus, king of, 288

The´mis. One of the six female Titans, 7, 12
goddess of justice, 34, 96, 101, 156

The-oph´a-ne. Maiden changed by Neptune into a sheep, 148

The´seus. Son of Ægeus and Æthra; hero of Athens, 175, 251–263, 268, 277
significance, 400, 401

Thes-mo-pho´ri-a. Festivals in Greece in honor of Ceres, 191

THES´SA-LY. A province of Greece, 315
    fight of the gods in, 13
    Admetus, king of, 54
    Ceyx, king of, 208
    Æson, king of, 275
    Protesilaus of, 321
THE´TIS.
    1. Mother of Achilles, 319
        a sea nymph, 10
    2. One of the Titanides, 7, 10
        marriage feast of, 310
        Olympus visited by, 324
        Achilles comforted by, 331
        Achilles' armor brought by,
        331, 332
        Achilles instructed by, 334
THIS´BE. Babylonian maiden loved by
    Pyramus, 109, 110
THRACE. Country on the Black Sea;
    the home of Mars, 131, 222, 269, 370
    significance, 409
THYR´SUS. The vine-encircled wand
    borne by the followers of Bacchus, 178
TI´BER. River in Italy, 197, 199, 201
    Æneas sails up the, 370, 380, 381, 382
TIME. Same as Cronus, Saturn, 8
TI-RE´SI-AS. The blind seer visited by
    Ulysses on the Cimmerian shore, 356,
    359
TI-SIPH´O-NE. One of the three Furies,
    or Eumenides, 159, 170
TI-TAN´I-DES. The six daughters of
    Uranus and Gæa, 7
TI´TANS. Name given to the six sons of
    Uranus and Gæa, 7, 8
    revolt of, 8, 12, 13–15

significance, 407
TI-THO´NUS. Trojan prince who visited
    Aurora, 80
TIT´Y-US. Giant in Tartarus, whose
    prostrate body covered nine acres,
    163–164
TRA-CHIN´I-A. Land where Hercules
    died, 215
TRI-NA´CRI-A. Land visited by
    Ulysses, whose men slay the cattle of
    the sun, 315
TRIP-TOL´E-MUS. Nursling and protégé
    of Ceres, 184
TRI´TON. Son of Neptune and Amphitrite;
    father of the Tritons, 95, 149, 151,
    306
    significance, 406
TRŒ-ZE´NE. Ancient city in Argolis, 147
    birthplace of Theseus, 251
    significance, 400
TRO´JANS. Inhabitants of Troy, 144,
    146, 321–340, 367–385
TROY. City of Asia Minor, ruled by
    Laomedon and Priam, 32, 90
    walls built by Neptune, 55
    war of, 309–342, 367–384
    significance, 403
TUC´CI-A. Vestal virgin who stood the
    test of purity, 197
TUR´NUS. Chief of the Rutules;
    wars against Æneas, 380–385
TUS´CANS. People of Tuscania in Italy,
    governed by Evander;
    allies of Æneas, 381
TYN-DA´RE-US. Stepfather of Helen;
    binds her suitors by oath, 315

Ty-phœ´us. Same as Typhon; monster sent to dethrone Jupiter, 13, 14

Tyre. City in Phœnicia, governed by Sychæus and Dido, 374

U-lys´ses. Same as Odysseus, hero of the *Odyssey*; King of Ithaca, 212, 318, 319, 320, 335, 337, 338 adventures of, 343–366 significance, 395, 404

U-ra´ni-a. Muse of astronomy, daughter of Jupiter and Mnemosyne, 78

U´ra-nus (Heaven). Husband of Gæa, created by her, 3, 7, 8 significance, 393

Ve´nus. Same as Aphrodite, goddess of beauty, 95–122 loved by Mars, 133 day of, 203 Hippomenes aided by, 280 Juno and Minerva dispute with, 310–311 Paris advised by, 314 Paris saved by, 325 Æneas, son of, 367, 369, 374, 375, 378, 382, 384 significance, 403

Ver-tum´nus. God of the orchards; loved by Pomona, 306

Ves´ta. Same as Hestia, goddess of fire and of the family hearth, 133, 197–200 birth of, 12 significance, 385, 408

Ves-ta´li-a. Festivals in honor of Vesta, held in Rome, 199

Ves´tals. Virgins dedicated to the service of Vesta, 133, 195–199, 385

Vic-to´ri-a. Same as Nice, goddess of victory, 31

Vol´scians. Tribe in Italy who join the Rutules against Æneas, 381, 382

Vul´can. Same as Hephæstus, god of the forge, 137–141 son of Juno, 42 Jupiter's head cleft by, 45 Venus, wife of, 98 Periphetes, son of, 251 armor made by, 331, 335 significance, 408

Vul-ca-na´li-a. Festivals celebrated in honor of Vulcan, 141

Zeph´y-rus. God of the south wind; son of Æolus and Aurora, 211 Hyacinthus slain by, 57 Venus conducted by, 95 Psyche saved by, 114, 119 Cloud enveloping Arethusa blown away by, 188 Flora, wife of, 305

Ze´tes. Son of Boreas and Orithyia; took part in Argonautic expedition, and drove away Harpies, 213

Ze´thus. Twin brother of Amphion; son of Jupiter and Antiope, 71

Zeus. Same as Jupiter, 10, 12 father of the gods, 29 significance, 388, 392, 393, 397, 404